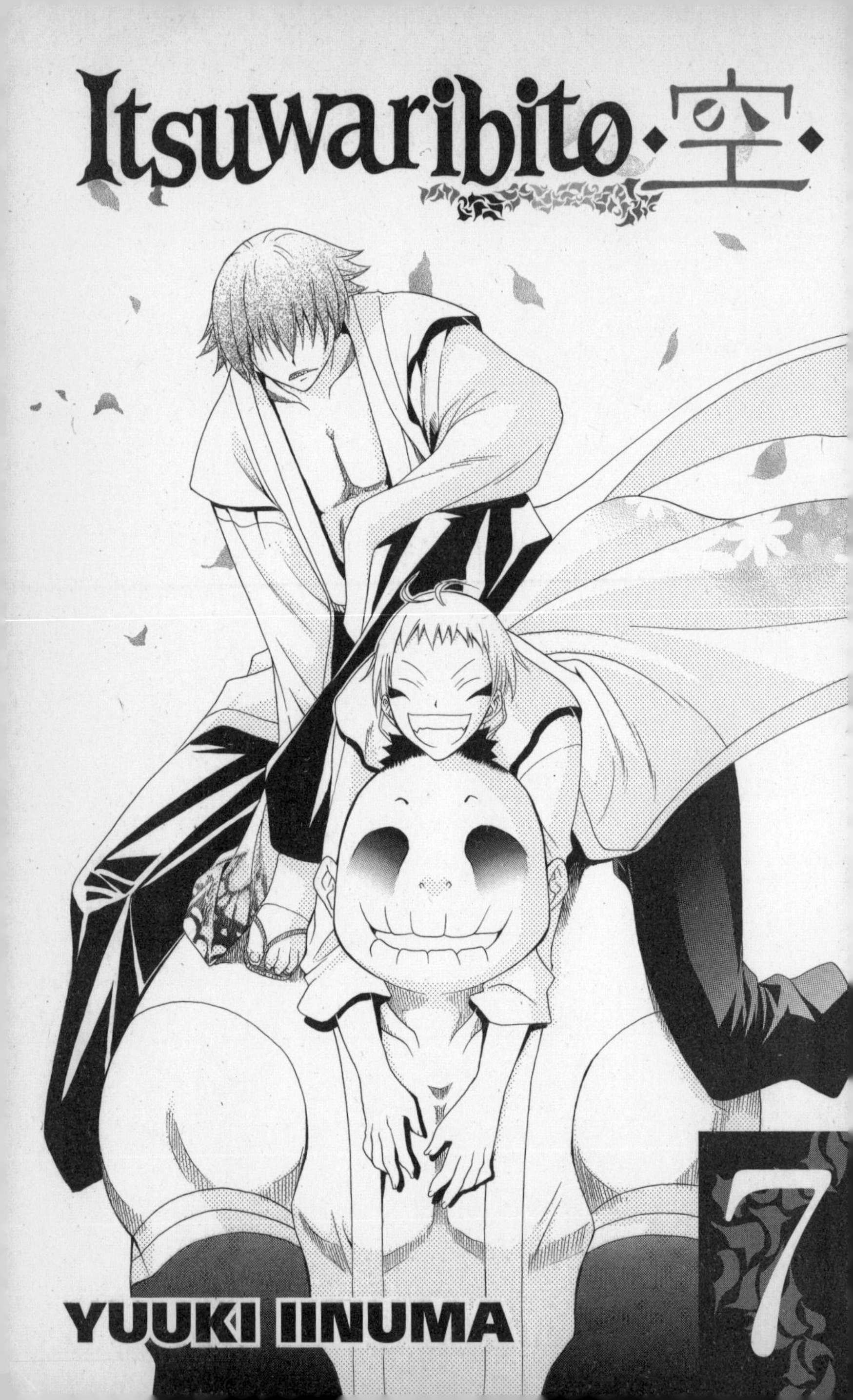
Itsuwaribito・空・
7
YUUKI IINUMA

Contents

Chapter 58 The Lord's True Identity

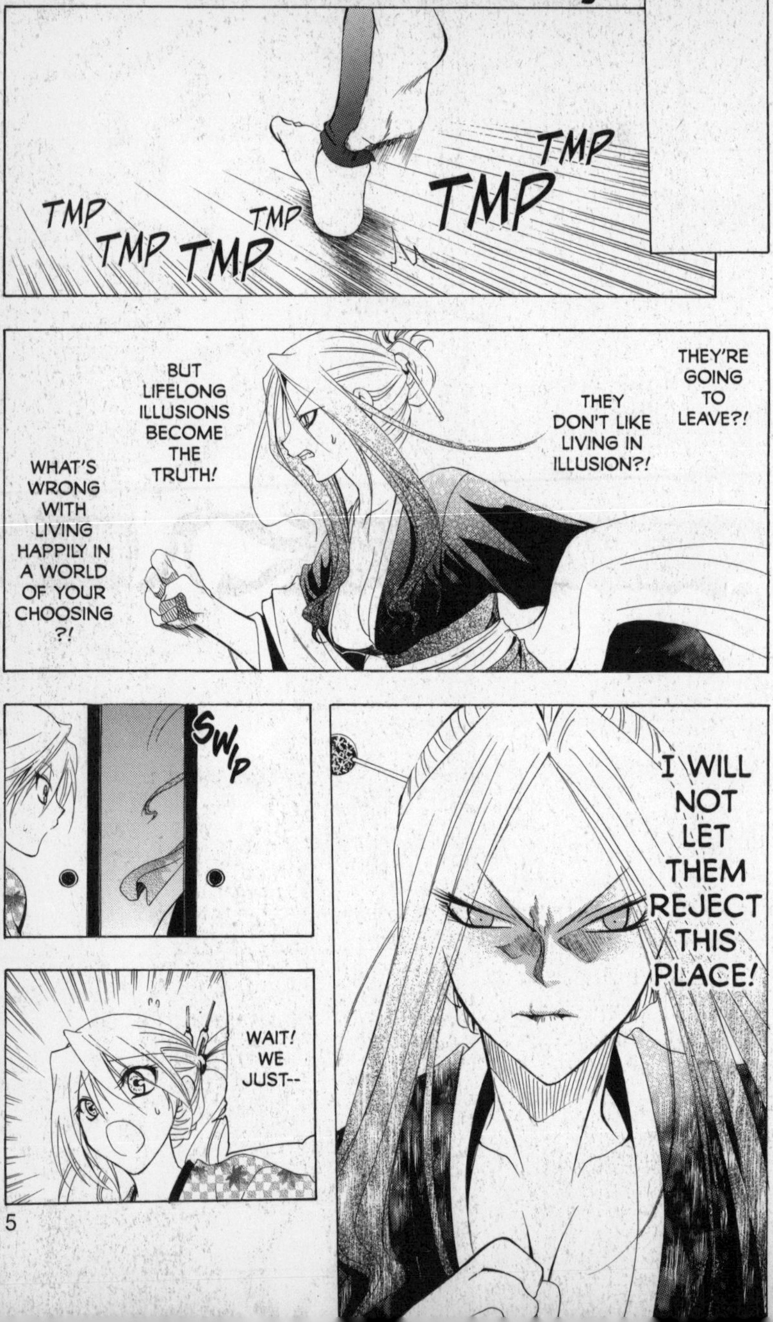
TMP
TMP
TMP
TMP
TMP
TMP
THEY'RE GOING TO LEAVE?!
THEY DON'T LIKE LIVING IN ILLUSION?!
BUT LIFELONG ILLUSIONS BECOME THE TRUTH!
WHAT'S WRONG WITH LIVING HAPPILY IN A WORLD OF YOUR CHOOSING ?!
I WILL NOT LET THEM REJECT THIS PLACE!
SWIP
WAIT! WE JUST--

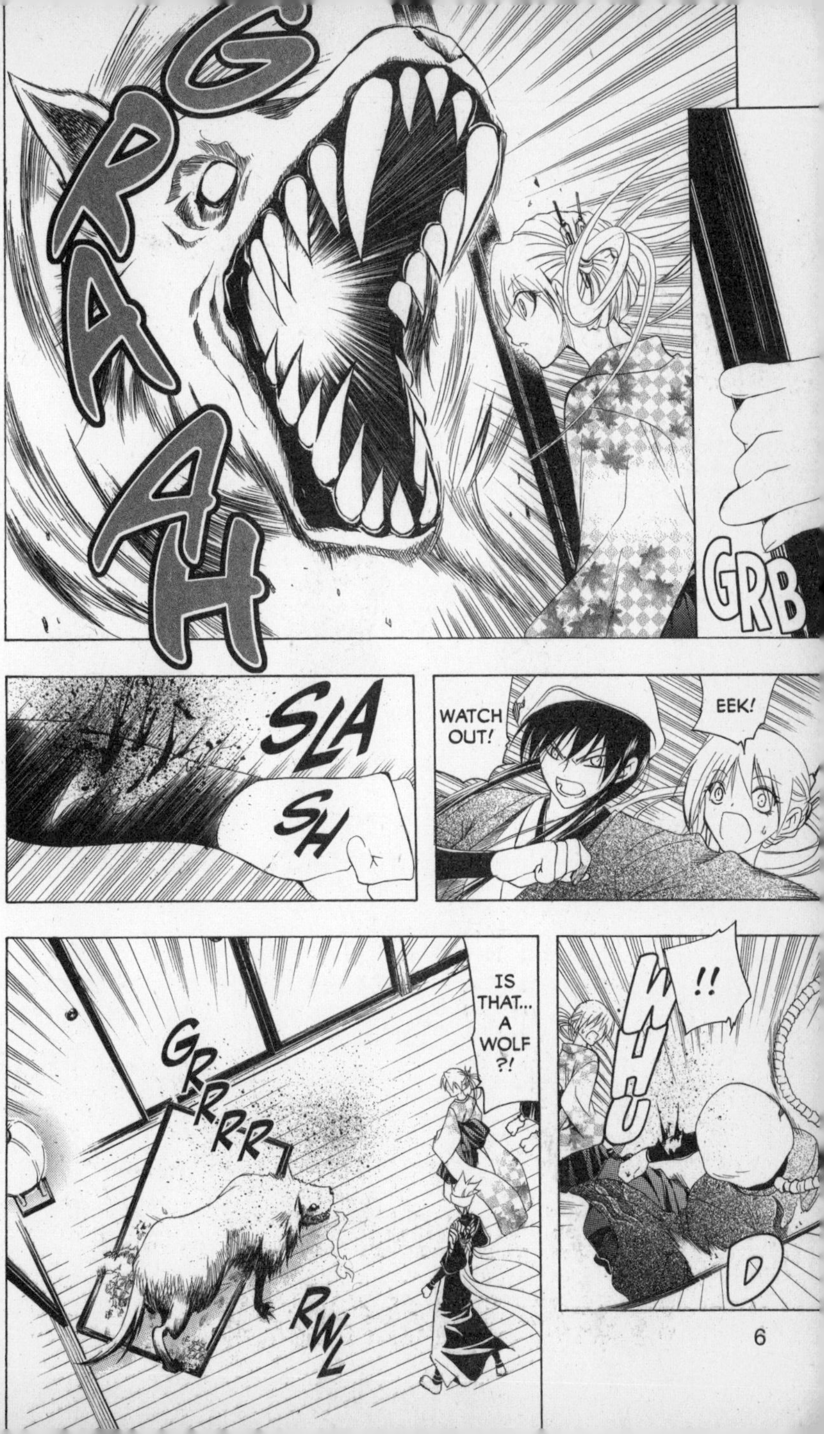
GRAAAH
GRB
EEK!
WATCH OUT!
SLASH
!!
WHUD
IS THAT... A WOLF?!
GRRRRR
RWL

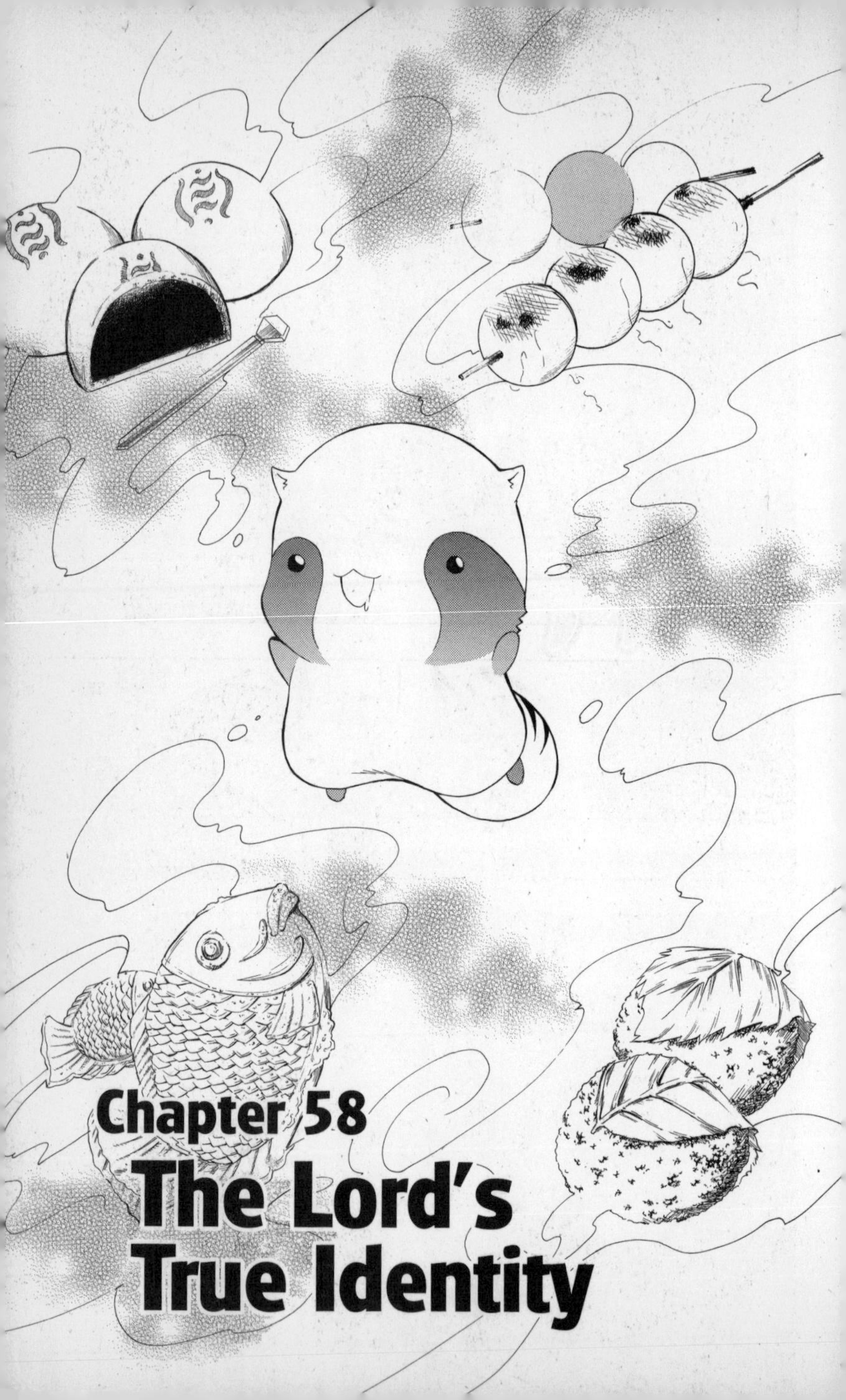

Chapter 58
The Lord's True Identity

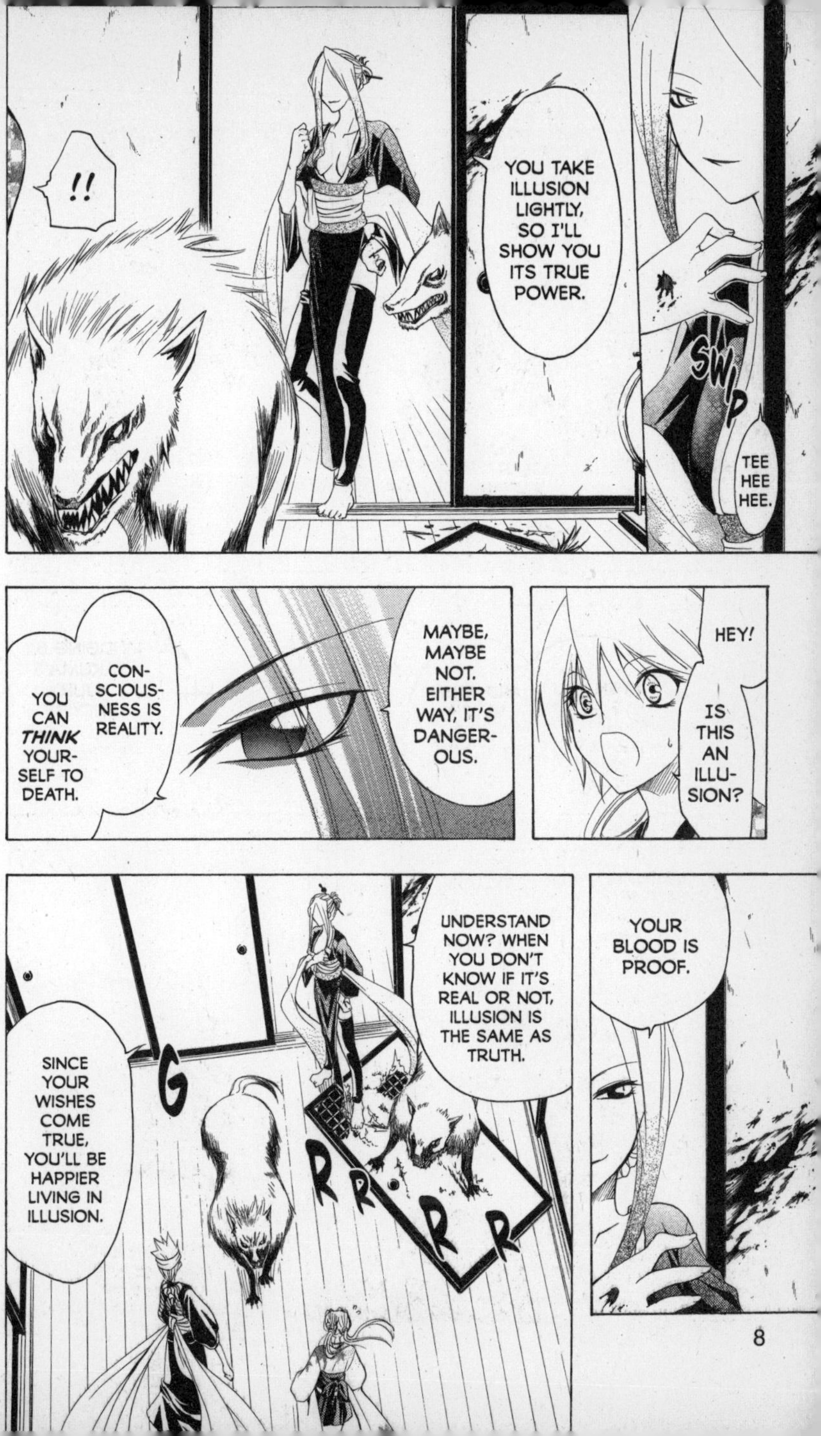
YOU TAKE ILLUSION LIGHTLY, SO I'LL SHOW YOU ITS TRUE POWER.
SWIP
TEE HEE HEE.
!!
HEY!
IS THIS AN ILLUSION?
MAYBE, MAYBE NOT. EITHER WAY, IT'S DANGEROUS.
CONSCIOUSNESS IS REALITY.
YOU CAN *THINK* YOURSELF TO DEATH.
YOUR BLOOD IS PROOF.
UNDERSTAND NOW? WHEN YOU DON'T KNOW IF IT'S REAL OR NOT, ILLUSION IS THE SAME AS TRUTH.
SINCE YOUR WISHES COME TRUE, YOU'LL BE HAPPIER LIVING IN ILLUSION.
GRRRR

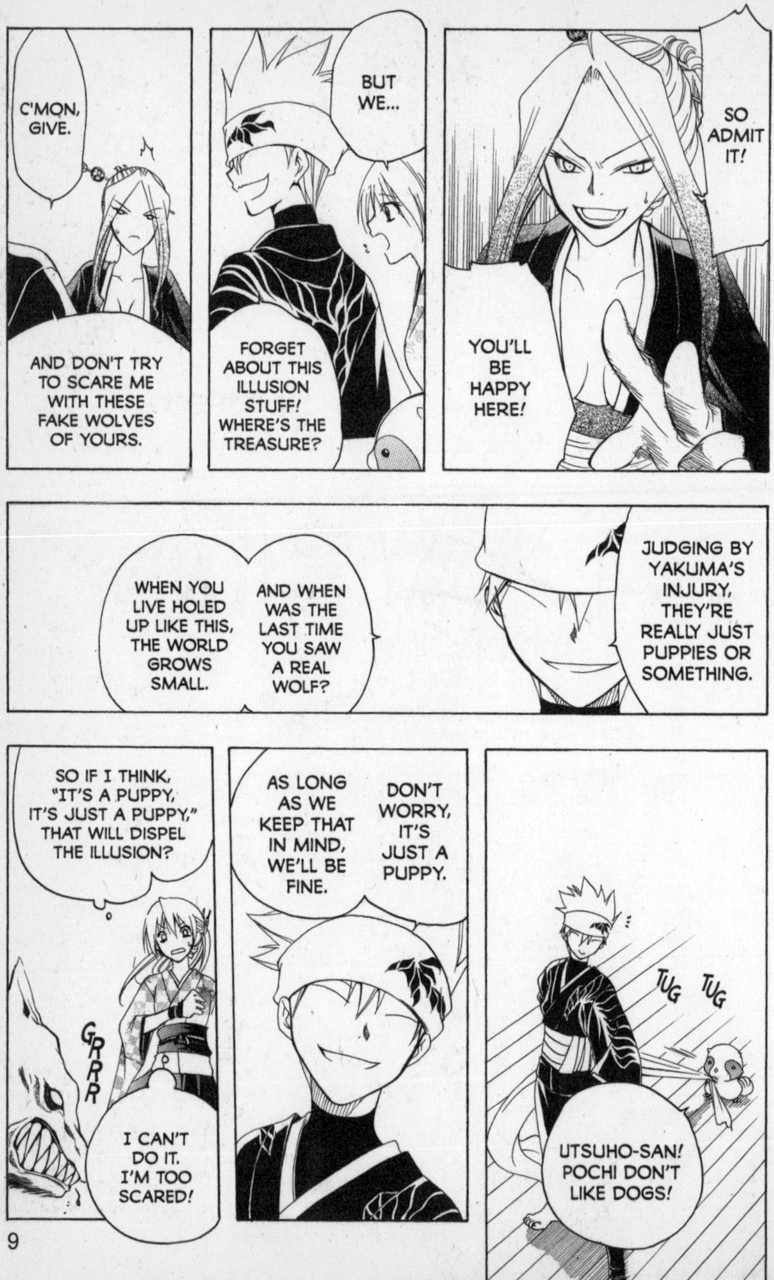
SO ADMIT IT!
YOU'LL BE HAPPY HERE!
BUT WE...
FORGET ABOUT THIS ILLUSION STUFF! WHERE'S THE TREASURE?
C'MON, GIVE.
AND DON'T TRY TO SCARE ME WITH THESE FAKE WOLVES OF YOURS.
JUDGING BY YAKUMA'S INJURY, THEY'RE REALLY JUST PUPPIES OR SOMETHING.
AND WHEN WAS THE LAST TIME YOU SAW A REAL WOLF?
WHEN YOU LIVE HOLED UP LIKE THIS, THE WORLD GROWS SMALL.
TUG TUG
UTSUHO-SAN! POCHI DON'T LIKE DOGS!
DON'T WORRY, IT'S JUST A PUPPY.
AS LONG AS WE KEEP THAT IN MIND, WE'LL BE FINE.
SO IF I THINK, "IT'S A PUPPY, IT'S JUST A PUPPY," THAT WILL DISPEL THE ILLUSION?
GRRR
I CAN'T DO IT. I'M TOO SCARED!

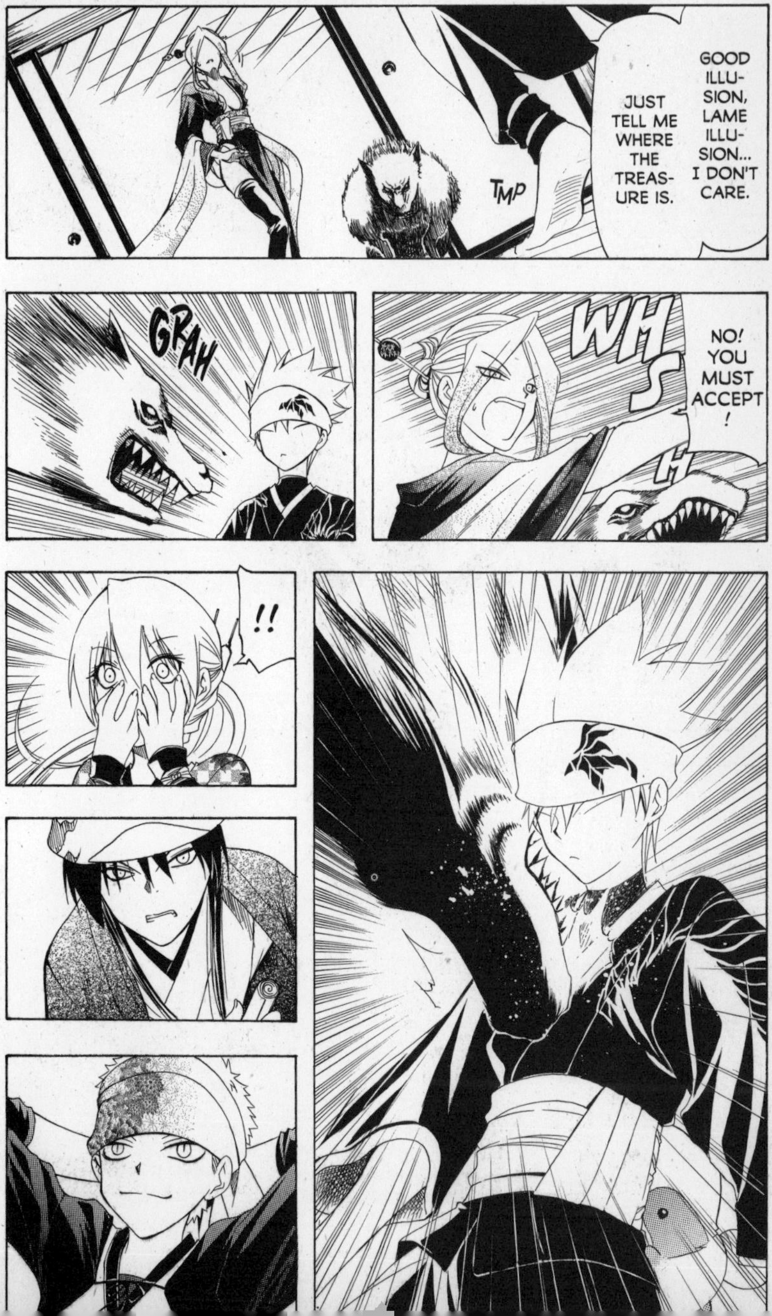
GOOD ILLUSION, LAME ILLUSION... I DON'T CARE.
JUST TELL ME WHERE THE TREASURE IS.
TMP
NO! YOU MUST ACCEPT!
WHSH
GRAH
!!

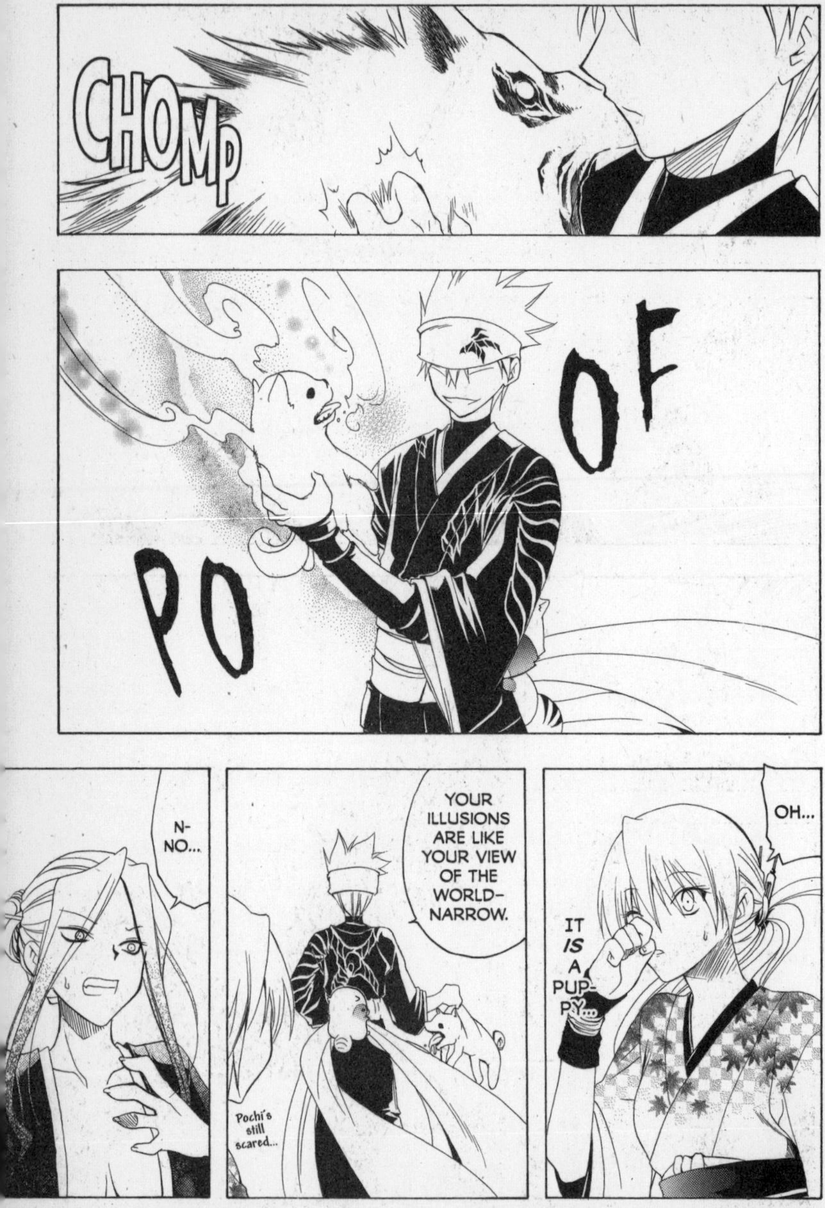
CHOMP
POOF
OH...
IT IS A PUPPY...
YOUR ILLUSIONS ARE LIKE YOUR VIEW OF THE WORLD—NARROW.
Pochi's still scared...
N-NO...

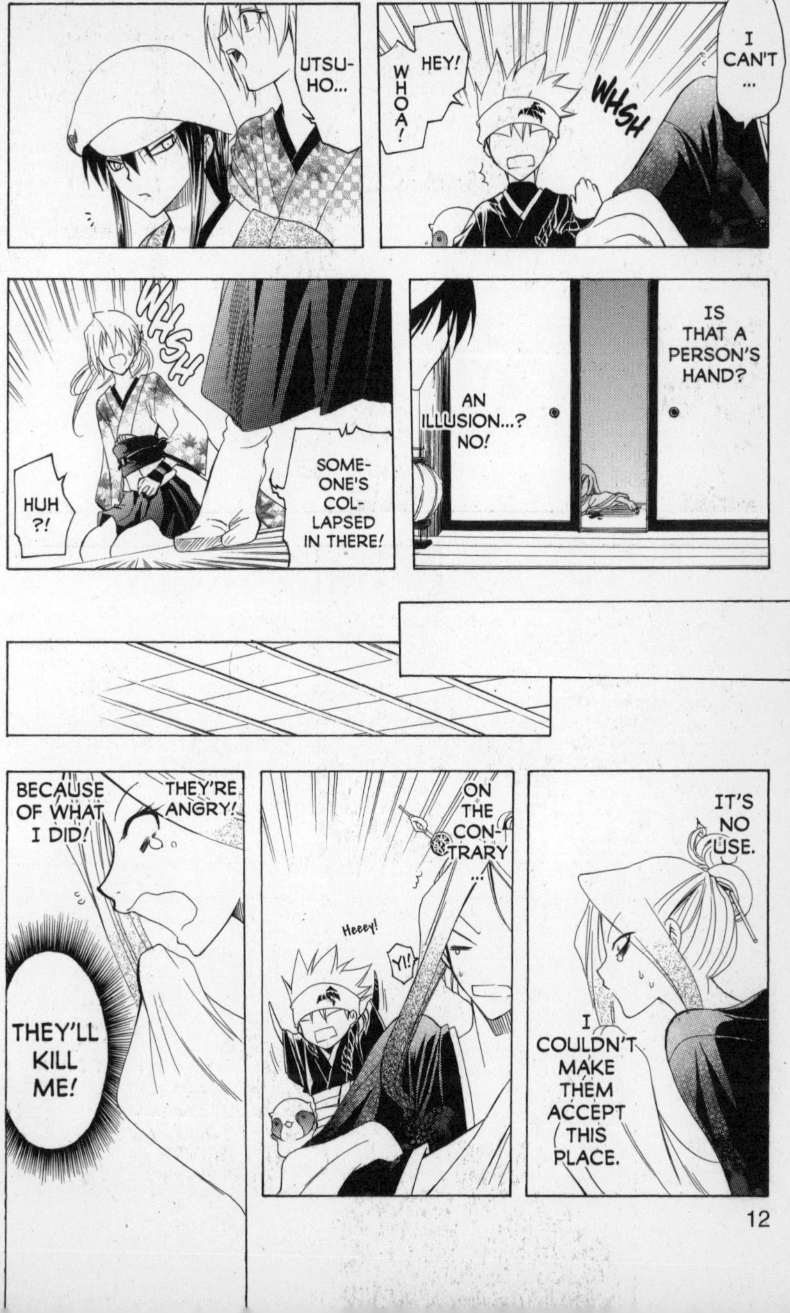
I CAN'T ...
WHSH
HEY!
WHOA!
UTSU-HO...
IS THAT A PERSON'S HAND?
AN ILLUSION...? NO!
WHSH
SOME-ONE'S COL-LAPSED IN THERE!
HUH ?!
IT'S NO USE.
I COULDN'T MAKE THEM ACCEPT THIS PLACE.
ON THE CON-TRARY ...
YI!
Heeey!
THEY'RE ANGRY!
BECAUSE OF WHAT I DID!
THEY'LL KILL ME!

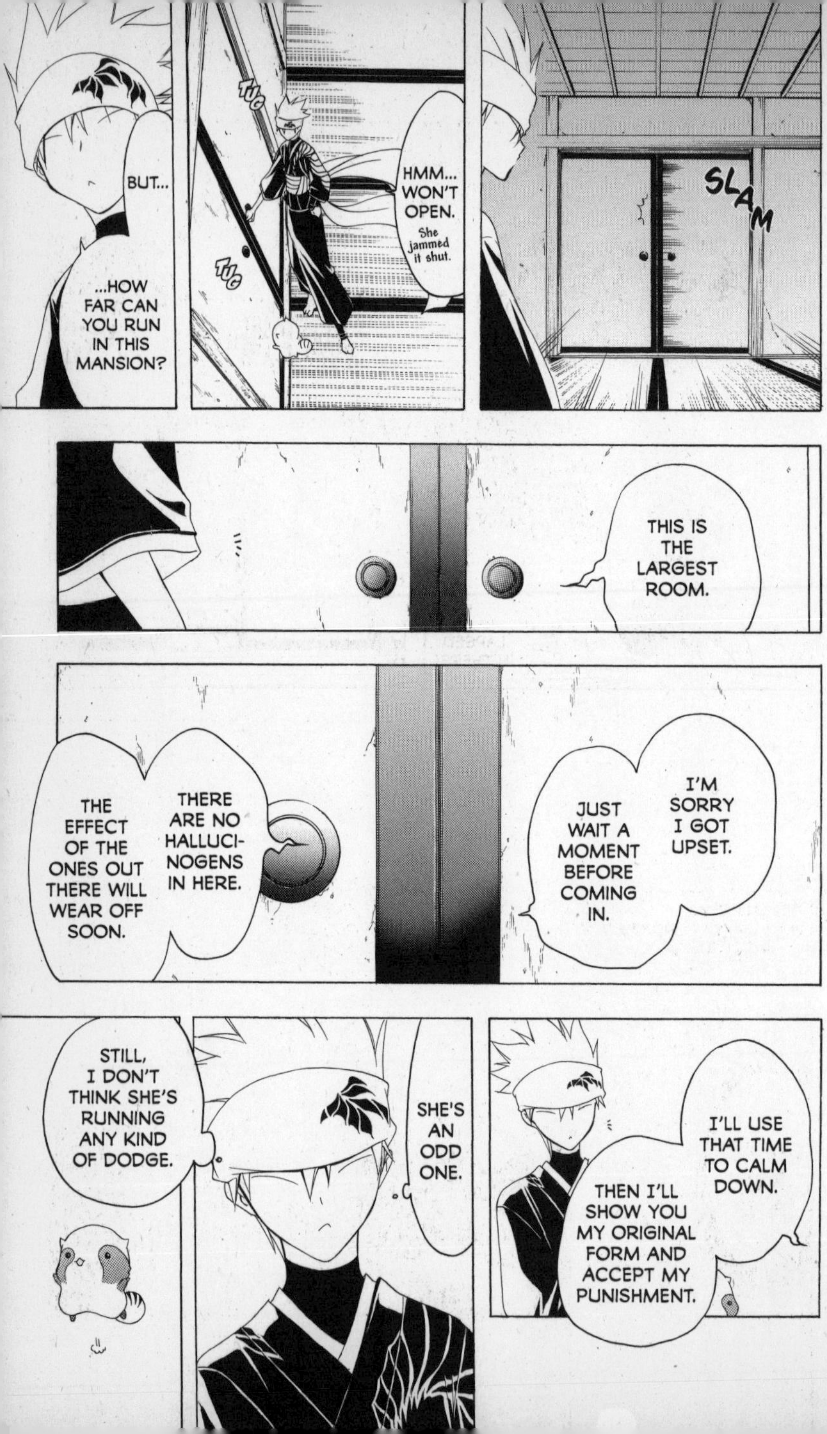
SLAM
TUG
TUG
HMM... WON'T OPEN.
She jammed it shut.
BUT...
...HOW FAR CAN YOU RUN IN THIS MANSION?
THIS IS THE LARGEST ROOM.
I'M SORRY I GOT UPSET.
JUST WAIT A MOMENT BEFORE COMING IN.
THERE ARE NO HALLUCINOGENS IN HERE.
THE EFFECT OF THE ONES OUT THERE WILL WEAR OFF SOON.
I'LL USE THAT TIME TO CALM DOWN.
THEN I'LL SHOW YOU MY ORIGINAL FORM AND ACCEPT MY PUNISHMENT.
SHE'S AN ODD ONE.
STILL, I DON'T THINK SHE'S RUNNING ANY KIND OF DODGE.

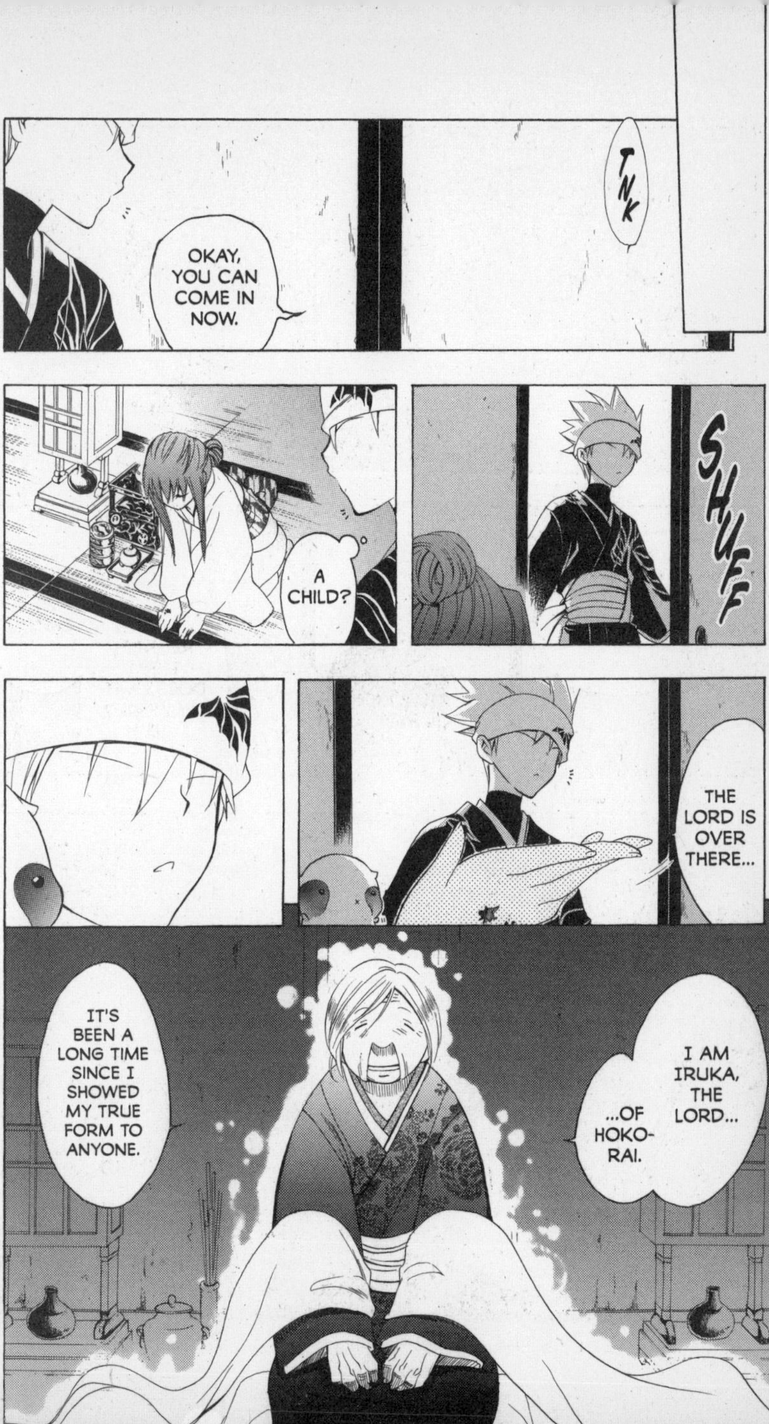
TNK
OKAY, YOU CAN COME IN NOW.
SHUFF
A CHILD?
THE LORD IS OVER THERE...
I AM IRUKA, THE LORD...
...OF HOKO-RAI.
IT'S BEEN A LONG TIME SINCE I SHOWED MY TRUE FORM TO ANYONE.

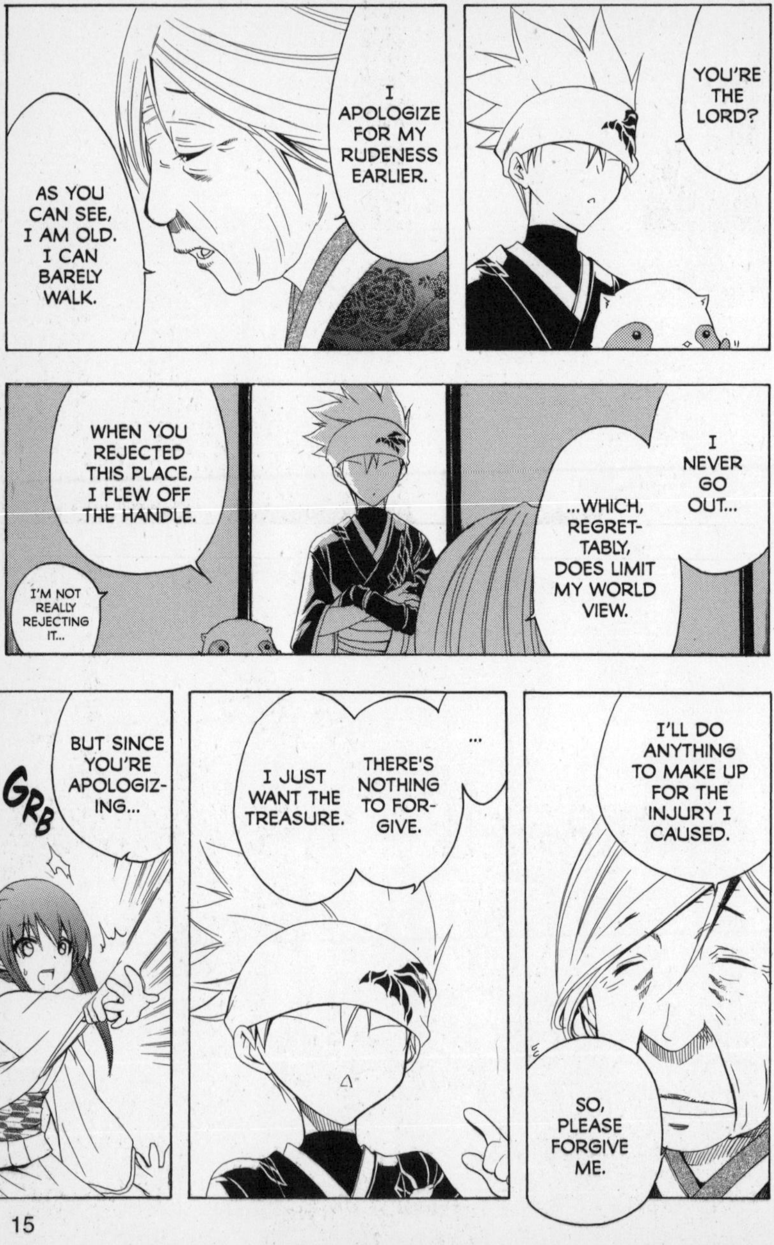
YOU'RE THE LORD?
I APOLOGIZE FOR MY RUDENESS EARLIER.
AS YOU CAN SEE, I AM OLD. I CAN BARELY WALK.
I NEVER GO OUT...
...WHICH, REGRETTABLY, DOES LIMIT MY WORLD VIEW.
WHEN YOU REJECTED THIS PLACE, I FLEW OFF THE HANDLE.
I'M NOT REALLY REJECTING IT...
I'LL DO ANYTHING TO MAKE UP FOR THE INJURY I CAUSED.
SO, PLEASE FORGIVE ME.
...
THERE'S NOTHING TO FORGIVE.
I JUST WANT THE TREASURE.
BUT SINCE YOU'RE APOLOGIZING...
GRB

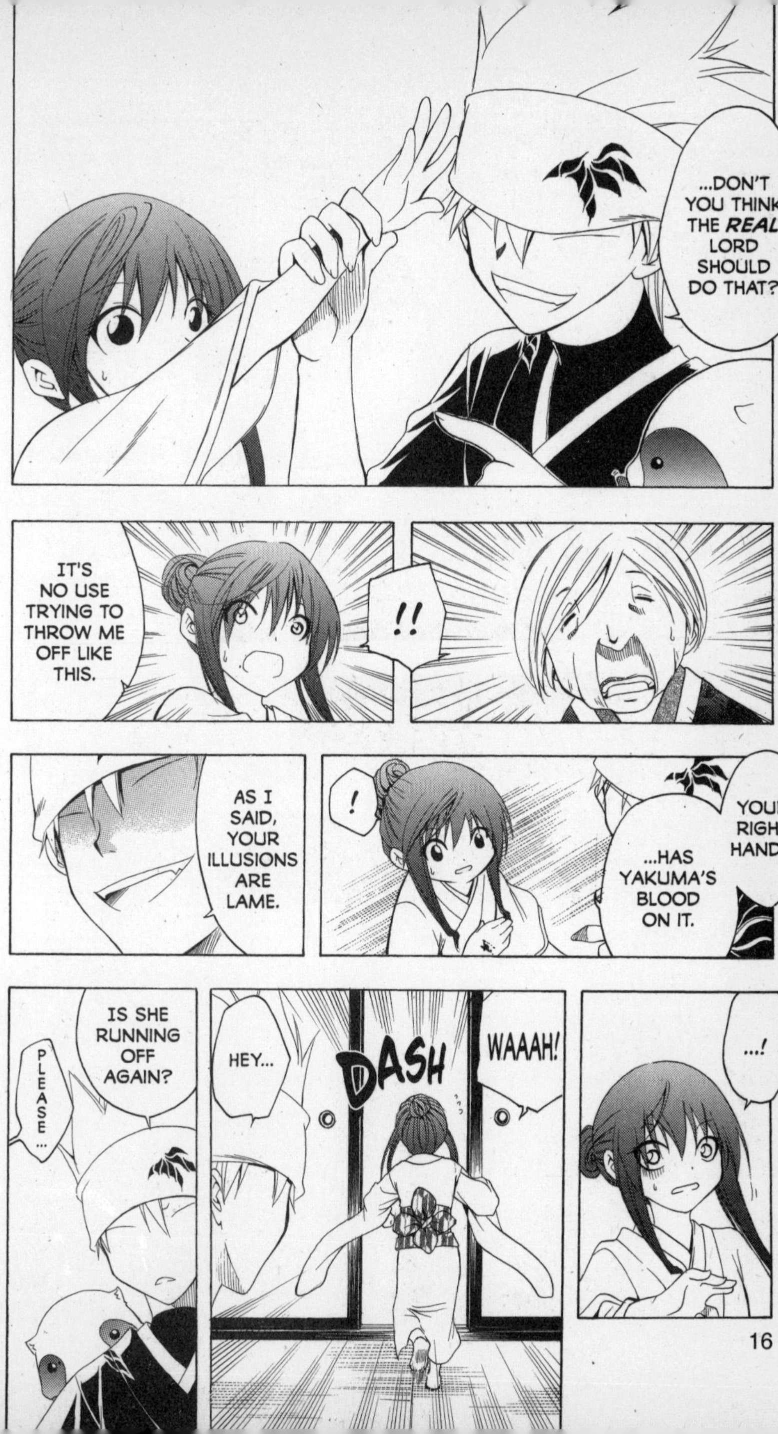
...DON'T YOU THINK THE *REAL* LORD SHOULD DO THAT?
!!
IT'S NO USE TRYING TO THROW ME OFF LIKE THIS.
YOUR RIGHT HAND...
...HAS YAKUMA'S BLOOD ON IT.
!
AS I SAID, YOUR ILLUSIONS ARE LAME.
...!
WAAAH!
DASH
HEY...
IS SHE RUNNING OFF AGAIN?
PLEASE...

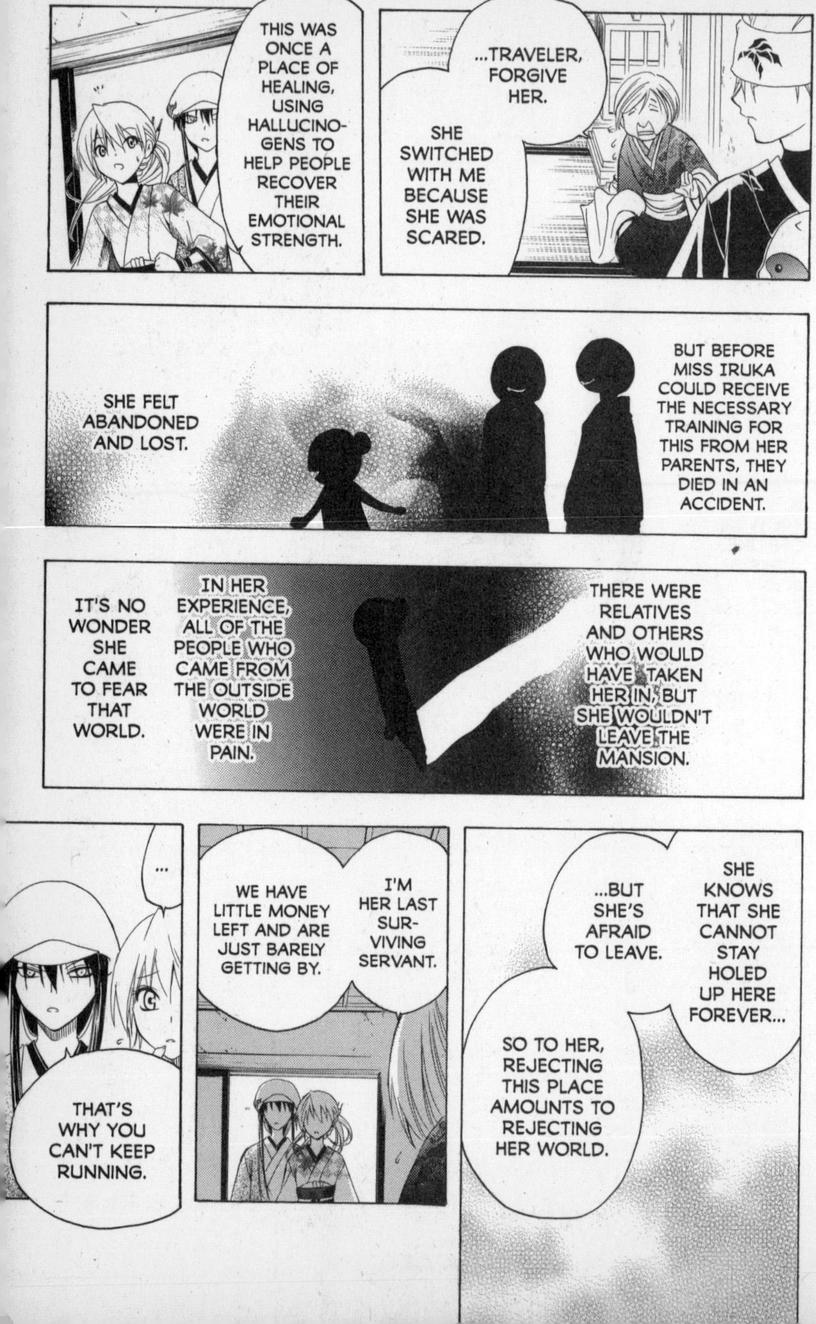
...TRAVELER, FORGIVE HER.
SHE SWITCHED WITH ME BECAUSE SHE WAS SCARED.
THIS WAS ONCE A PLACE OF HEALING, USING HALLUCINO-GENS TO HELP PEOPLE RECOVER THEIR EMOTIONAL STRENGTH.
BUT BEFORE MISS IRUKA COULD RECEIVE THE NECESSARY TRAINING FOR THIS FROM HER PARENTS, THEY DIED IN AN ACCIDENT.
SHE FELT ABANDONED AND LOST.
THERE WERE RELATIVES AND OTHERS WHO WOULD HAVE TAKEN HER IN, BUT SHE WOULDN'T LEAVE THE MANSION.
IN HER EXPERIENCE, ALL OF THE PEOPLE WHO CAME FROM THE OUTSIDE WORLD WERE IN PAIN.
IT'S NO WONDER SHE CAME TO FEAR THAT WORLD.
SHE KNOWS THAT SHE CANNOT STAY HOLED UP HERE FOREVER...
...BUT SHE'S AFRAID TO LEAVE.
SO TO HER, REJECTING THIS PLACE AMOUNTS TO REJECTING HER WORLD.
I'M HER LAST SUR-VIVING SERVANT.
WE HAVE LITTLE MONEY LEFT AND ARE JUST BARELY GETTING BY.
...
THAT'S WHY YOU CAN'T KEEP RUNNING.

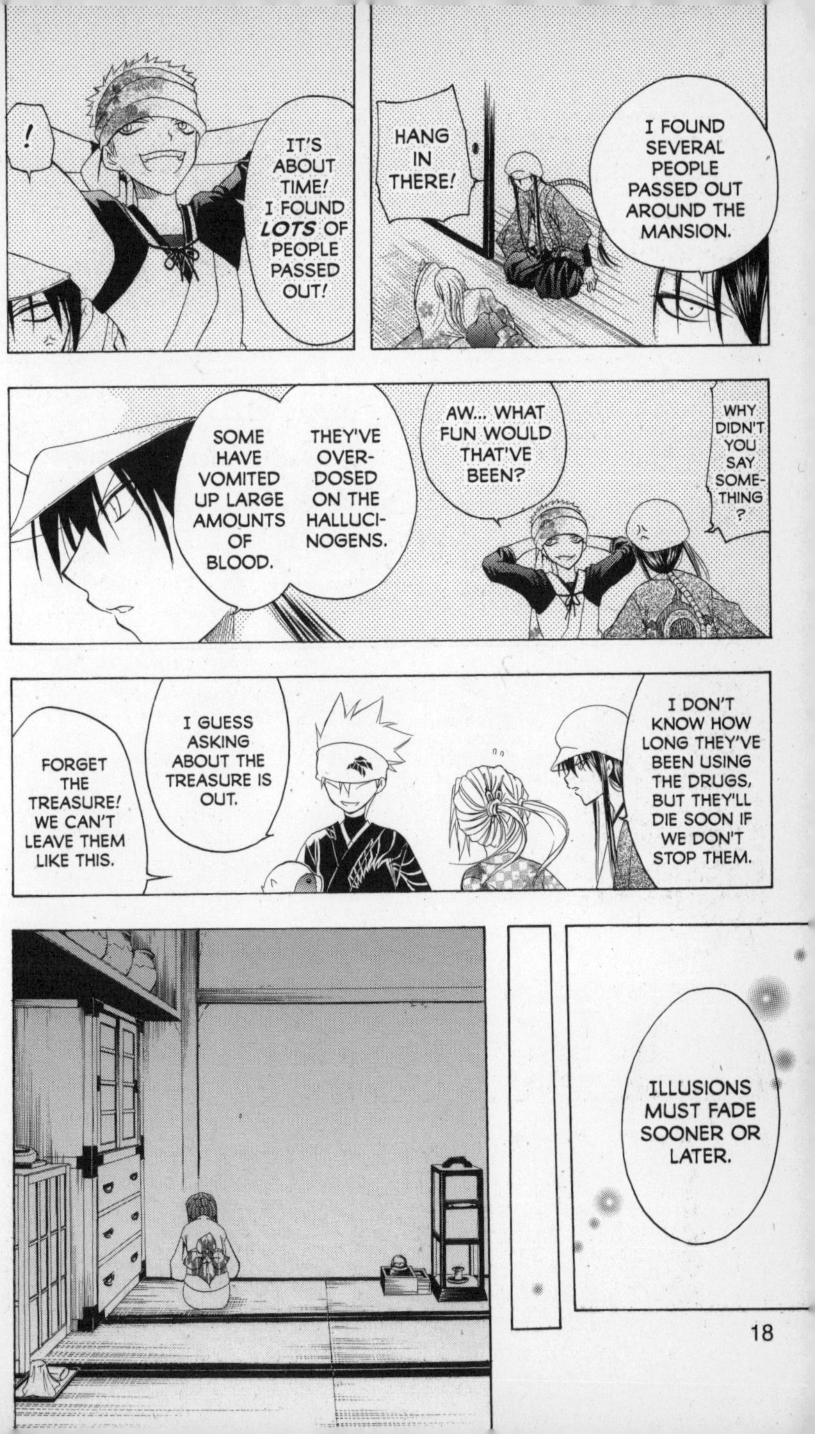
I FOUND SEVERAL PEOPLE PASSED OUT AROUND THE MANSION.
HANG IN THERE!
IT'S ABOUT TIME! I FOUND *LOTS* OF PEOPLE PASSED OUT!
!
WHY DIDN'T YOU SAY SOME-THING?
AW... WHAT FUN WOULD THAT'VE BEEN?
THEY'VE OVER-DOSED ON THE HALLUCI-NOGENS.
SOME HAVE VOMITED UP LARGE AMOUNTS OF BLOOD.
I DON'T KNOW HOW LONG THEY'VE BEEN USING THE DRUGS, BUT THEY'LL DIE SOON IF WE DON'T STOP THEM.
I GUESS ASKING ABOUT THE TREASURE IS OUT.
FORGET THE TREASURE! WE CAN'T LEAVE THEM LIKE THIS.
ILLUSIONS MUST FADE SOONER OR LATER.

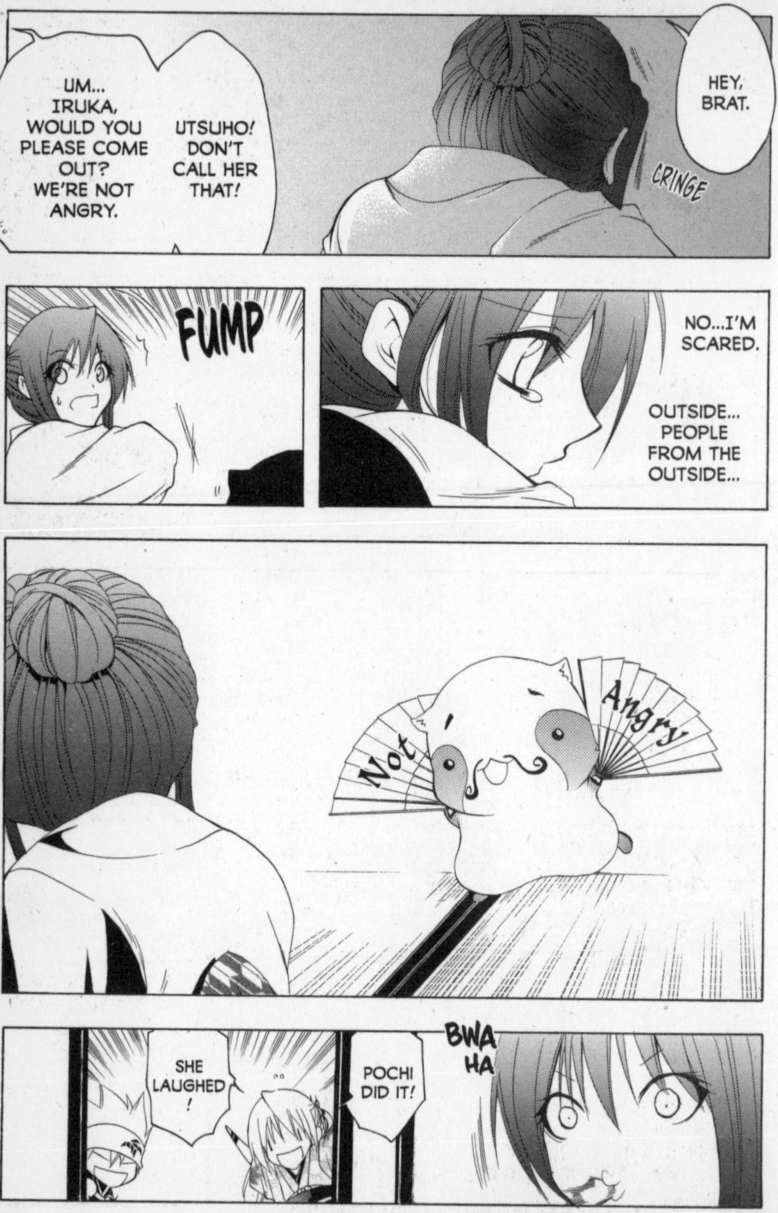
HEY, BRAT.
CRINGE
UTSUHO! DON'T CALL HER THAT!
UM... IRUKA, WOULD YOU PLEASE COME OUT? WE'RE NOT ANGRY.
NO...I'M SCARED.
OUTSIDE... PEOPLE FROM THE OUTSIDE...
FUMP
Not Angry
BWA HA
POCHI DID IT!
SHE LAUGHED!

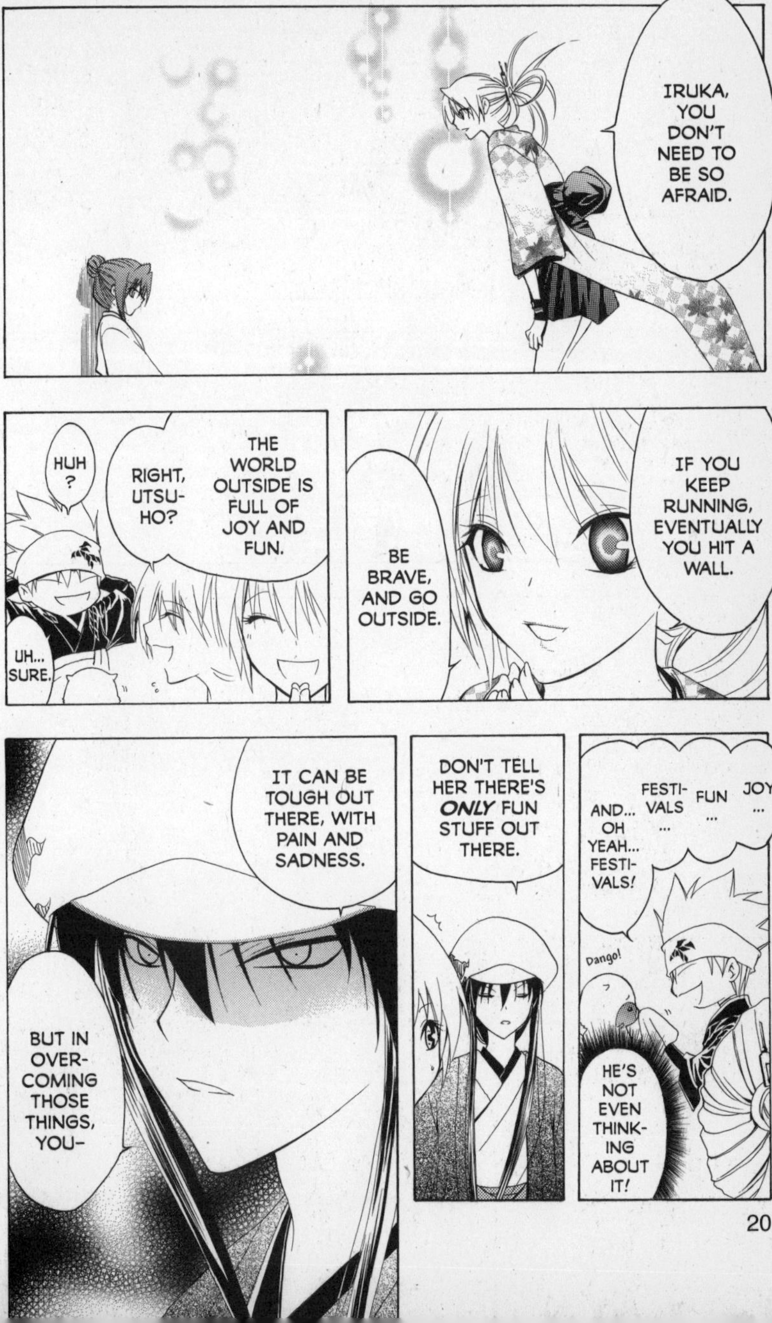
IRUKA, YOU DON'T NEED TO BE SO AFRAID.
IF YOU KEEP RUNNING, EVENTUALLY YOU HIT A WALL.
BE BRAVE, AND GO OUTSIDE.
THE WORLD OUTSIDE IS FULL OF JOY AND FUN.
RIGHT, UTSU-HO?
HUH?
UH... SURE.
JOY...
FUN...
FESTIVALS...
AND... OH YEAH... FESTIVALS!
Dango!
HE'S NOT EVEN THINKING ABOUT IT!
DON'T TELL HER THERE'S *ONLY* FUN STUFF OUT THERE.
IT CAN BE TOUGH OUT THERE, WITH PAIN AND SADNESS.
BUT IN OVERCOMING THOSE THINGS, YOU–

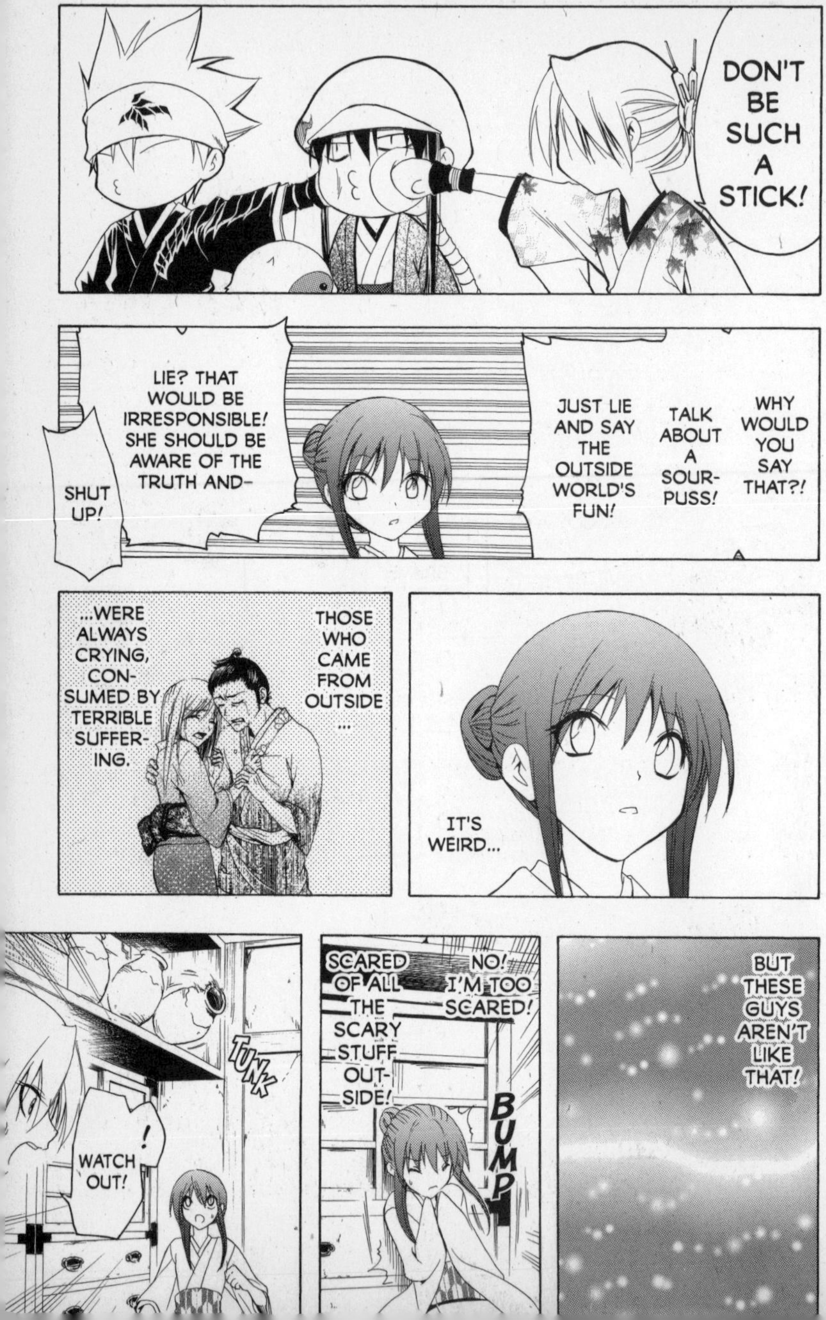
DON'T BE SUCH A STICK!
WHY WOULD YOU SAY THAT?!
TALK ABOUT A SOUR-PUSS!
JUST LIE AND SAY THE OUTSIDE WORLD'S FUN!
LIE? THAT WOULD BE IRRESPONSIBLE! SHE SHOULD BE AWARE OF THE TRUTH AND-
SHUT UP!
IT'S WEIRD...
THOSE WHO CAME FROM OUTSIDE ...
...WERE ALWAYS CRYING, CON-SUMED BY TERRIBLE SUFFER-ING.
BUT THESE GUYS AREN'T LIKE THAT!
NO! I'M TOO SCARED!
SCARED OF ALL THE SCARY STUFF OUT-SIDE!
BUMP
TUNK
!
WATCH OUT!

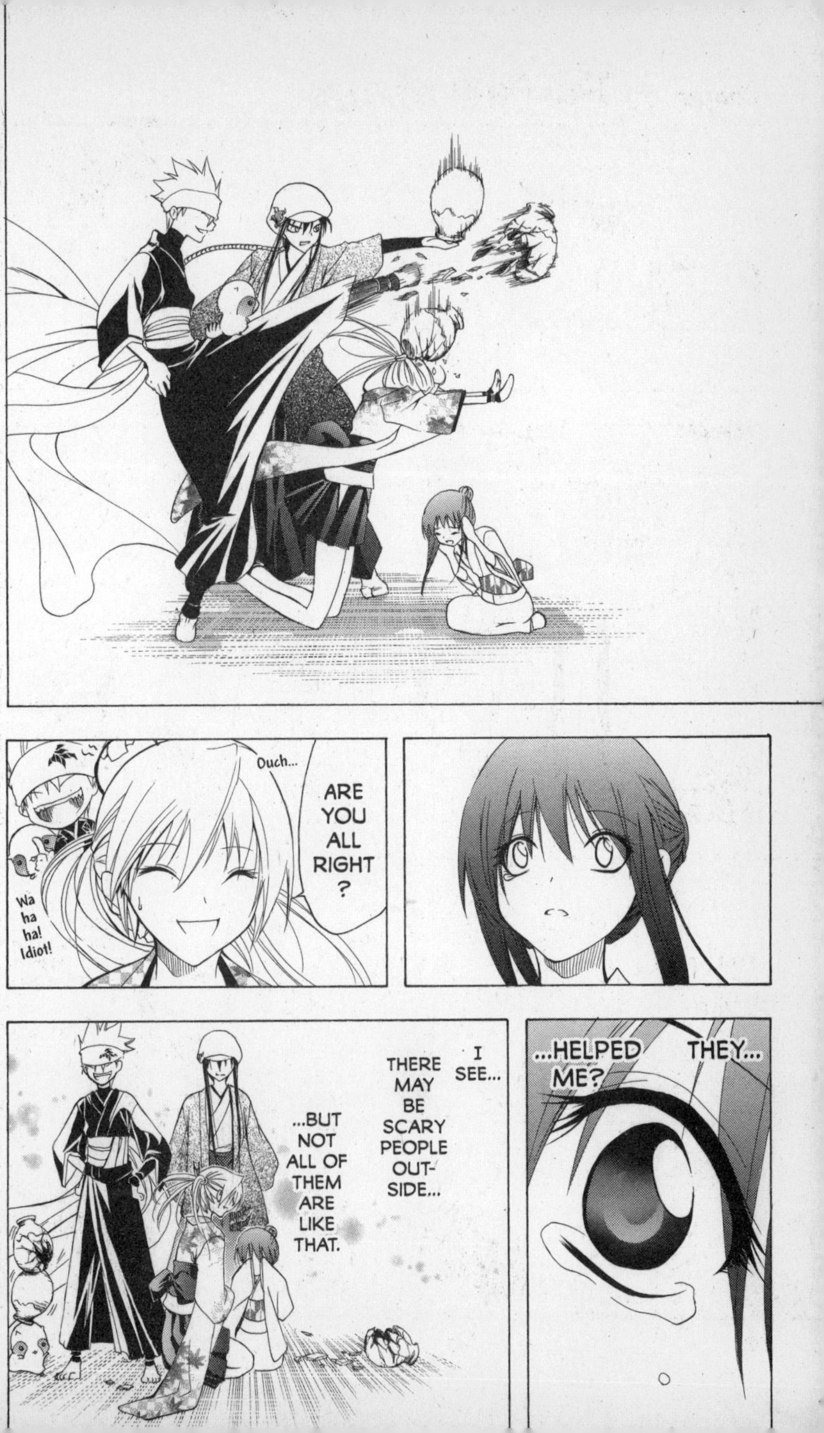
Ouch...
ARE YOU ALL RIGHT?
Wa ha ha! Idiot!
THEY...
...HELPED ME?
I SEE...
THERE MAY BE SCARY PEOPLE OUTSIDE...
...BUT NOT ALL OF THEM ARE LIKE THAT.

Chapter 59 The Path of God

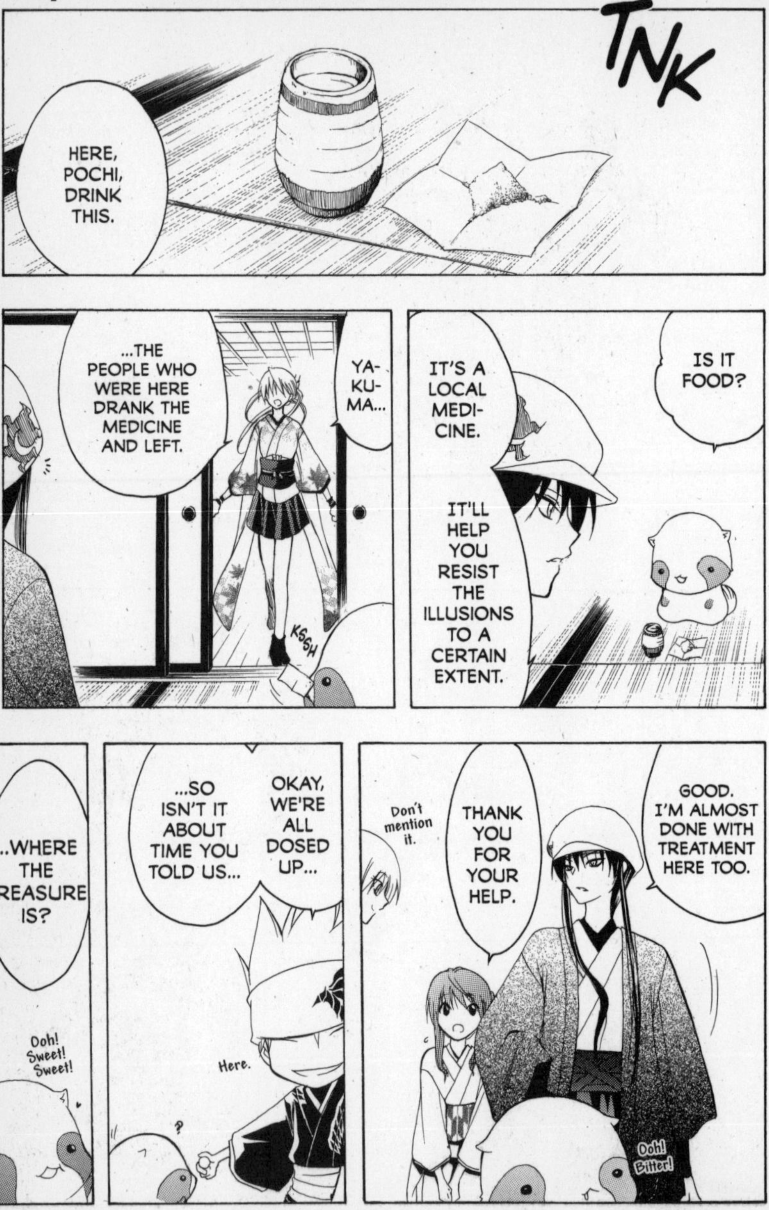
TNK
HERE, POCHI, DRINK THIS.
IS IT FOOD?
IT'S A LOCAL MEDI-CINE.
IT'LL HELP YOU RESIST THE ILLUSIONS TO A CERTAIN EXTENT.
YA-KU-MA...
...THE PEOPLE WHO WERE HERE DRANK THE MEDICINE AND LEFT.
KSSH
GOOD. I'M ALMOST DONE WITH TREATMENT HERE TOO.
THANK YOU FOR YOUR HELP.
Don't mention it.
Ooh! Bitter!
OKAY, WE'RE ALL DOSED UP...
...SO ISN'T IT ABOUT TIME YOU TOLD US...
Here.
...WHERE THE TREASURE IS?
Ooh! Sweet! Sweet!

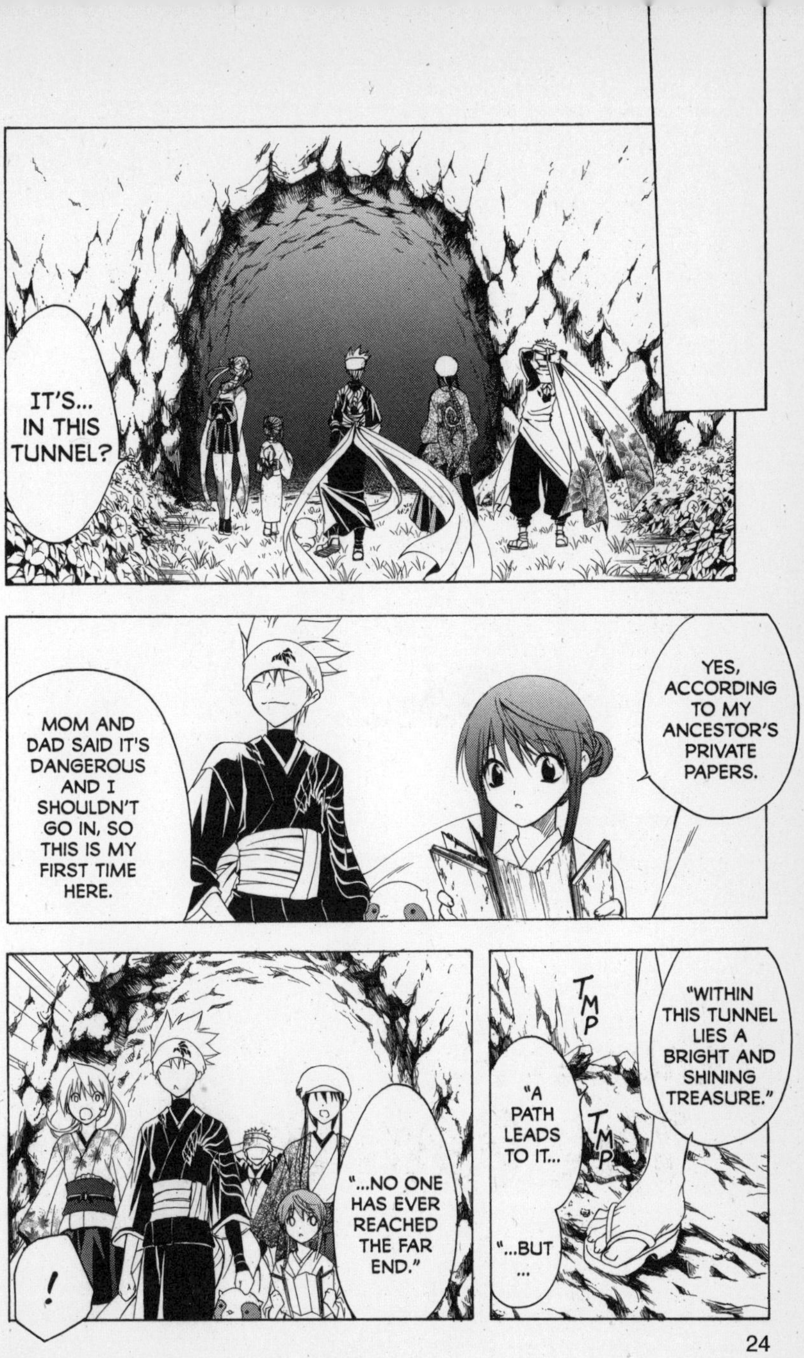
IT'S... IN THIS TUNNEL?
YES, ACCORDING TO MY ANCESTOR'S PRIVATE PAPERS.
MOM AND DAD SAID IT'S DANGEROUS AND I SHOULDN'T GO IN, SO THIS IS MY FIRST TIME HERE.
"WITHIN THIS TUNNEL LIES A BRIGHT AND SHINING TREASURE."
TMP
TMP
"A PATH LEADS TO IT...
"...BUT ...
"...NO ONE HAS EVER REACHED THE FAR END."
!

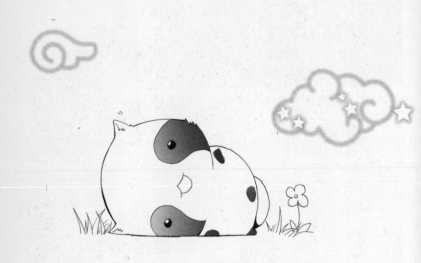

Chapter 59
The Path of God

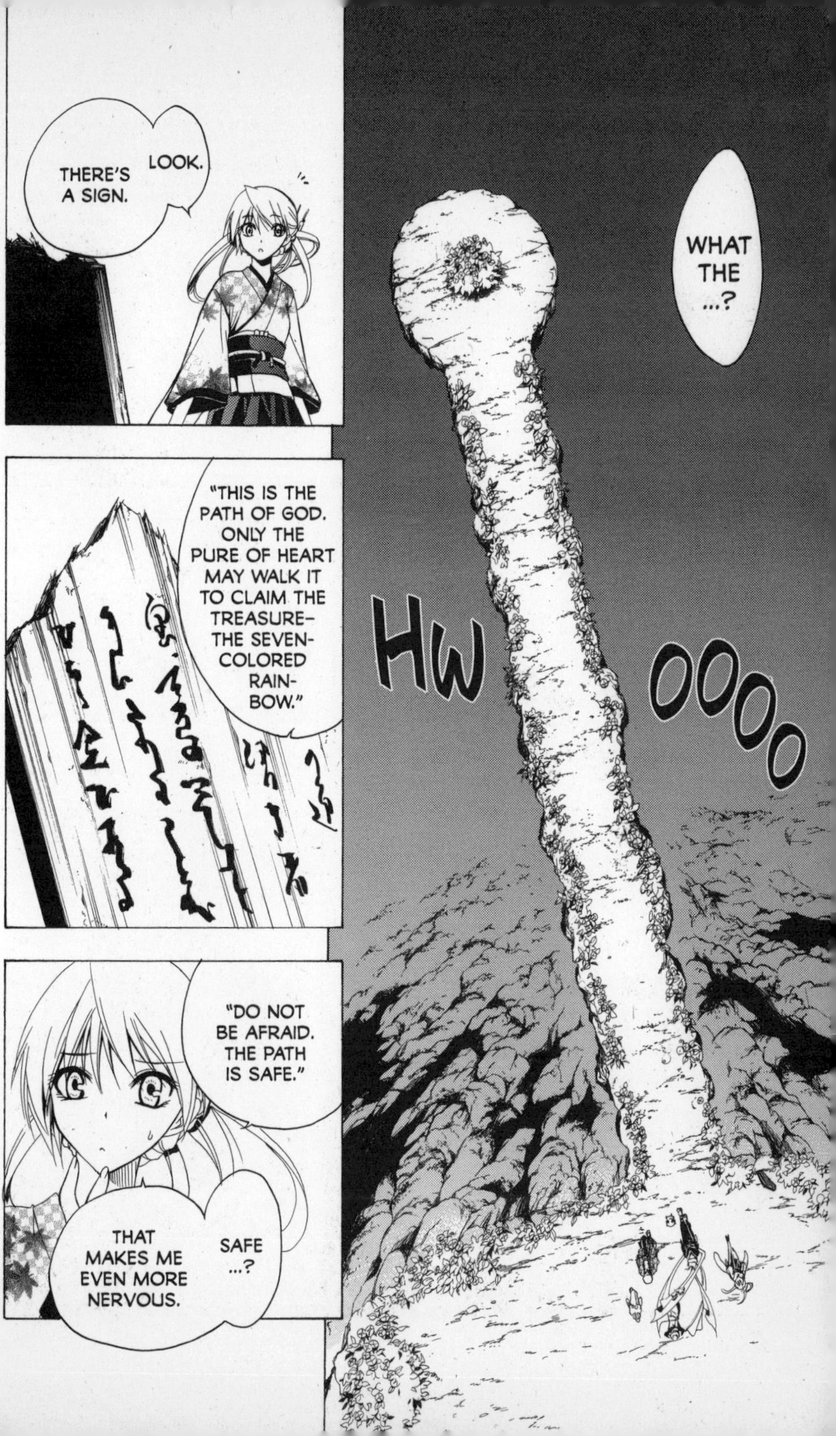
WHAT THE ...?
HWOOOO
LOOK. THERE'S A SIGN.
"THIS IS THE PATH OF GOD. ONLY THE PURE OF HEART MAY WALK IT TO CLAIM THE TREASURE—THE SEVEN-COLORED RAIN-BOW."
"DO NOT BE AFRAID. THE PATH IS SAFE."
SAFE ...?
THAT MAKES ME EVEN MORE NERVOUS.

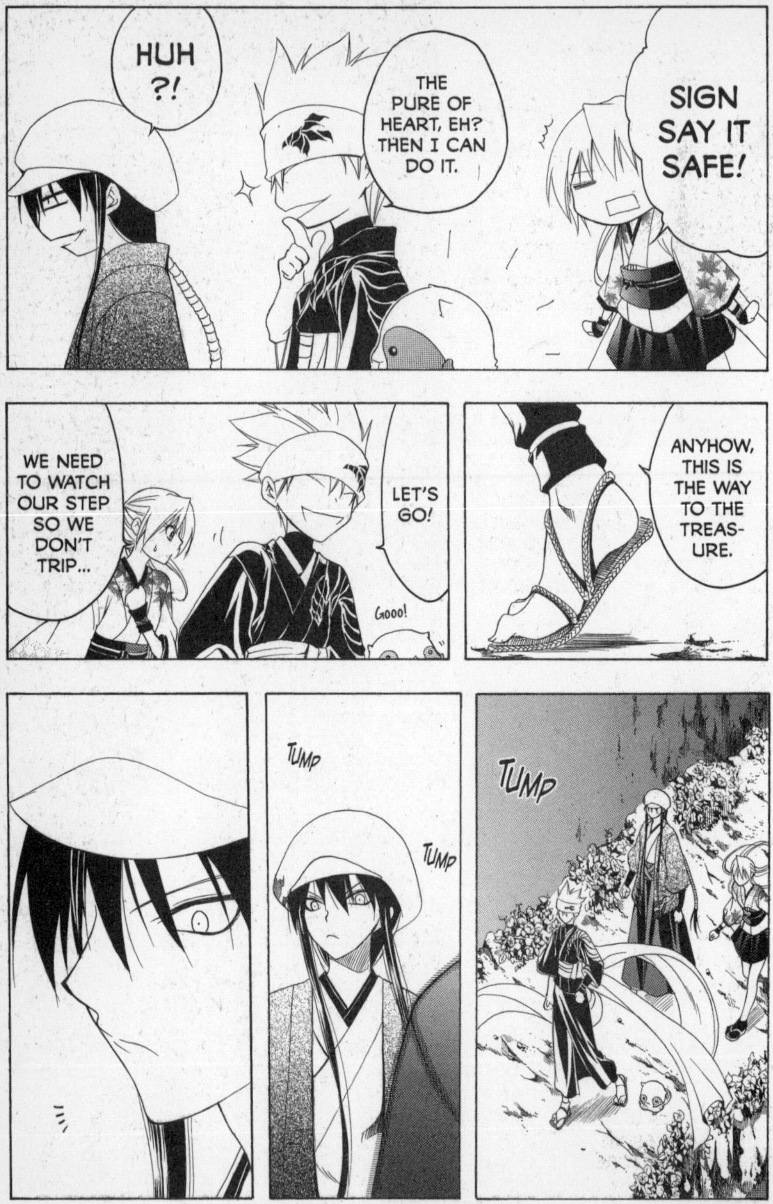
SIGN SAY IT SAFE!
THE PURE OF HEART, EH? THEN I CAN DO IT.
HUH ?!
ANYHOW, THIS IS THE WAY TO THE TREAS-URE.
LET'S GO!
GOOO!
WE NEED TO WATCH OUR STEP SO WE DON'T TRIP...
TUMP
TUMP
TUMP

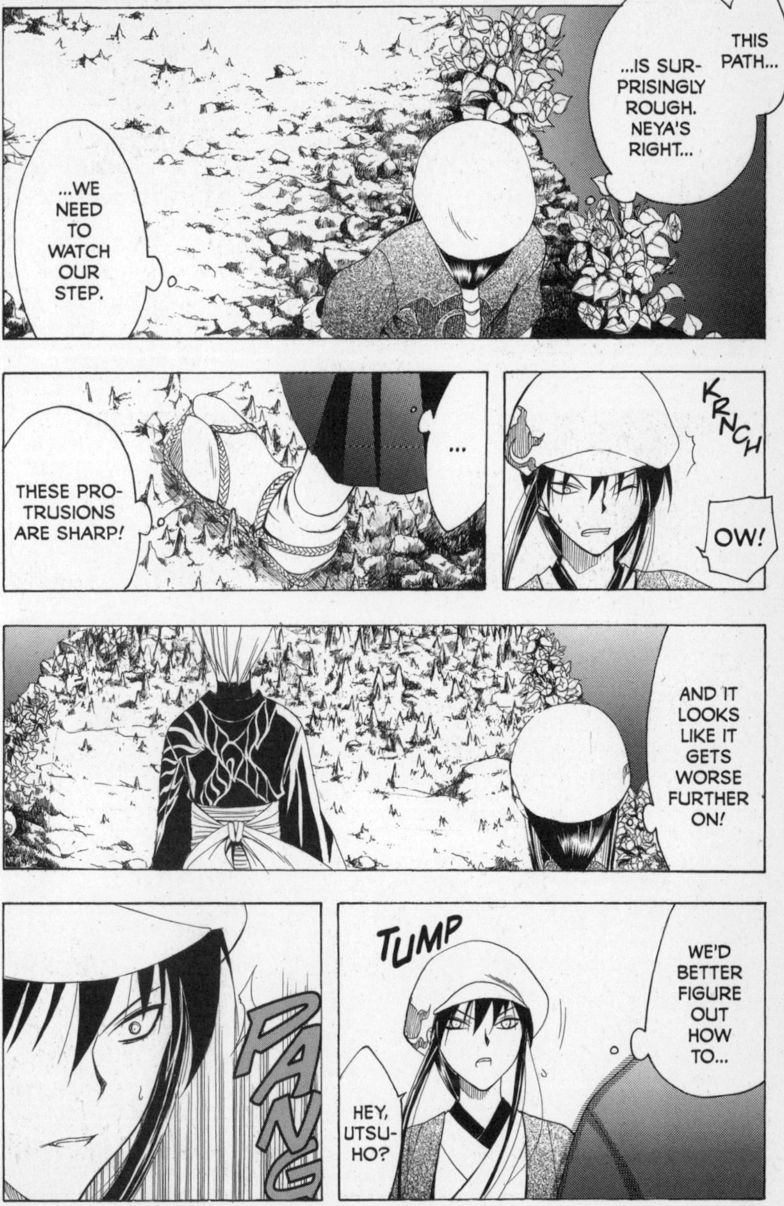
THIS PATH...
...IS SURPRISINGLY ROUGH. NEYA'S RIGHT...
...WE NEED TO WATCH OUR STEP.
KRNCH
OW!
...
THESE PROTRUSIONS ARE SHARP!
AND IT LOOKS LIKE IT GETS WORSE FURTHER ON!
TUMP
WE'D BETTER FIGURE OUT HOW TO...
HEY, UTSUHO?
PANG

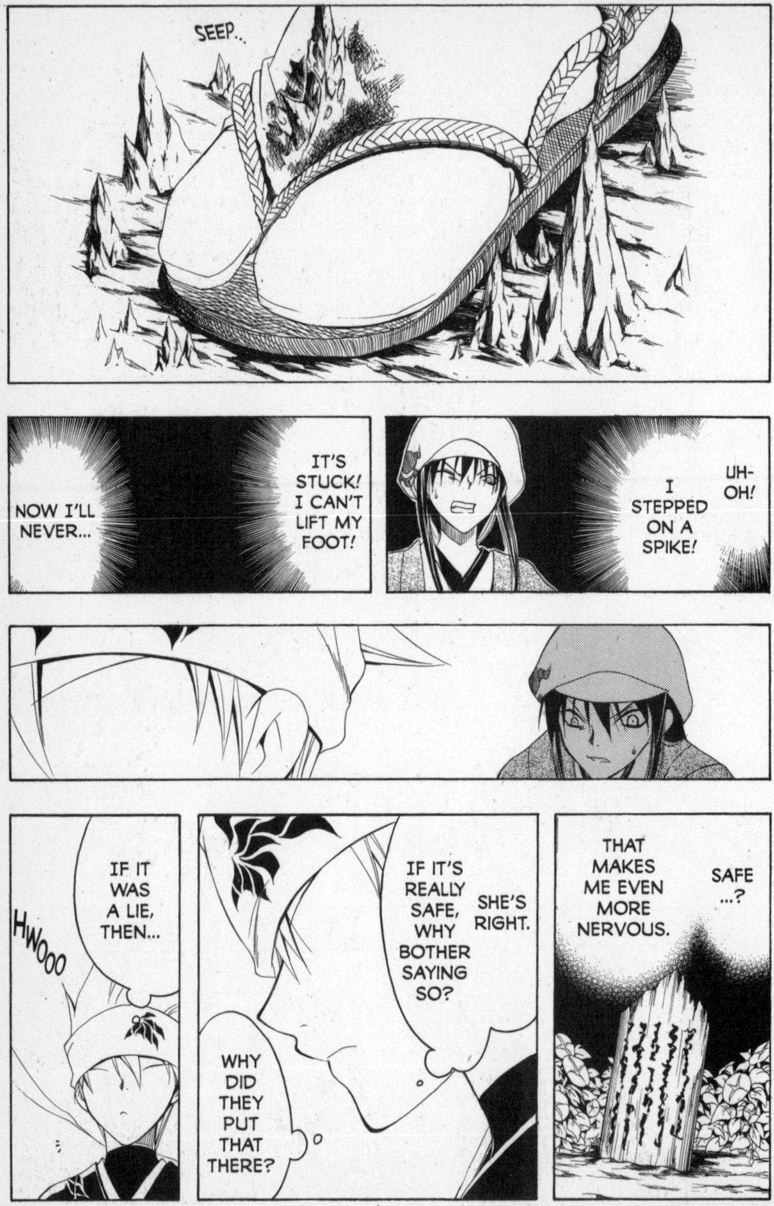
SEEP...
UH-OH!
I STEPPED ON A SPIKE!
IT'S STUCK! I CAN'T LIFT MY FOOT!
NOW I'LL NEVER...
SAFE ...?
THAT MAKES ME EVEN MORE NERVOUS.
SHE'S RIGHT.
IF IT'S REALLY SAFE, WHY BOTHER SAYING SO?
WHY DID THEY PUT THAT THERE?
IF IT WAS A LIE, THEN...
HWOOO

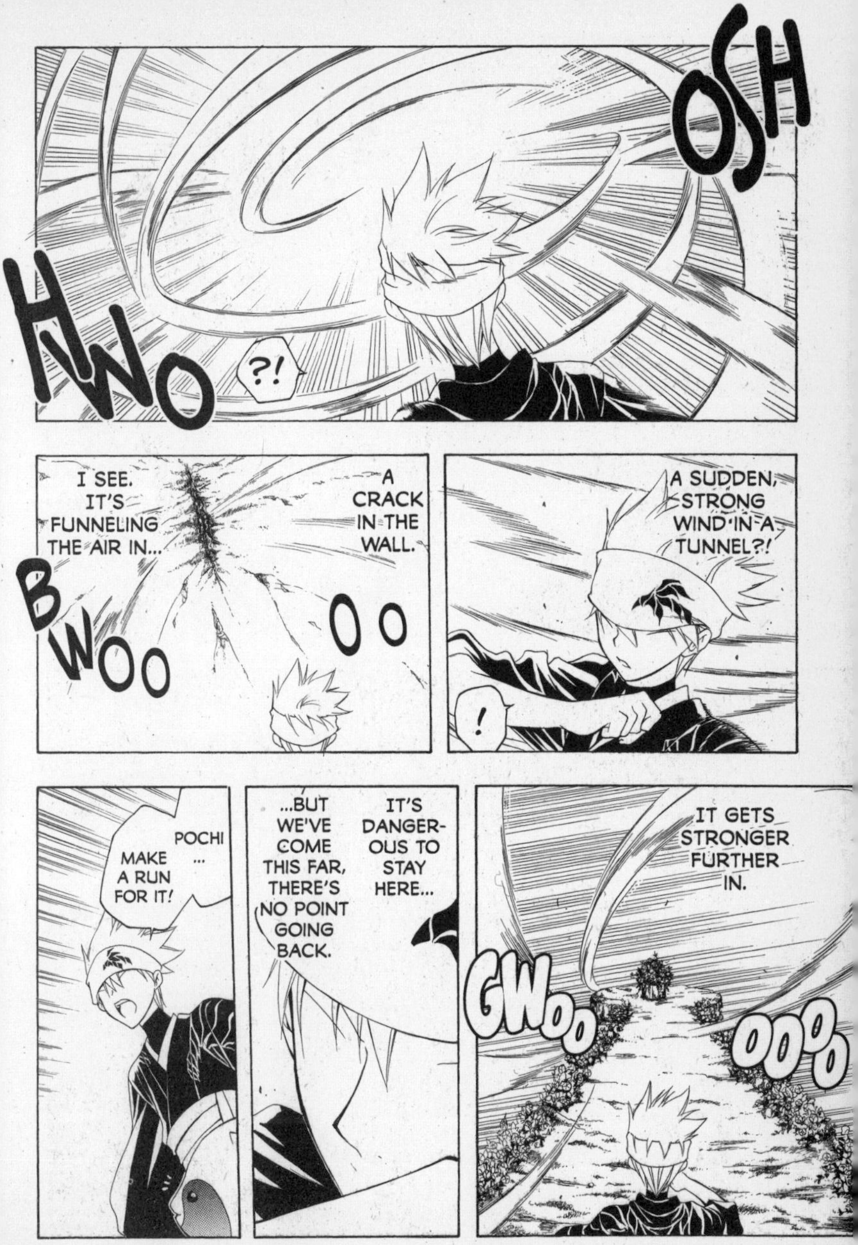
HWO
OSH
?!
A SUDDEN, STRONG WIND IN A TUNNEL?!
!
A CRACK IN THE WALL.
I SEE. IT'S FUNNELING THE AIR IN...
BWOO
OO
IT GETS STRONGER FURTHER IN.
GWOO
OOOO
IT'S DANGER-OUS TO STAY HERE...
...BUT WE'VE COME THIS FAR, THERE'S NO POINT GOING BACK.
POCHI ...
MAKE A RUN FOR IT!

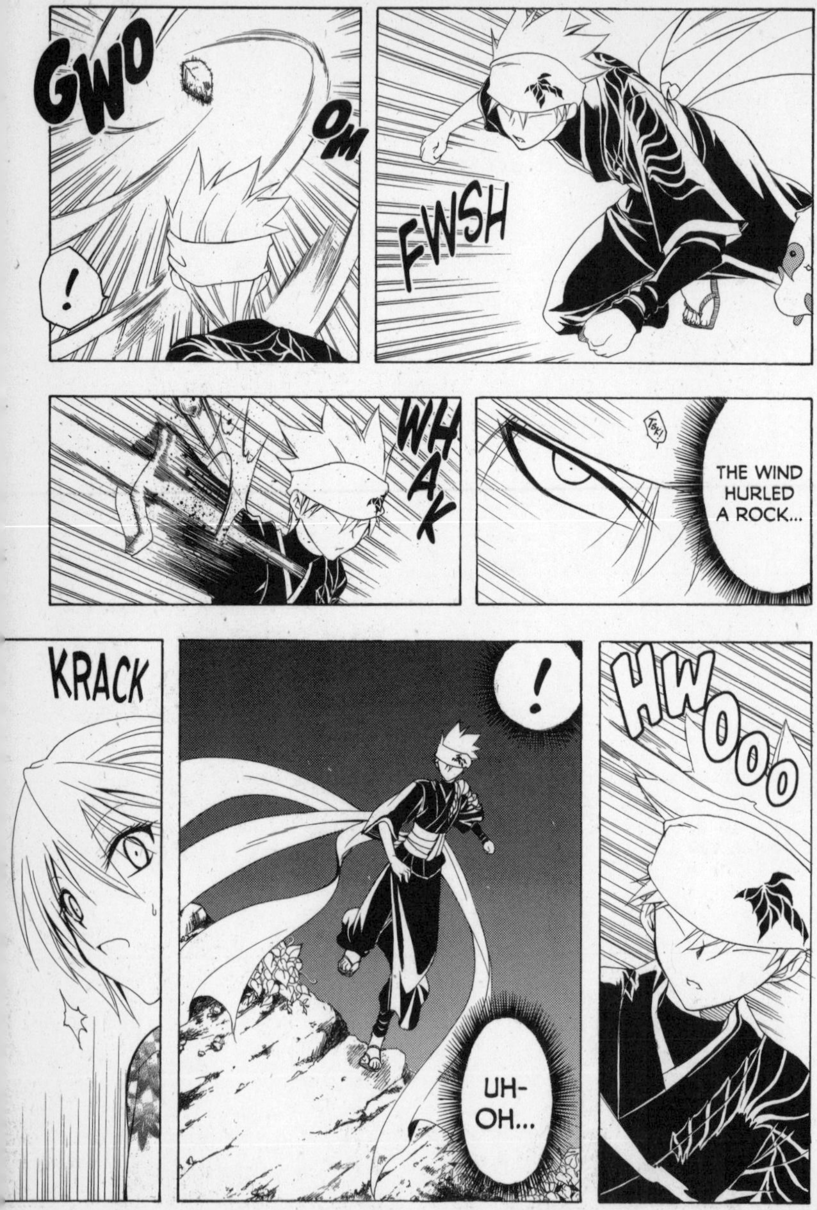
FWSH
GWO
OM
!
TSK!
THE WIND HURLED A ROCK...
WHAK
HWOOO
!
UH-OH...
KRACK

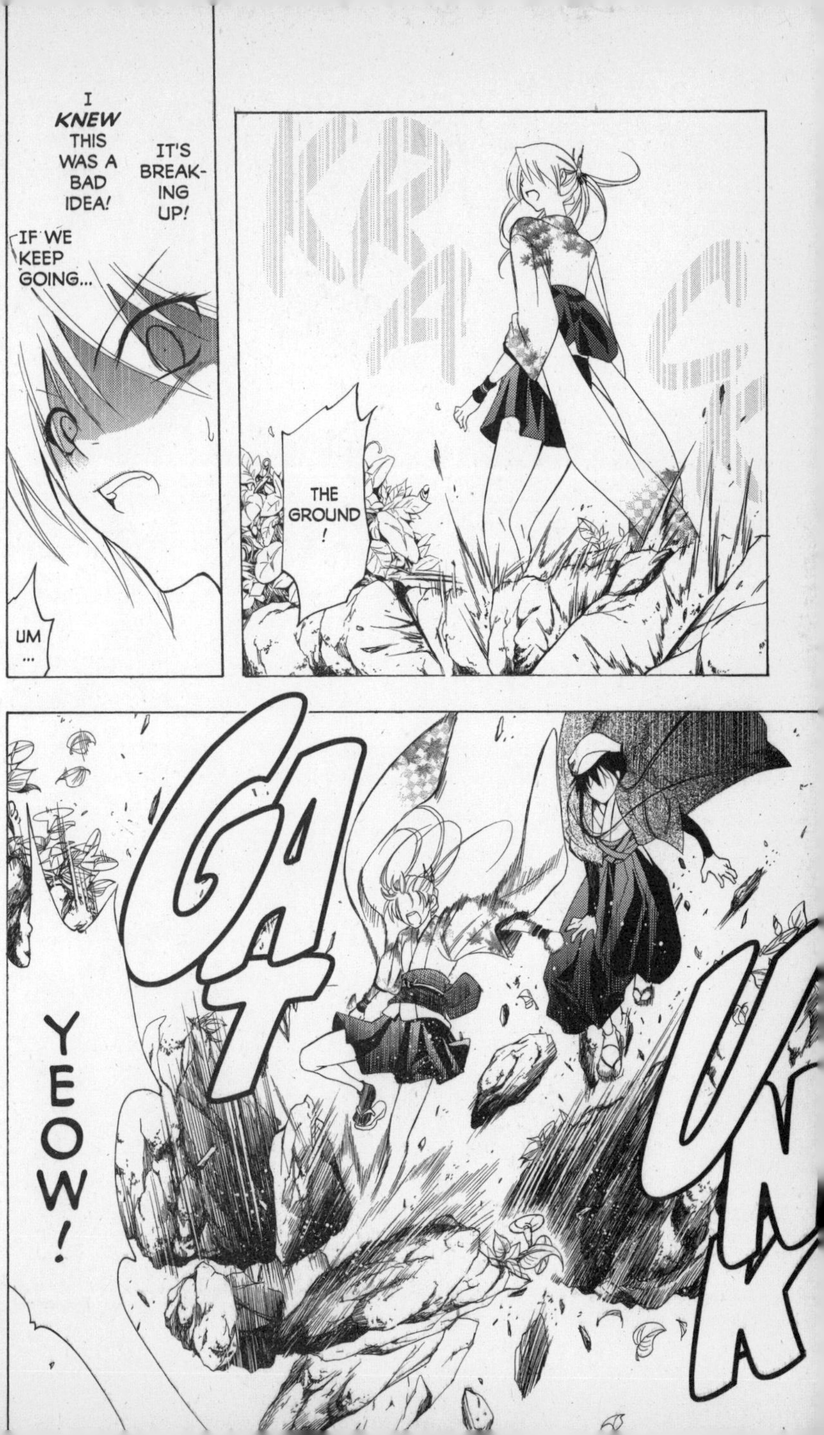
THE GROUND!
IT'S BREAKING UP!
I KNEW THIS WAS A BAD IDEA!
IF WE KEEP GOING...
UM...
GA
YEOW!

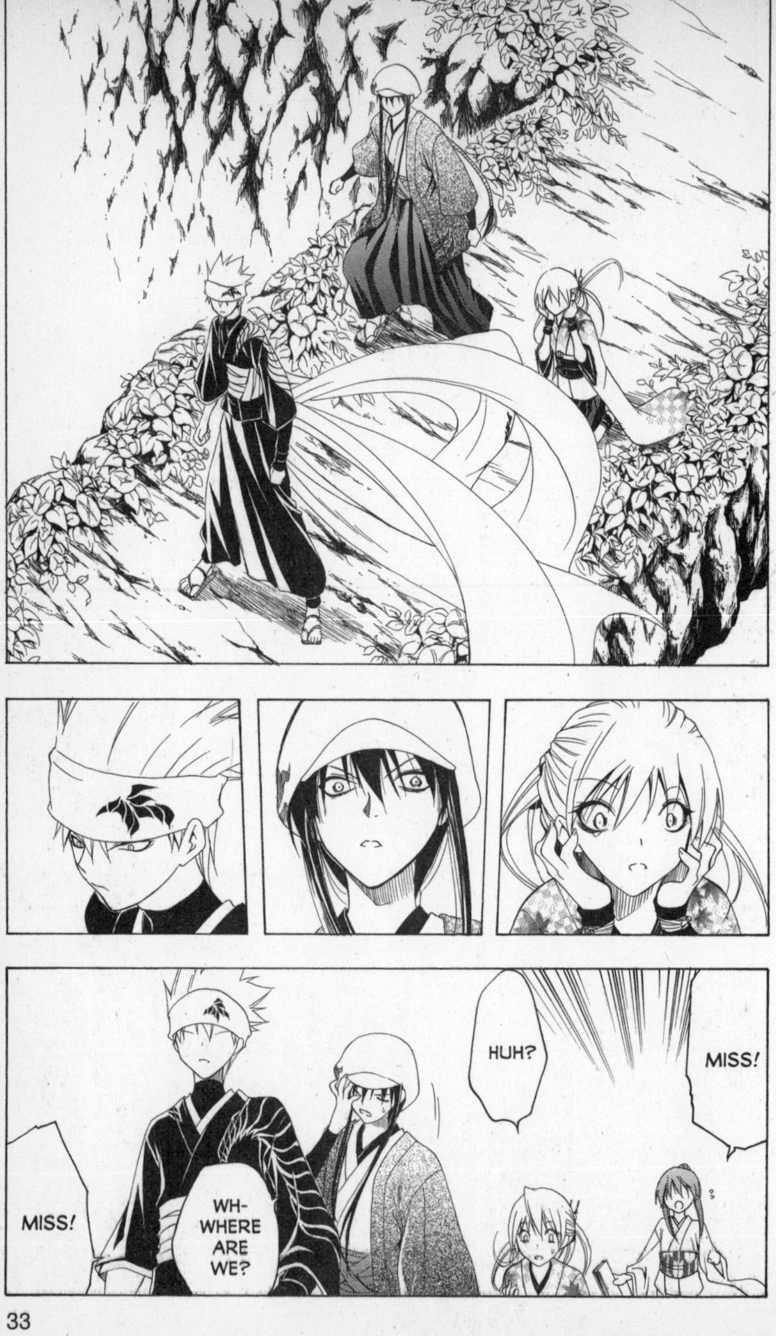
MISS!
HUH?
WH-WHERE ARE WE?
MISS!

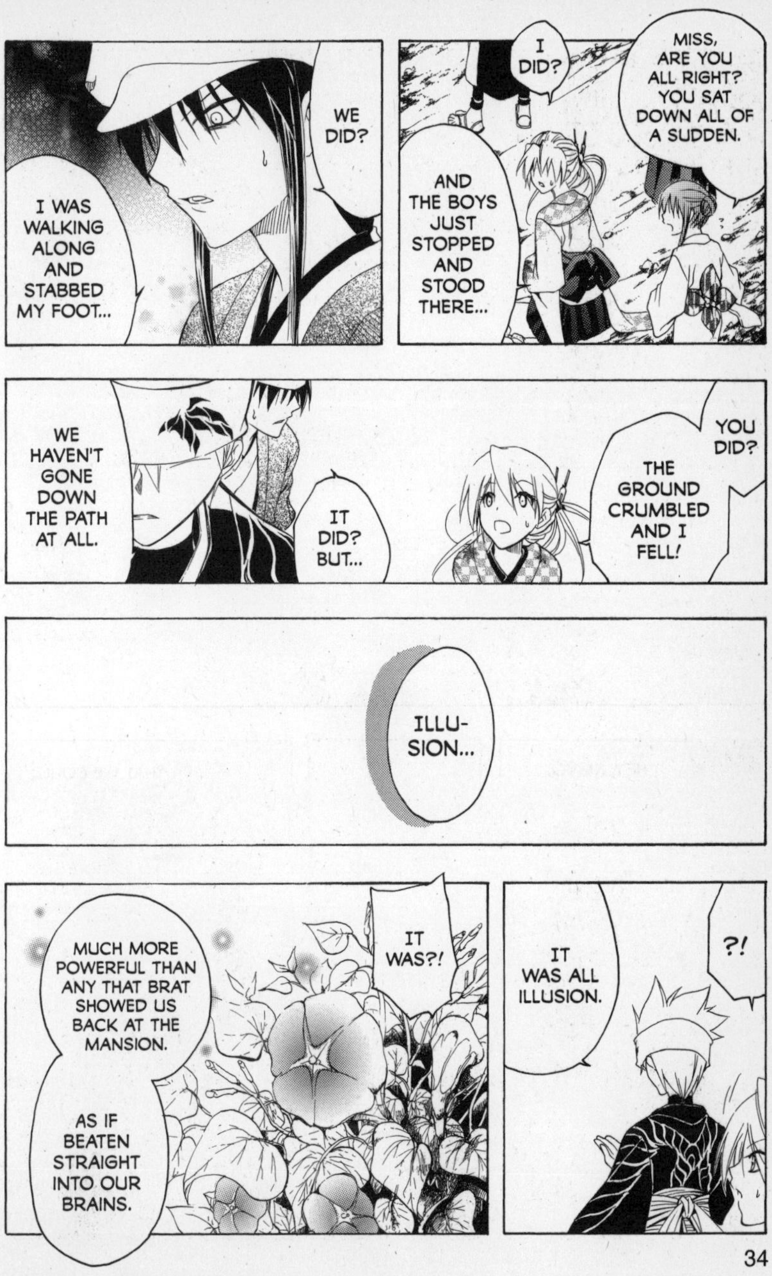
MISS, ARE YOU ALL RIGHT? YOU SAT DOWN ALL OF A SUDDEN.
I DID?
AND THE BOYS JUST STOPPED AND STOOD THERE...
WE DID?
I WAS WALKING ALONG AND STABBED MY FOOT...
YOU DID?
THE GROUND CRUMBLED AND I FELL!
IT DID? BUT...
WE HAVEN'T GONE DOWN THE PATH AT ALL.
ILLUSION...
?!
IT WAS ALL ILLUSION.
IT WAS?!
MUCH MORE POWERFUL THAN ANY THAT BRAT SHOWED US BACK AT THE MANSION.
AS IF BEATEN STRAIGHT INTO OUR BRAINS.

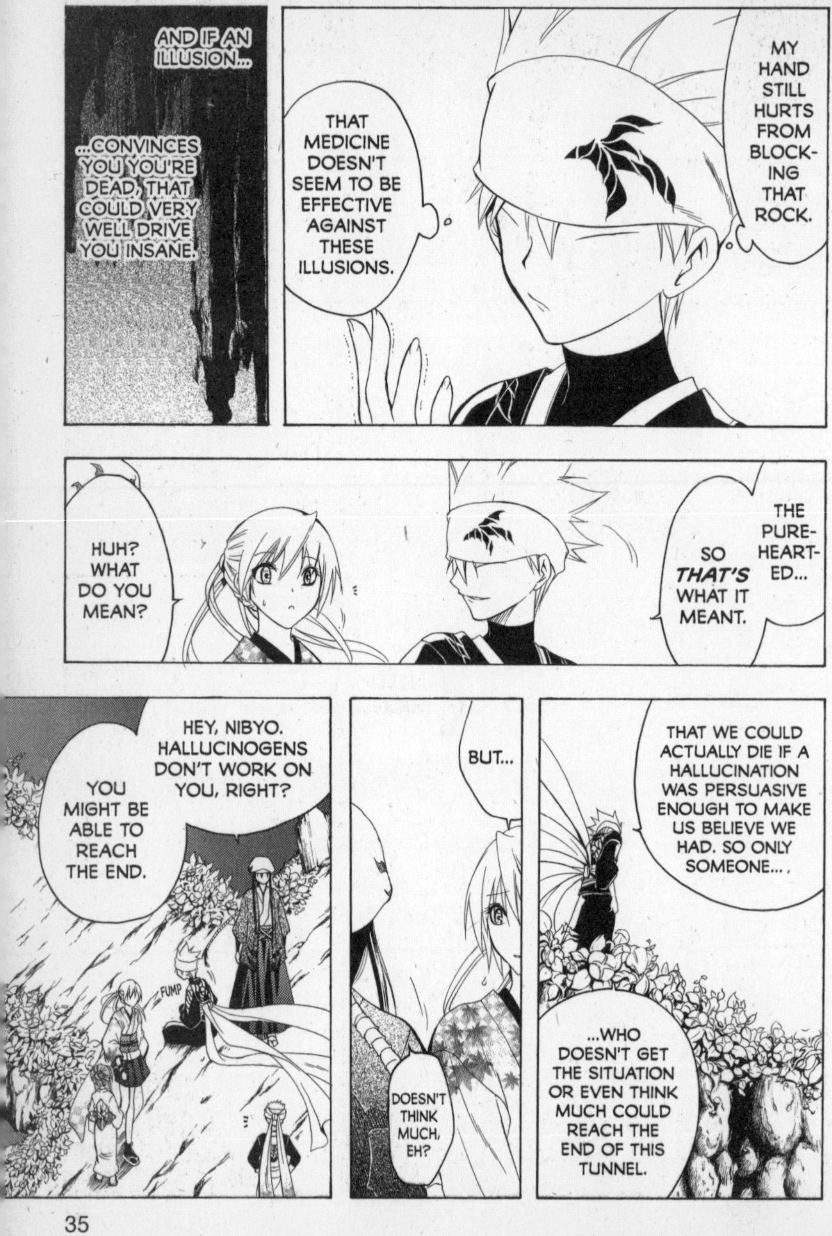
MY HAND STILL HURTS FROM BLOCKING THAT ROCK.
THAT MEDICINE DOESN'T SEEM TO BE EFFECTIVE AGAINST THESE ILLUSIONS.
AND IF AN ILLUSION...
...CONVINCES YOU YOU'RE DEAD, THAT COULD VERY WELL DRIVE YOU INSANE.
THE PURE-HEARTED...
SO *THAT'S* WHAT IT MEANT.
HUH? WHAT DO YOU MEAN?
THAT WE COULD ACTUALLY DIE IF A HALLUCINATION WAS PERSUASIVE ENOUGH TO MAKE US BELIEVE WE HAD. SO ONLY SOMEONE....
...WHO DOESN'T GET THE SITUATION OR EVEN THINK MUCH COULD REACH THE END OF THIS TUNNEL.
BUT...
DOESN'T THINK MUCH, EH?
HEY, NIBYO. HALLUCINOGENS DON'T WORK ON YOU, RIGHT?
YOU MIGHT BE ABLE TO REACH THE END.
FUMP

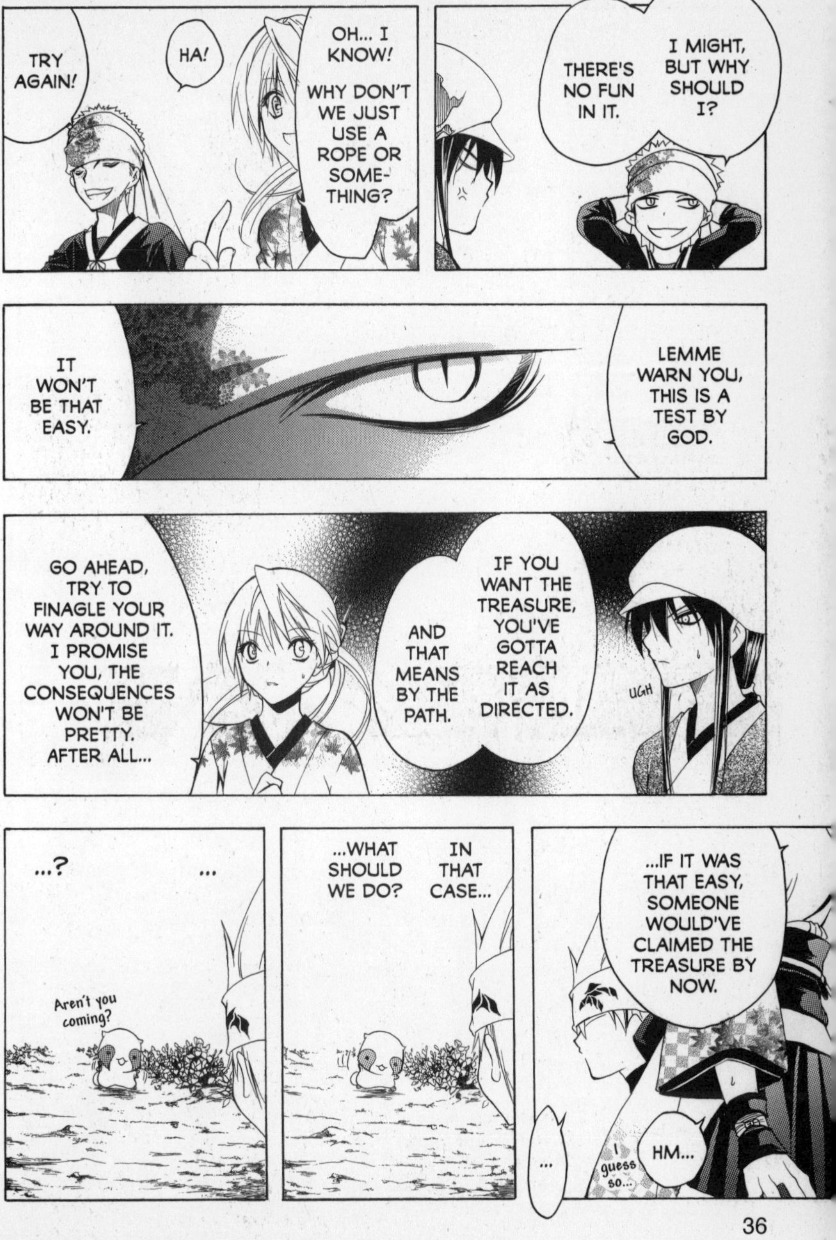
I MIGHT, BUT WHY SHOULD I?
THERE'S NO FUN IN IT.
OH... I KNOW!
WHY DON'T WE JUST USE A ROPE OR SOME-THING?
HA!
TRY AGAIN!
LEMME WARN YOU, THIS IS A TEST BY GOD.
IT WON'T BE THAT EASY.
IF YOU WANT THE TREASURE, YOU'VE GOTTA REACH IT AS DIRECTED.
AND THAT MEANS BY THE PATH.
UGH
GO AHEAD, TRY TO FINAGLE YOUR WAY AROUND IT. I PROMISE YOU, THE CONSEQUENCES WON'T BE PRETTY. AFTER ALL...
...IF IT WAS THAT EASY, SOMEONE WOULD'VE CLAIMED THE TREASURE BY NOW.
HM...
I guess so...
...
IN THAT CASE...
...WHAT SHOULD WE DO?
...
...?
Aren't you coming?

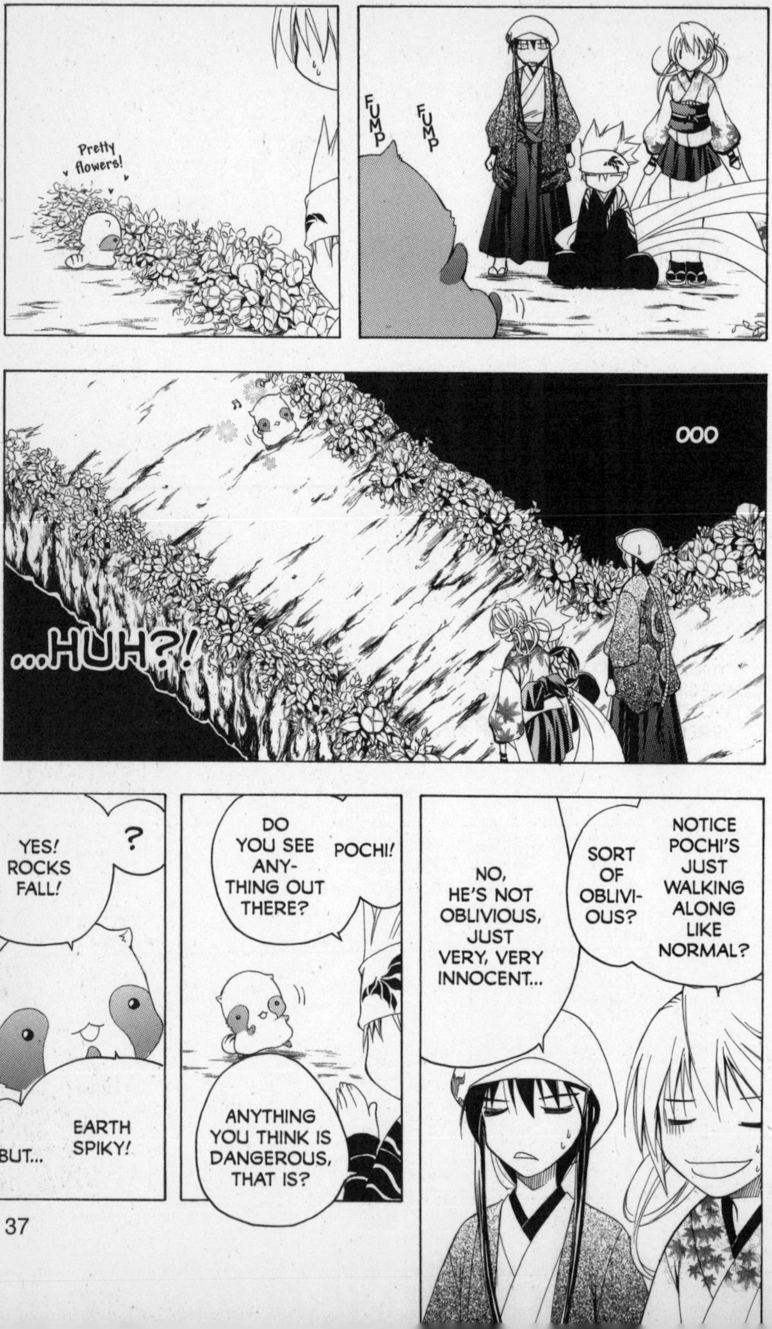
FUMP
FUMP
Pretty flowers!
ooo
...HUH?!
NOTICE POCHI'S JUST WALKING ALONG LIKE NORMAL?
SORT OF OBLIVIOUS?
NO, HE'S NOT OBLIVIOUS, JUST VERY, VERY INNOCENT...
POCHI!
DO YOU SEE ANY-THING OUT THERE?
ANYTHING YOU THINK IS DANGEROUS, THAT IS?
?
YES! ROCKS FALL!
BUT... EARTH SPIKY!

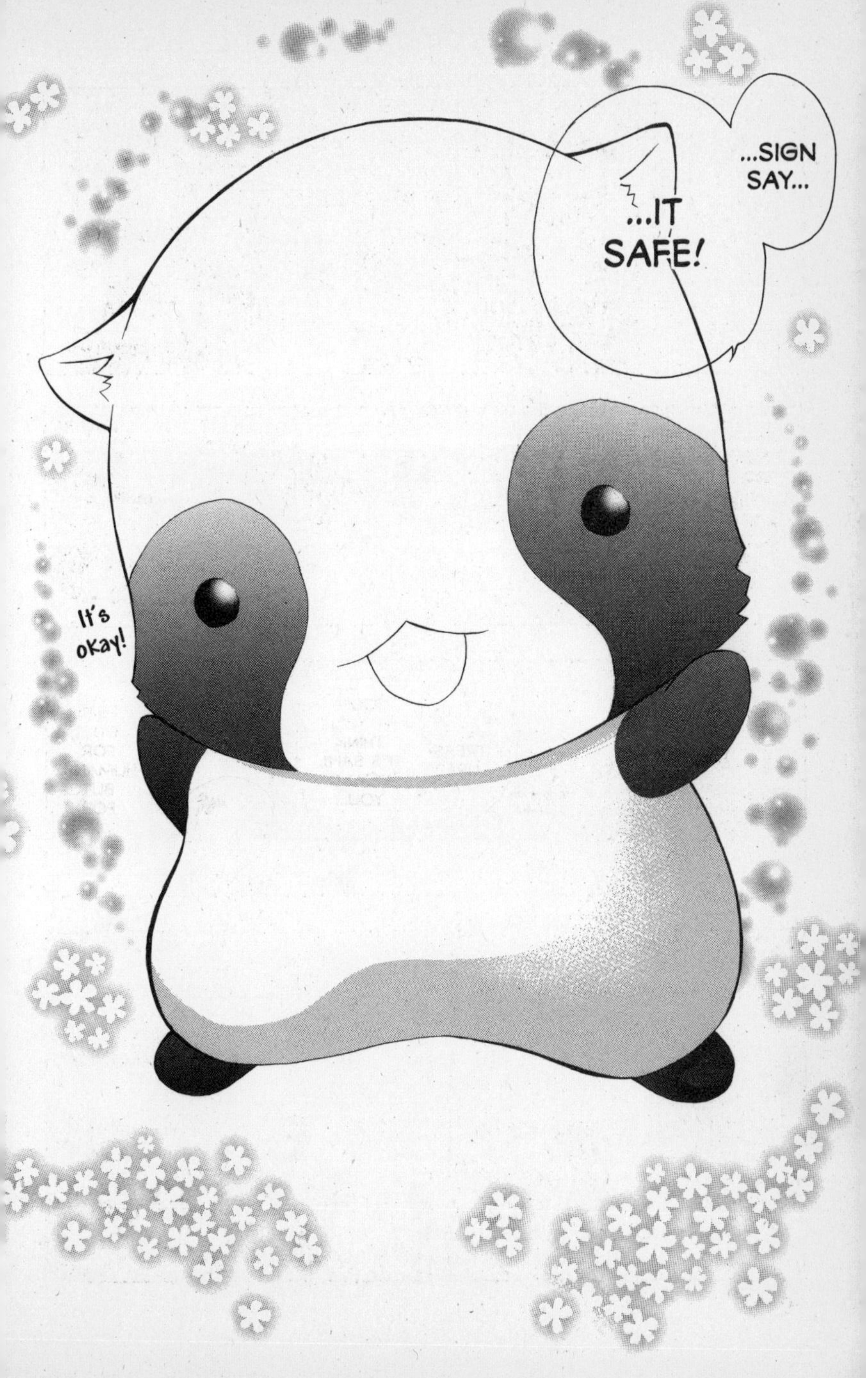
...SIGN SAY...
...IT SAFE!
It's okay!

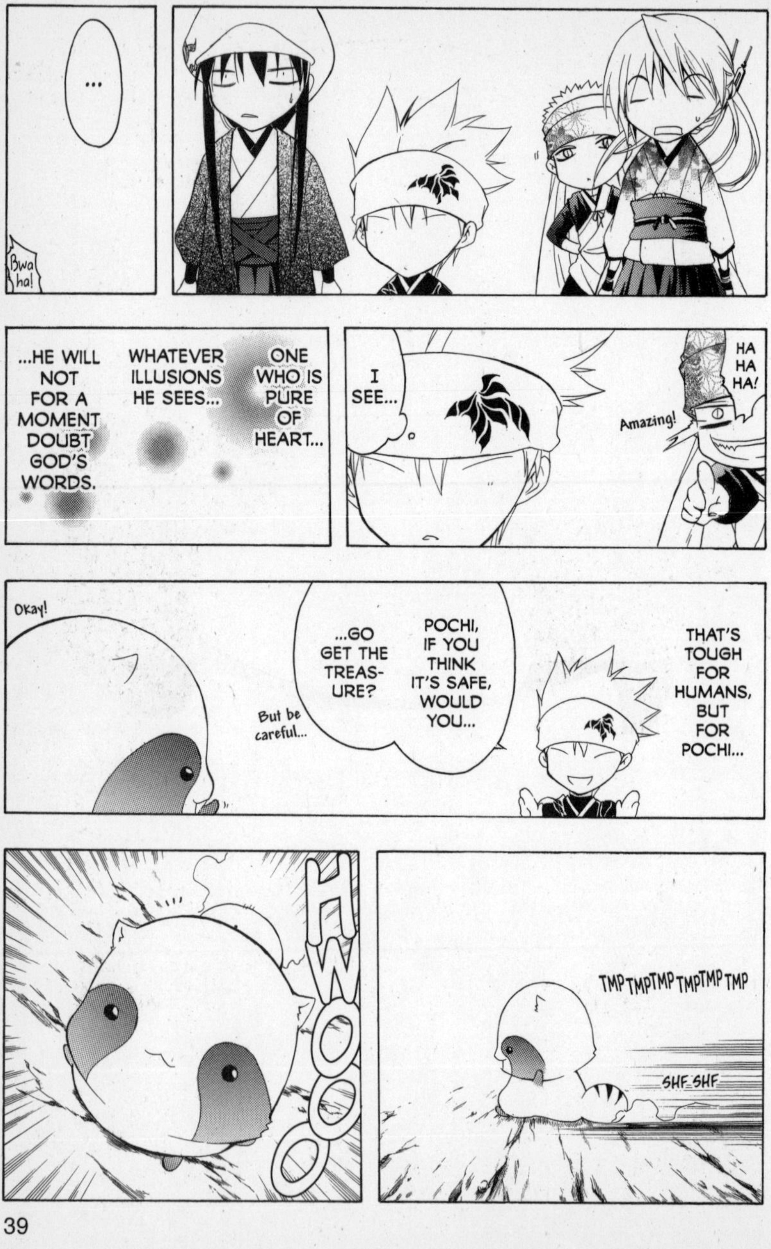
...
Bwa ha!
HA HA HA!
Amazing!
I SEE...
ONE WHO IS PURE OF HEART...
WHATEVER ILLUSIONS HE SEES...
...HE WILL NOT FOR A MOMENT DOUBT GOD'S WORDS.
THAT'S TOUGH FOR HUMANS, BUT FOR POCHI...
POCHI, IF YOU THINK IT'S SAFE, WOULD YOU...
...GO GET THE TREASURE?
But be careful...
Okay!
TMP TMPTMP TMPTMP TMP
SHF SHF
HWOOOO

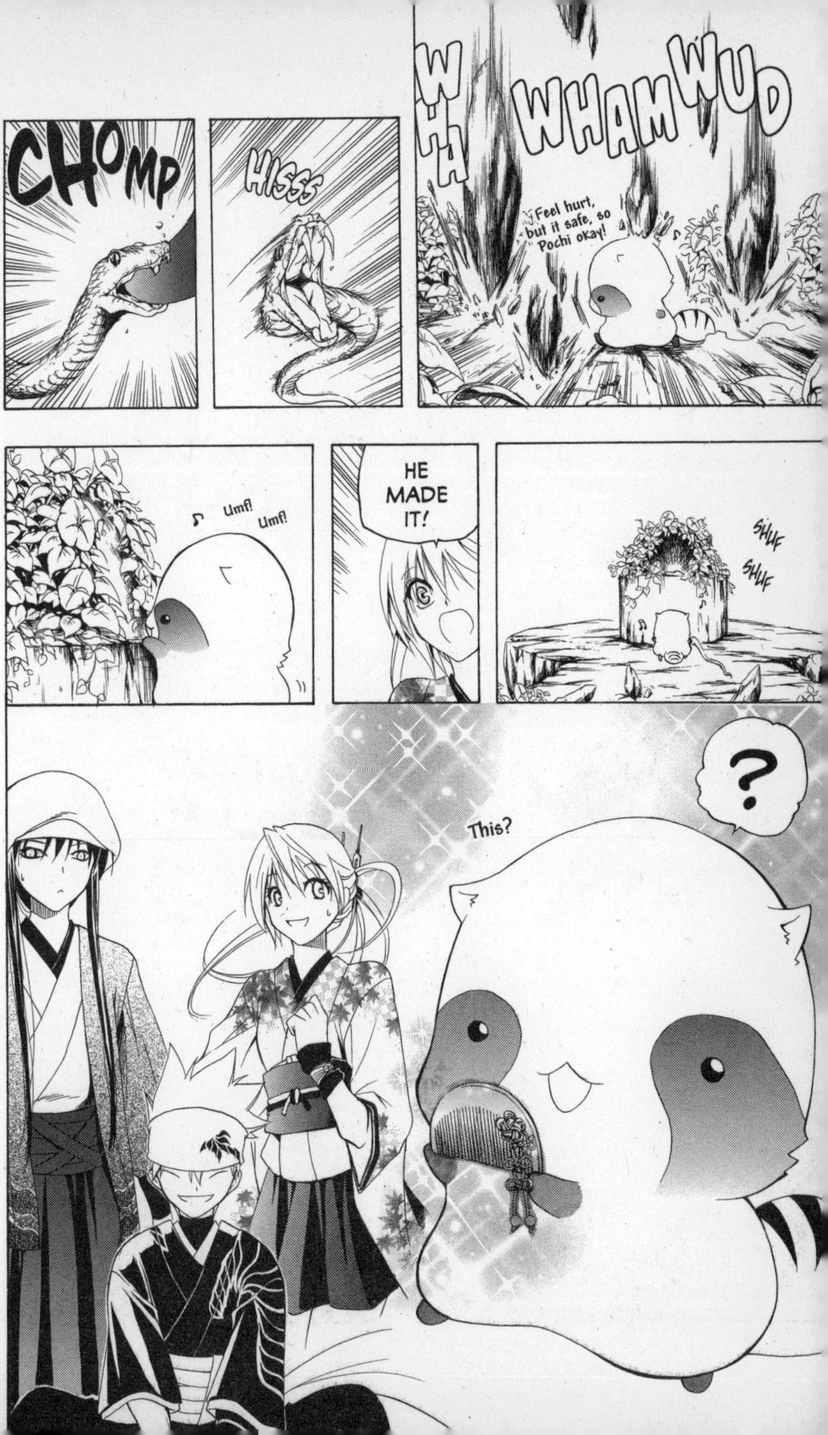

WHAM
WHA
WUD
Feel hurt, but it safe, so Pochi okay!
HISSS
CHOMP
SHUF
SHUF
HE MADE IT!
Umf!
Umf!
?
This?

Chapter 60 Closed Island

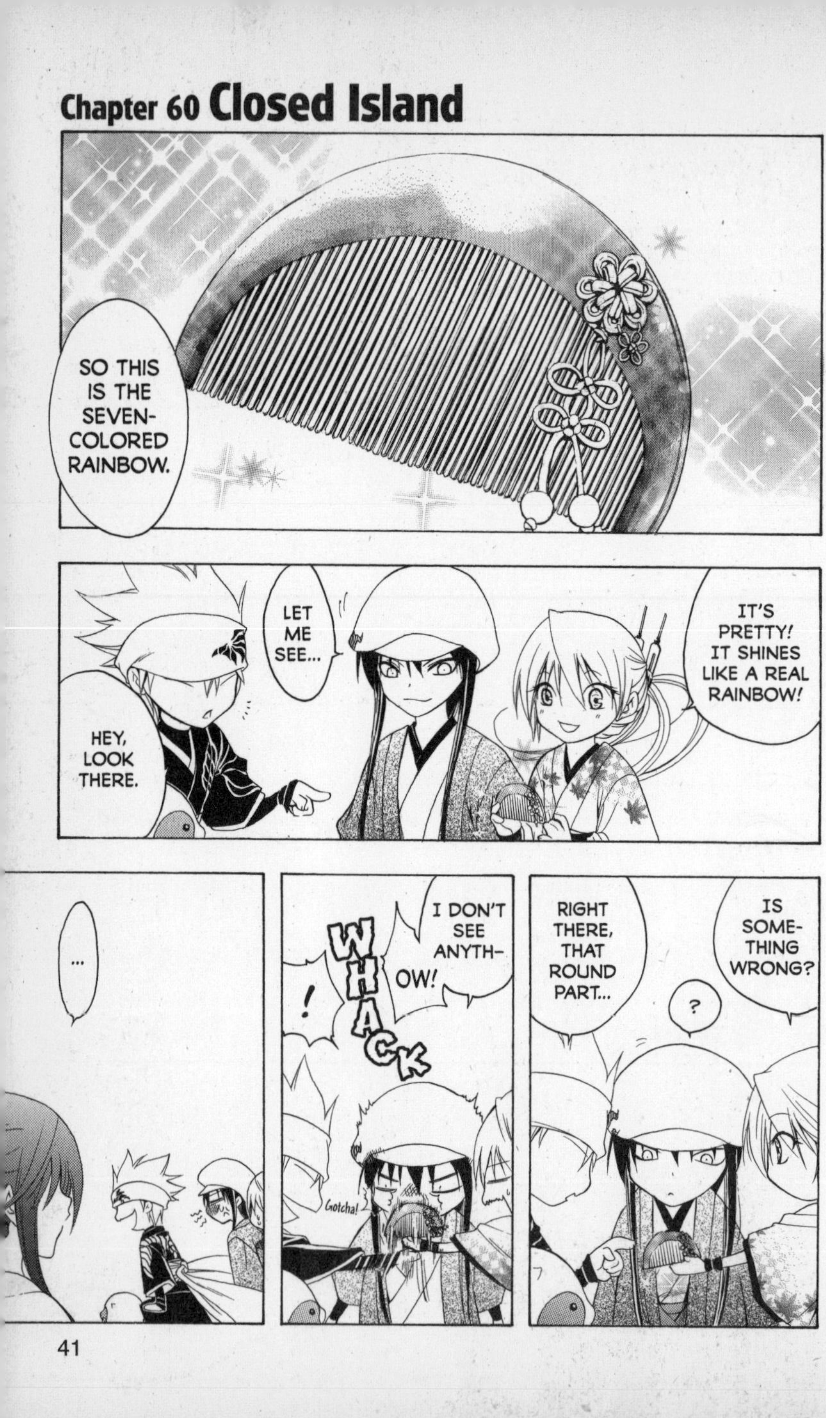

SO THIS IS THE SEVEN-COLORED RAINBOW.
IT'S PRETTY! IT SHINES LIKE A REAL RAINBOW!
LET ME SEE...
HEY, LOOK THERE.
IS SOMETHING WRONG?
?
RIGHT THERE, THAT ROUND PART...
I DON'T SEE ANYTH-
OW!
WHACK
!
Gotcha!
...

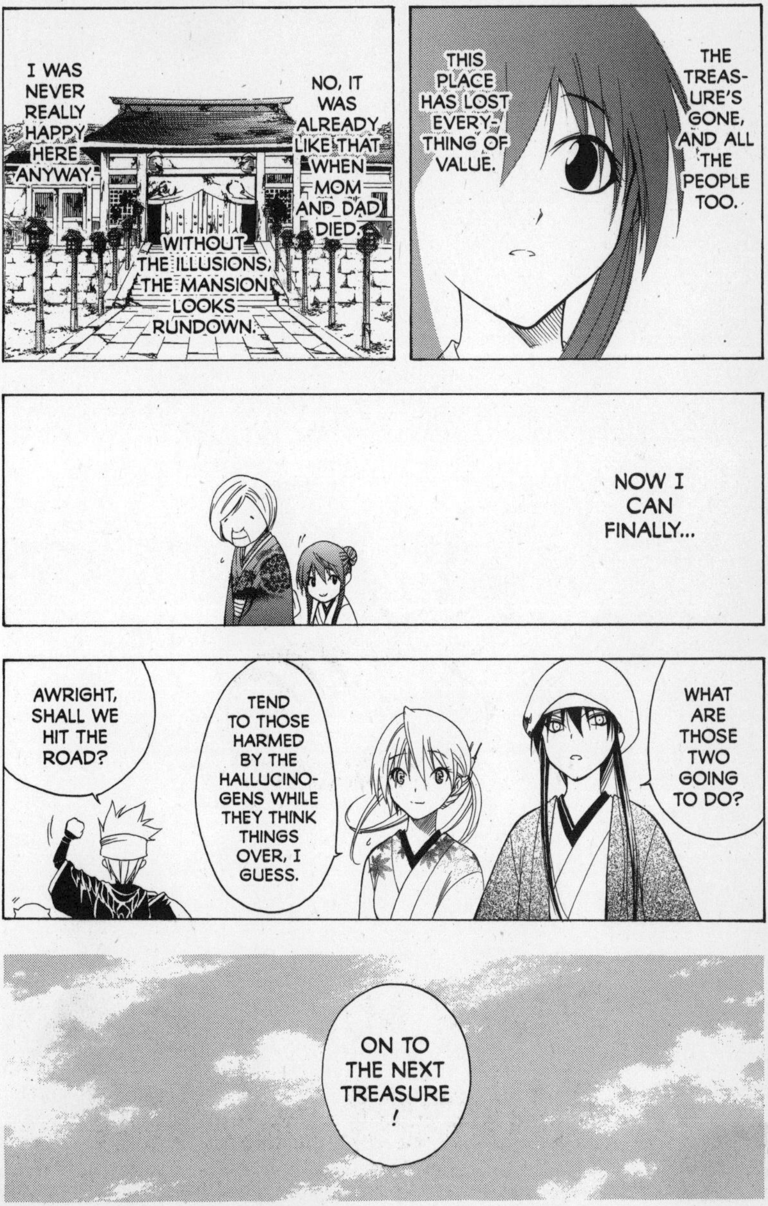
THE TREASURE'S GONE, AND ALL THE PEOPLE TOO.
THIS PLACE HAS LOST EVERYTHING OF VALUE.
NO, IT WAS ALREADY LIKE THAT WHEN MOM AND DAD DIED.
I WAS NEVER REALLY HAPPY HERE ANYWAY.
WITHOUT THE ILLUSIONS, THE MANSION LOOKS RUNDOWN.
NOW I CAN FINALLY...
WHAT ARE THOSE TWO GOING TO DO?
TEND TO THOSE HARMED BY THE HALLUCINOGENS WHILE THEY THINK THINGS OVER, I GUESS.
AWRIGHT, SHALL WE HIT THE ROAD?
ON TO THE NEXT TREASURE!

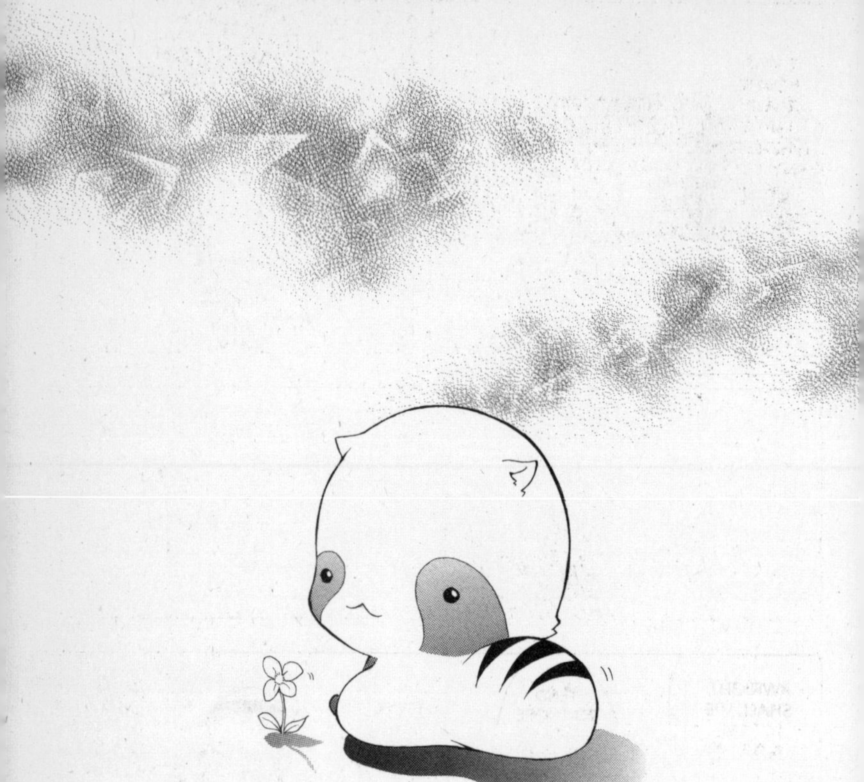

Chapter 60
Closed Island

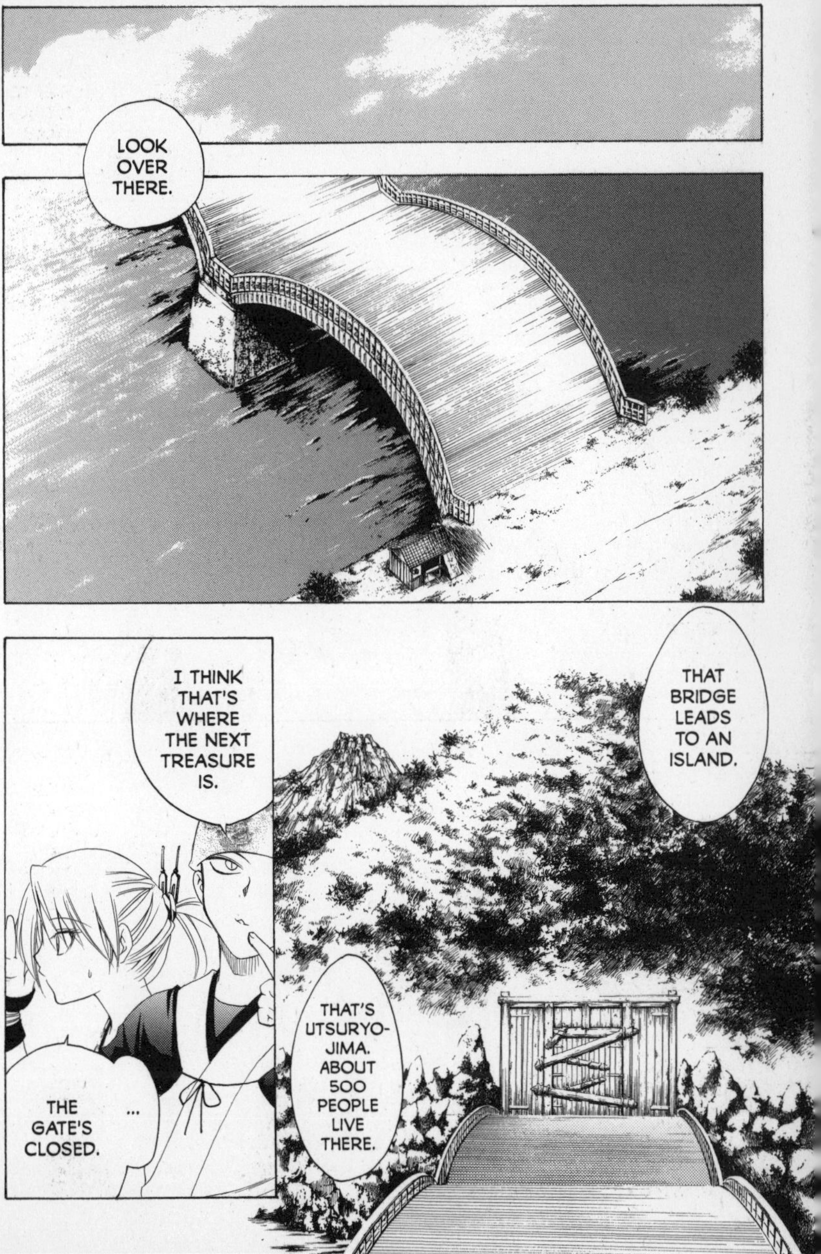
LOOK OVER THERE.
THAT BRIDGE LEADS TO AN ISLAND.
THAT'S UTSURYO-JIMA. ABOUT 500 PEOPLE LIVE THERE.
I THINK THAT'S WHERE THE NEXT TREASURE IS.
...
THE GATE'S CLOSED.

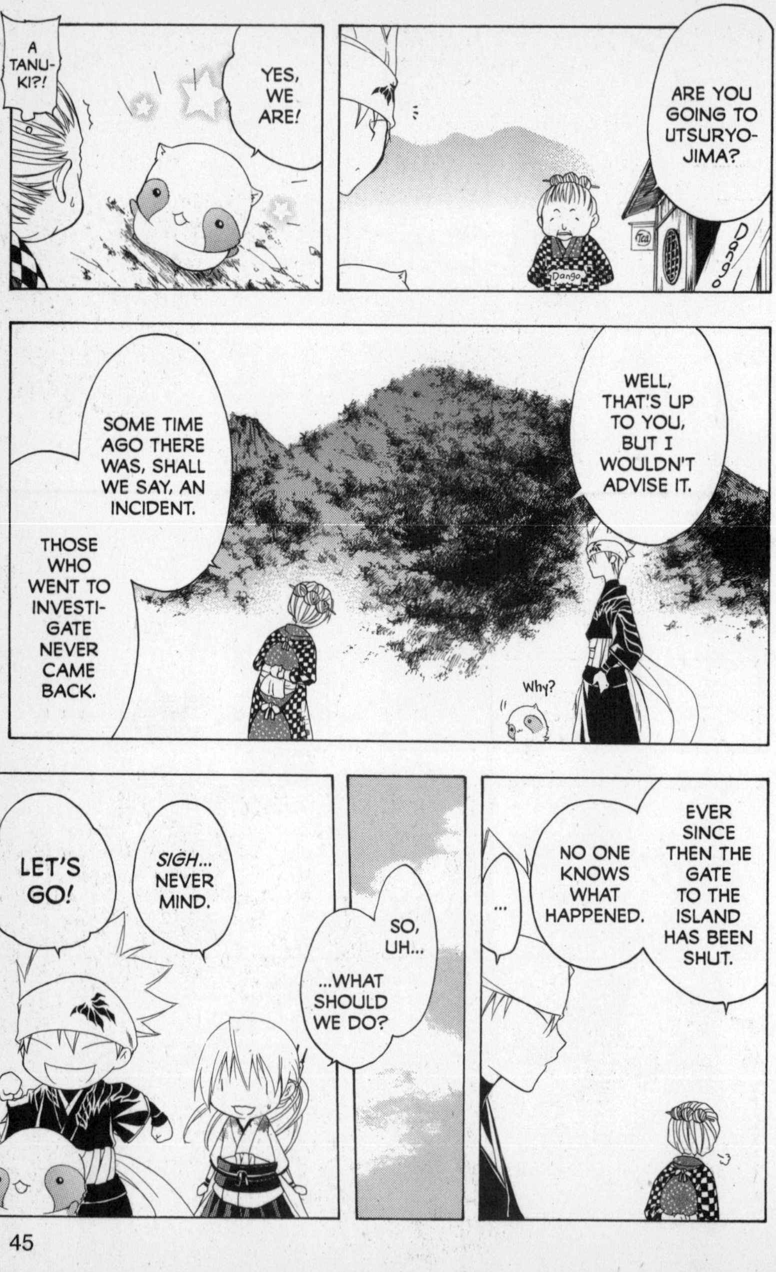
ARE YOU GOING TO UTSURYO-JIMA?
Dango
Tea
Dango
YES, WE ARE!
A TANU-KI?!
WELL, THAT'S UP TO YOU, BUT I WOULDN'T ADVISE IT.
Why?
SOME TIME AGO THERE WAS, SHALL WE SAY, AN INCIDENT.
THOSE WHO WENT TO INVESTI-GATE NEVER CAME BACK.
EVER SINCE THEN THE GATE TO THE ISLAND HAS BEEN SHUT.
NO ONE KNOWS WHAT HAPPENED.
...
SO, UH...
...WHAT SHOULD WE DO?
SIGH... NEVER MIND.
LET'S GO!

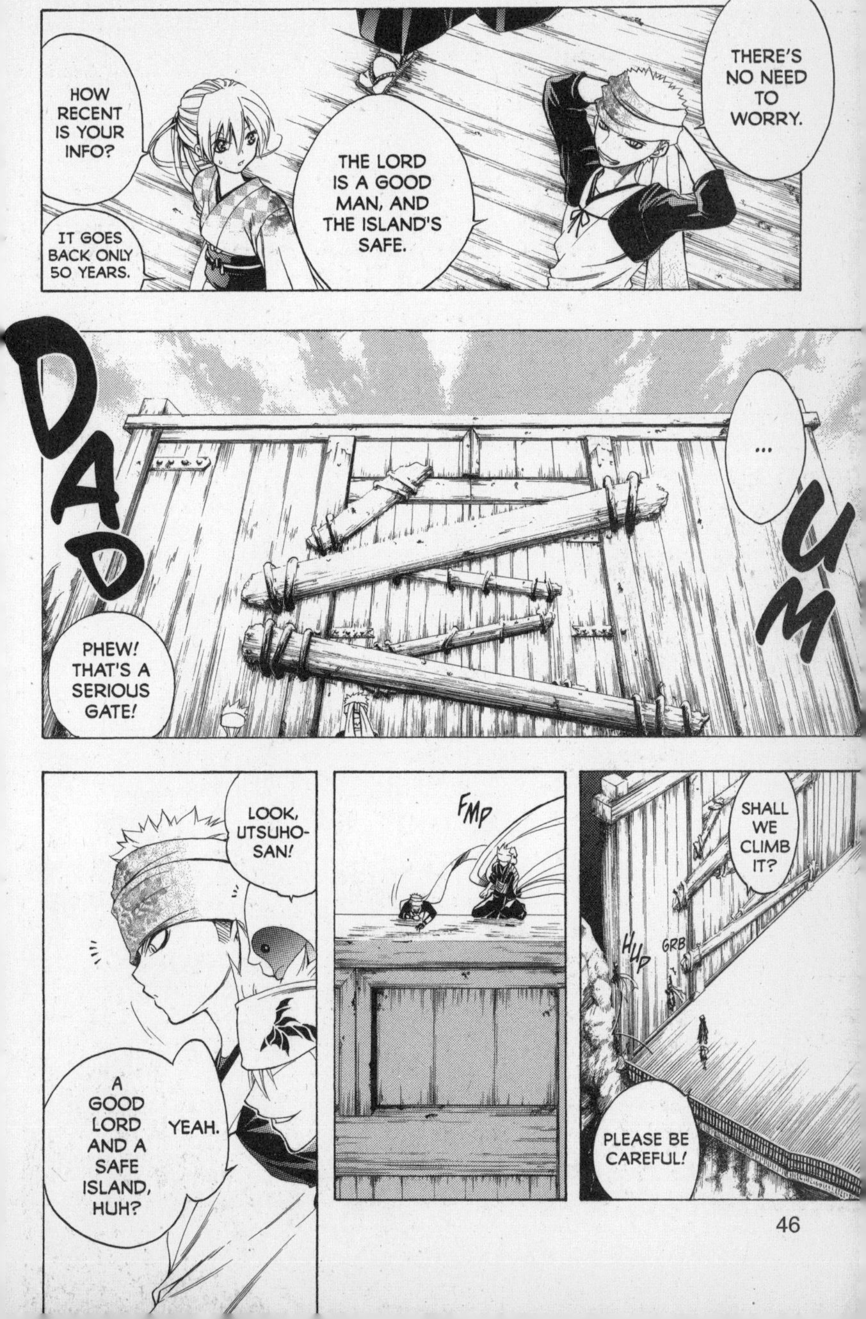
THERE'S NO NEED TO WORRY.
THE LORD IS A GOOD MAN, AND THE ISLAND'S SAFE.
HOW RECENT IS YOUR INFO?
IT GOES BACK ONLY 50 YEARS.
...
DAD
UM
PHEW! THAT'S A SERIOUS GATE!
SHALL WE CLIMB IT?
HUP
GRB
PLEASE BE CAREFUL!
FMP
LOOK, UTSUHO-SAN!
YEAH.
A GOOD LORD AND A SAFE ISLAND, HUH?

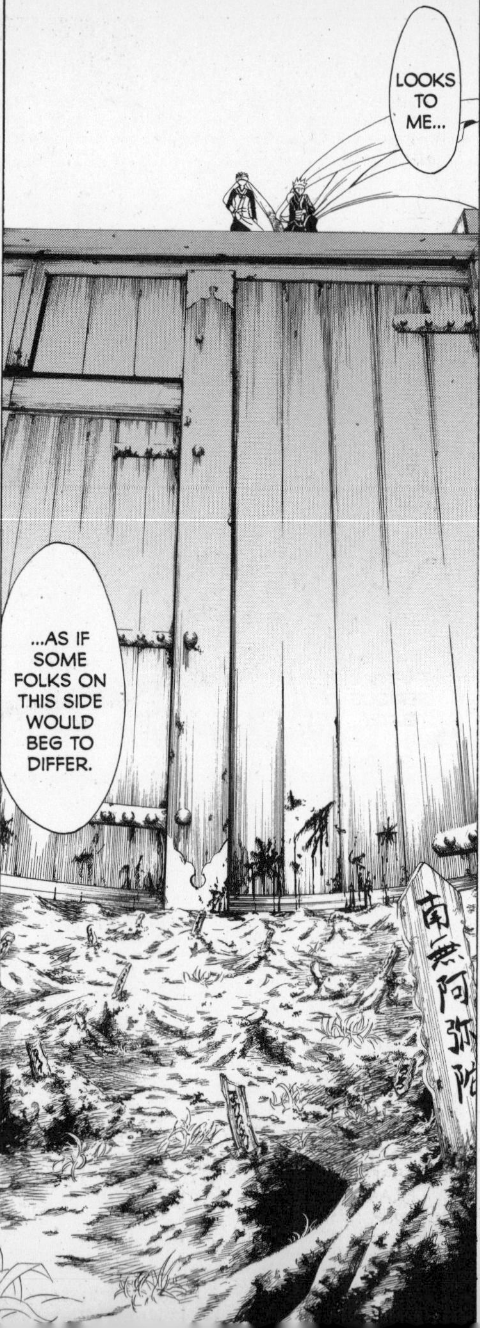
LOOKS TO ME...
...AS IF SOME FOLKS ON THIS SIDE WOULD BEG TO DIFFER.
南無阿弥陀

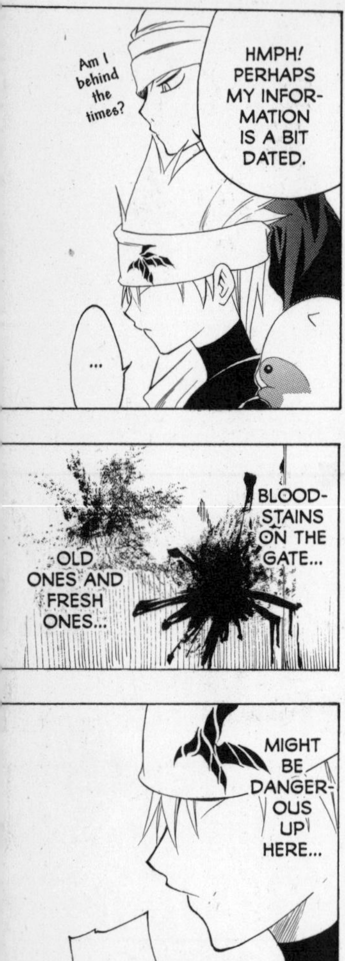
HMPH! PERHAPS MY INFOR-MATION IS A BIT DATED.
Am I behind the times?
...
BLOOD-STAINS ON THE GATE...
OLD ONES AND FRESH ONES...
MIGHT BE DANGER-OUS UP HERE...
HEY, YOU!
TWANG

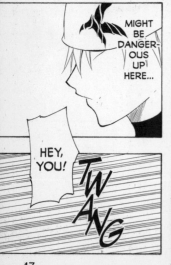

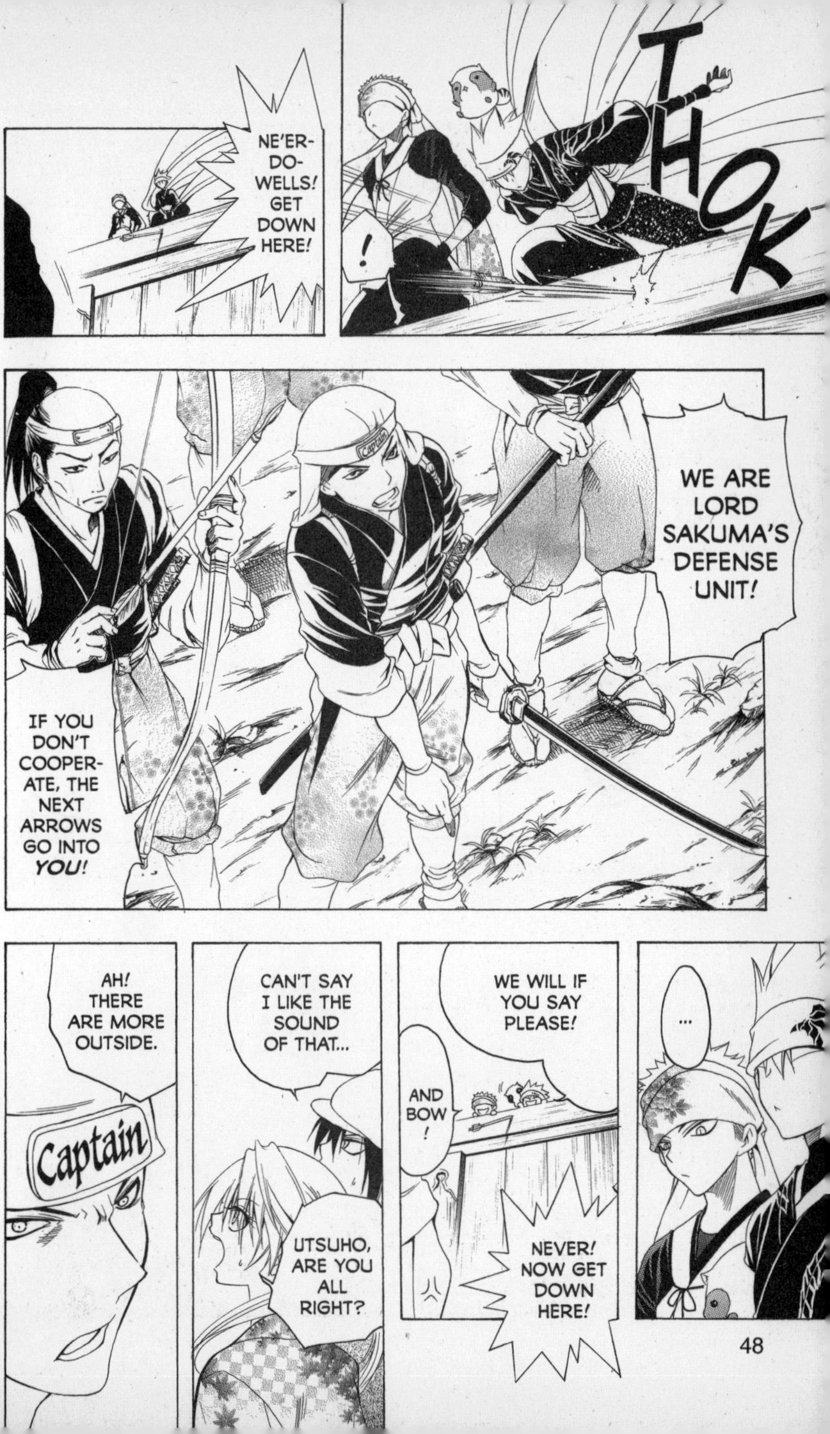
THOK
!
NE'ER-DO-WELLS! GET DOWN HERE!
WE ARE LORD SAKUMA'S DEFENSE UNIT!
IF YOU DON'T COOPERATE, THE NEXT ARROWS GO INTO *YOU*!
...
WE WILL IF YOU SAY PLEASE!
AND BOW!
NEVER! NOW GET DOWN HERE!
CAN'T SAY I LIKE THE SOUND OF THAT...
UTSUHO, ARE YOU ALL RIGHT?
AH! THERE ARE MORE OUTSIDE.
Captain

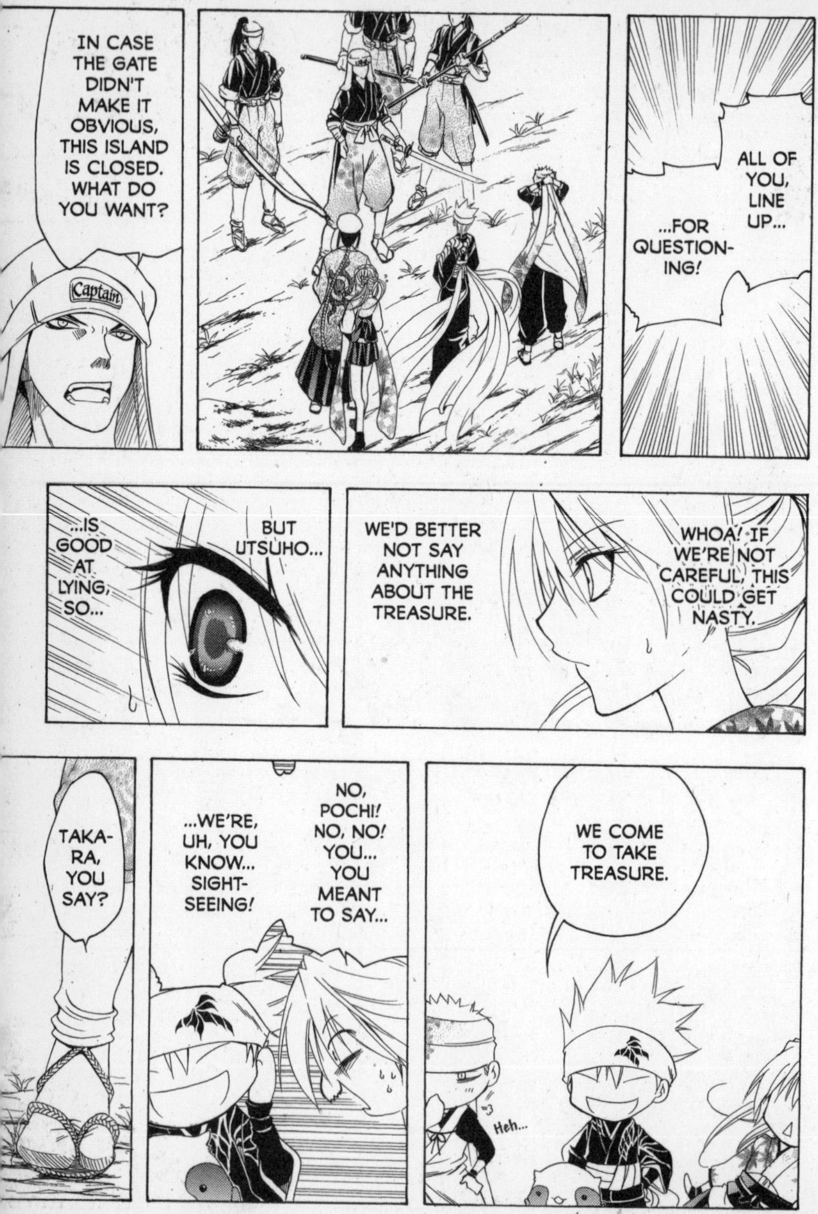
ALL OF YOU, LINE UP...
...FOR QUESTIONING!
IN CASE THE GATE DIDN'T MAKE IT OBVIOUS, THIS ISLAND IS CLOSED. WHAT DO YOU WANT?
Captain
WHOA! IF WE'RE NOT CAREFUL, THIS COULD GET NASTY.
WE'D BETTER NOT SAY ANYTHING ABOUT THE TREASURE.
BUT UTSUHO...
...IS GOOD AT LYING, SO...
WE COME TO TAKE TREASURE.
Heh...
NO, POCHI! NO, NO! YOU... YOU MEANT TO SAY...
...WE'RE, UH, YOU KNOW... SIGHT-SEEING!
TAKA-RA, YOU SAY?

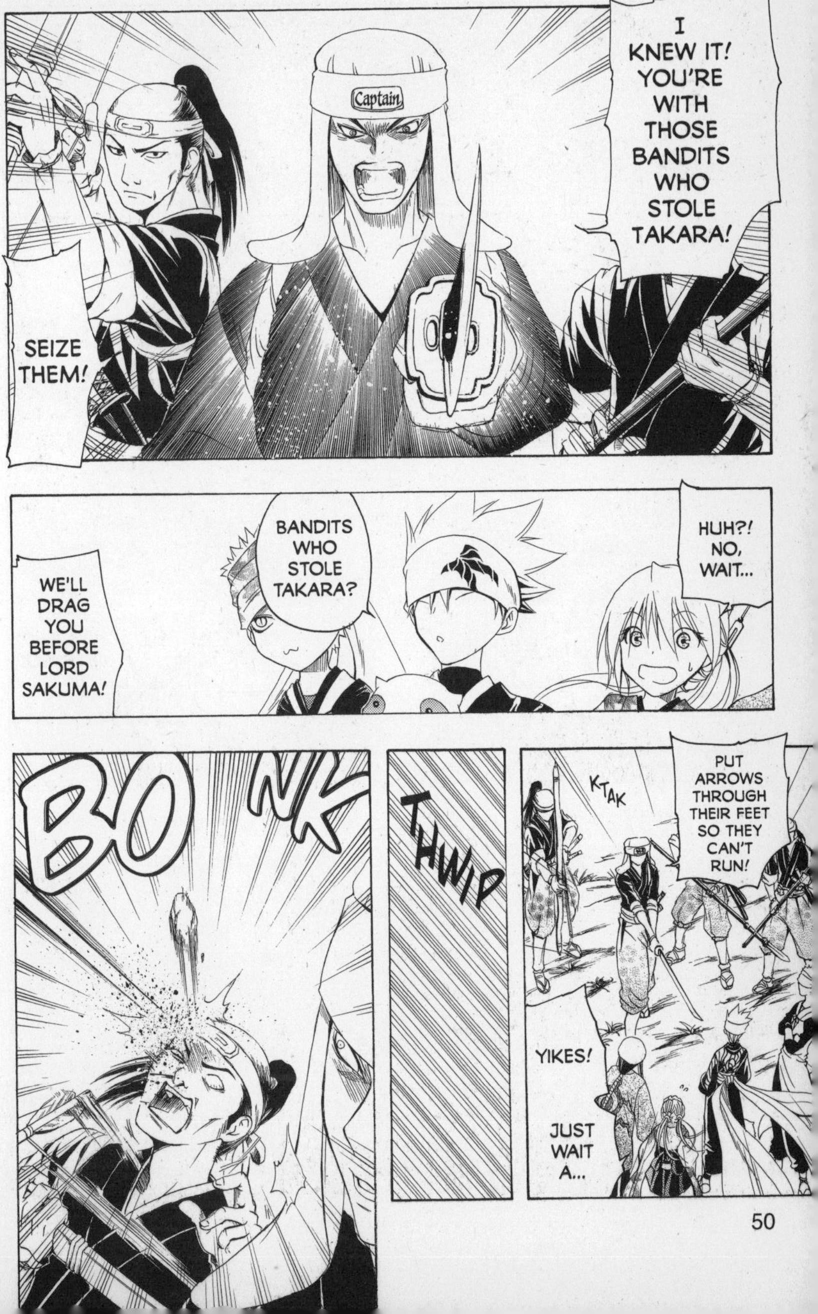
I KNEW IT! YOU'RE WITH THOSE BANDITS WHO STOLE TAKARA!
SEIZE THEM!
HUH?! NO, WAIT...
BANDITS WHO STOLE TAKARA?
WE'LL DRAG YOU BEFORE LORD SAKUMA!
PUT ARROWS THROUGH THEIR FEET SO THEY CAN'T RUN!
KTAK
YIKES!
JUST WAIT A...
THWIP
BONK

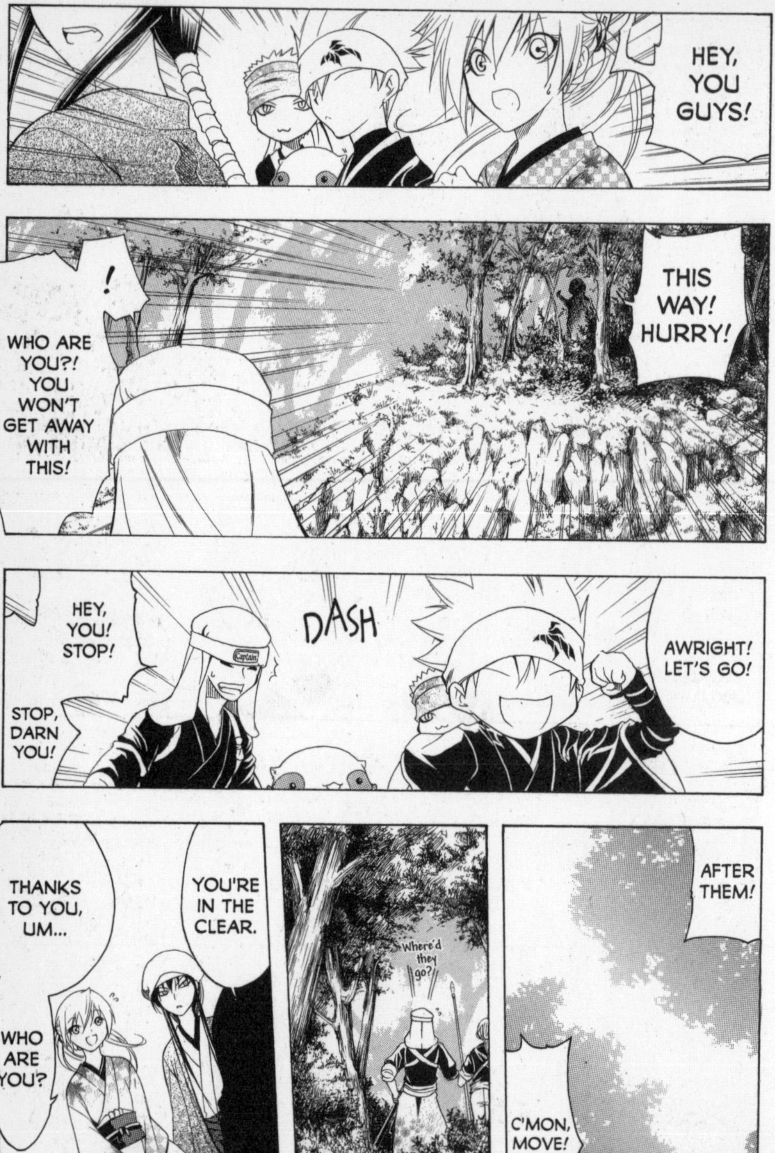
HEY, YOU GUYS!
THIS WAY! HURRY!
!
WHO ARE YOU?! YOU WON'T GET AWAY WITH THIS!
AWRIGHT! LET'S GO!
DASH
Captain
HEY, YOU! STOP!
STOP, DARN YOU!
AFTER THEM!
C'MON, MOVE!
Where'd they go?
YOU'RE IN THE CLEAR.
THANKS TO YOU, UM...
WHO ARE YOU?

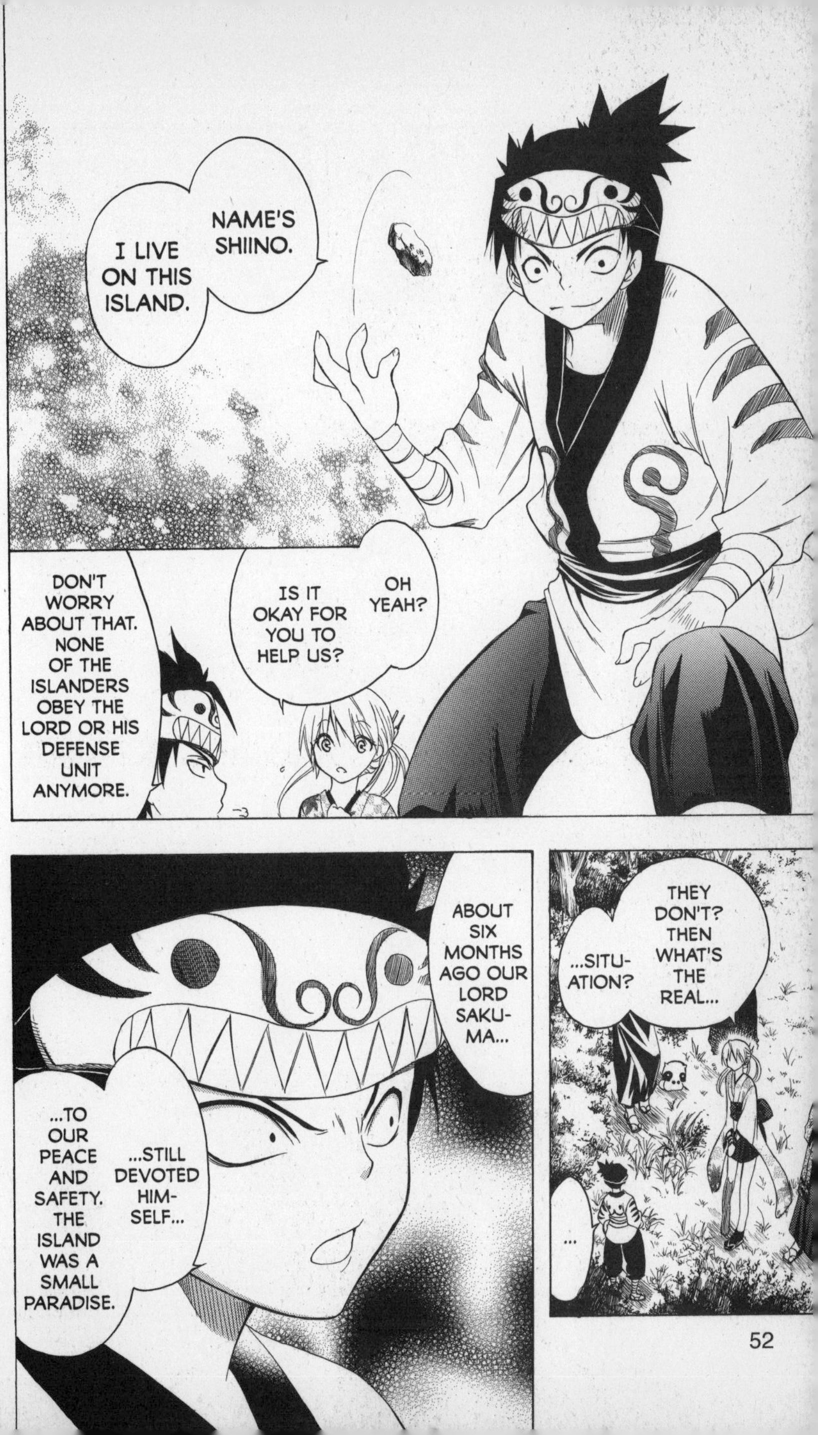
NAME'S SHIINO.
I LIVE ON THIS ISLAND.
OH YEAH?
IS IT OKAY FOR YOU TO HELP US?
DON'T WORRY ABOUT THAT. NONE OF THE ISLANDERS OBEY THE LORD OR HIS DEFENSE UNIT ANYMORE.
THEY DON'T? THEN WHAT'S THE REAL...
...SITUATION?
...
ABOUT SIX MONTHS AGO OUR LORD SAKUMA...
...STILL DEVOTED HIMSELF...
...TO OUR PEACE AND SAFETY. THE ISLAND WAS A SMALL PARADISE.

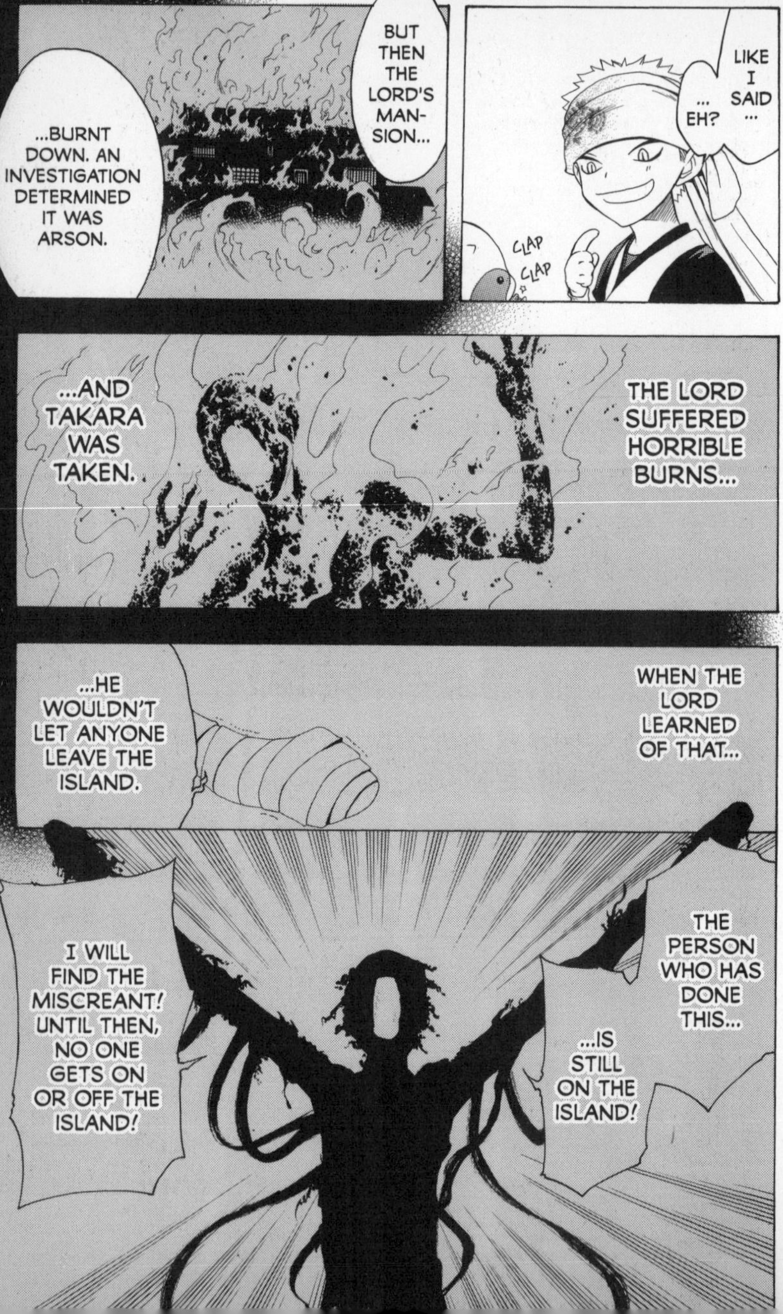
LIKE I SAID ...
... EH?
CLAP
CLAP
BUT THEN THE LORD'S MAN-SION...
...BURNT DOWN. AN INVESTIGATION DETERMINED IT WAS ARSON.
THE LORD SUFFERED HORRIBLE BURNS...
...AND TAKARA WAS TAKEN.
WHEN THE LORD LEARNED OF THAT...
...HE WOULDN'T LET ANYONE LEAVE THE ISLAND.
THE PERSON WHO HAS DONE THIS...
...IS STILL ON THE ISLAND!
I WILL FIND THE MISCREANT! UNTIL THEN, NO ONE GETS ON OR OFF THE ISLAND!

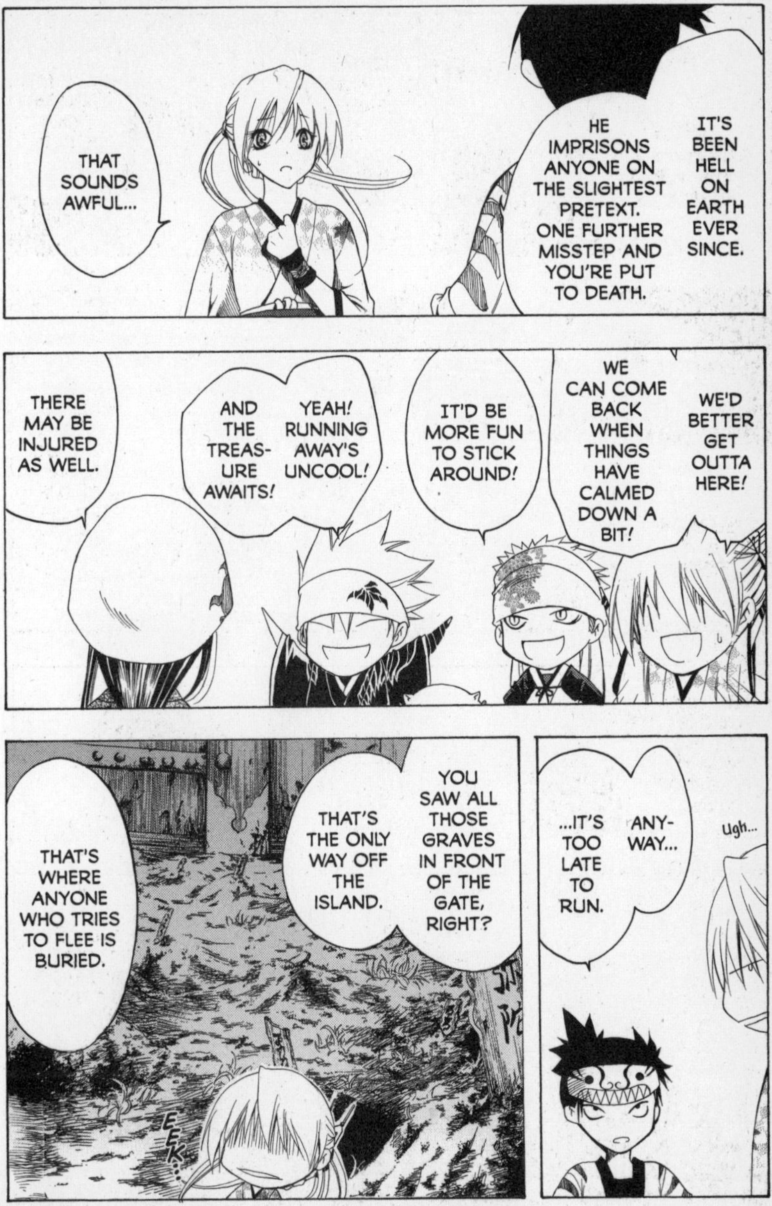
IT'S BEEN HELL ON EARTH EVER SINCE.
HE IMPRISONS ANYONE ON THE SLIGHTEST PRETEXT. ONE FURTHER MISSTEP AND YOU'RE PUT TO DEATH.
THAT SOUNDS AWFUL...
WE'D BETTER GET OUTTA HERE!
WE CAN COME BACK WHEN THINGS HAVE CALMED DOWN A BIT!
IT'D BE MORE FUN TO STICK AROUND!
YEAH! RUNNING AWAY'S UNCOOL!
AND THE TREAS-URE AWAITS!
THERE MAY BE INJURED AS WELL.
Ugh...
ANY-WAY...
...IT'S TOO LATE TO RUN.
YOU SAW ALL THOSE GRAVES IN FRONT OF THE GATE, RIGHT?
THAT'S THE ONLY WAY OFF THE ISLAND.
THAT'S WHERE ANYONE WHO TRIES TO FLEE IS BURIED.
EEK...

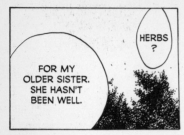

SO WHAT BROUGHT YOU HERE?
ME?
I CAME TO PICK HERBS.
HERBS?
FOR MY OLDER SISTER. SHE HASN'T BEEN WELL.
OUR PARENTS DIED YEARS AGO, LEAVING JUST THE TWO OF US.
MY SISTER ALWAYS DID EVERYTHING SHE COULD FOR ME...
...SO NOW IT'S MY TURN.
WELL...
...NO USE STANDING AROUND. I'LL TAKE YOU INTO TOWN.
IF YOU BLEND IN THERE, THE DEFENSE UNIT WON'T FIND YOU.
TWEEET
CHIRP
ANY-WAY...
...ABOUT MY SISTER...
...SHE'S...
...NOT...
... ...

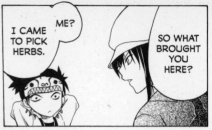

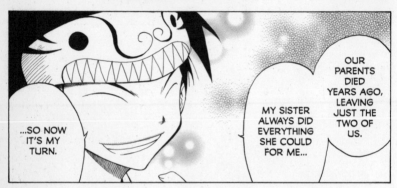

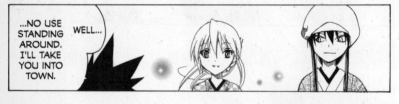

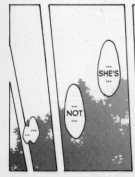

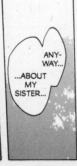

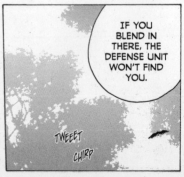

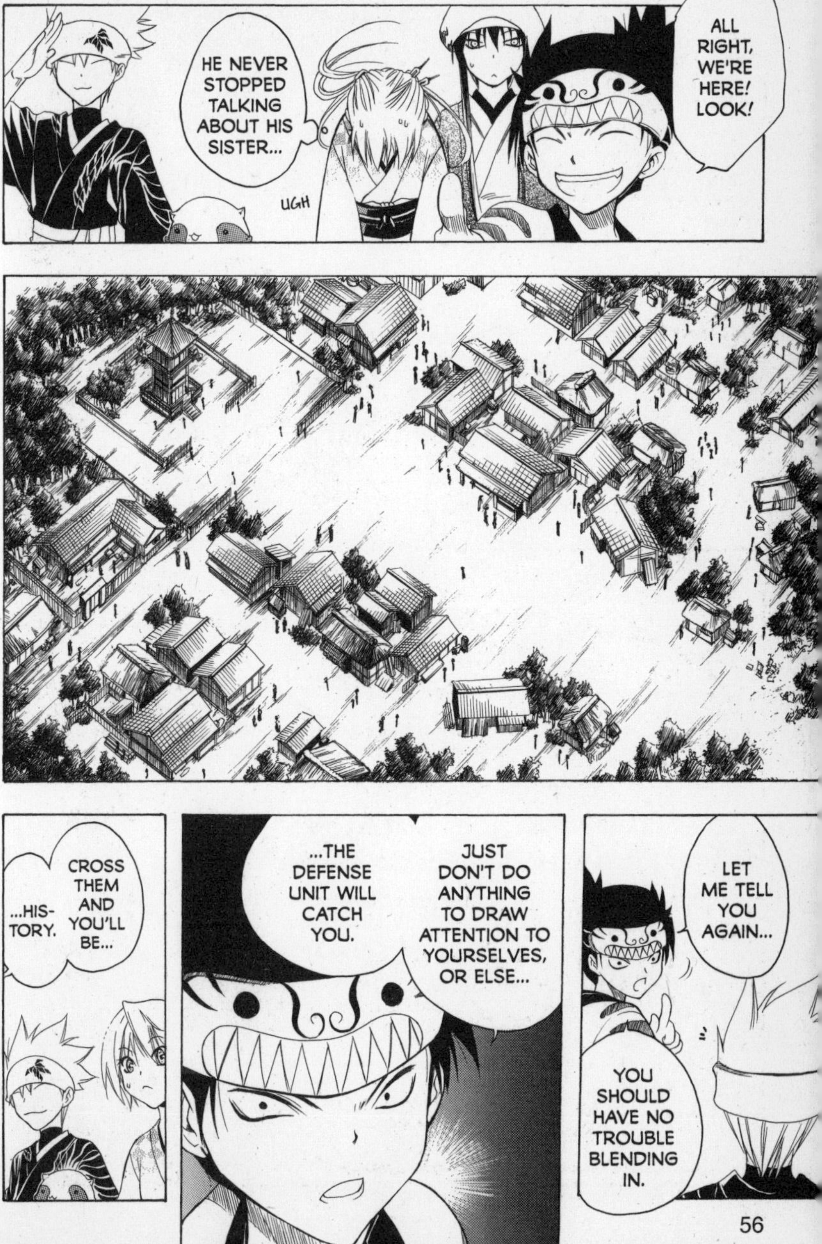
ALL RIGHT, WE'RE HERE! LOOK!
HE NEVER STOPPED TALKING ABOUT HIS SISTER...
UGH
LET ME TELL YOU AGAIN...
YOU SHOULD HAVE NO TROUBLE BLENDING IN.
JUST DON'T DO ANYTHING TO DRAW ATTENTION TO YOURSELVES, OR ELSE...
...THE DEFENSE UNIT WILL CATCH YOU.
CROSS THEM AND YOU'LL BE...
...HIS-TORY.

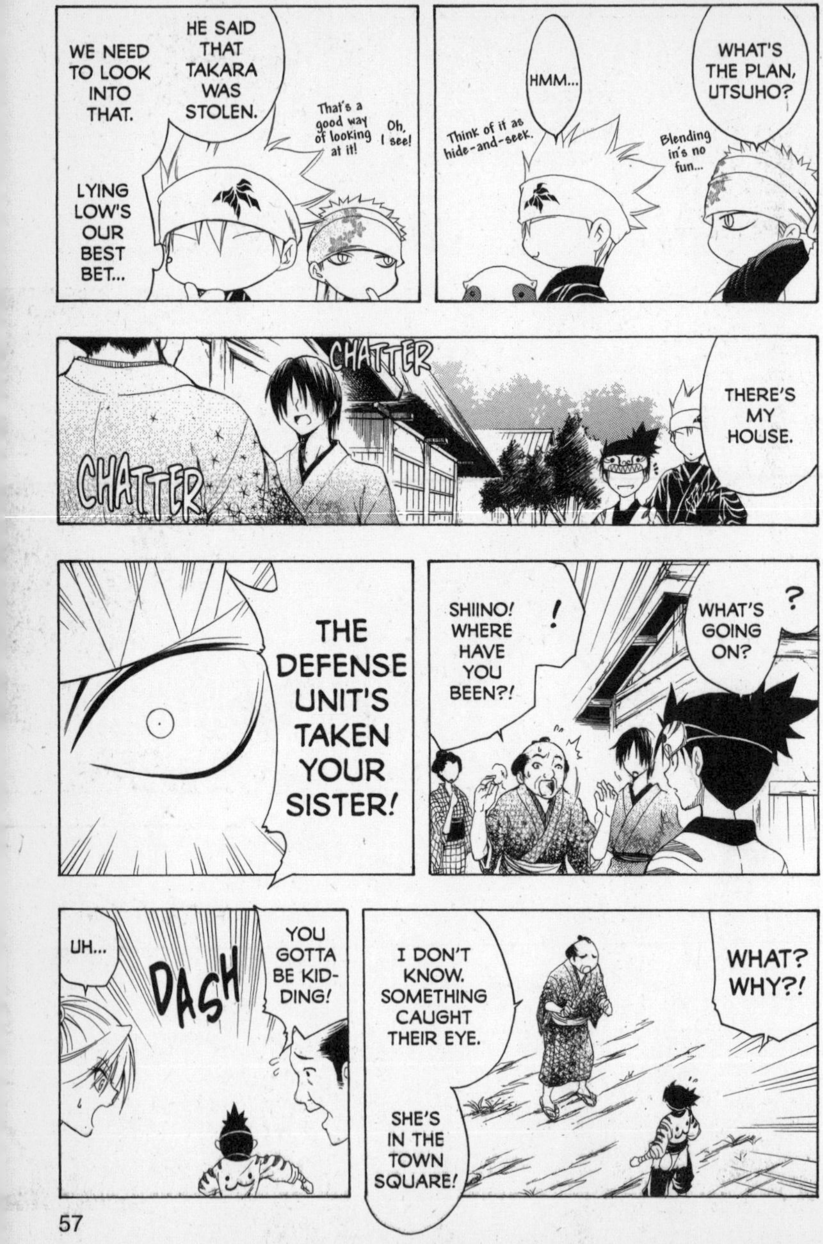
WHAT'S THE PLAN, UTSUHO?
Blending in's no fun...
HMM...
Think of it as hide-and-seek.
HE SAID THAT TAKARA WAS STOLEN.
Oh, I see!
That's a good way of looking at it!
WE NEED TO LOOK INTO THAT.
LYING LOW'S OUR BEST BET...
THERE'S MY HOUSE.
CHATTER
CHATTER
?
WHAT'S GOING ON?
!
SHIINO! WHERE HAVE YOU BEEN?!
THE DEFENSE UNIT'S TAKEN YOUR SISTER!
WHAT? WHY?!
I DON'T KNOW. SOMETHING CAUGHT THEIR EYE.
SHE'S IN THE TOWN SQUARE!
YOU GOTTA BE KID-DING!
DASH
UH...

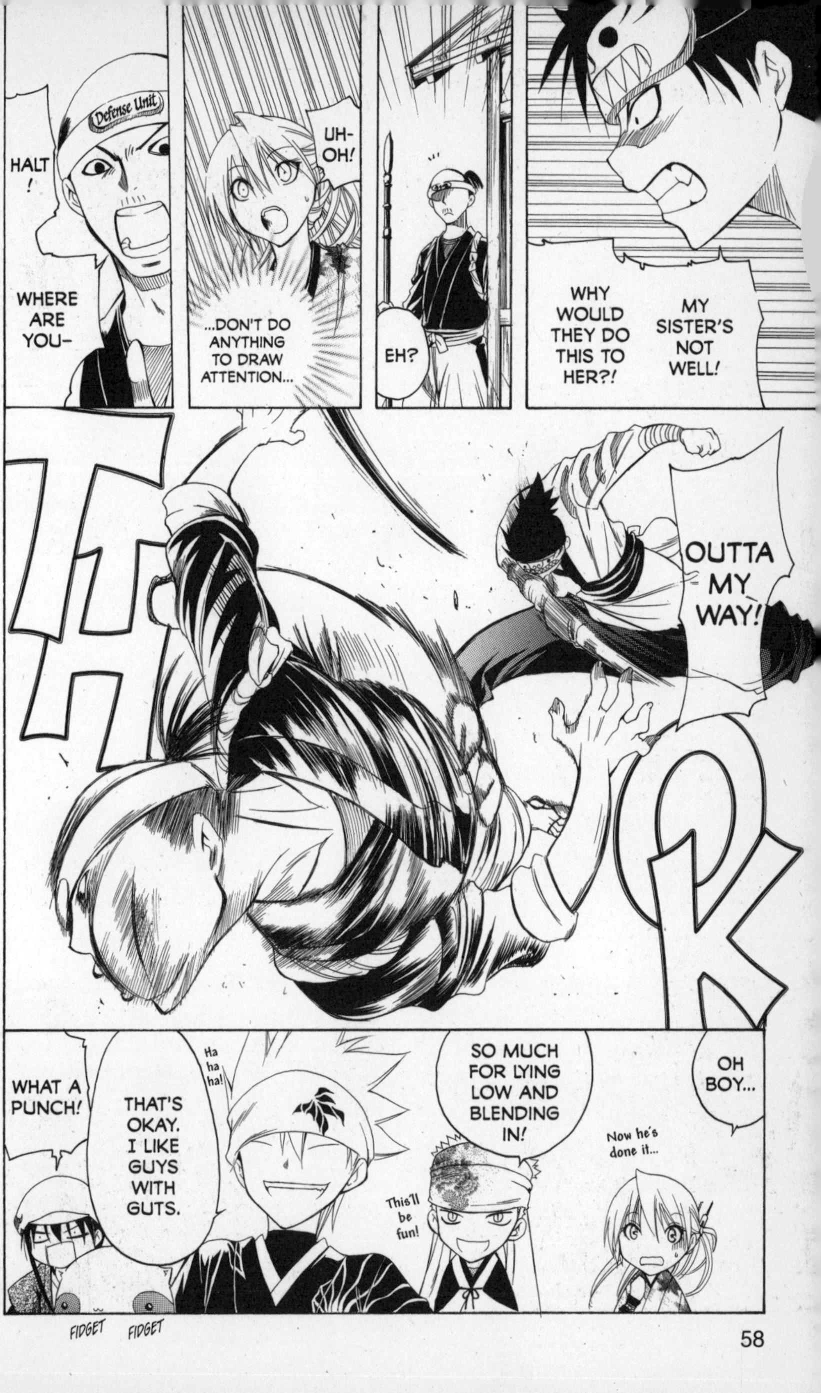
MY SISTER'S NOT WELL!
WHY WOULD THEY DO THIS TO HER?!
EH?
UH-OH!
...DON'T DO ANYTHING TO DRAW ATTENTION...
HALT!
WHERE ARE YOU-
OUTTA MY WAY!
OH BOY...
Now he's done it...
SO MUCH FOR LYING LOW AND BLENDING IN!
This'll be fun!
Ha ha ha!
THAT'S OKAY. I LIKE GUYS WITH GUTS.
WHAT A PUNCH!
FIDGET
FIDGET

Chapter 61 The True Culprit?!

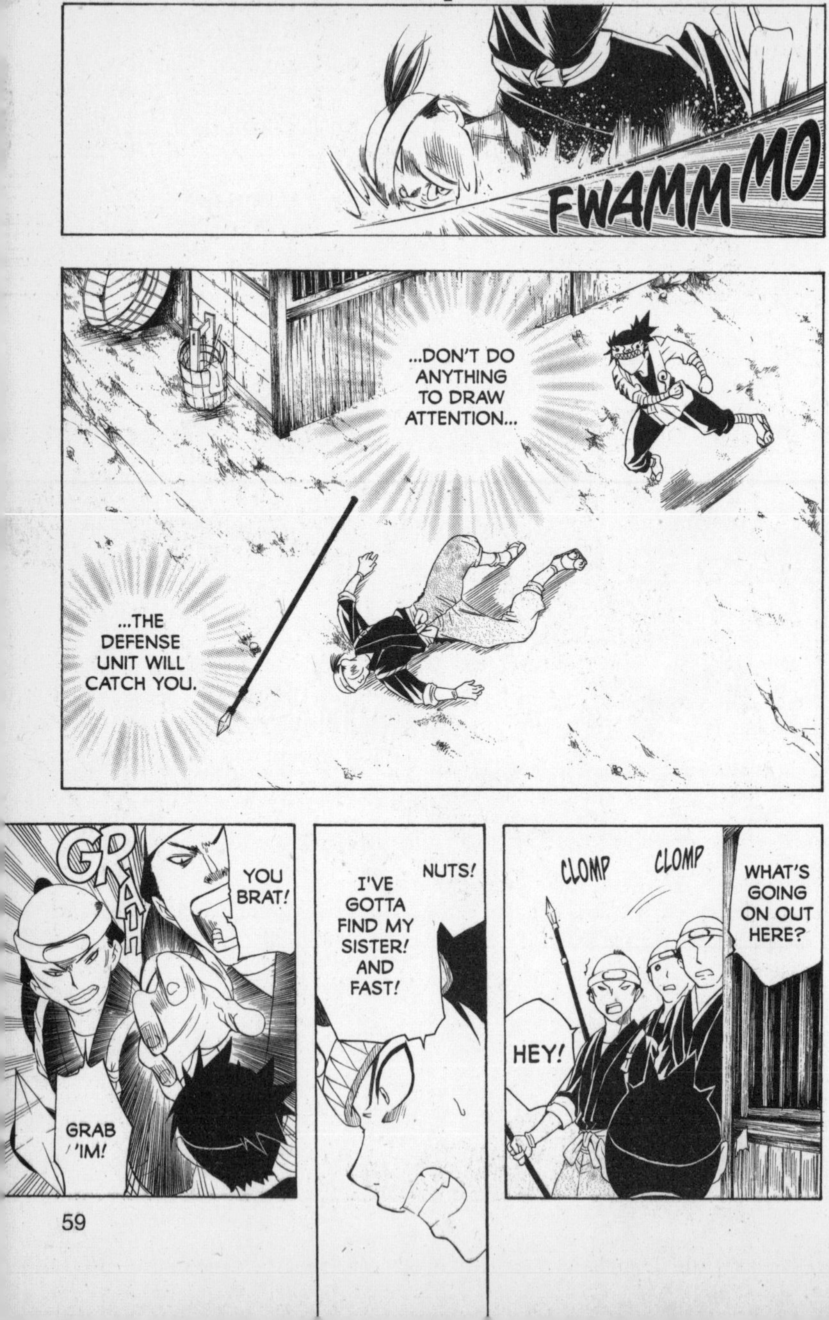

FWAMM MO
...DON'T DO ANYTHING TO DRAW ATTENTION...
...THE DEFENSE UNIT WILL CATCH YOU.
CLOMP
CLOMP
WHAT'S GOING ON OUT HERE?
HEY!
NUTS!
I'VE GOTTA FIND MY SISTER! AND FAST!
GRAH
YOU BRAT!
GRAB 'IM!

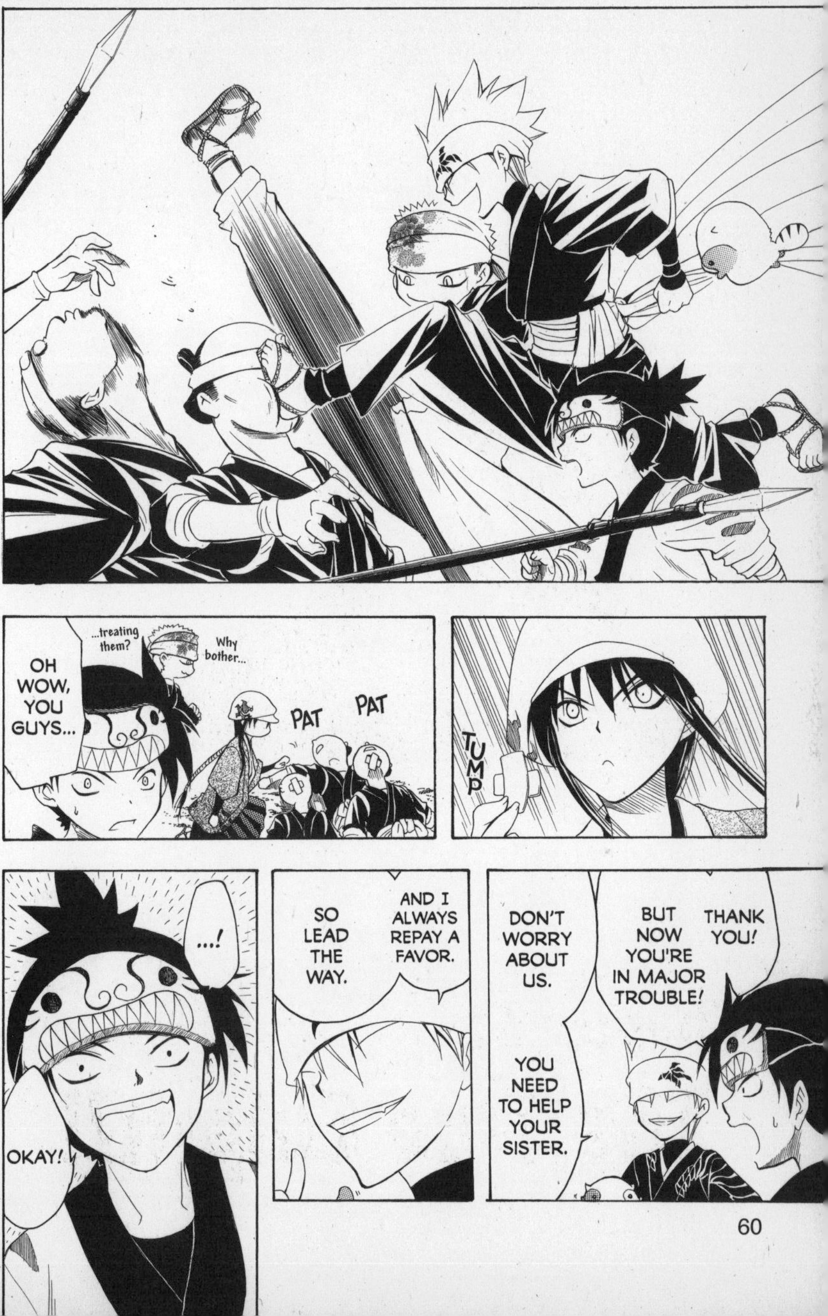
TUMP
PAT PAT
Why bother...
...treating them?
OH WOW, YOU GUYS...
THANK YOU!
BUT NOW YOU'RE IN MAJOR TROUBLE!
DON'T WORRY ABOUT US.
YOU NEED TO HELP YOUR SISTER.
AND I ALWAYS REPAY A FAVOR.
SO LEAD THE WAY.
...!
OKAY!

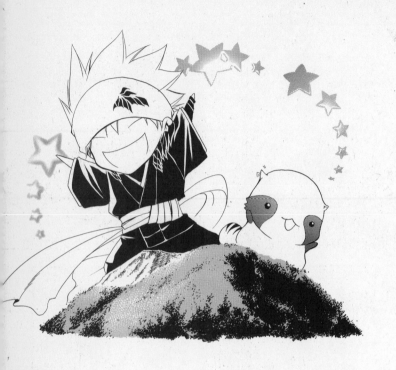

Chapter 61
The True Culprit?!

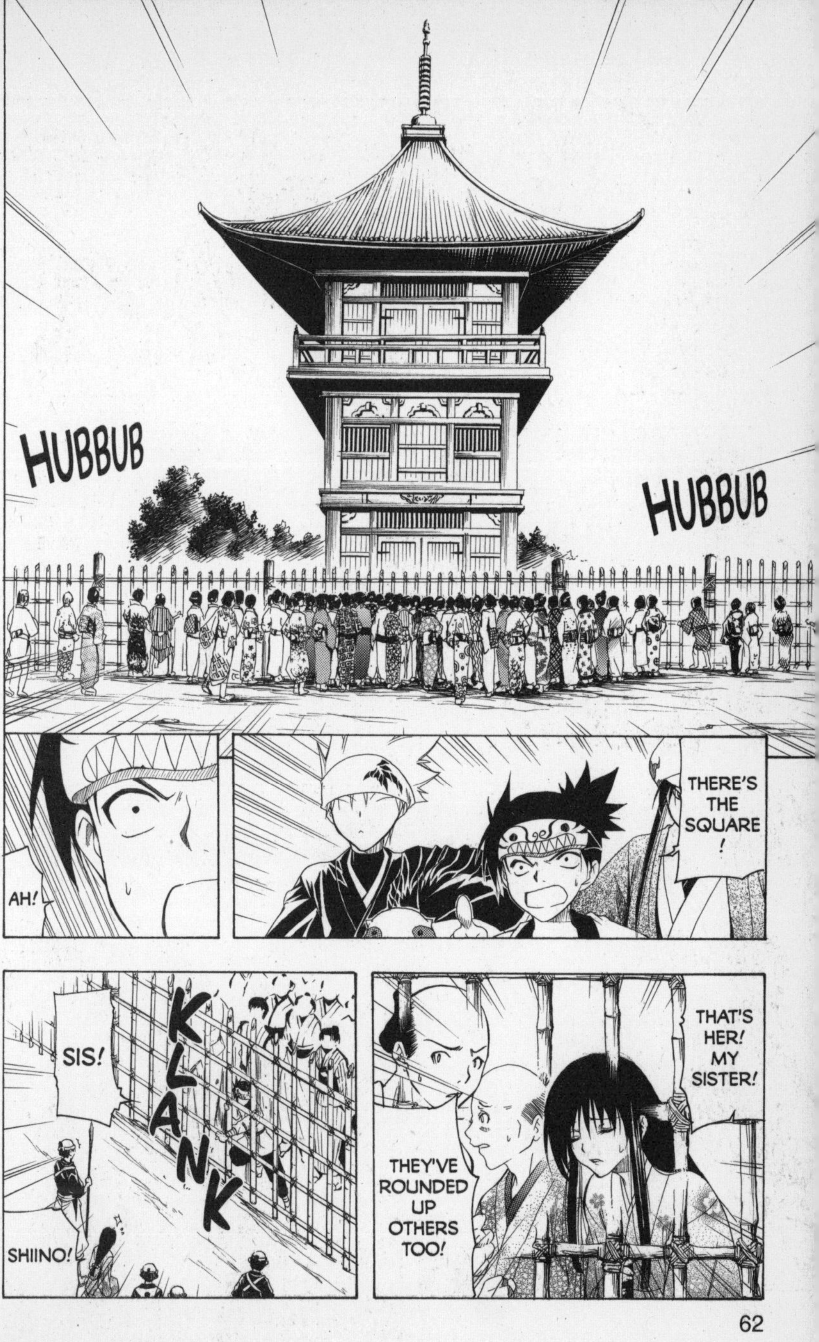
HUBBUB
HUBBUB
THERE'S THE SQUARE!
AH!
THAT'S HER! MY SISTER!
THEY'VE ROUNDED UP OTHERS TOO!
SIS!
KLANK
SHIINO!

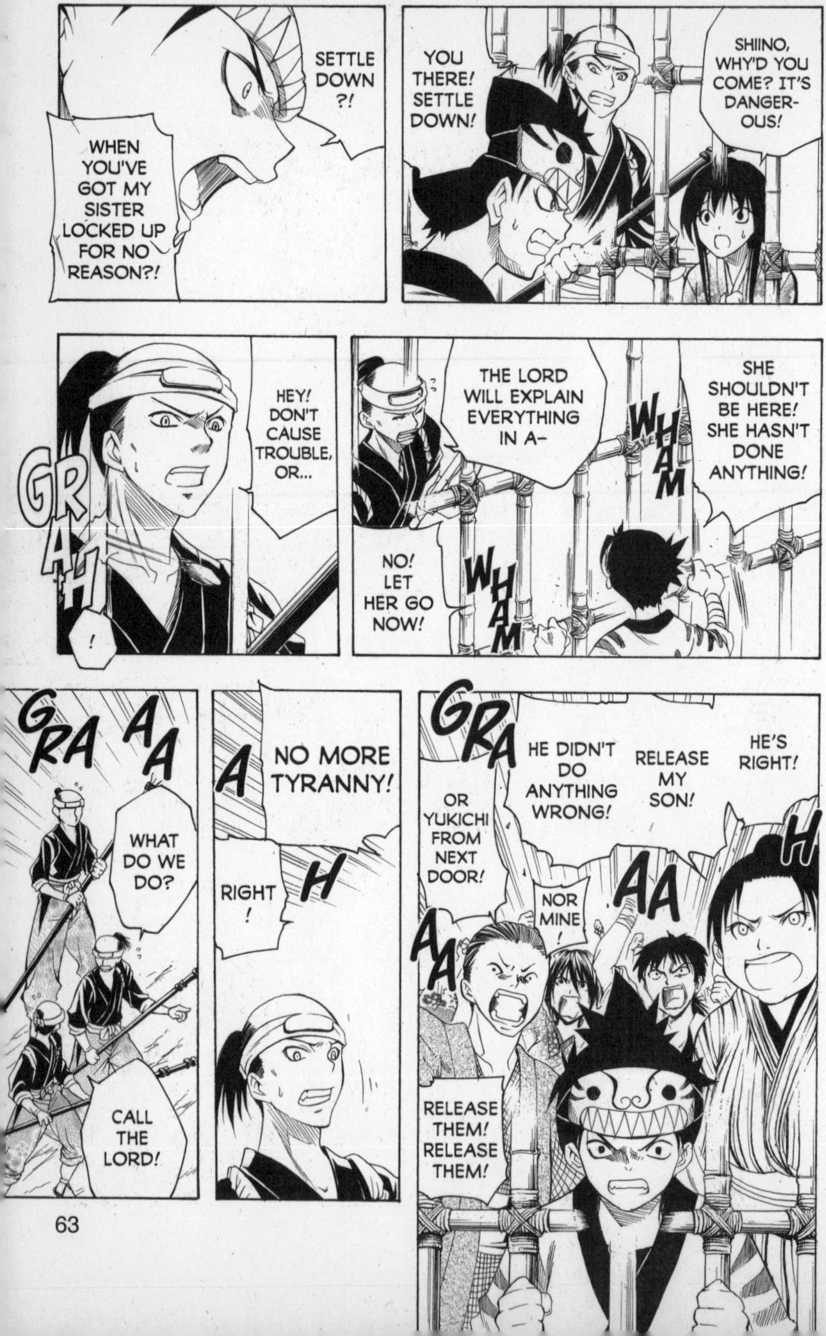
SHIINO, WHY'D YOU COME? IT'S DANGER-OUS!
YOU THERE! SETTLE DOWN!
SETTLE DOWN ?!
WHEN YOU'VE GOT MY SISTER LOCKED UP FOR NO REASON?!
SHE SHOULDN'T BE HERE! SHE HASN'T DONE ANYTHING!
WHAM
THE LORD WILL EXPLAIN EVERYTHING IN A-
NO! LET HER GO NOW!
WHAM
HEY! DON'T CAUSE TROUBLE, OR...
GRAH
!
HE'S RIGHT!
RELEASE MY SON!
HE DIDN'T DO ANYTHING WRONG!
GRA
OR YUKICHI FROM NEXT DOOR!
NOR MINE!
AAH
AA
RELEASE THEM! RELEASE THEM!
NO MORE TYRANNY!
A
RIGHT!
H
GRA
AA
WHAT DO WE DO?
CALL THE LORD!

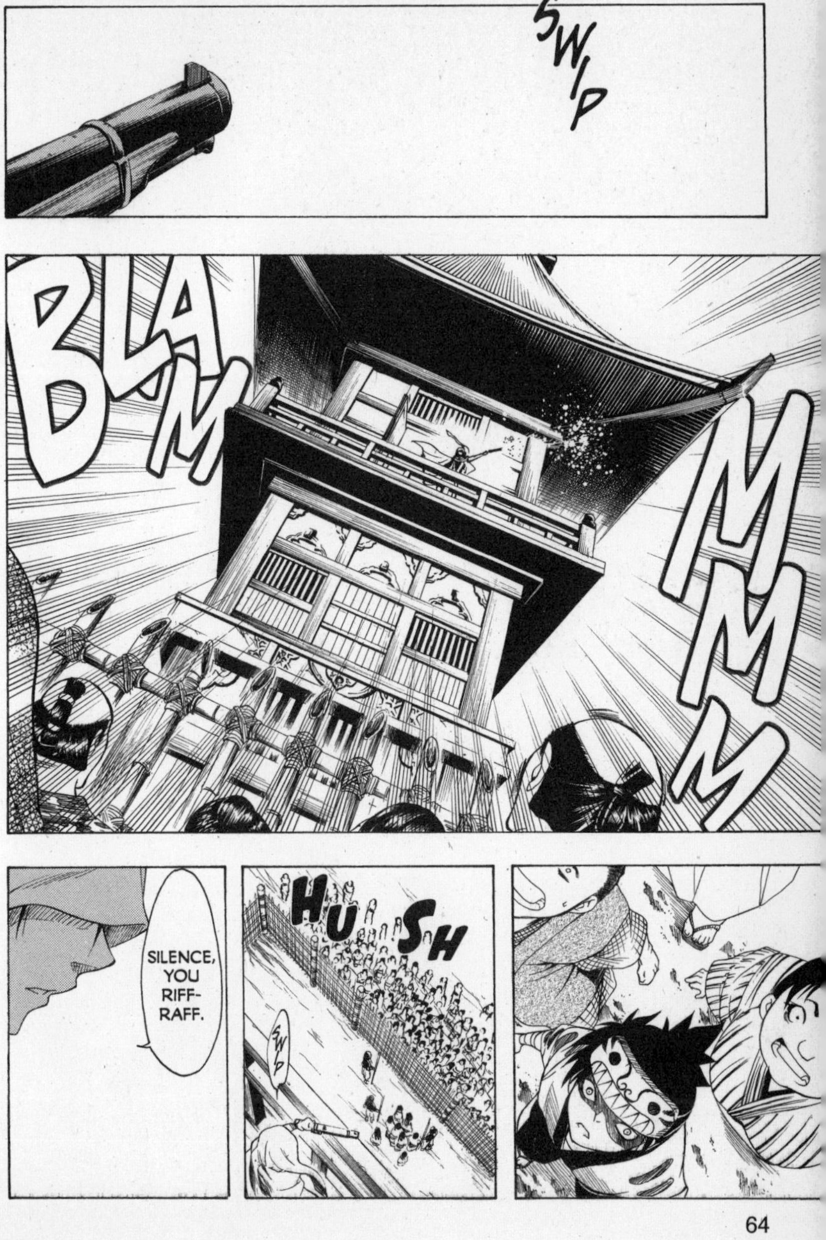
SWIP
BLAM
MMM
HUSH
SWIP
SILENCE, YOU RIFF-RAFF.

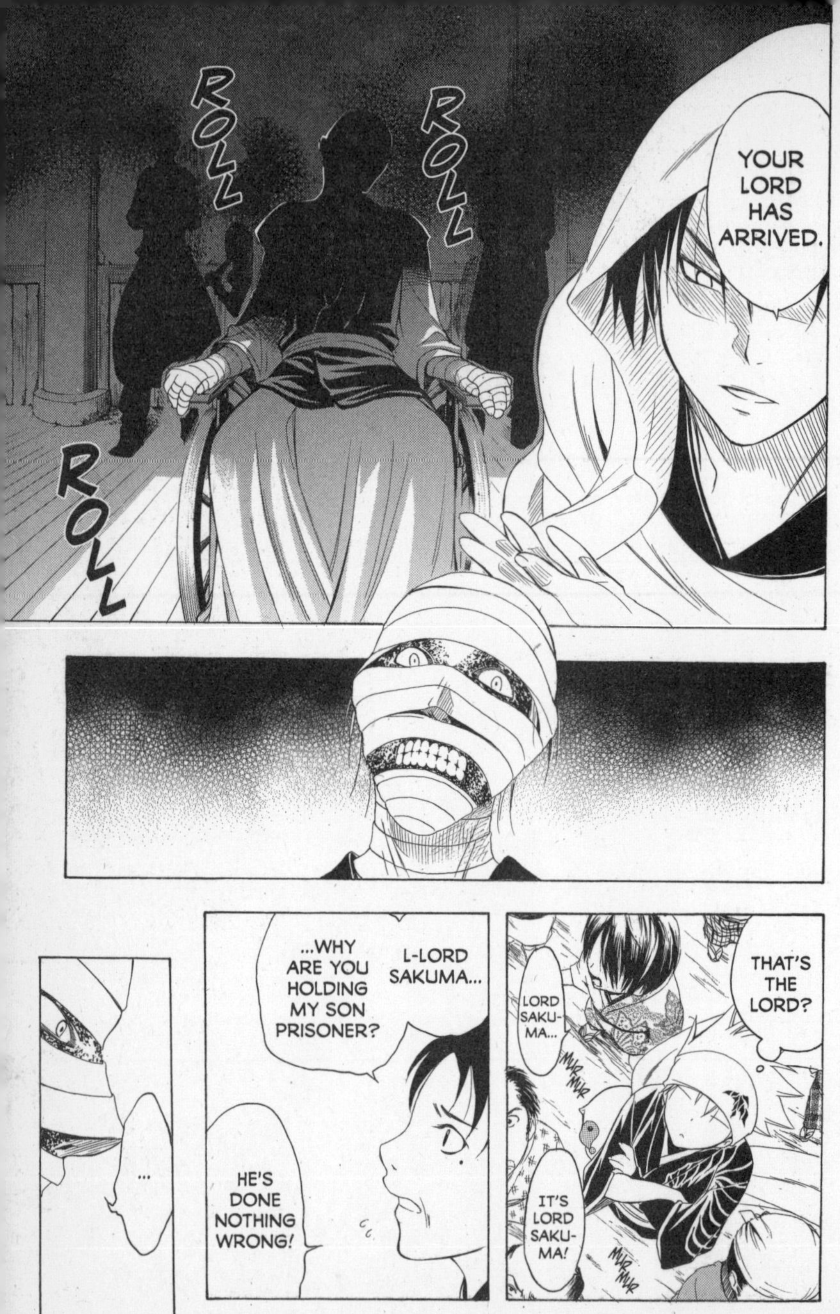
YOUR LORD HAS ARRIVED.
ROLL
ROLL
ROLL
THAT'S THE LORD?
LORD SAKU-MA...
MUR MUR
IT'S LORD SAKU-MA!
MUR MUR
L-LORD SAKUMA...
...WHY ARE YOU HOLDING MY SON PRISONER?
HE'S DONE NOTHING WRONG!
...

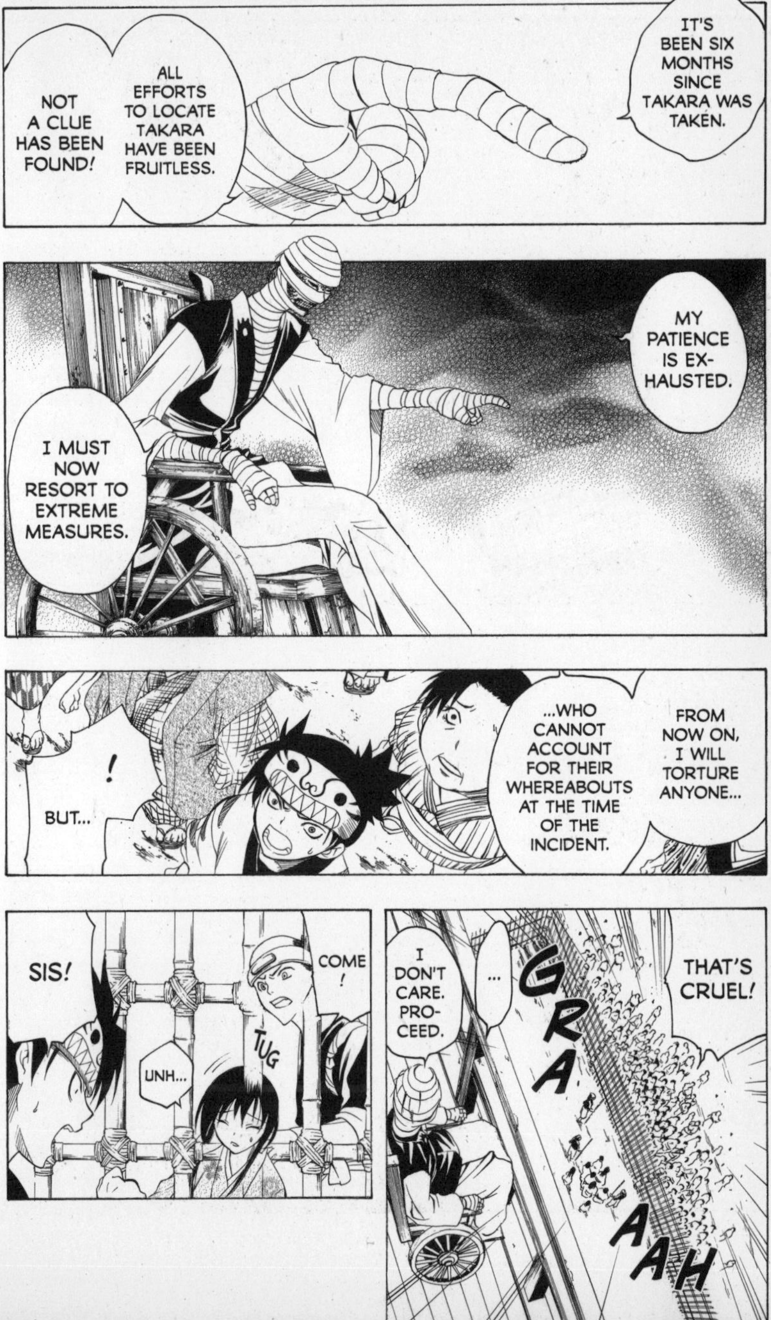
IT'S BEEN SIX MONTHS SINCE TAKARA WAS TAKEN.
ALL EFFORTS TO LOCATE TAKARA HAVE BEEN FRUITLESS.
NOT A CLUE HAS BEEN FOUND!
MY PATIENCE IS EX-HAUSTED.
I MUST NOW RESORT TO EXTREME MEASURES.
FROM NOW ON, I WILL TORTURE ANYONE...
...WHO CANNOT ACCOUNT FOR THEIR WHEREABOUTS AT THE TIME OF THE INCIDENT.
!
BUT...
THAT'S CRUEL!
GRAAAAH
...
I DON'T CARE. PRO-CEED.
COME!
TUG
SIS!
UNH...

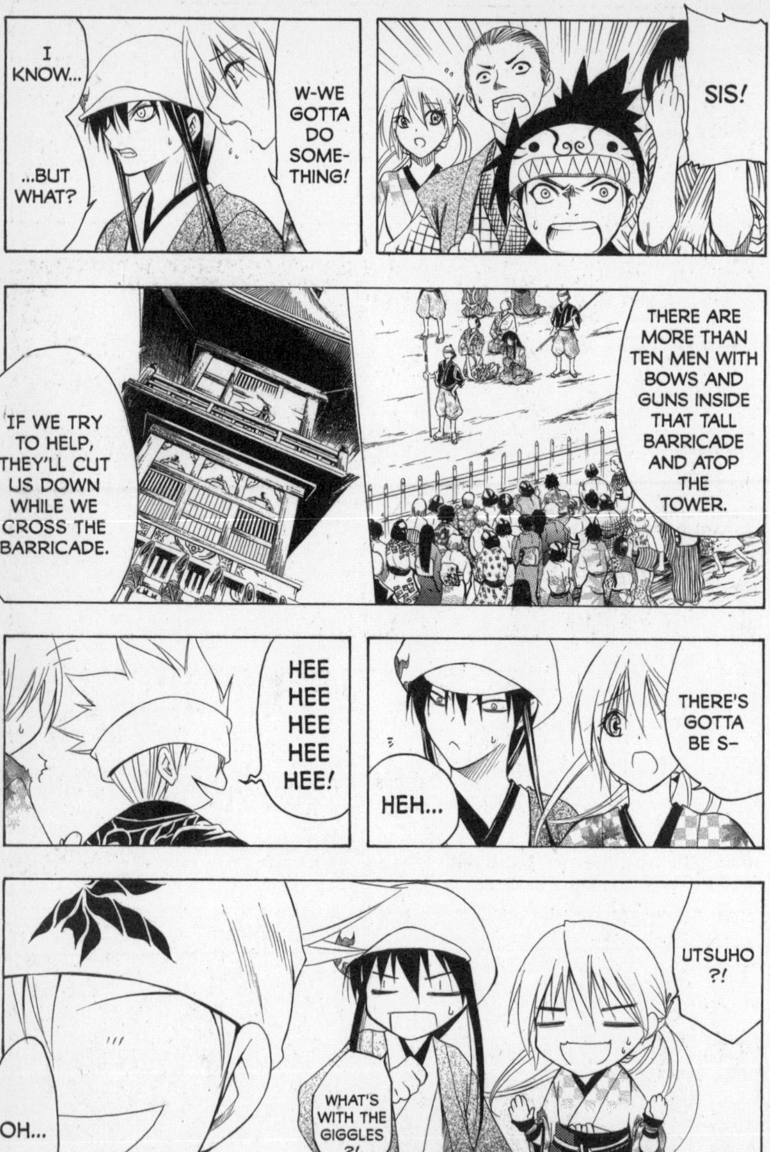
SIS!
W-WE GOTTA DO SOME-THING!
I KNOW...
...BUT WHAT?
THERE ARE MORE THAN TEN MEN WITH BOWS AND GUNS INSIDE THAT TALL BARRICADE AND ATOP THE TOWER.
IF WE TRY TO HELP, THEY'LL CUT US DOWN WHILE WE CROSS THE BARRICADE.
THERE'S GOTTA BE S-
HEH...
HEE HEE HEE HEE HEE!
UTSUHO ?!
WHAT'S WITH THE GIGGLES ?!
OH...

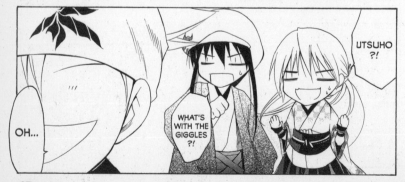

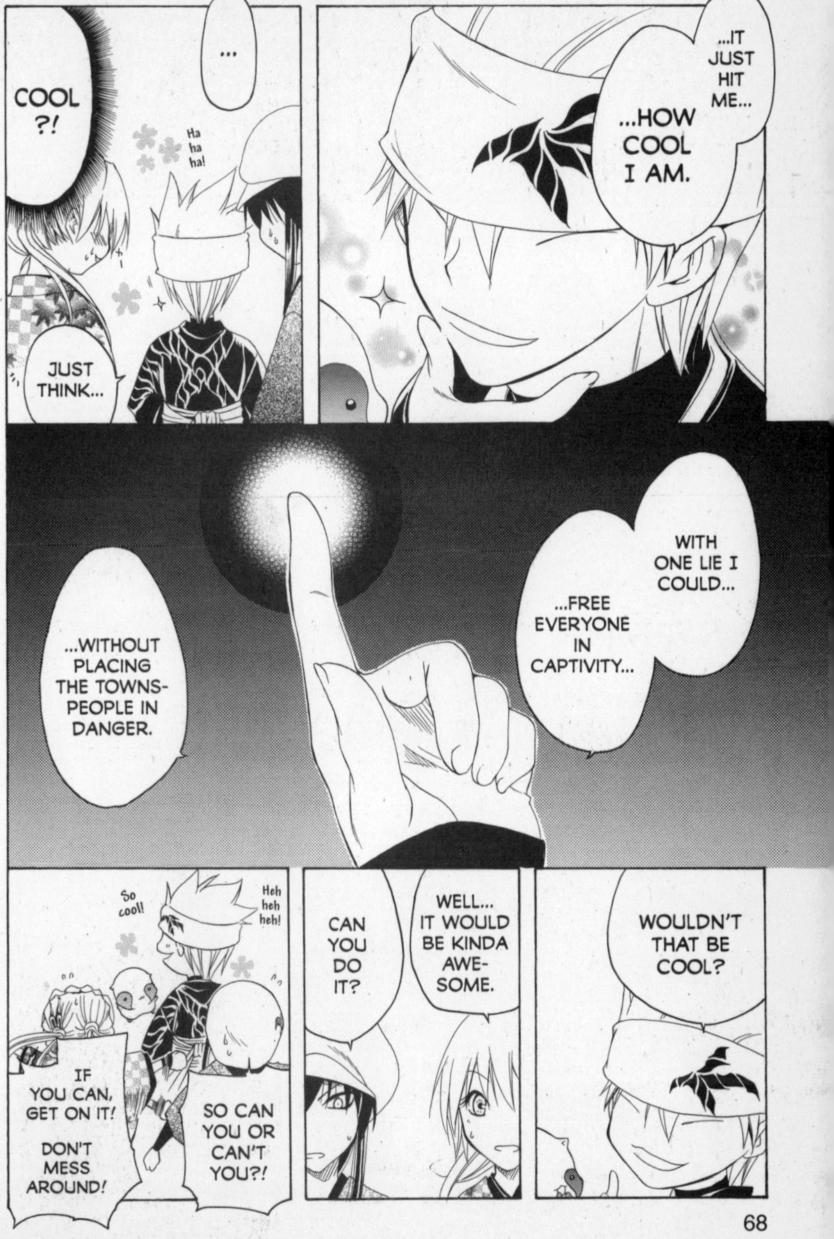
...IT JUST HIT ME...
...HOW COOL I AM.
...
COOL ?!
Ha ha ha!
JUST THINK...
WITH ONE LIE I COULD...
...FREE EVERYONE IN CAPTIVITY...
...WITHOUT PLACING THE TOWNS-PEOPLE IN DANGER.
WOULDN'T THAT BE COOL?
WELL... IT WOULD BE KINDA AWE-SOME.
CAN YOU DO IT?
Heh heh heh!
So cool!
SO CAN YOU OR CAN'T YOU?!
IF YOU CAN, GET ON IT!
DON'T MESS AROUND!

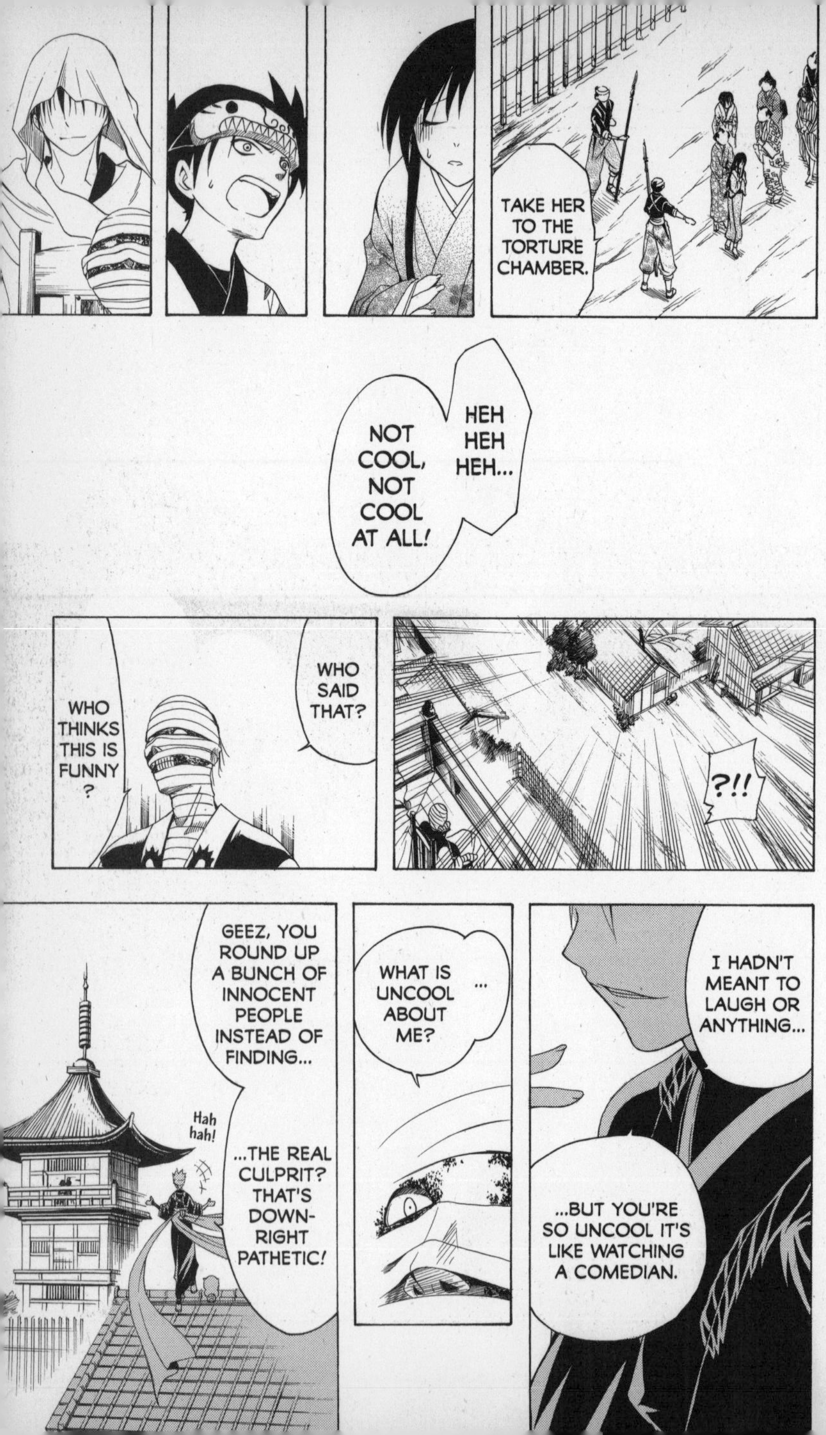
TAKE HER TO THE TORTURE CHAMBER.
HEH HEH HEH...
NOT COOL, NOT COOL AT ALL!
?!!
WHO SAID THAT?
WHO THINKS THIS IS FUNNY?
I HADN'T MEANT TO LAUGH OR ANYTHING...
...BUT YOU'RE SO UNCOOL IT'S LIKE WATCHING A COMEDIAN.
WHAT IS UNCOOL ABOUT ME? ...
GEEZ, YOU ROUND UP A BUNCH OF INNOCENT PEOPLE INSTEAD OF FINDING...
Hah hah!
...THE REAL CULPRIT? THAT'S DOWNRIGHT PATHETIC!

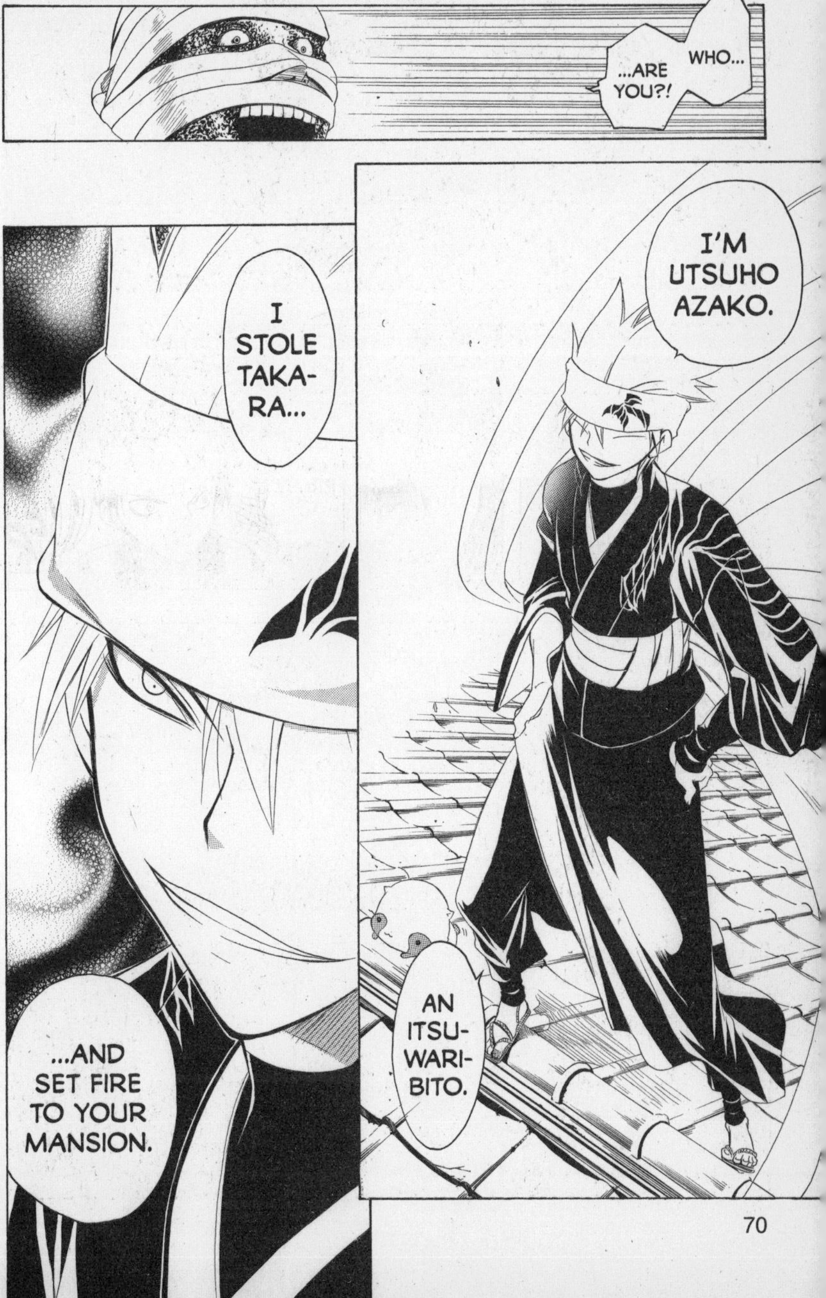
WHO...
...ARE YOU?!
I'M UTSUHO AZAKO.
AN ITSU-WARI-BITO.
I STOLE TAKA-RA...
...AND SET FIRE TO YOUR MANSION.

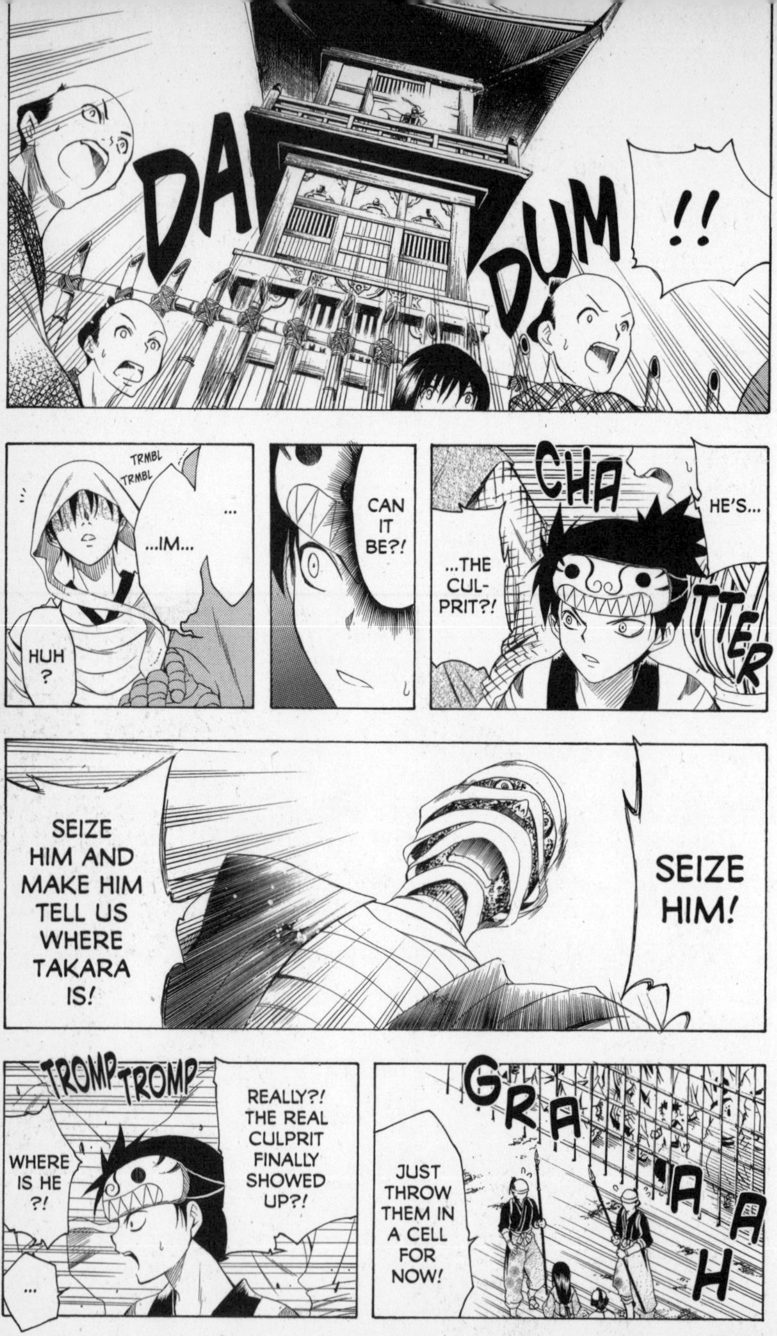

DA DUM
!!
HE'S...
...THE CULPRIT?!
CHATTER
CAN IT BE?!
TRMBL TRMBL
...
...IM...
HUH?
SEIZE HIM!
SEIZE HIM AND MAKE HIM TELL US WHERE TAKARA IS!
GRAAAAH
JUST THROW THEM IN A CELL FOR NOW!
TROMP TROMP
REALLY?! THE REAL CULPRIT FINALLY SHOWED UP?!
WHERE IS HE?!
...

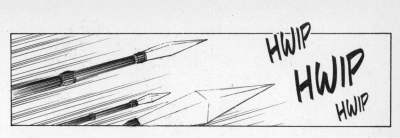

HWIP
HWIP
HWIP

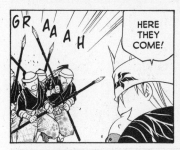

GR A A A H

HERE THEY COME!

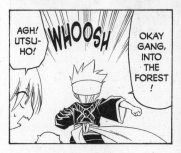

AGH! UTSU-HO!

WHOOSH

OKAY GANG, INTO THE FOREST!

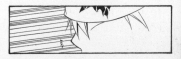

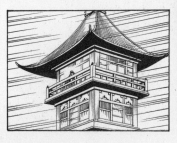

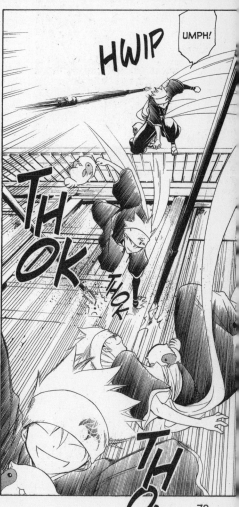

HWIP

UMPH!

TH OK

TH OK!

TH OK

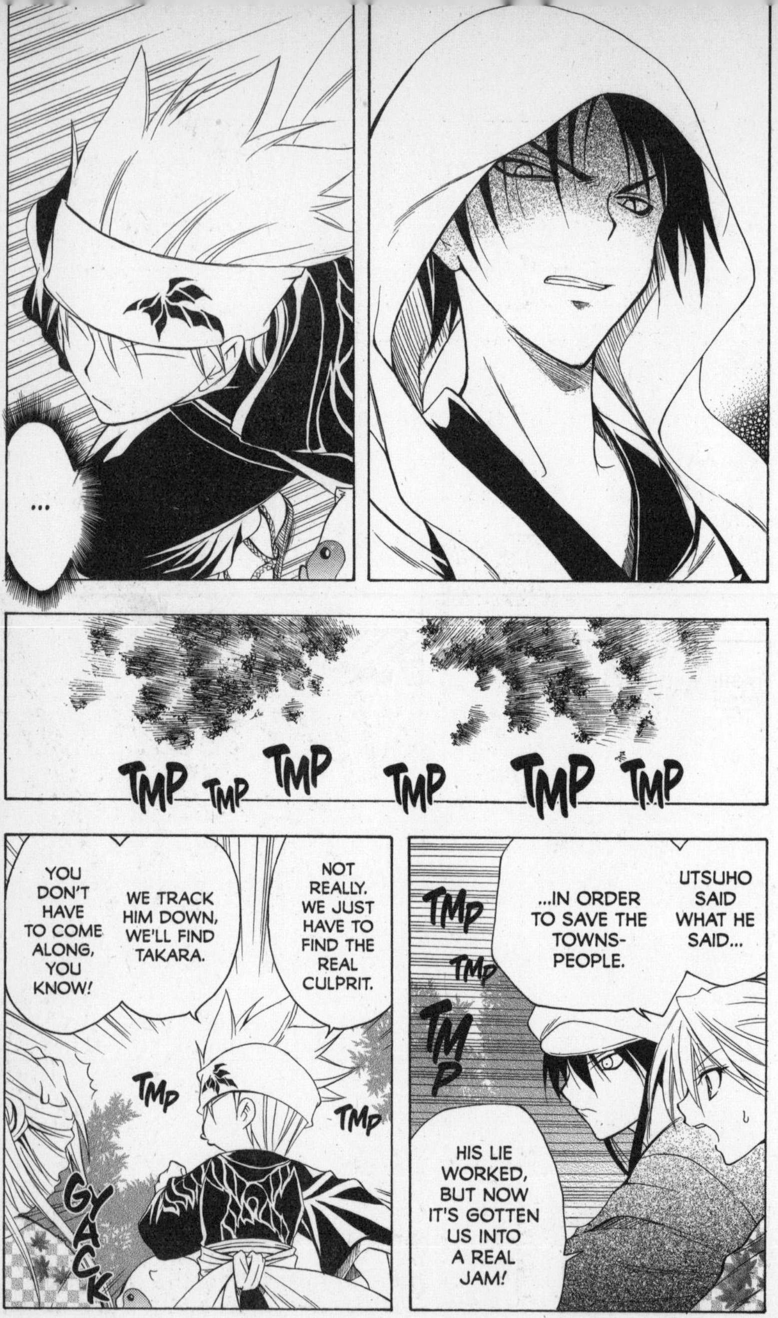
...
TMP TMP TMP TMP TMP TMP
UTSUHO SAID WHAT HE SAID...
...IN ORDER TO SAVE THE TOWNS-PEOPLE.
TMP TMP TMP
HIS LIE WORKED, BUT NOW IT'S GOTTEN US INTO A REAL JAM!
NOT REALLY. WE JUST HAVE TO FIND THE REAL CULPRIT.
WE TRACK HIM DOWN, WE'LL FIND TAKARA.
YOU DON'T HAVE TO COME ALONG, YOU KNOW!
TMP TMP
GYACK

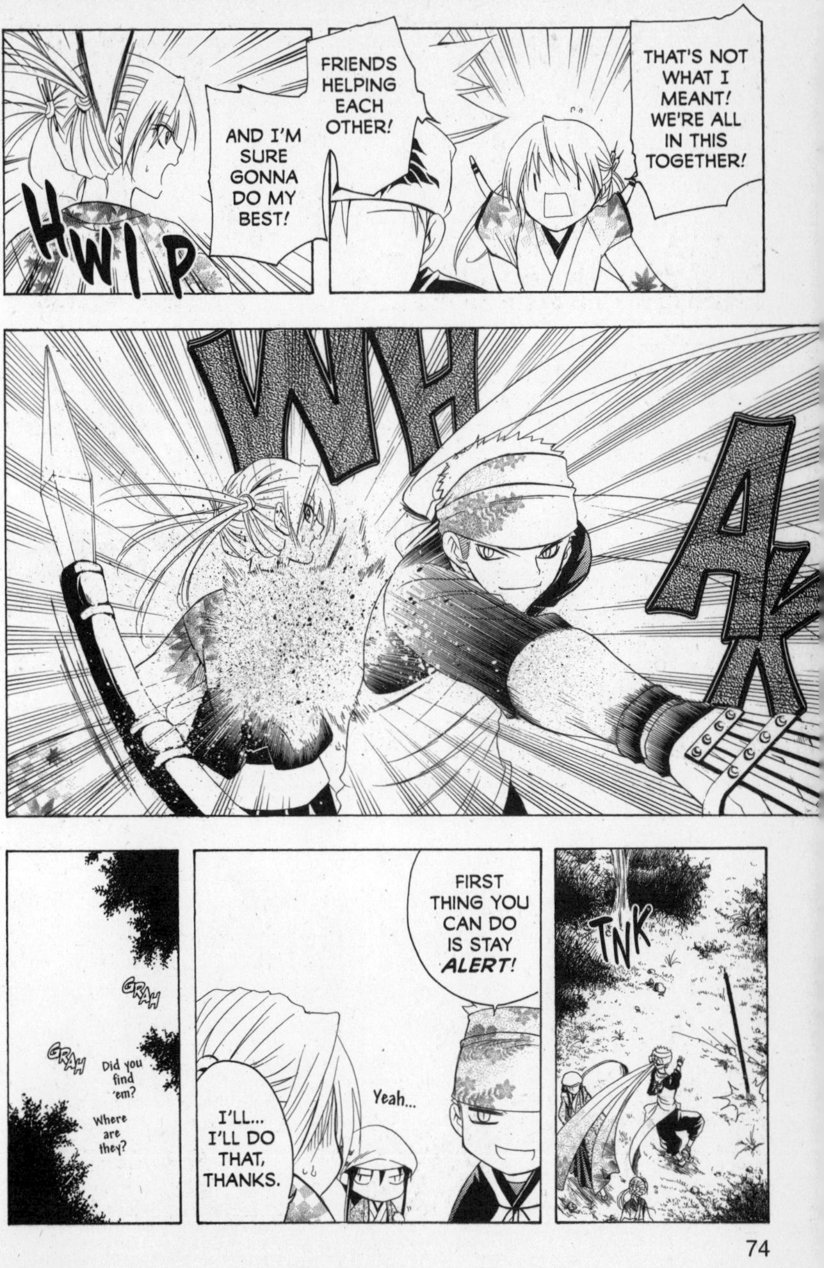
THAT'S NOT WHAT I MEANT! WE'RE ALL IN THIS TOGETHER!
FRIENDS HELPING EACH OTHER!
AND I'M SURE GONNA DO MY BEST!
HWIP
WHAK
TNK
FIRST THING YOU CAN DO IS STAY *ALERT*!
Yeah...
I'LL... I'LL DO THAT, THANKS.
GRAH
GRAH
Did you find 'em?
Where are they?

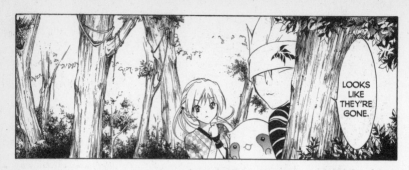

LOOKS LIKE THEY'RE GONE.
SO, WE NEED A PLAN.
CAPTURE MEANS TORTURE, SO LETS AVOID THAT!
OTHER-WISE, ALL THRILLING ♡ AND FUN ☆ OPTIONS ARE OPEN!
Skweek!
THEY WON'T CAPTURE *ME*, NO MATTER WHAT!
Me neither!
HOW CAN THEY BE SO SURE?
CLAP ☆ CLAP
WELL, NEVER MIND THAT!
THIS IS MY CHANCE TO SHOW UTSUHO I'M NOT SOME USELESS TAG-A-LONG!
RUSTLE

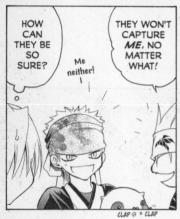

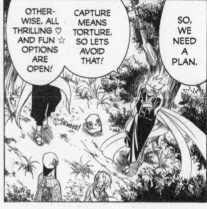

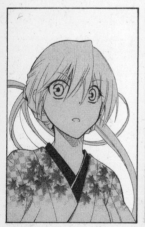

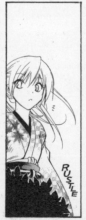

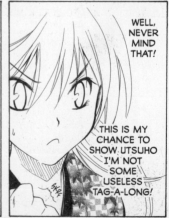

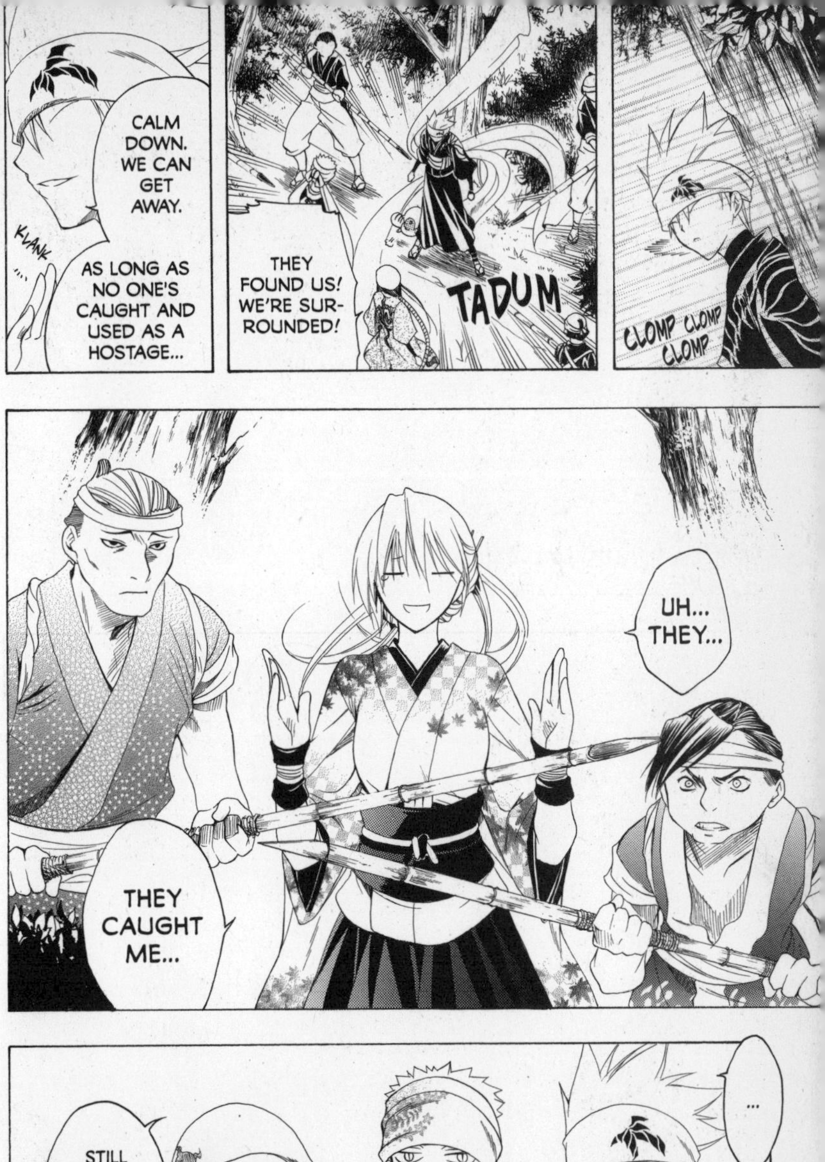
CLOMP CLOMP CLOMP
THEY FOUND US! WE'RE SUR-ROUNDED!
TADUM
CALM DOWN. WE CAN GET AWAY.
KLANK
...
AS LONG AS NO ONE'S CAUGHT AND USED AS A HOSTAGE...
UH... THEY...
THEY CAUGHT ME...
...
STILL WORKING ON THAT ALERTNESS, EH?

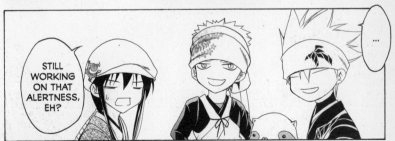

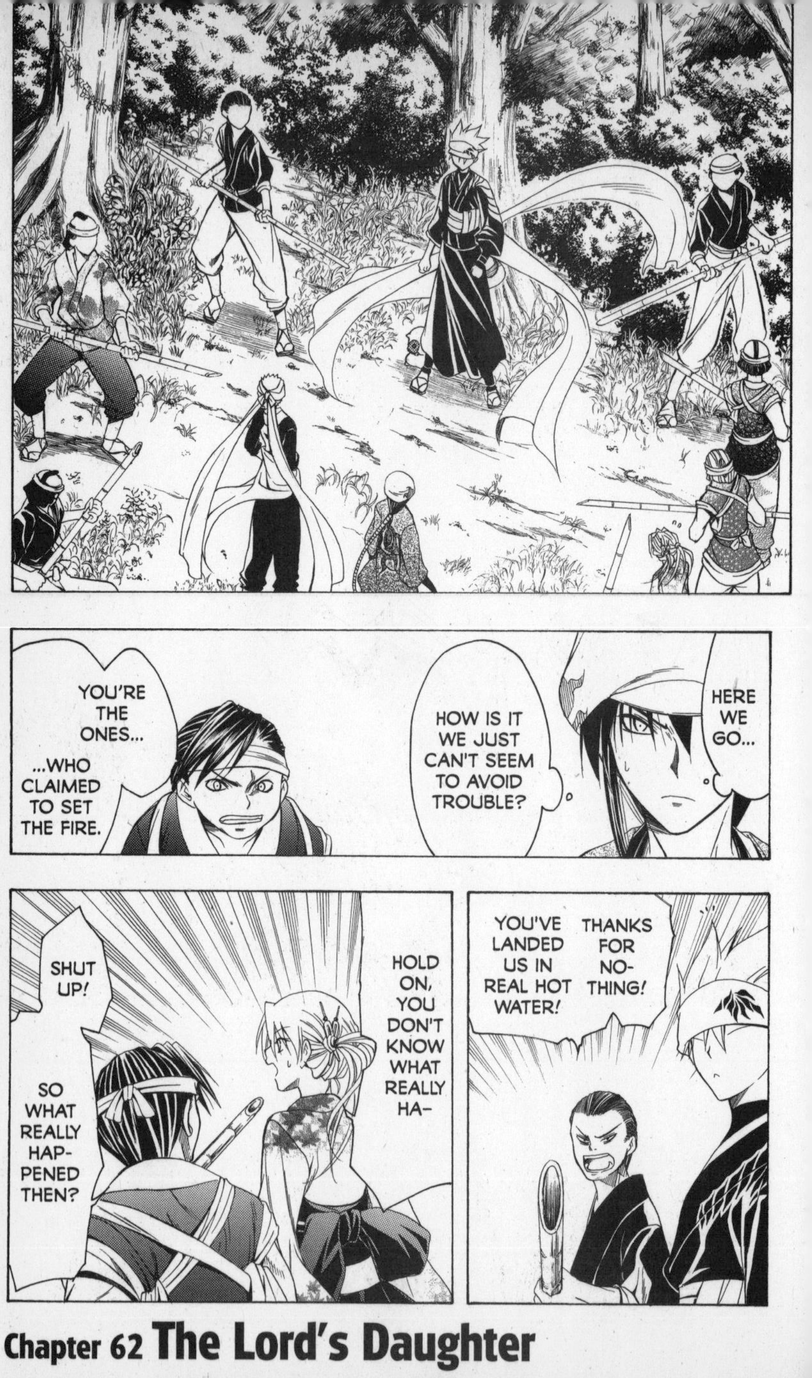
HERE WE GO...
HOW IS IT WE JUST CAN'T SEEM TO AVOID TROUBLE?
YOU'RE THE ONES...
...WHO CLAIMED TO SET THE FIRE.
THANKS FOR NO-THING!
YOU'VE LANDED US IN REAL HOT WATER!
HOLD ON, YOU DON'T KNOW WHAT REALLY HA-
SHUT UP!
SO WHAT REALLY HAP-PENED THEN?

Chapter 62 The Lord's Daughter

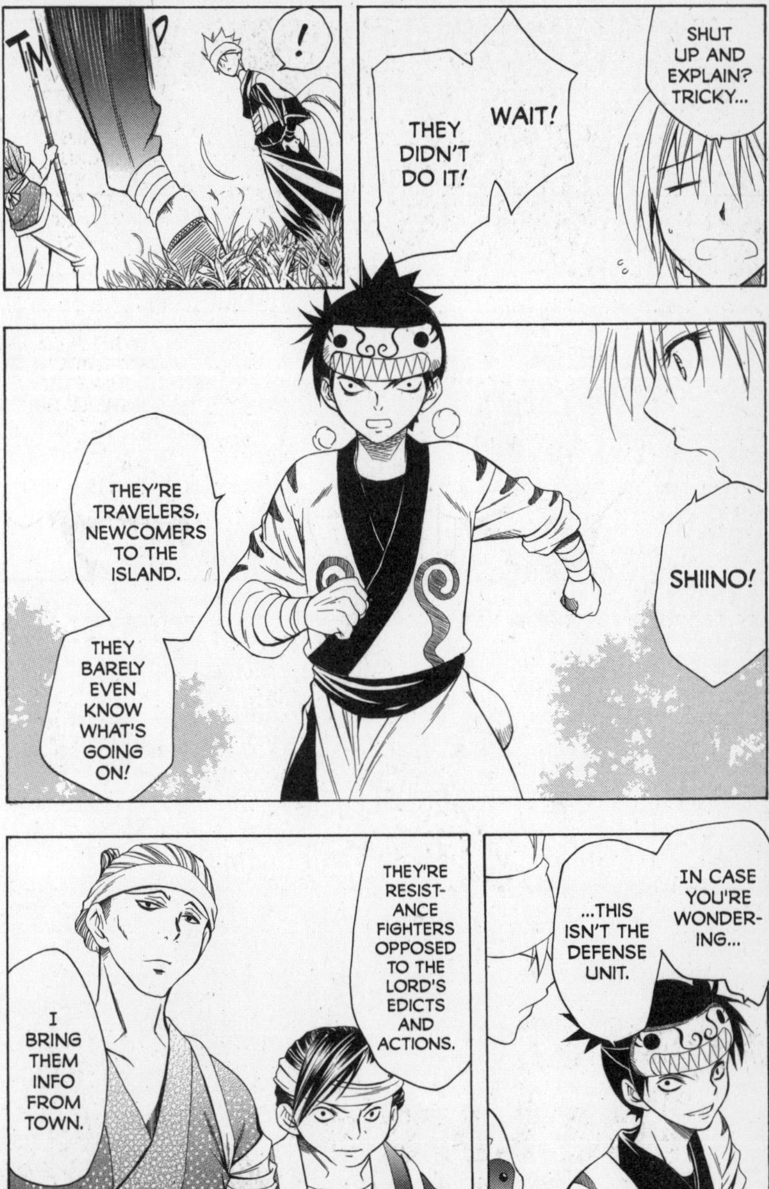
SHUT UP AND EXPLAIN? TRICKY...
WAIT!
THEY DIDN'T DO IT!
TMP
!
SHIINO!
THEY'RE TRAVELERS, NEWCOMERS TO THE ISLAND.
THEY BARELY EVEN KNOW WHAT'S GOING ON!
IN CASE YOU'RE WONDER-ING...
...THIS ISN'T THE DEFENSE UNIT.
THEY'RE RESIST-ANCE FIGHTERS OPPOSED TO THE LORD'S EDICTS AND ACTIONS.
I BRING THEM INFO FROM TOWN.

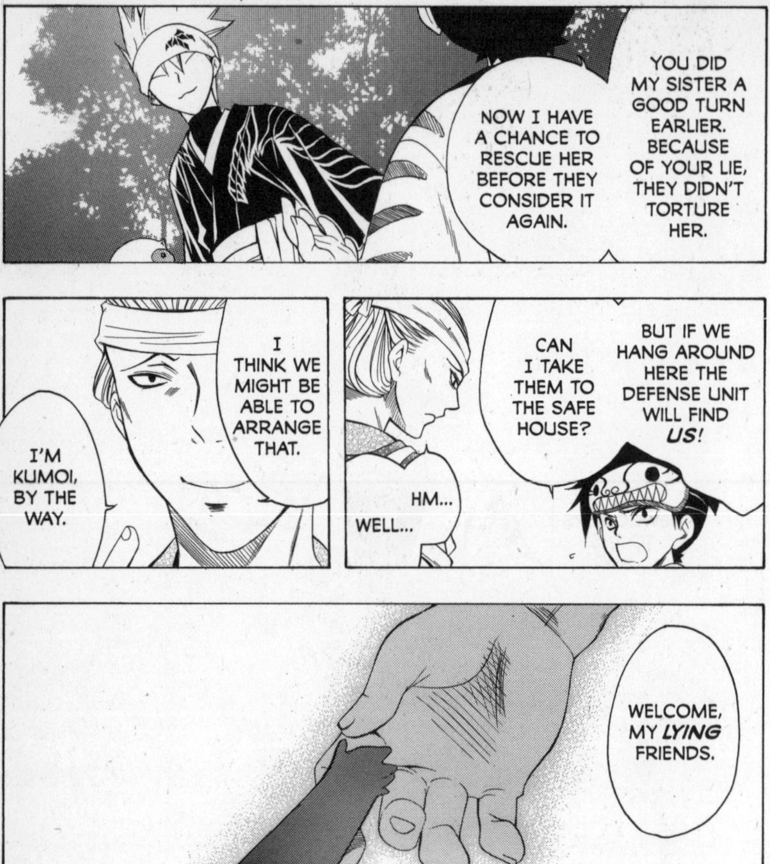
YOU DID MY SISTER A GOOD TURN EARLIER. BECAUSE OF YOUR LIE, THEY DIDN'T TORTURE HER.
NOW I HAVE A CHANCE TO RESCUE HER BEFORE THEY CONSIDER IT AGAIN.
BUT IF WE HANG AROUND HERE THE DEFENSE UNIT WILL FIND *US!*
CAN I TAKE THEM TO THE SAFE HOUSE?
HM... WELL...
I THINK WE MIGHT BE ABLE TO ARRANGE THAT.
I'M KUMOI, BY THE WAY.
WELCOME, MY *LYING* FRIENDS.

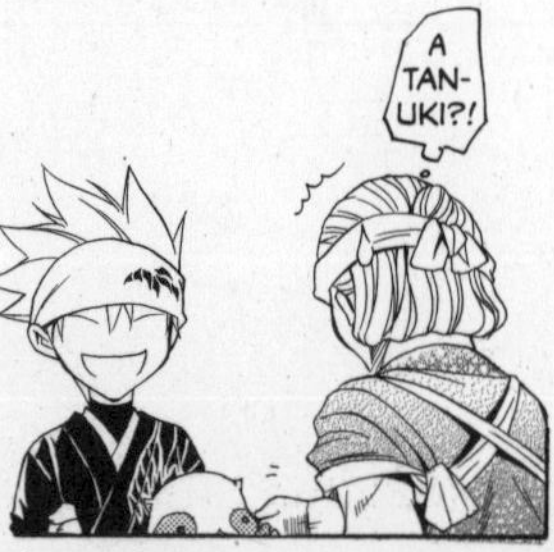
A TAN-UKI?!

Chapter 62 The Lord's Daughter

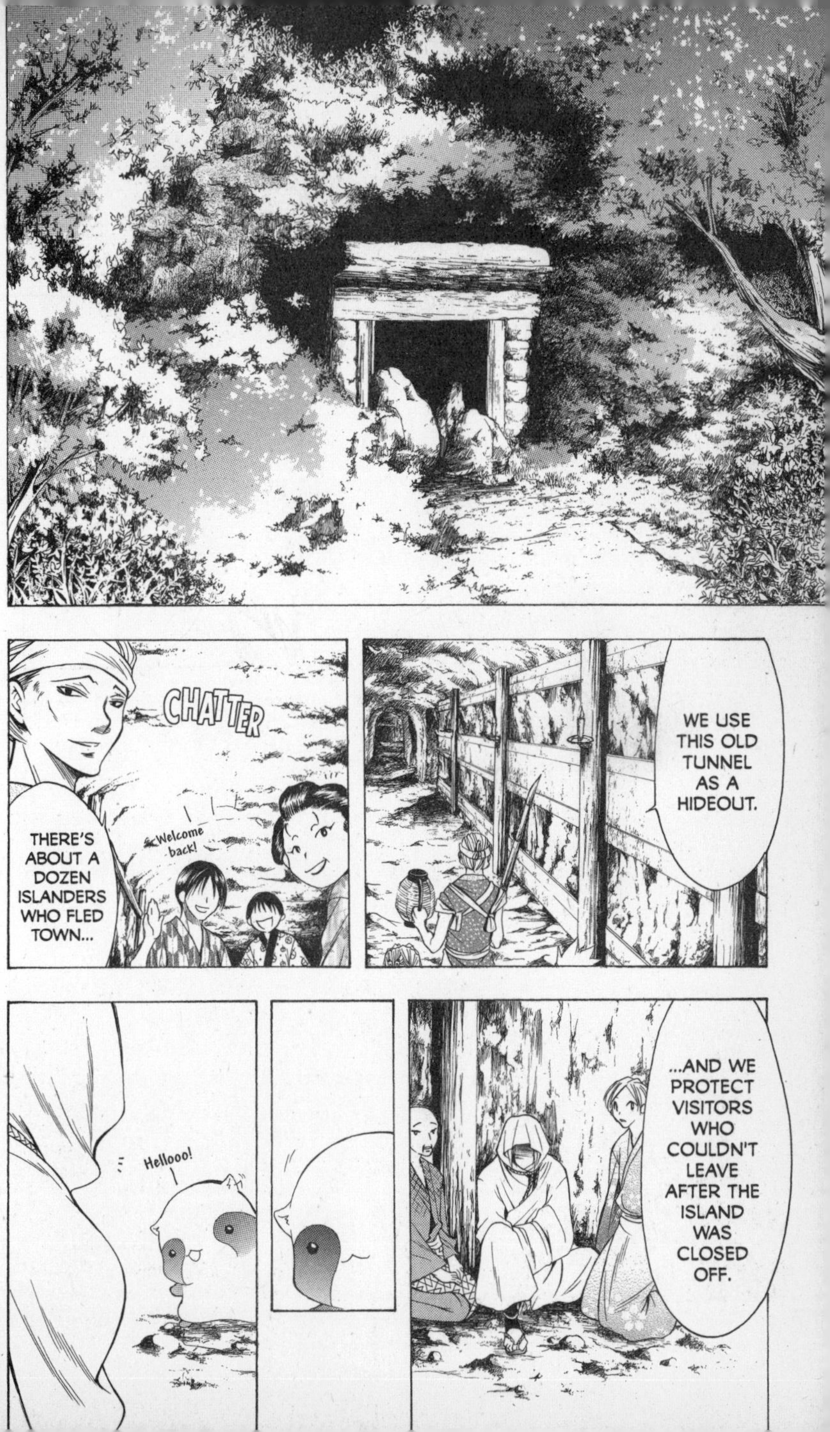
WE USE THIS OLD TUNNEL AS A HIDEOUT.
CHATTER
Welcome back!
THERE'S ABOUT A DOZEN ISLANDERS WHO FLED TOWN...
...AND WE PROTECT VISITORS WHO COULDN'T LEAVE AFTER THE ISLAND WAS CLOSED OFF.
Hellooo!

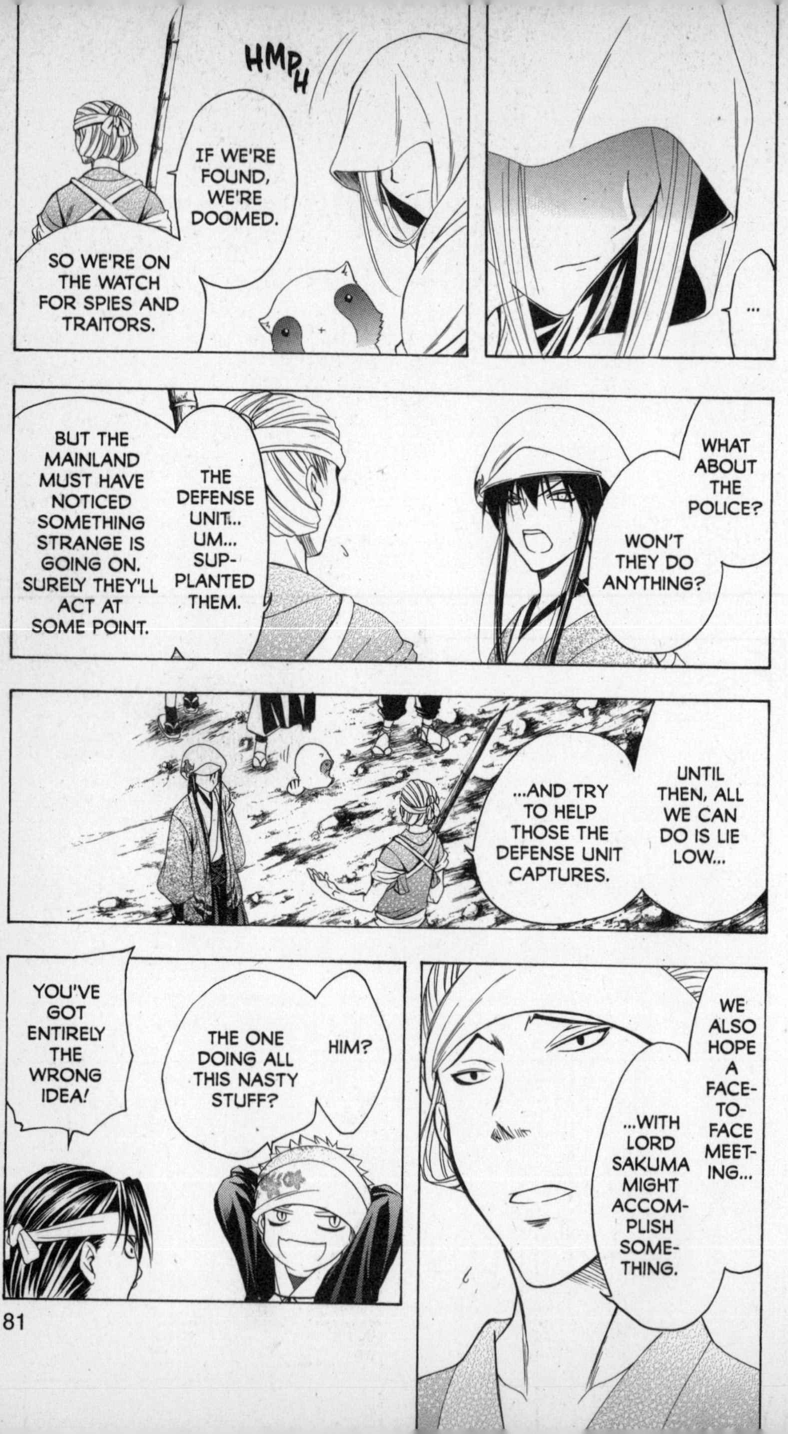
...
HMPH
IF WE'RE FOUND, WE'RE DOOMED.
SO WE'RE ON THE WATCH FOR SPIES AND TRAITORS.
WHAT ABOUT THE POLICE?
WON'T THEY DO ANYTHING?
THE DEFENSE UNIT... UM... SUP-PLANTED THEM.
BUT THE MAINLAND MUST HAVE NOTICED SOMETHING STRANGE IS GOING ON. SURELY THEY'LL ACT AT SOME POINT.
UNTIL THEN, ALL WE CAN DO IS LIE LOW...
...AND TRY TO HELP THOSE THE DEFENSE UNIT CAPTURES.
WE ALSO HOPE A FACE-TO-FACE MEET-ING...
...WITH LORD SAKUMA MIGHT ACCOM-PLISH SOME-THING.
HIM?
THE ONE DOING ALL THIS NASTY STUFF?
YOU'VE GOT ENTIRELY THE WRONG IDEA!

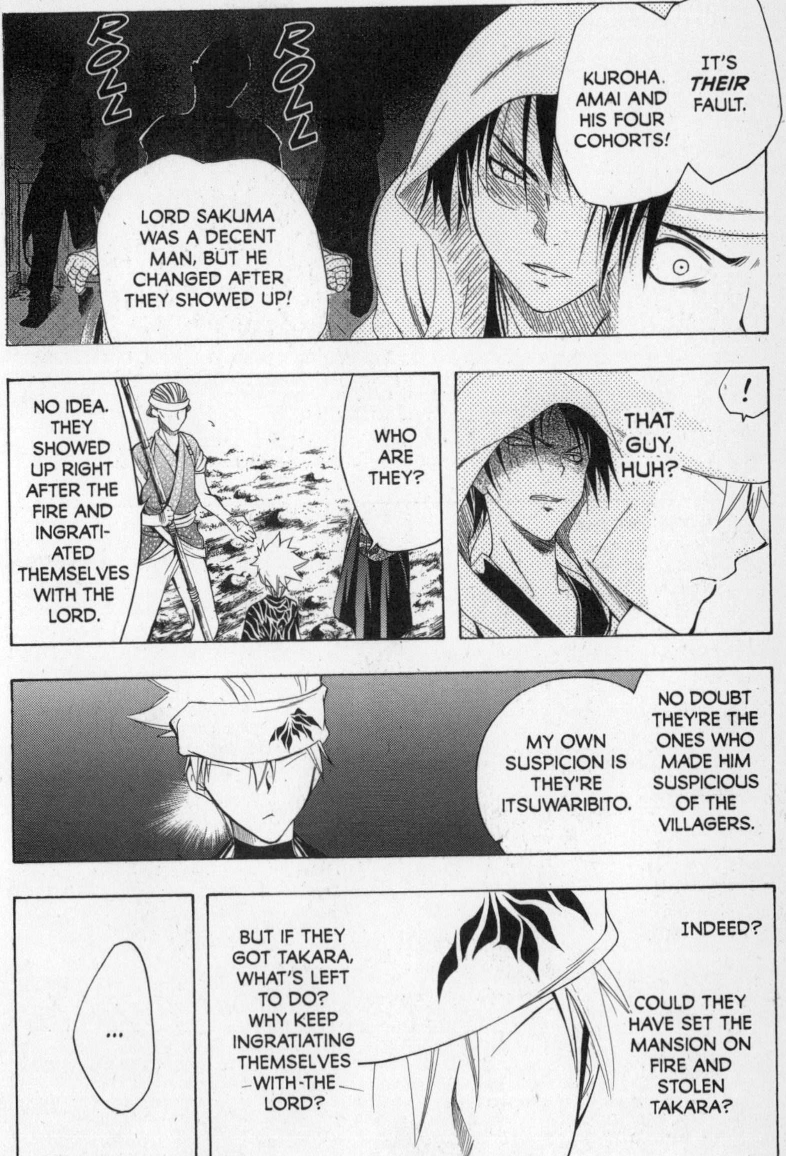
IT'S ***THEIR*** FAULT.
KUROHA. AMAI AND HIS FOUR COHORTS!
LORD SAKUMA WAS A DECENT MAN, BUT HE CHANGED AFTER THEY SHOWED UP!
ROLL
ROLL
!
THAT GUY, HUH?
WHO ARE THEY?
NO IDEA. THEY SHOWED UP RIGHT AFTER THE FIRE AND INGRATI-ATED THEMSELVES WITH THE LORD.
NO DOUBT THEY'RE THE ONES WHO MADE HIM SUSPICIOUS OF THE VILLAGERS.
MY OWN SUSPICION IS THEY'RE ITSUWARIBITO.
INDEED?
COULD THEY HAVE SET THE MANSION ON FIRE AND STOLEN TAKARA?
BUT IF THEY GOT TAKARA, WHAT'S LEFT TO DO? WHY KEEP INGRATIATING THEMSELVES WITH THE LORD?
...

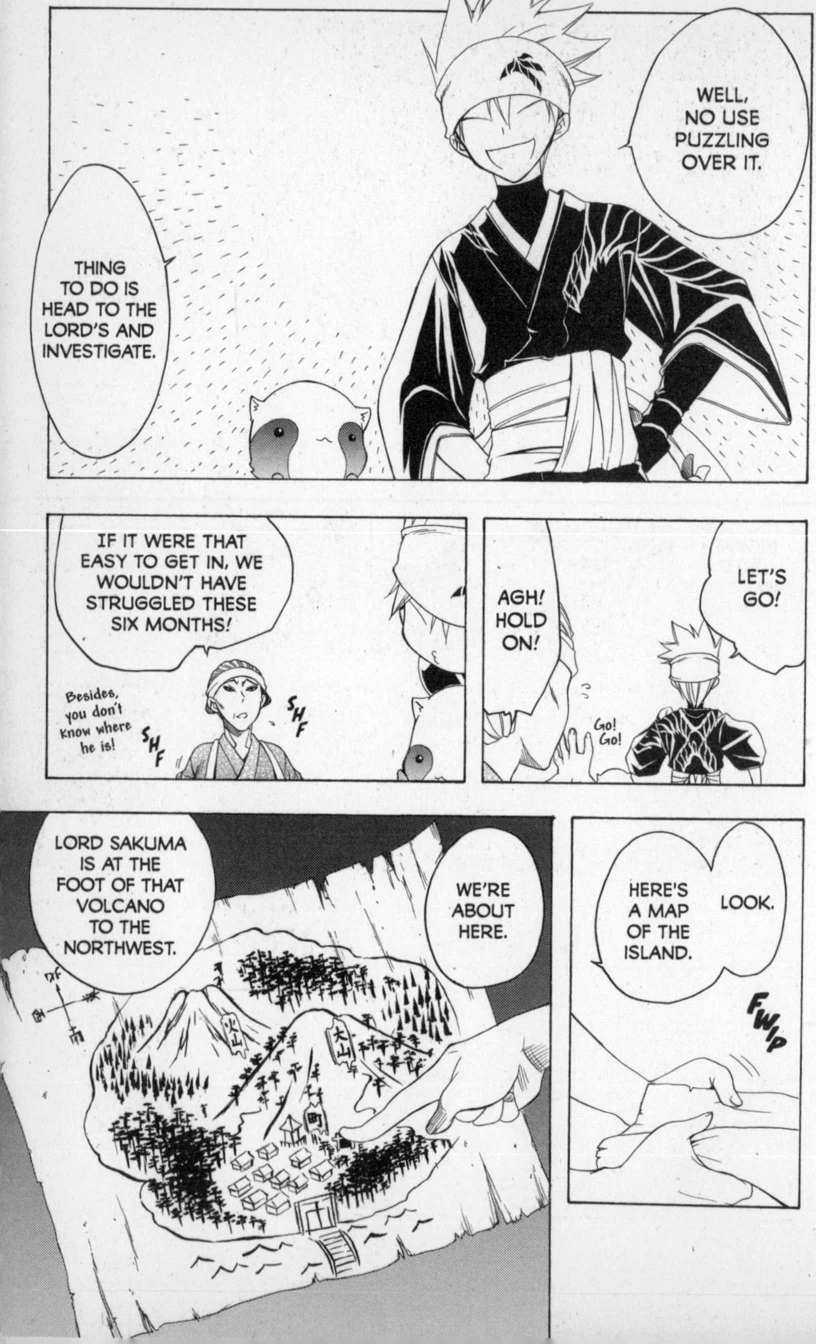
WELL, NO USE PUZZLING OVER IT.
THING TO DO IS HEAD TO THE LORD'S AND INVESTIGATE.
LET'S GO!
Go! Go!
AGH! HOLD ON!
IF IT WERE THAT EASY TO GET IN, WE WOULDN'T HAVE STRUGGLED THESE SIX MONTHS!
Besides, you don't know where he is!
SHF
SHF
LOOK.
HERE'S A MAP OF THE ISLAND.
FWIP
WE'RE ABOUT HERE.
LORD SAKUMA IS AT THE FOOT OF THAT VOLCANO TO THE NORTHWEST.
火山
大山
町

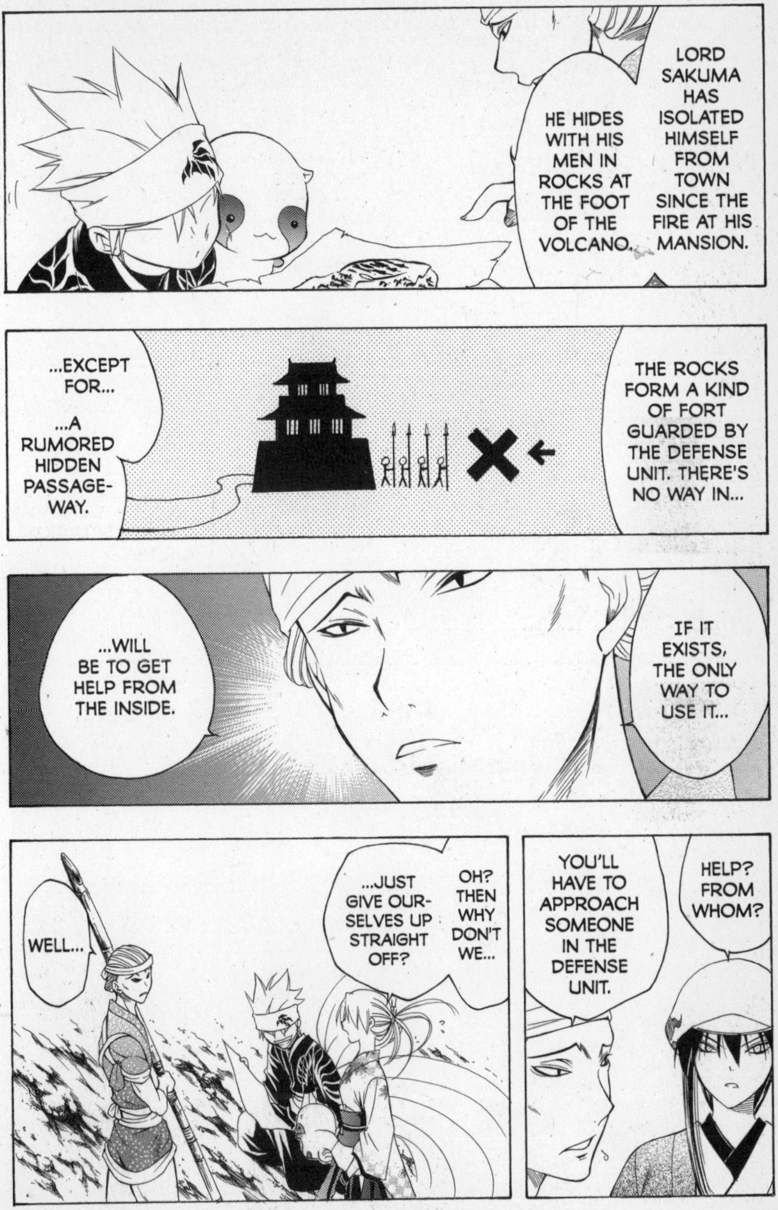
LORD SAKUMA HAS ISOLATED HIMSELF FROM TOWN SINCE THE FIRE AT HIS MANSION.
HE HIDES WITH HIS MEN IN ROCKS AT THE FOOT OF THE VOLCANO.
THE ROCKS FORM A KIND OF FORT GUARDED BY THE DEFENSE UNIT. THERE'S NO WAY IN...
...EXCEPT FOR...
...A RUMORED HIDDEN PASSAGE-WAY.
IF IT EXISTS, THE ONLY WAY TO USE IT...
...WILL BE TO GET HELP FROM THE INSIDE.
HELP? FROM WHOM?
YOU'LL HAVE TO APPROACH SOMEONE IN THE DEFENSE UNIT.
OH? THEN WHY DON'T WE...
...JUST GIVE OUR-SELVES UP STRAIGHT OFF?
WELL...

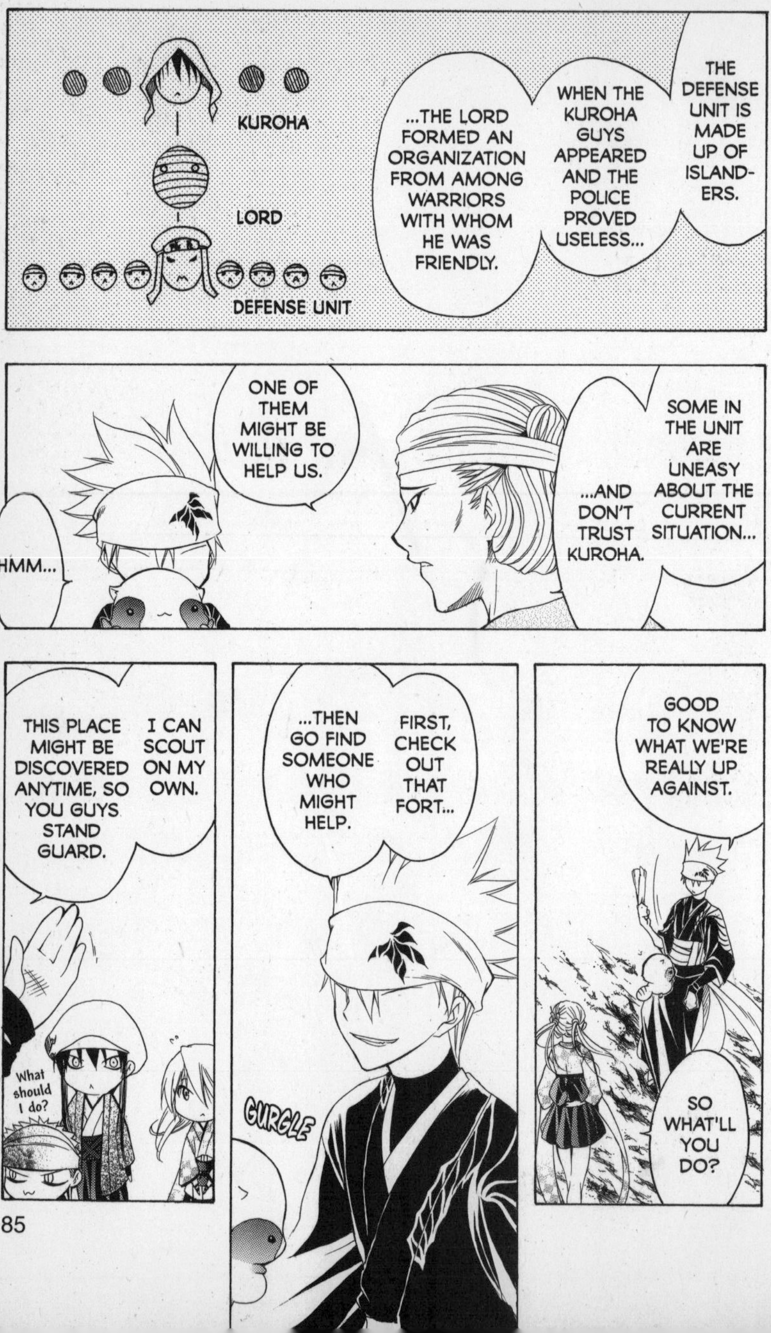
THE DEFENSE UNIT IS MADE UP OF ISLANDERS.
WHEN THE KUROHA GUYS APPEARED AND THE POLICE PROVED USELESS...
...THE LORD FORMED AN ORGANIZATION FROM AMONG WARRIORS WITH WHOM HE WAS FRIENDLY.
KUROHA
LORD
DEFENSE UNIT
SOME IN THE UNIT ARE UNEASY ABOUT THE CURRENT SITUATION...
...AND DON'T TRUST KUROHA.
ONE OF THEM MIGHT BE WILLING TO HELP US.
HMM...
GOOD TO KNOW WHAT WE'RE REALLY UP AGAINST.
SO WHAT'LL YOU DO?
FIRST, CHECK OUT THAT FORT...
...THEN GO FIND SOMEONE WHO MIGHT HELP.
GURGLE
I CAN SCOUT ON MY OWN.
THIS PLACE MIGHT BE DISCOVERED ANYTIME, SO YOU GUYS STAND GUARD.
What should I do?

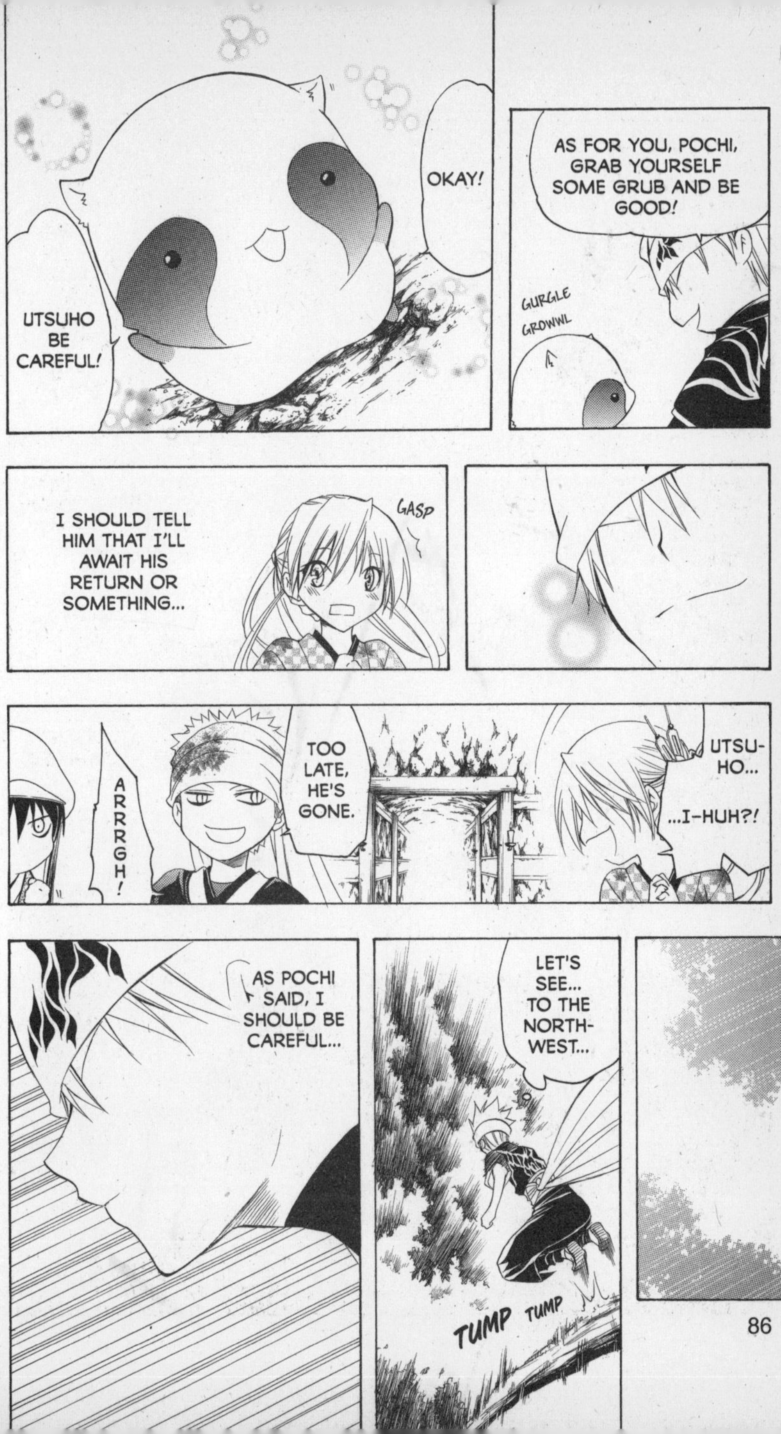
AS FOR YOU, POCHI, GRAB YOURSELF SOME GRUB AND BE GOOD!
GURGLE
GROWWL
OKAY!
UTSUHO BE CAREFUL!
GASP
I SHOULD TELL HIM THAT I'LL AWAIT HIS RETURN OR SOMETHING...
UTSU-HO...
...I-HUH?!
TOO LATE, HE'S GONE.
ARRRGH!
LET'S SEE... TO THE NORTH-WEST...
TUMP TUMP
AS POCHI SAID, I SHOULD BE CAREFUL...

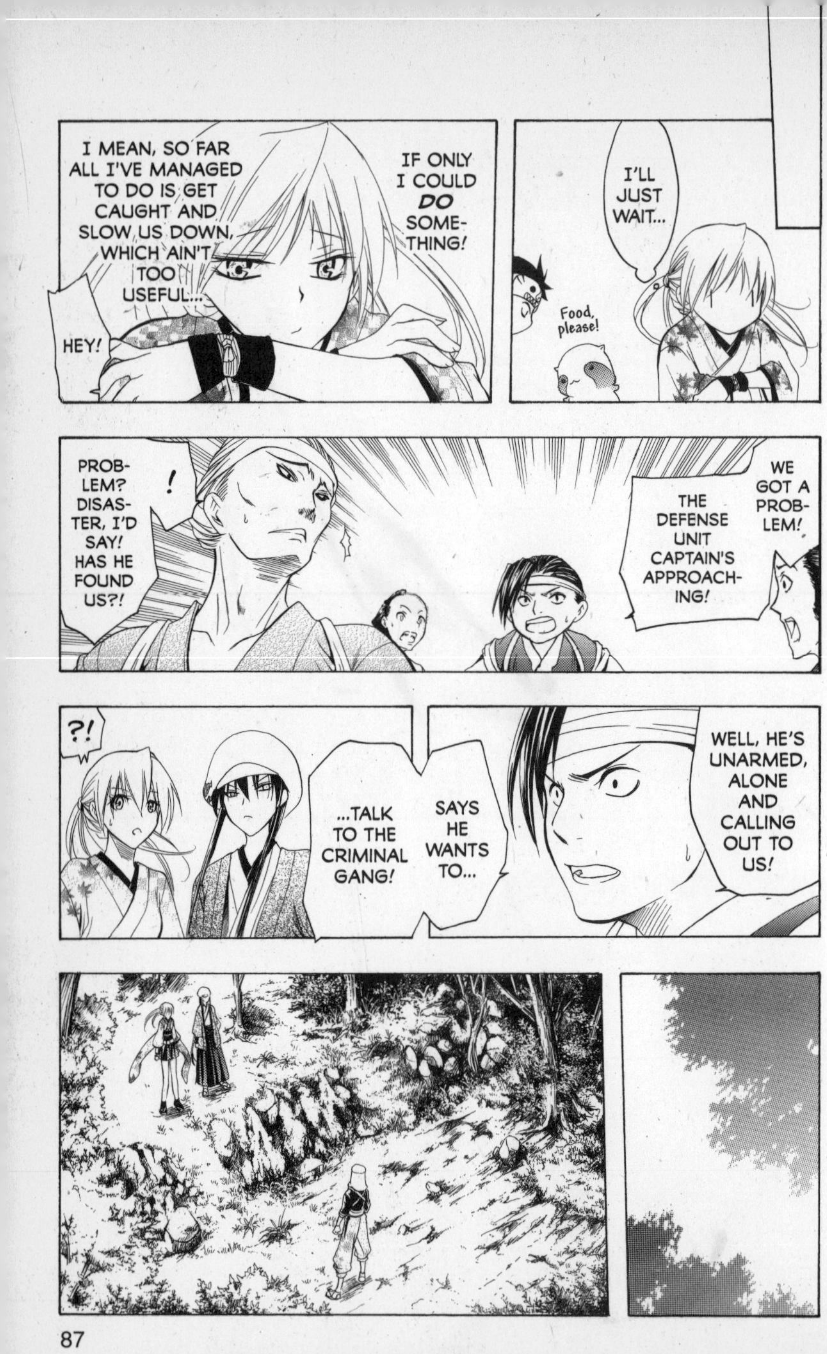
I'LL JUST WAIT...
Food, please!
IF ONLY I COULD *DO* SOMETHING!
I MEAN, SO FAR ALL I'VE MANAGED TO DO IS GET CAUGHT AND SLOW US DOWN, WHICH AIN'T TOO USEFUL...
HEY!
WE GOT A PROBLEM!
THE DEFENSE UNIT CAPTAIN'S APPROACHING!
!
PROBLEM? DISASTER, I'D SAY! HAS HE FOUND US?!
WELL, HE'S UNARMED, ALONE AND CALLING OUT TO US!
SAYS HE WANTS TO...
...TALK TO THE CRIMINAL GANG!
?!

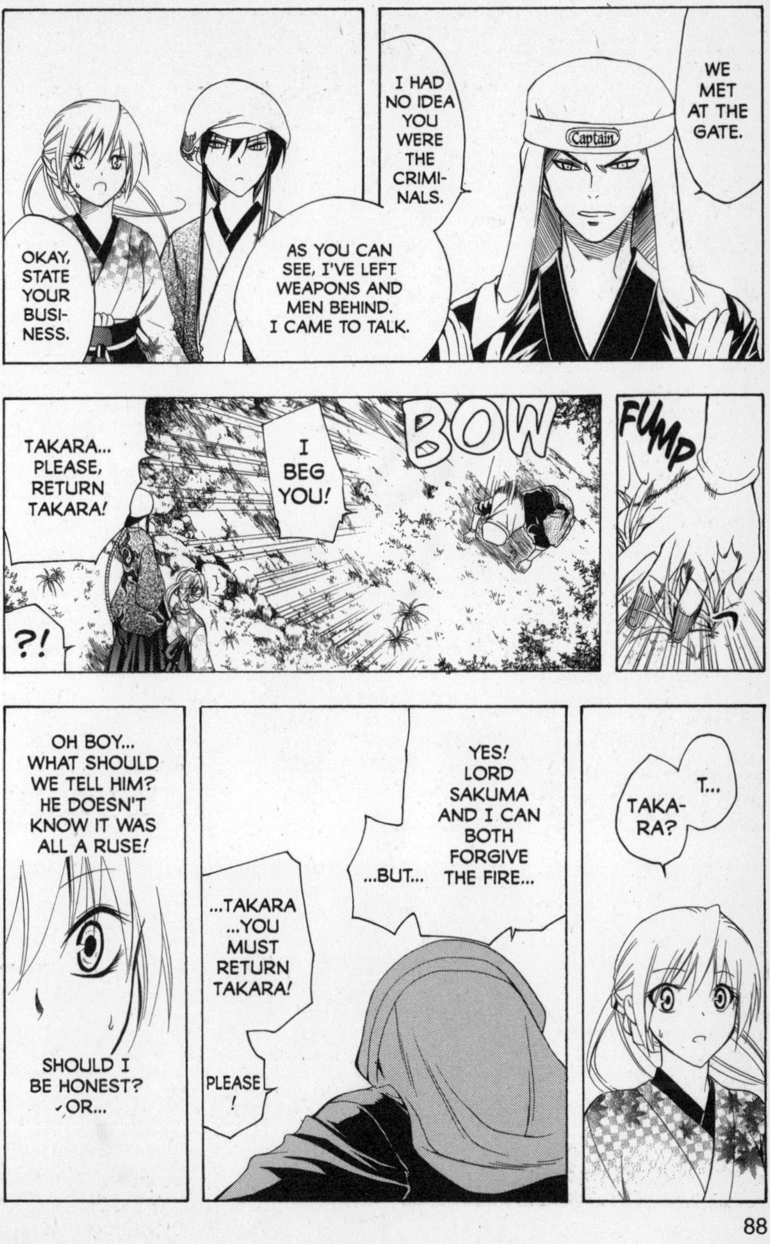
WE MET AT THE GATE.
I HAD NO IDEA YOU WERE THE CRIMINALS.
AS YOU CAN SEE, I'VE LEFT WEAPONS AND MEN BEHIND. I CAME TO TALK.
OKAY, STATE YOUR BUSINESS.
FUMP
BOW
I BEG YOU!
TAKARA... PLEASE, RETURN TAKARA!
?!
T... TAKA-RA?
YES! LORD SAKUMA AND I CAN BOTH FORGIVE THE FIRE...
...BUT...
...TAKARA ...YOU MUST RETURN TAKARA!
PLEASE!
OH BOY... WHAT SHOULD WE TELL HIM? HE DOESN'T KNOW IT WAS ALL A RUSE!
SHOULD I BE HONEST? ...OR...

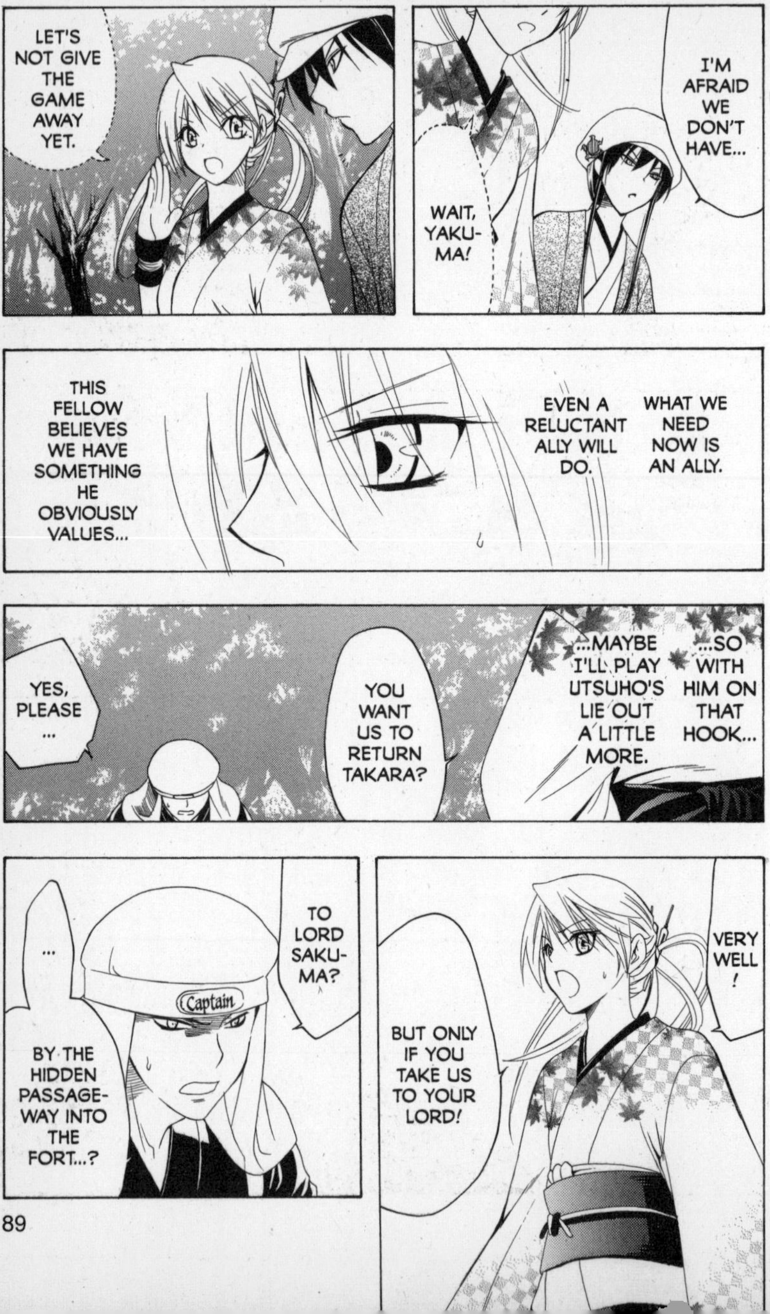
I'M AFRAID WE DON'T HAVE...
WAIT, YAKU-MA!
LET'S NOT GIVE THE GAME AWAY YET.
WHAT WE NEED NOW IS AN ALLY.
EVEN A RELUCTANT ALLY WILL DO.
THIS FELLOW BELIEVES WE HAVE SOMETHING HE OBVIOUSLY VALUES...
...SO WITH HIM ON THAT HOOK...
...MAYBE I'LL PLAY UTSUHO'S LIE OUT A LITTLE MORE.
YOU WANT US TO RETURN TAKARA?
YES, PLEASE ...
VERY WELL!
BUT ONLY IF YOU TAKE US TO YOUR LORD!
TO LORD SAKU-MA?
...
Captain
BY THE HIDDEN PASSAGE-WAY INTO THE FORT...?

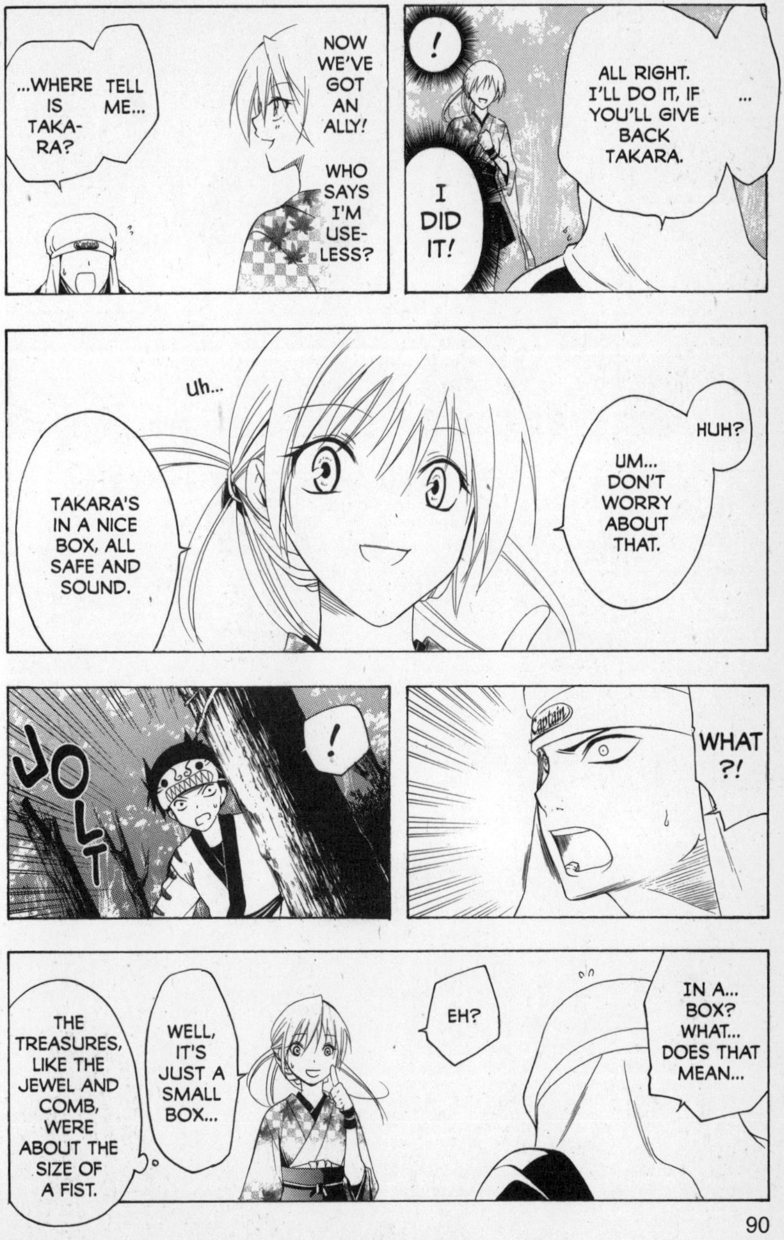
ALL RIGHT. I'LL DO IT, IF YOU'LL GIVE BACK TAKARA.
...
!
I DID IT!
NOW WE'VE GOT AN ALLY!
WHO SAYS I'M USELESS?
TELL ME...
...WHERE IS TAKARA?
HUH?
UM... DON'T WORRY ABOUT THAT.
Uh...
TAKARA'S IN A NICE BOX, ALL SAFE AND SOUND.
Captain
WHAT ?!
!
JOLT
IN A... BOX? WHAT... DOES THAT MEAN...
EH?
WELL, IT'S JUST A SMALL BOX...
THE TREASURES, LIKE THE JEWEL AND COMB, WERE ABOUT THE SIZE OF A FIST.

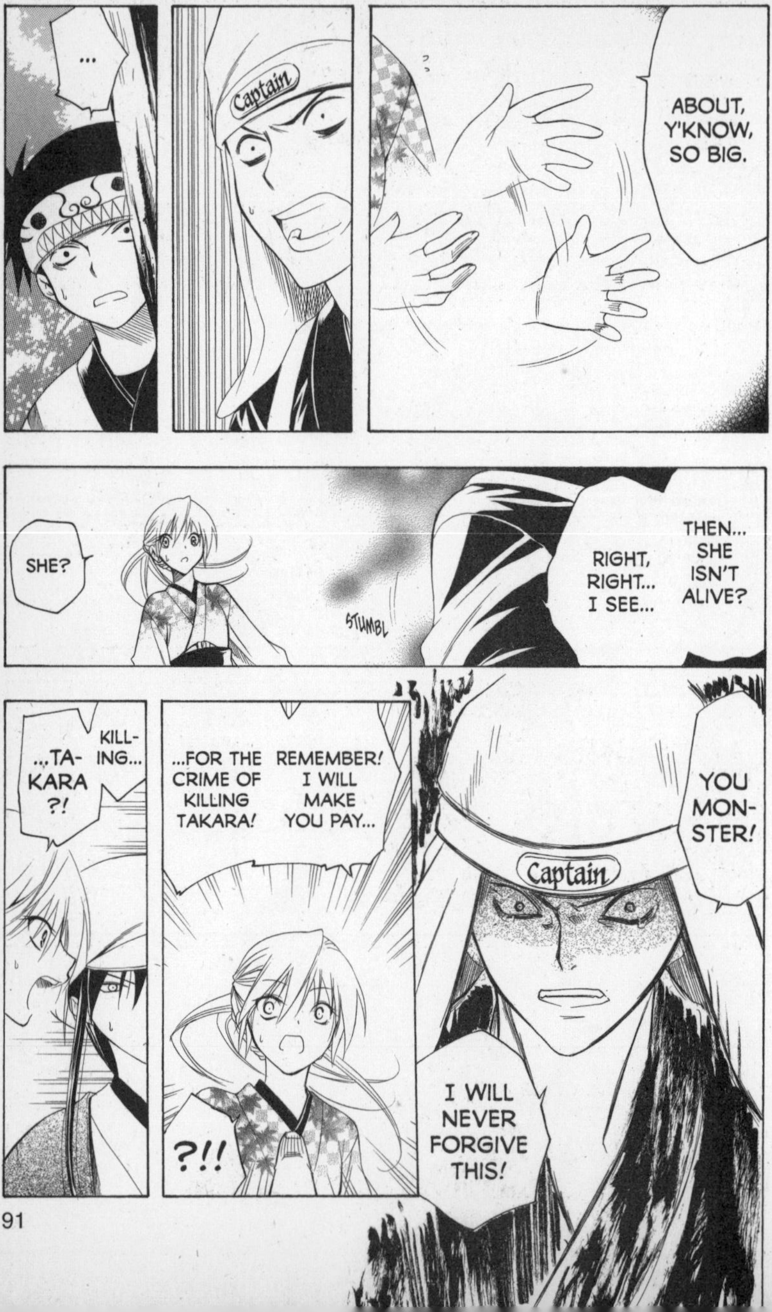
ABOUT, Y'KNOW, SO BIG.
Captain
...
THEN... SHE ISN'T ALIVE?
RIGHT, RIGHT... I SEE...
STUMBL
SHE?
YOU MON-STER!
Captain
I WILL NEVER FORGIVE THIS!
REMEMBER! I WILL MAKE YOU PAY...
...FOR THE CRIME OF KILLING TAKARA!
?!!
KILL-ING...
...TA-KARA ?!

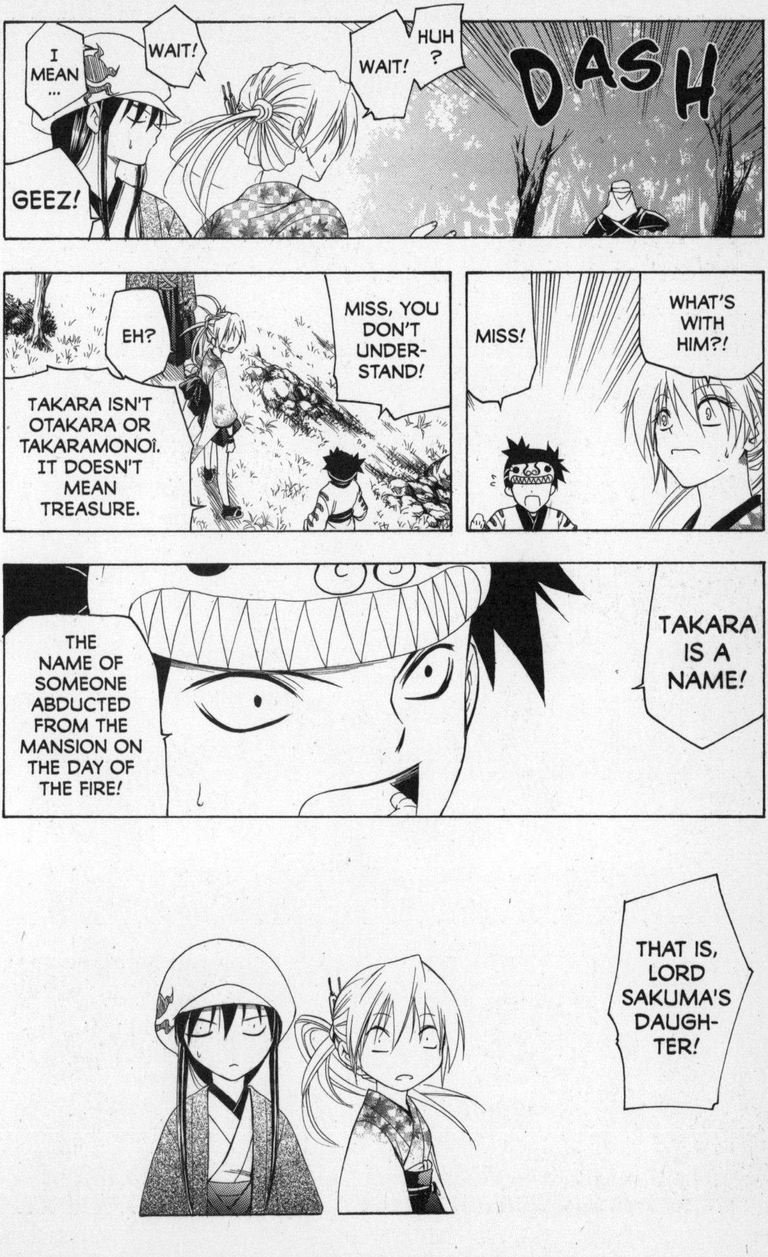
DASH
HUH ?
WAIT!
WAIT!
I MEAN ...
GEEZ!
WHAT'S WITH HIM?!
MISS!
MISS, YOU DON'T UNDER-STAND!
EH?
TAKARA ISN'T OTAKARA OR TAKARAMONOÎ. IT DOESN'T MEAN TREASURE.
TAKARA IS A NAME!
THE NAME OF SOMEONE ABDUCTED FROM THE MANSION ON THE DAY OF THE FIRE!
THAT IS, LORD SAKUMA'S DAUGH-TER!

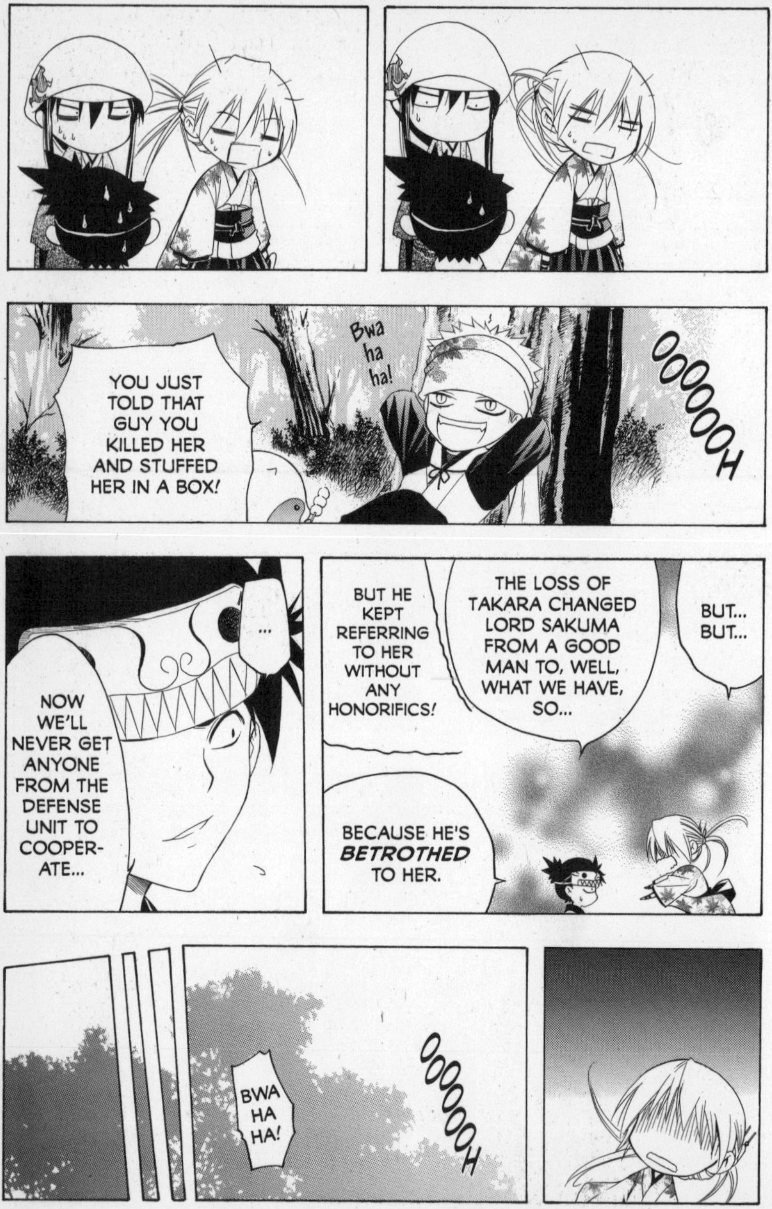
OOOOOOH
Bwa ha ha!
YOU JUST TOLD THAT GUY YOU KILLED HER AND STUFFED HER IN A BOX!
BUT... BUT...
THE LOSS OF TAKARA CHANGED LORD SAKUMA FROM A GOOD MAN TO, WELL, WHAT WE HAVE, SO...
BUT HE KEPT REFERRING TO HER WITHOUT ANY HONORIFICS!
BECAUSE HE'S *BETROTHED* TO HER.
...
NOW WE'LL NEVER GET ANYONE FROM THE DEFENSE UNIT TO COOPER-ATE...
OOOOOH
BWA HA HA!

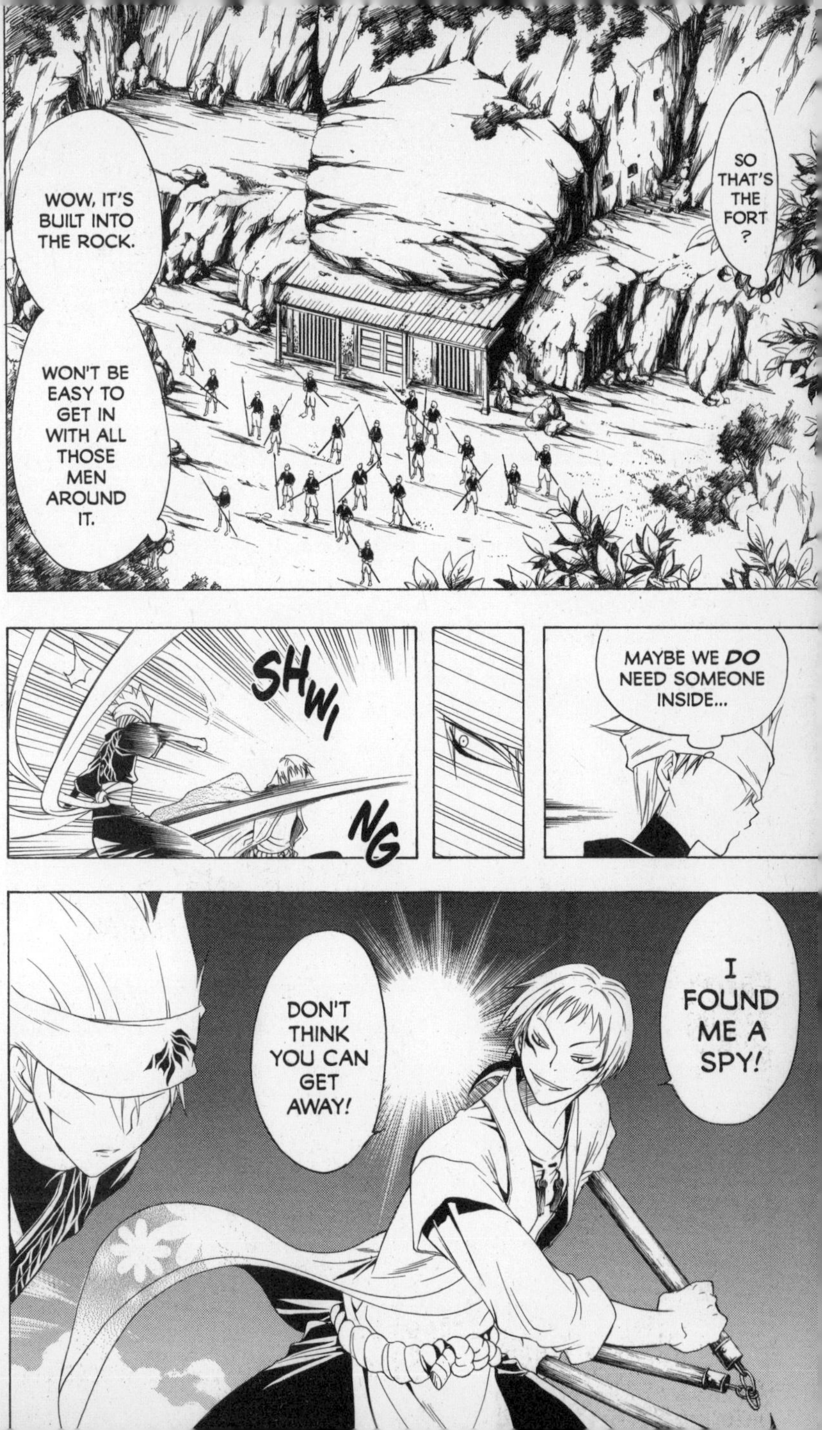
SO THAT'S THE FORT?
WOW, IT'S BUILT INTO THE ROCK.
WON'T BE EASY TO GET IN WITH ALL THOSE MEN AROUND IT.
MAYBE WE *DO* NEED SOMEONE INSIDE...
SHWING
I FOUND ME A SPY!
DON'T THINK YOU CAN GET AWAY!

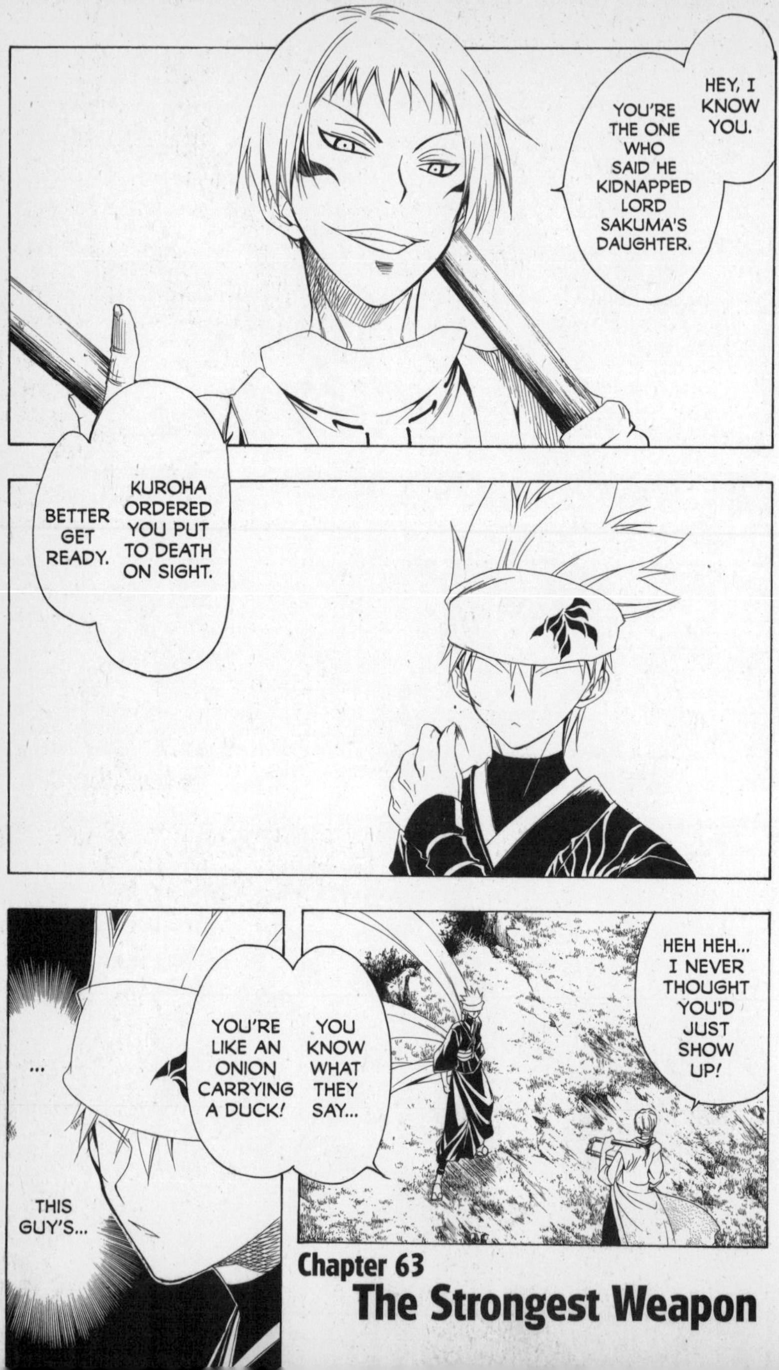
HEY, I KNOW YOU.
YOU'RE THE ONE WHO SAID HE KIDNAPPED LORD SAKUMA'S DAUGHTER.
KUROHA ORDERED YOU PUT TO DEATH ON SIGHT.
BETTER GET READY.
HEH HEH... I NEVER THOUGHT YOU'D JUST SHOW UP!
YOU KNOW WHAT THEY SAY...
YOU'RE LIKE AN ONION CARRYING A DUCK!
...
THIS GUY'S...

Chapter 63
The Strongest Weapon

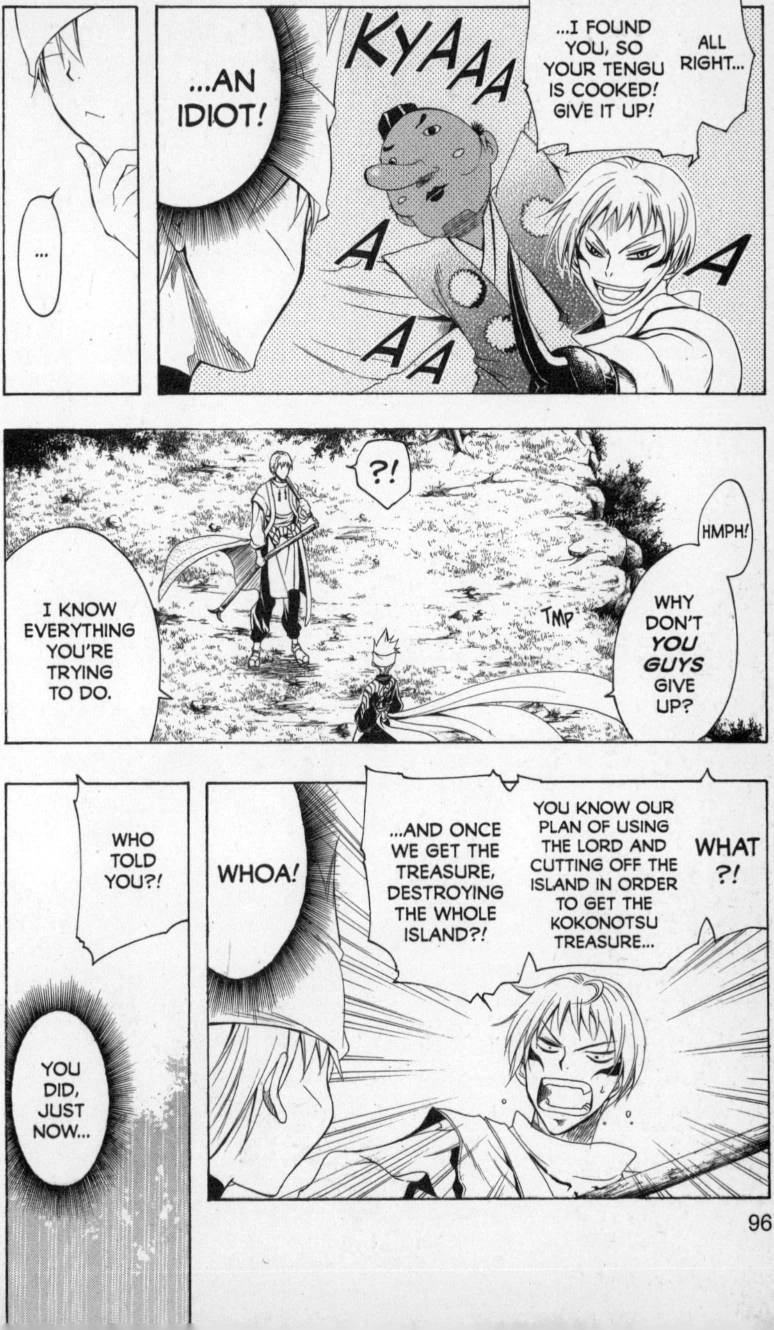
ALL RIGHT...
...I FOUND YOU, SO YOUR TENGU IS COOKED! GIVE IT UP!
KYAAAAAAA
...AN IDIOT!
...
HMPH!
WHY DON'T *YOU GUYS* GIVE UP?
?!
TMP
I KNOW EVERYTHING YOU'RE TRYING TO DO.
WHAT?!
YOU KNOW OUR PLAN OF USING THE LORD AND CUTTING OFF THE ISLAND IN ORDER TO GET THE KOKONOTSU TREASURE...
...AND ONCE WE GET THE TREASURE, DESTROYING THE WHOLE ISLAND?!
WHOA!
WHO TOLD YOU?!
YOU DID, JUST NOW...

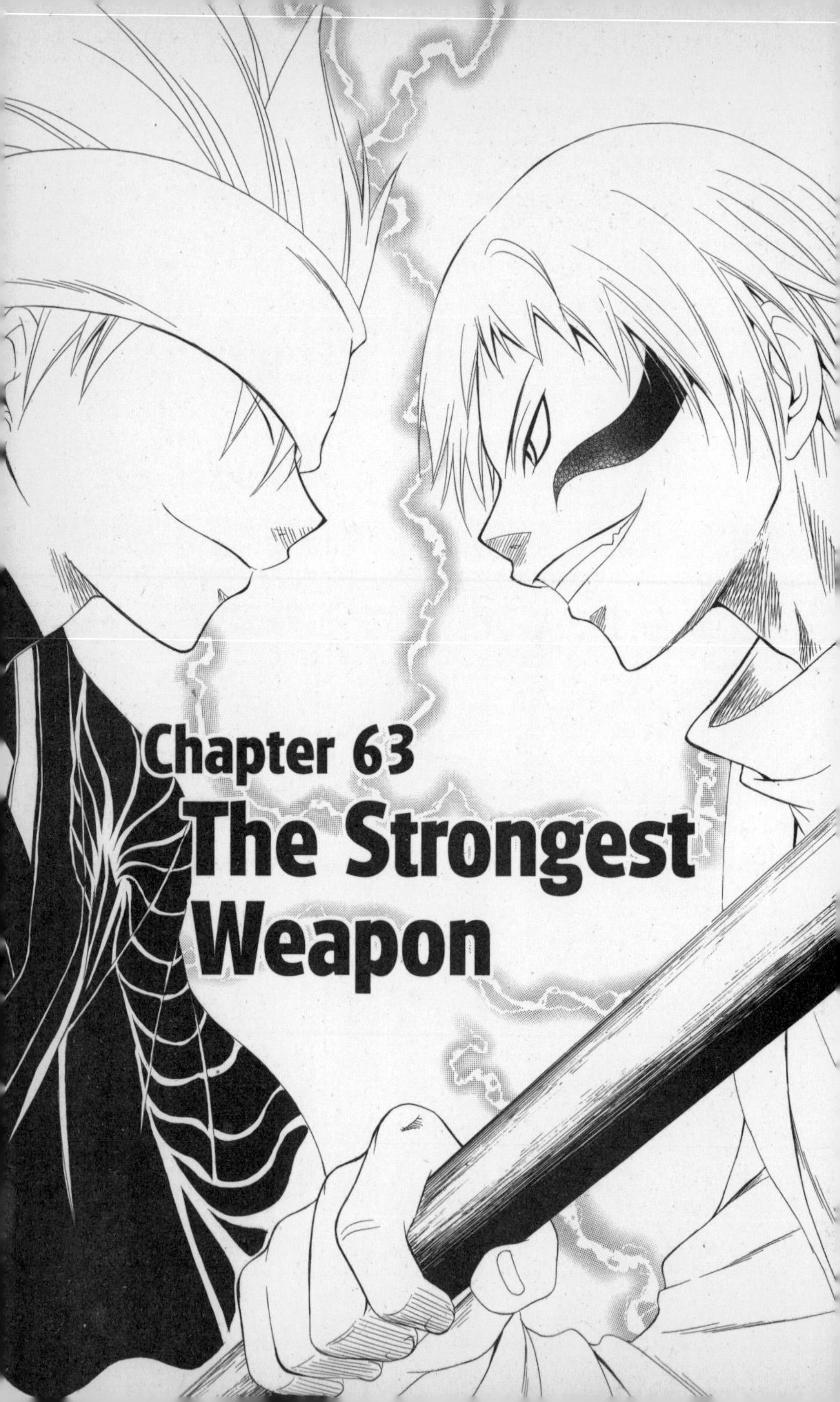
Chapter 63
The Strongest Weapon

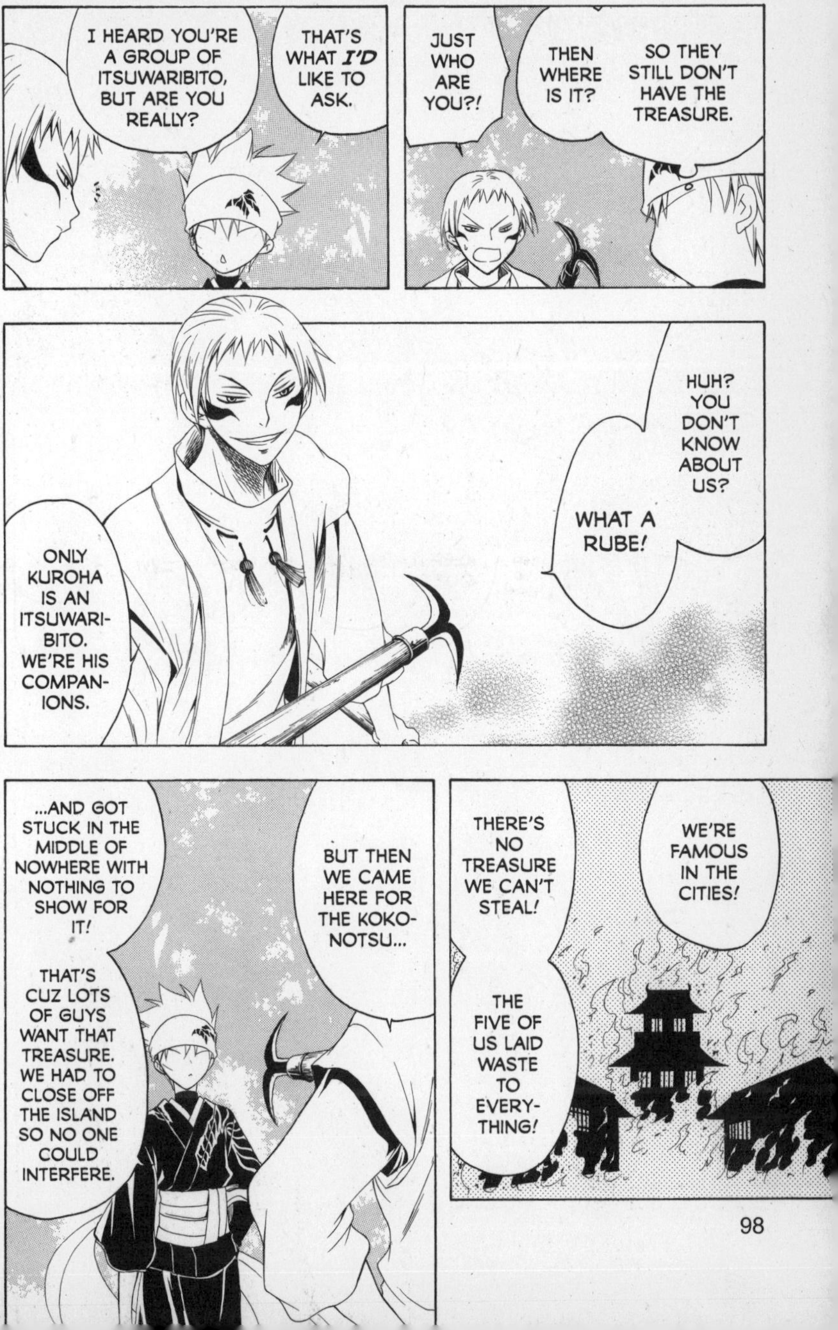
SO THEY STILL DON'T HAVE THE TREASURE.
THEN WHERE IS IT?
JUST WHO ARE YOU?!
THAT'S WHAT *I'D* LIKE TO ASK.
I HEARD YOU'RE A GROUP OF ITSUWARIBITO, BUT ARE YOU REALLY?
HUH? YOU DON'T KNOW ABOUT US?
WHAT A RUBE!
ONLY KUROHA IS AN ITSUWARI-BITO. WE'RE HIS COMPAN-IONS.
WE'RE FAMOUS IN THE CITIES!
THERE'S NO TREASURE WE CAN'T STEAL!
THE FIVE OF US LAID WASTE TO EVERY-THING!
BUT THEN WE CAME HERE FOR THE KOKO-NOTSU...
...AND GOT STUCK IN THE MIDDLE OF NOWHERE WITH NOTHING TO SHOW FOR IT!
THAT'S CUZ LOTS OF GUYS WANT THAT TREASURE. WE HAD TO CLOSE OFF THE ISLAND SO NO ONE COULD INTERFERE.

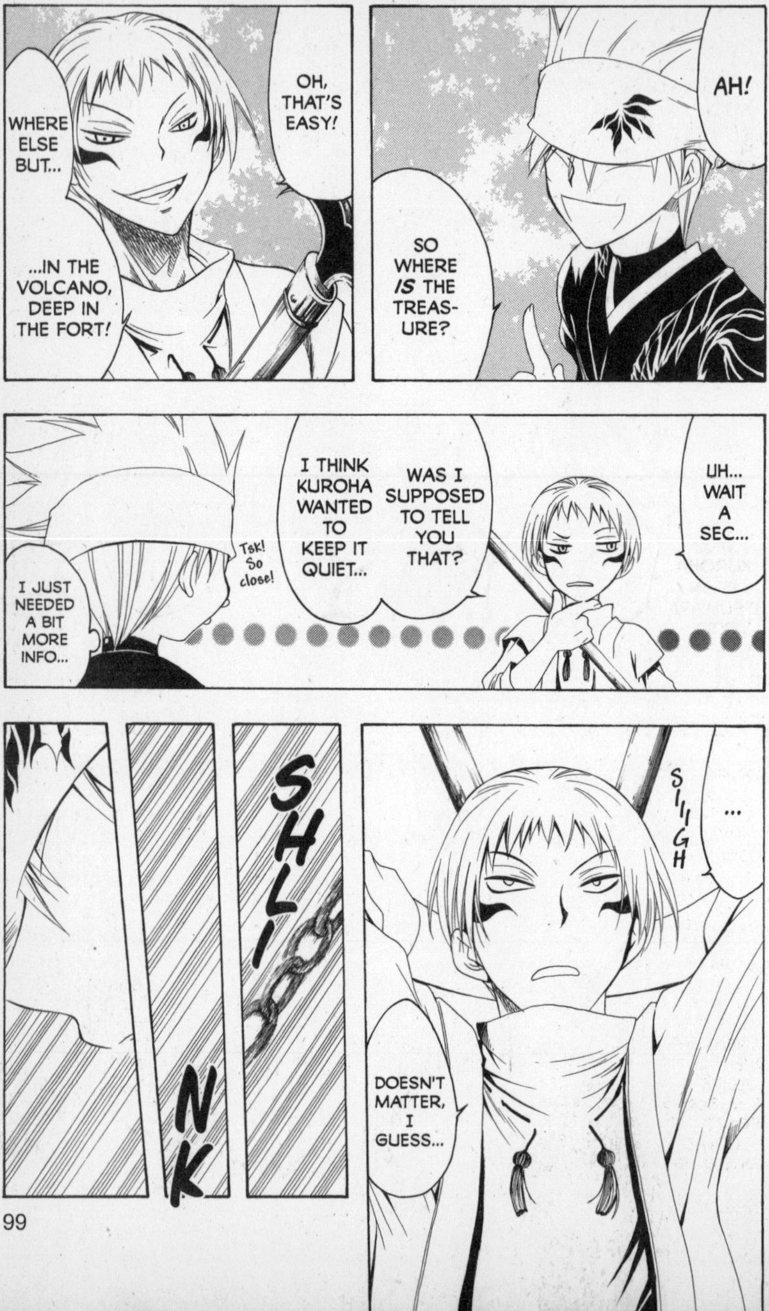
AH!
SO WHERE *IS* THE TREASURE?
OH, THAT'S EASY!
WHERE ELSE BUT...
...IN THE VOLCANO, DEEP IN THE FORT!
UH... WAIT A SEC...
WAS I SUPPOSED TO TELL YOU THAT?
I THINK KUROHA WANTED TO KEEP IT QUIET...
Tsk! So close!
I JUST NEEDED A BIT MORE INFO...
SIIIGH
...
DOESN'T MATTER, I GUESS...
SHLIINK

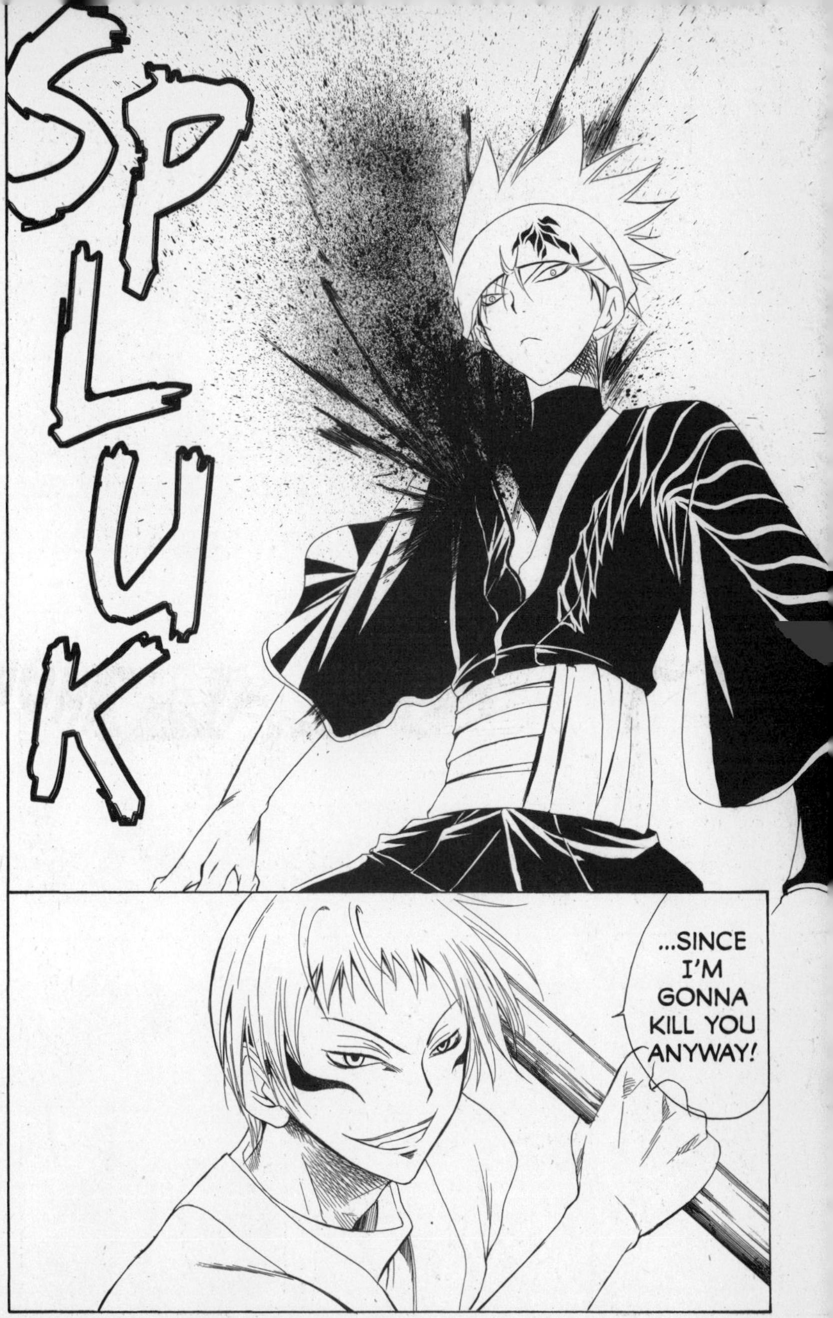
SPLUK
...SINCE I'M GONNA KILL YOU ANYWAY!

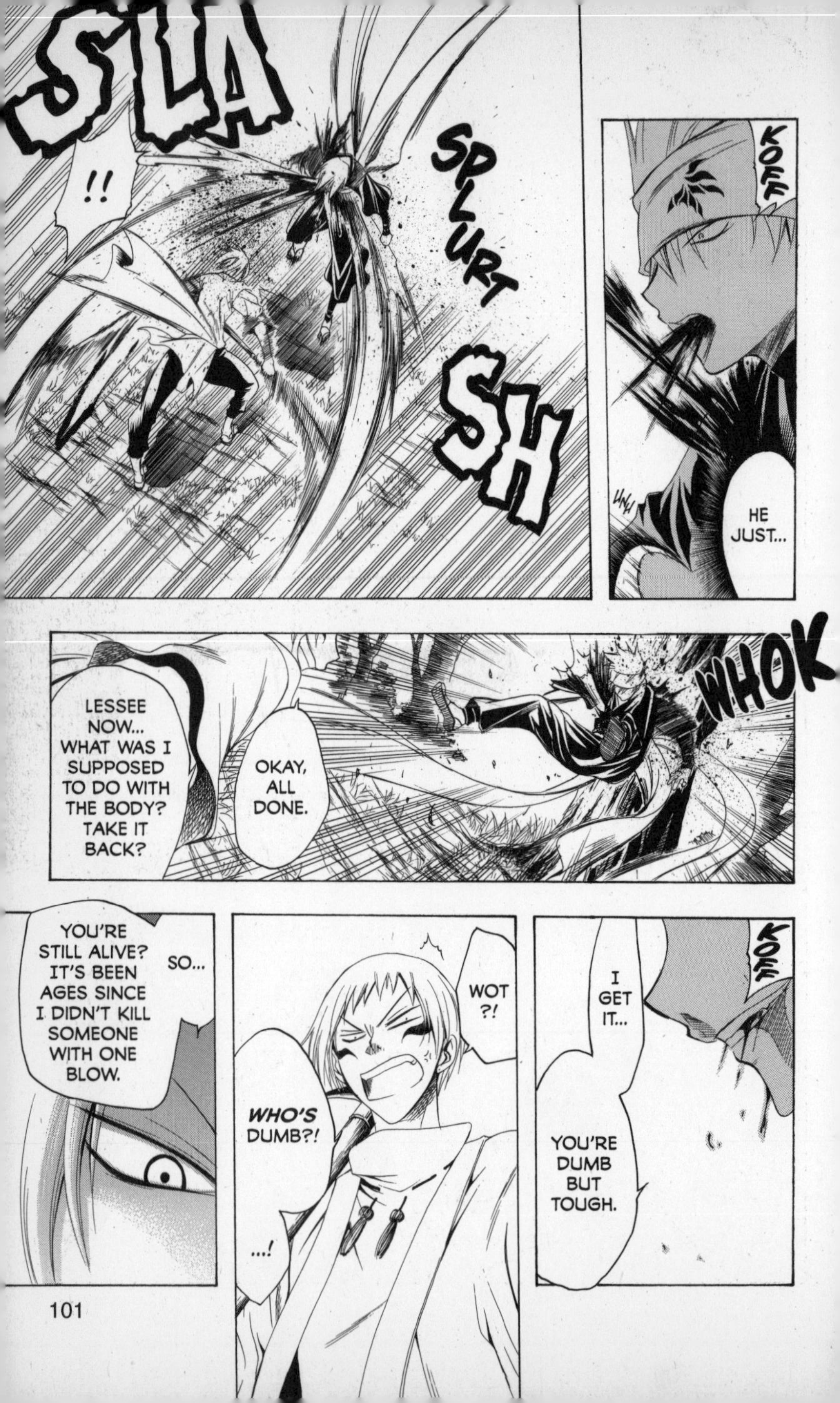
KOFF
UNH
HE JUST...
SLA
!!
SPLURT
SH
WHOK
OKAY, ALL DONE.
LESSEE NOW... WHAT WAS I SUPPOSED TO DO WITH THE BODY? TAKE IT BACK?
KOFF
I GET IT...
YOU'RE DUMB BUT TOUGH.
WOT?!
WHO'S DUMB?!
...!
SO...
YOU'RE STILL ALIVE? IT'S BEEN AGES SINCE I DIDN'T KILL SOMEONE WITH ONE BLOW.

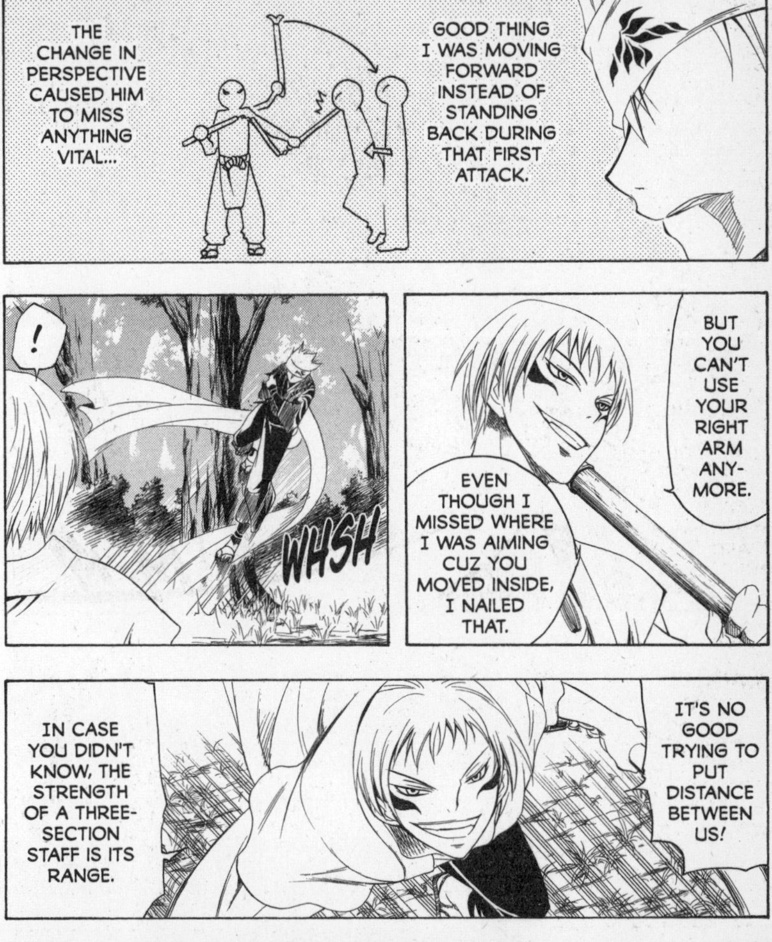
GOOD THING I WAS MOVING FORWARD INSTEAD OF STANDING BACK DURING THAT FIRST ATTACK.
THE CHANGE IN PERSPECTIVE CAUSED HIM TO MISS ANYTHING VITAL...
BUT YOU CAN'T USE YOUR RIGHT ARM ANY-MORE.
EVEN THOUGH I MISSED WHERE I WAS AIMING CUZ YOU MOVED INSIDE, I NAILED THAT.
!
WHSH
IT'S NO GOOD TRYING TO PUT DISTANCE BETWEEN US!
IN CASE YOU DIDN'T KNOW, THE STRENGTH OF A THREE-SECTION STAFF IS ITS RANGE.
YOU CAN FOLD IT DOWN FOR CLOSE FIGHTING...
SWOOSH
...OR EXTEND IT FOR A MAXIMUM RANGE OF ABOUT...

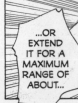

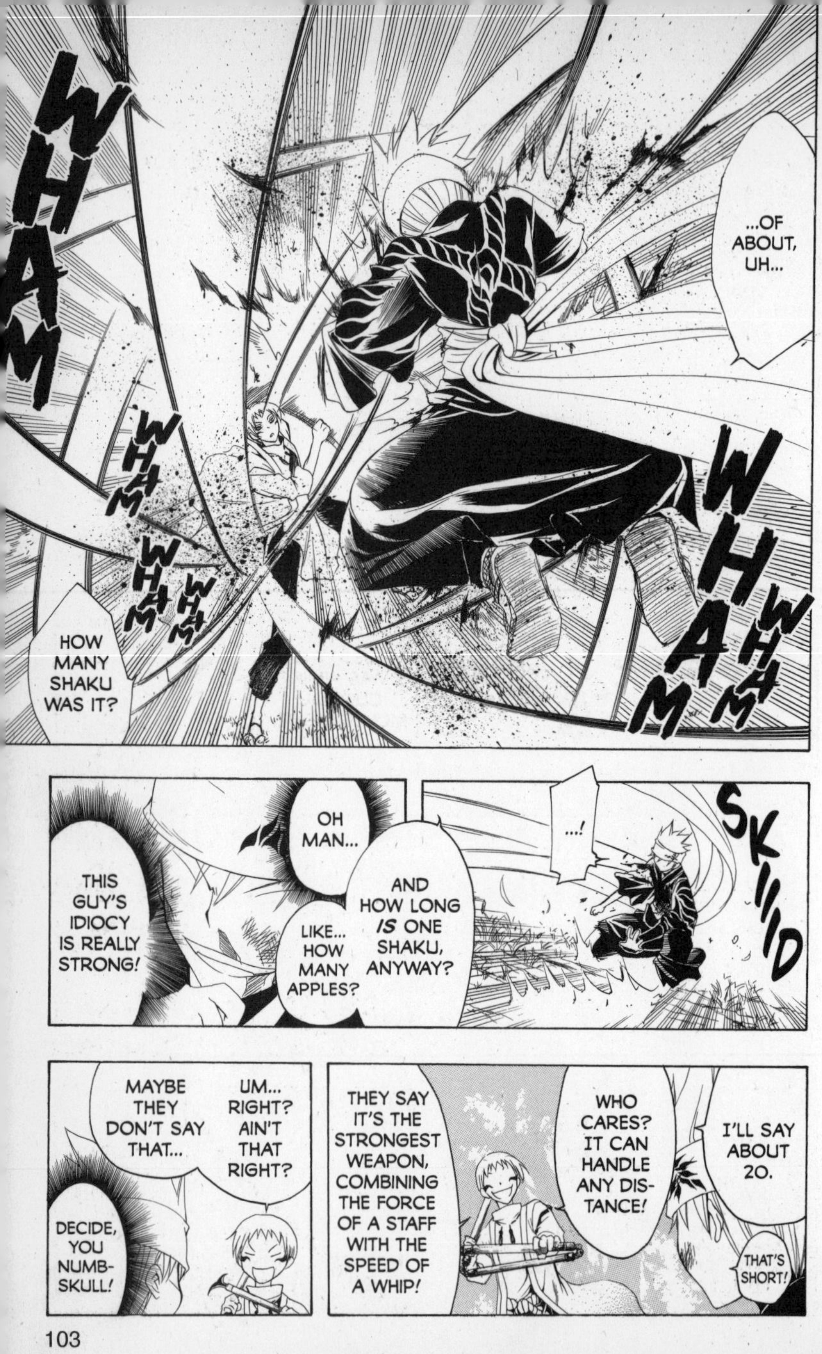

...OF ABOUT, UH...
WHAM
WHAM
WHAM
WHAM
WHAM
WHAM
HOW MANY SHAKU WAS IT?
...!
SKIIIID
OH MAN...
AND HOW LONG *IS* ONE SHAKU, ANYWAY?
LIKE... HOW MANY APPLES?
THIS GUY'S IDIOCY IS REALLY STRONG!
I'LL SAY ABOUT 20.
WHO CARES? IT CAN HANDLE ANY DISTANCE!
THAT'S SHORT!
THEY SAY IT'S THE STRONGEST WEAPON, COMBINING THE FORCE OF A STAFF WITH THE SPEED OF A WHIP!
UM... RIGHT? AIN'T THAT RIGHT?
MAYBE THEY DON'T SAY THAT...
DECIDE, YOU NUMBSKULL!

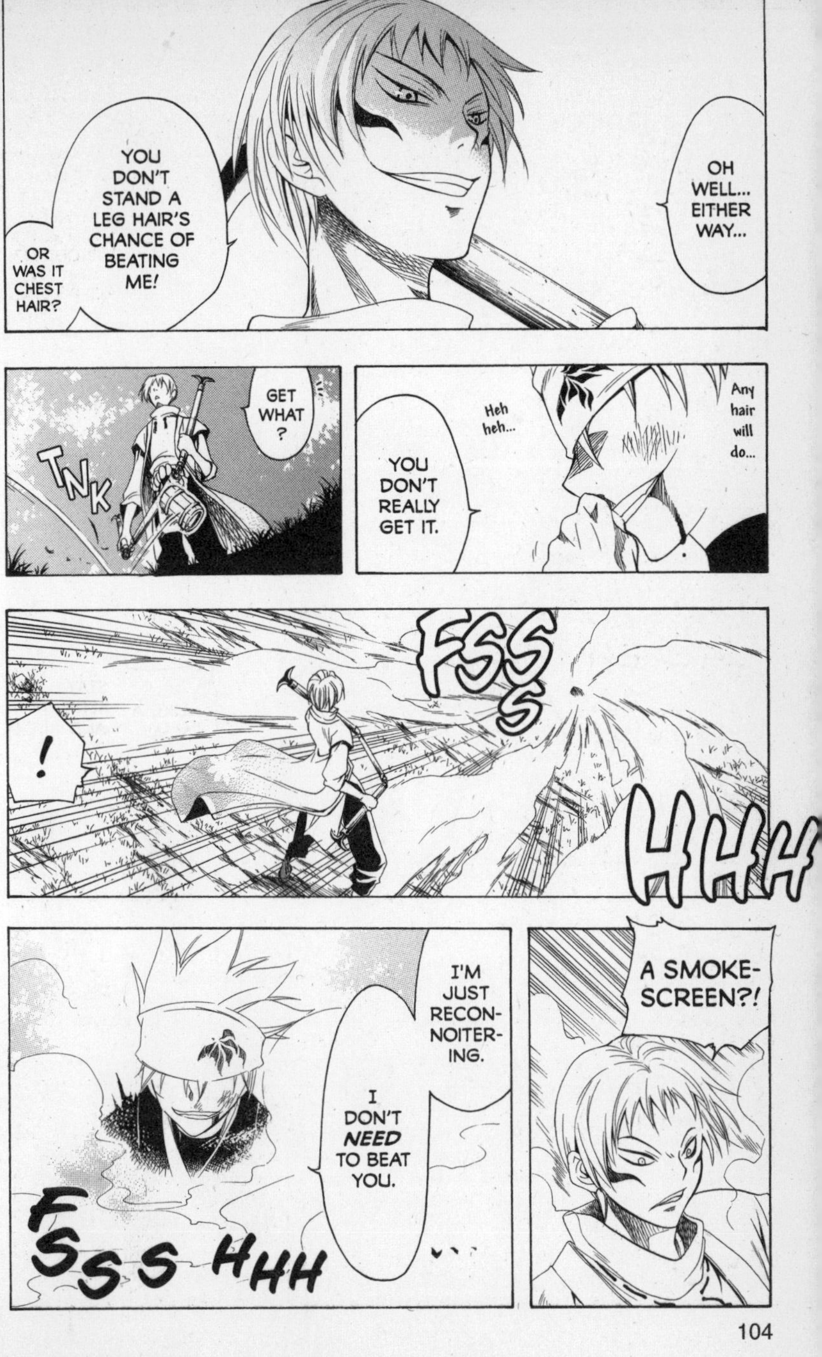
OH WELL... EITHER WAY...
YOU DON'T STAND A LEG HAIR'S CHANCE OF BEATING ME!
OR WAS IT CHEST HAIR?
Any hair will do...
Heh heh...
YOU DON'T REALLY GET IT.
GET WHAT?
TNK
FSSS
HHH
!
A SMOKE-SCREEN?!
I'M JUST RECONNOITERING.
I DON'T *NEED* TO BEAT YOU.
FSSS HHH

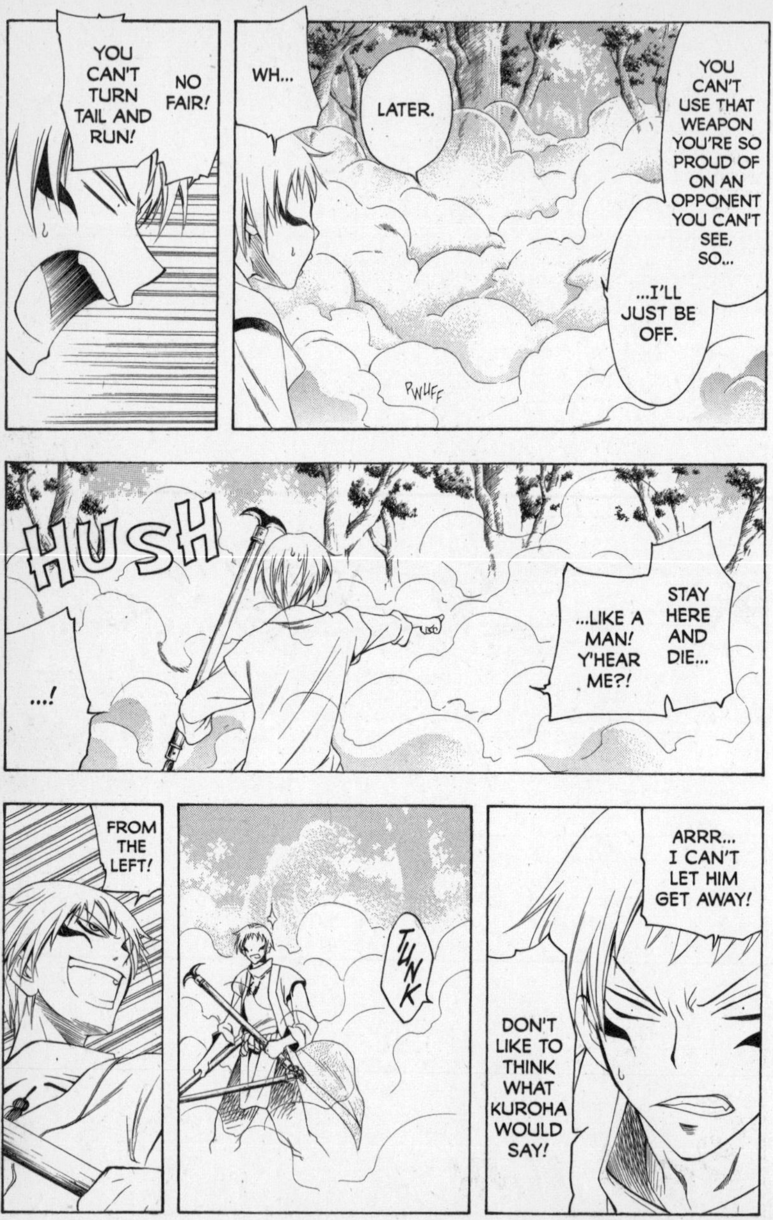

YOU CAN'T USE THAT WEAPON YOU'RE SO PROUD OF ON AN OPPONENT YOU CAN'T SEE, SO...
...I'LL JUST BE OFF.
LATER.
PWUFF
WH...
NO FAIR!
YOU CAN'T TURN TAIL AND RUN!
STAY HERE AND DIE...
...LIKE A MAN! Y'HEAR ME?!
HUSH
...!
ARRR... I CAN'T LET HIM GET AWAY!
DON'T LIKE TO THINK WHAT KUROHA WOULD SAY!
TUNK
FROM THE LEFT!

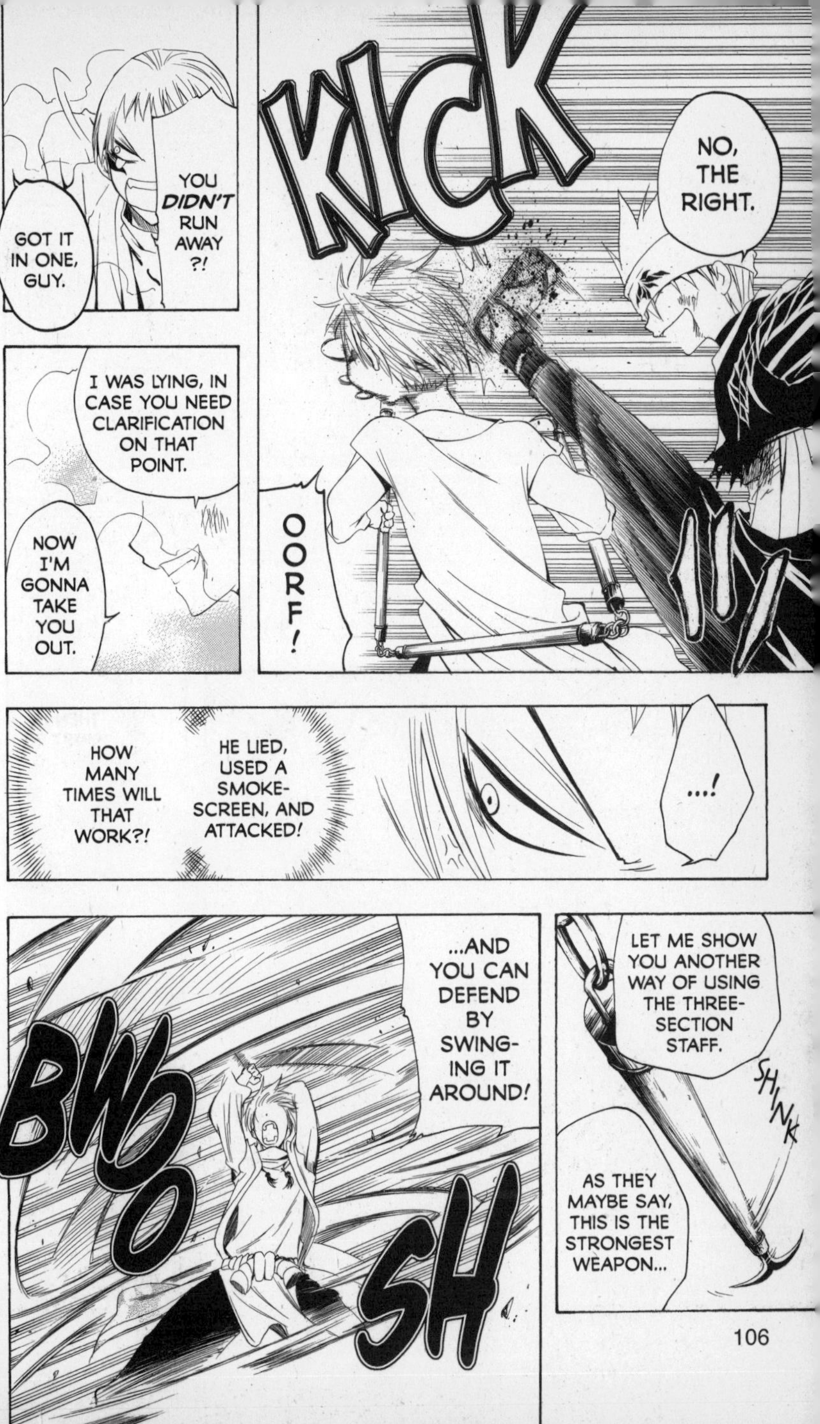
KICK
NO, THE RIGHT.
OORF!
YOU DIDN'T RUN AWAY?!
GOT IT IN ONE, GUY.
I WAS LYING, IN CASE YOU NEED CLARIFICATION ON THAT POINT.
NOW I'M GONNA TAKE YOU OUT.
...!
HE LIED, USED A SMOKE-SCREEN, AND ATTACKED!
HOW MANY TIMES WILL THAT WORK?!
LET ME SHOW YOU ANOTHER WAY OF USING THE THREE-SECTION STAFF.
SHINK
AS THEY MAYBE SAY, THIS IS THE STRONGEST WEAPON...
...AND YOU CAN DEFEND BY SWING-ING IT AROUND!
BWOOSH

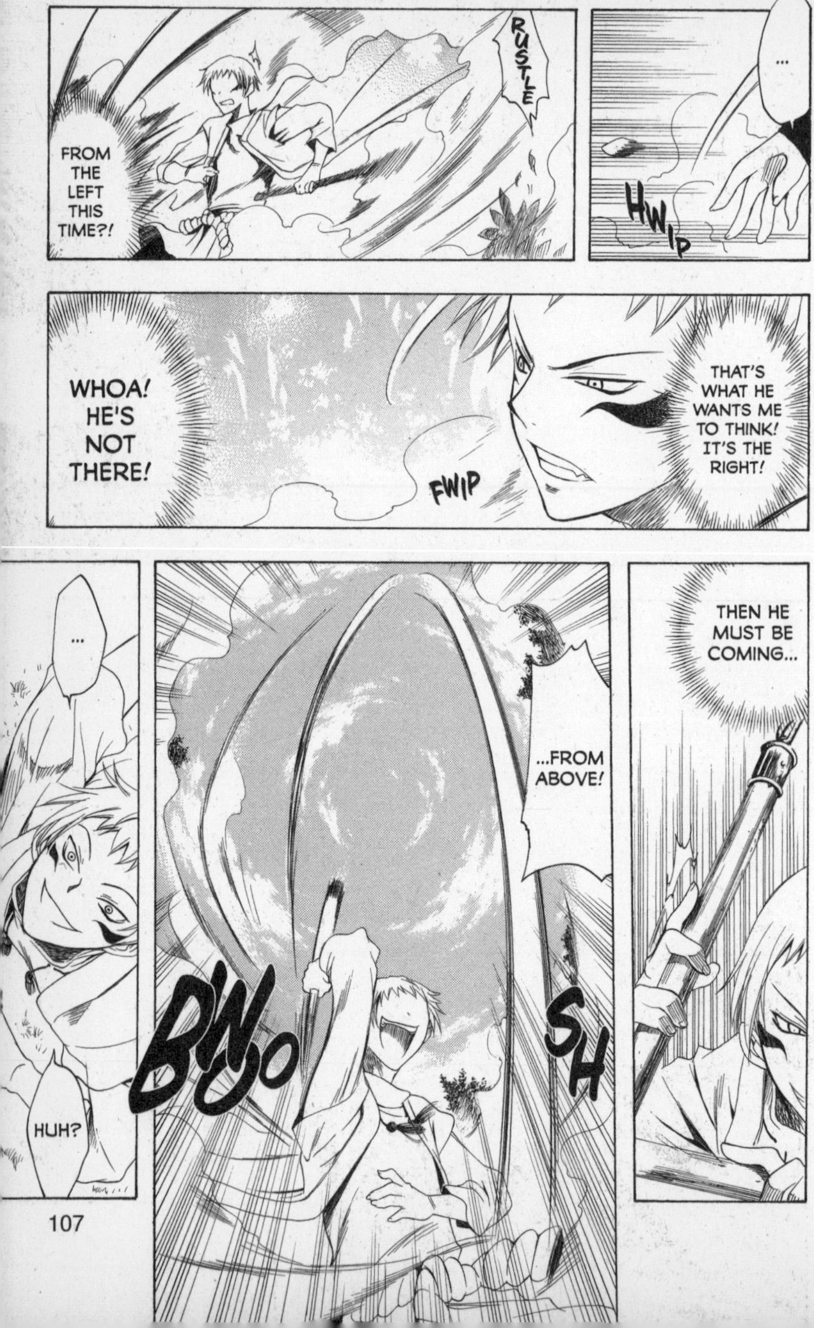
...
HWIP
RUSTLE
FROM THE LEFT THIS TIME?!
THAT'S WHAT HE WANTS ME TO THINK! IT'S THE RIGHT!
FWIP
WHOA! HE'S NOT THERE!
THEN HE MUST BE COMING...
...FROM ABOVE!
SH
BWOO
...
HUH?

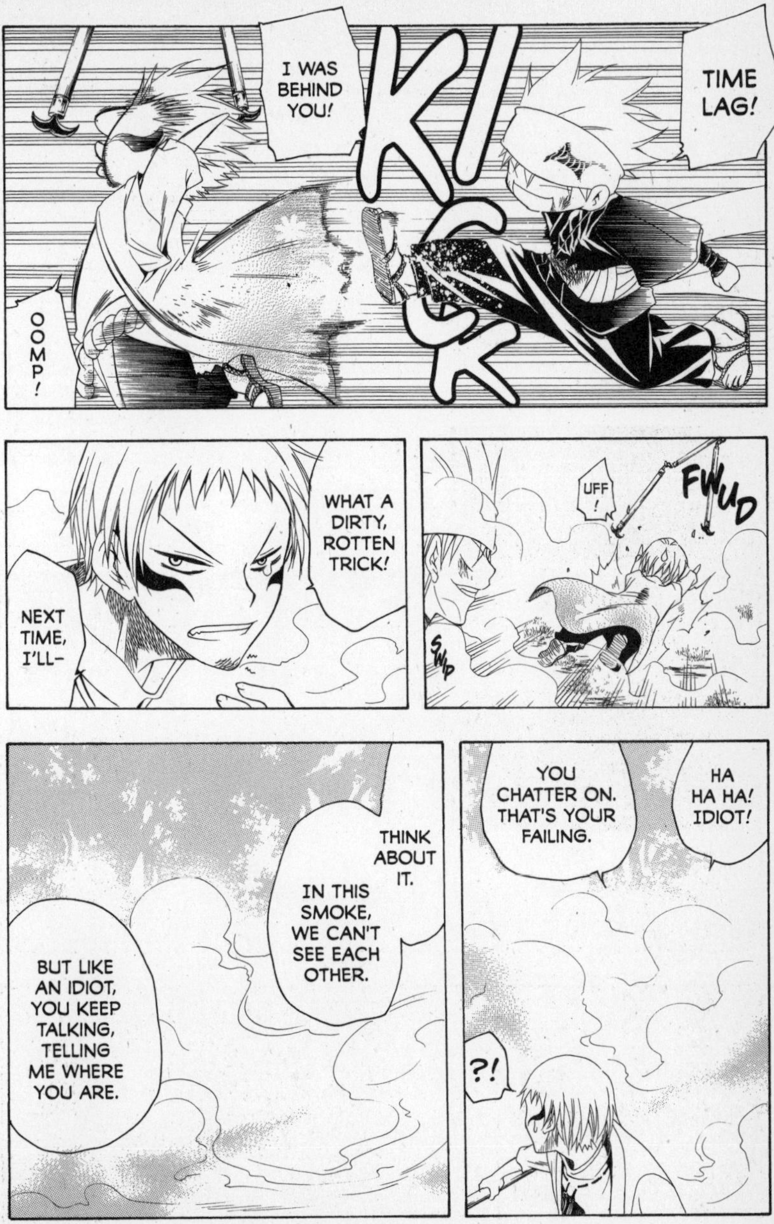
TIME LAG!
KICK
I WAS BEHIND YOU!
OOMP!
FWUD
UFF!
SWIP
WHAT A DIRTY, ROTTEN TRICK!
NEXT TIME, I'LL–
HA HA HA! IDIOT!
YOU CHATTER ON. THAT'S YOUR FAILING.
?!
THINK ABOUT IT.
IN THIS SMOKE, WE CAN'T SEE EACH OTHER.
BUT LIKE AN IDIOT, YOU KEEP TALKING, TELLING ME WHERE YOU ARE.

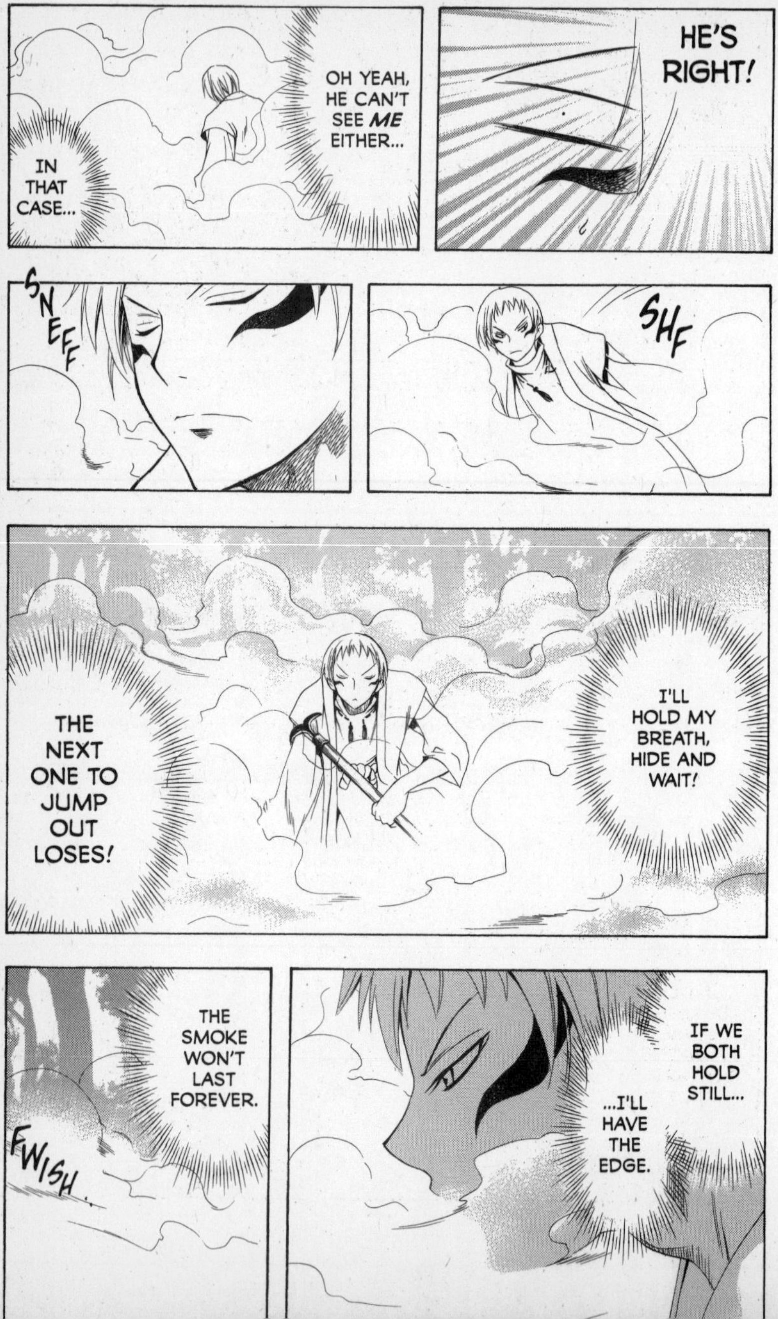
HE'S RIGHT!
OH YEAH, HE CAN'T SEE *ME* EITHER...
IN THAT CASE...
SHF
SNEFF
I'LL HOLD MY BREATH, HIDE AND WAIT!
THE NEXT ONE TO JUMP OUT LOSES!
IF WE BOTH HOLD STILL...
...I'LL HAVE THE EDGE.
THE SMOKE WON'T LAST FOREVER.
FWISH

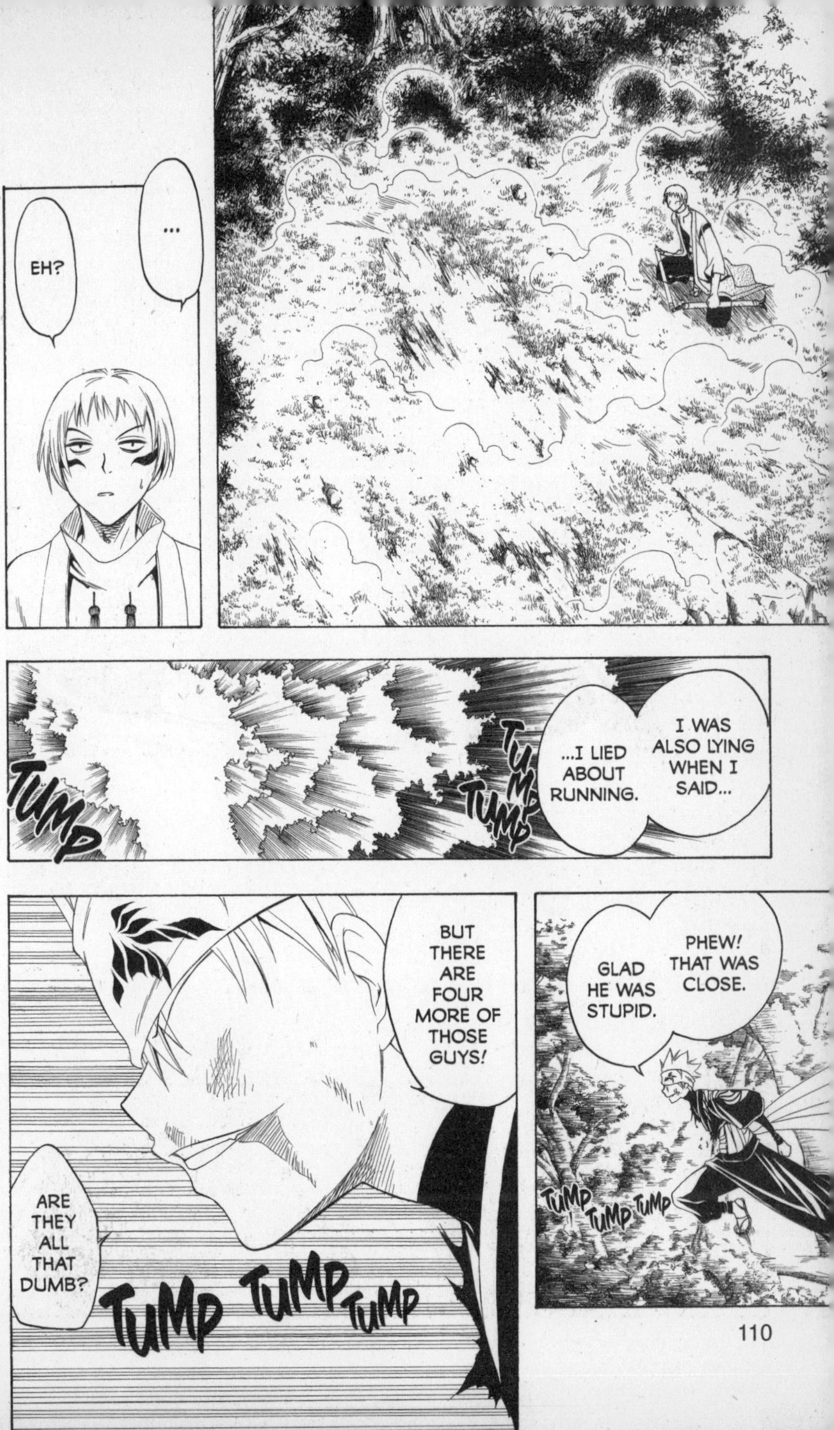
...
EH?
I WAS ALSO LYING WHEN I SAID...
...I LIED ABOUT RUNNING.
TUMP TUMP
TUMP
PHEW! THAT WAS CLOSE.
GLAD HE WAS STUPID.
TUMP TUMP TUMP
BUT THERE ARE FOUR MORE OF THOSE GUYS!
ARE THEY ALL THAT DUMB?
TUMP TUMP TUMP

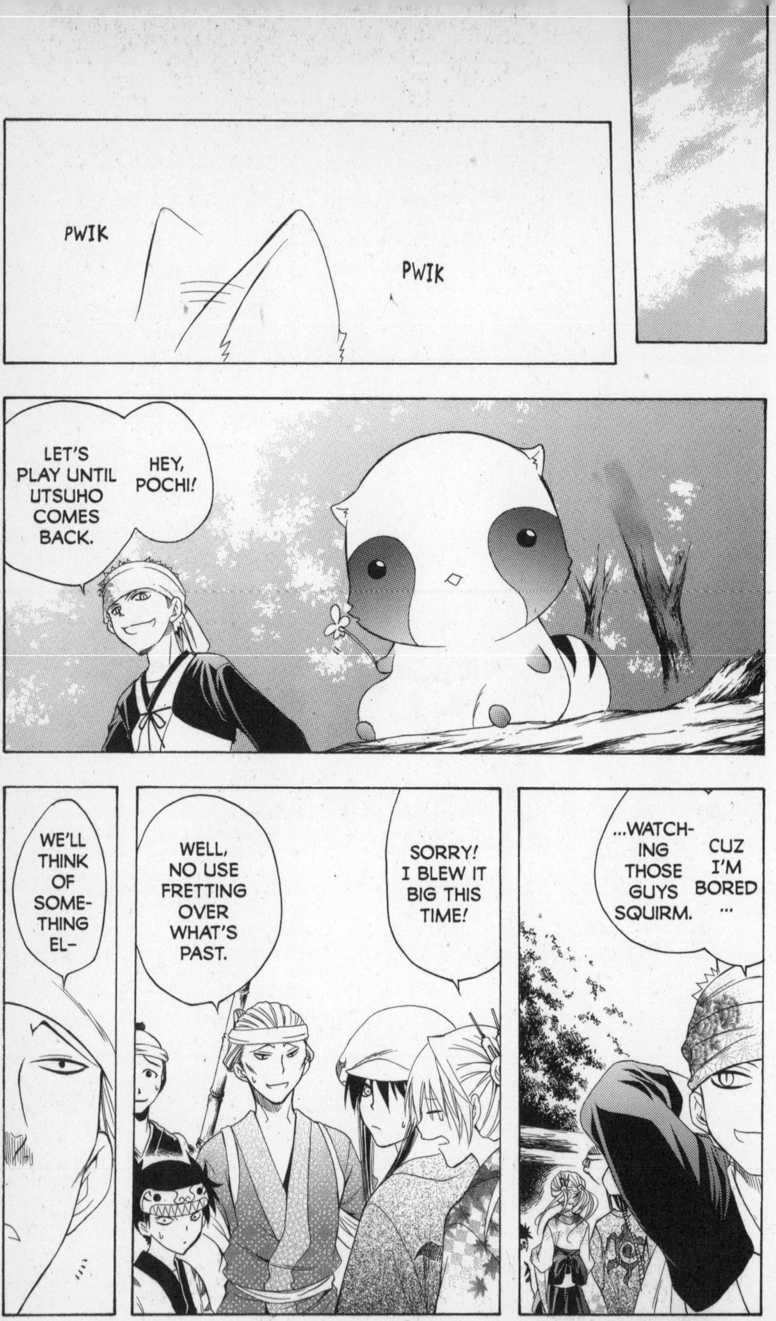
PWIK
PWIK
HEY, POCHI!
LET'S PLAY UNTIL UTSUHO COMES BACK.
CUZ I'M BORED ...
...WATCHING THOSE GUYS SQUIRM.
SORRY! I BLEW IT BIG THIS TIME!
WELL, NO USE FRETTING OVER WHAT'S PAST.
WE'LL THINK OF SOMETHING EL-

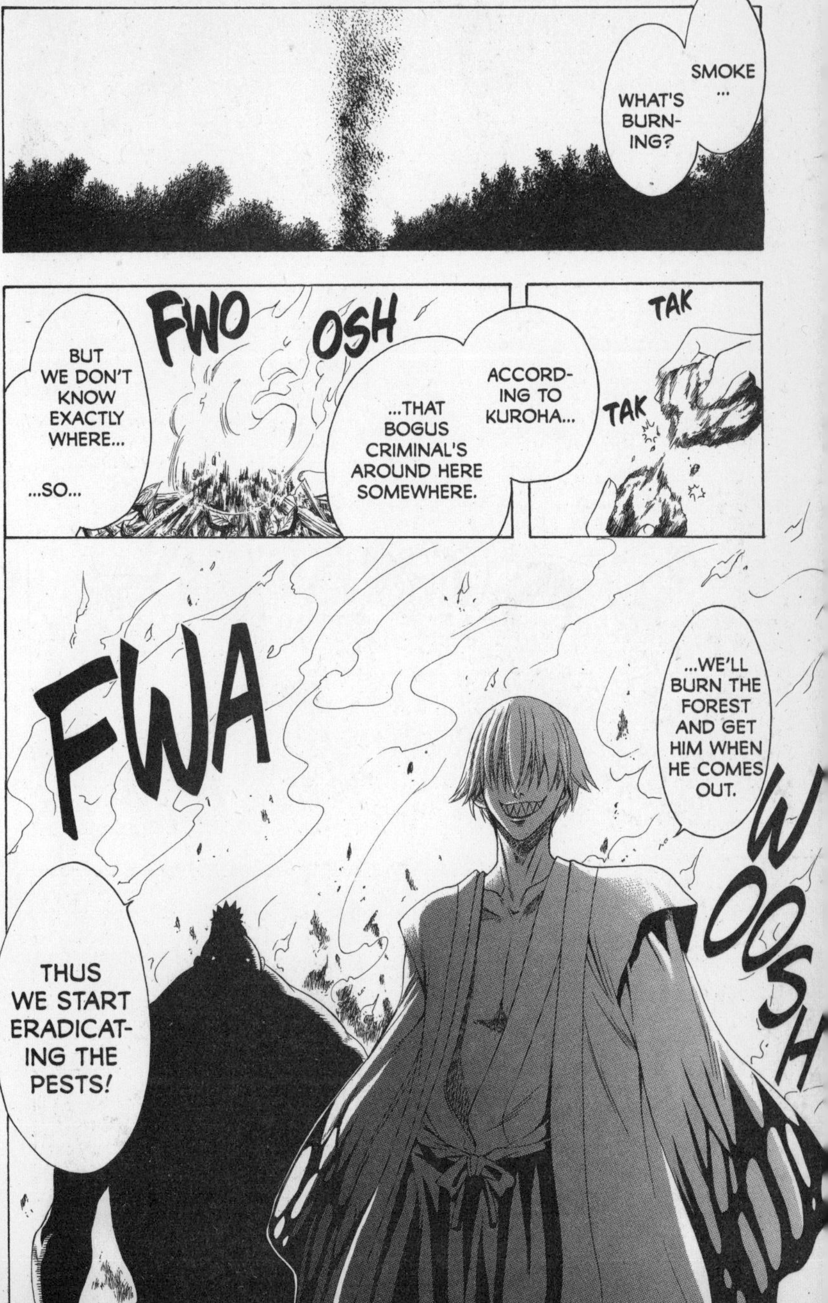
SMOKE ...
WHAT'S BURNING?
TAK
TAK
ACCORDING TO KUROHA...
...THAT BOGUS CRIMINAL'S AROUND HERE SOMEWHERE.
FWOOSH
BUT WE DON'T KNOW EXACTLY WHERE...
...SO...
...WE'LL BURN THE FOREST AND GET HIM WHEN HE COMES OUT.
WOOSH
FWA
THUS WE START ERADICATING THE PESTS!

Chapter 64 Hikae Dies?!

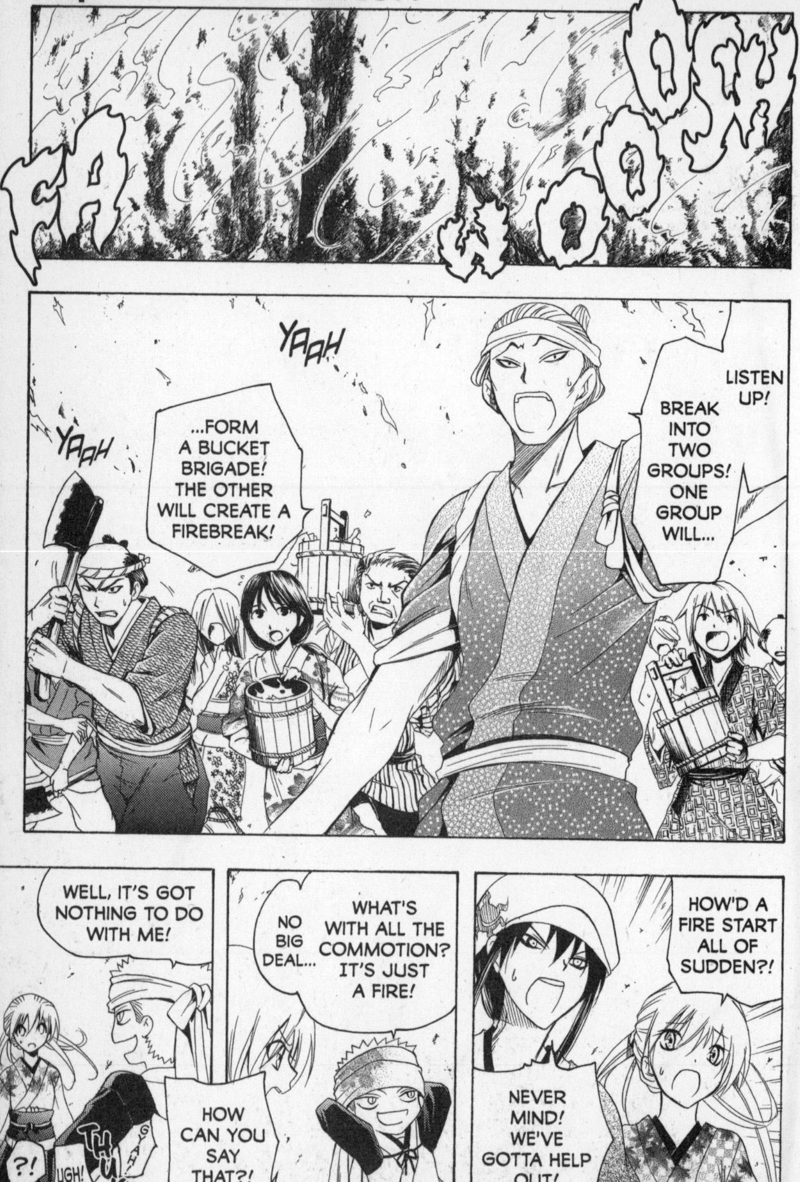

LISTEN UP!
BREAK INTO TWO GROUPS! ONE GROUP WILL...
...FORM A BUCKET BRIGADE! THE OTHER WILL CREATE A FIREBREAK!
YAAH
YAAH
HOW'D A FIRE START ALL OF SUDDEN?!
NEVER MIND! WE'VE GOTTA HELP OUT!
WHAT'S WITH ALL THE COMMOTION? IT'S JUST A FIRE!
NO BIG DEAL...
HOW CAN YOU SAY THAT?!
WELL, IT'S GOT NOTHING TO DO WITH ME!
THUK
GYAH!
UGH!
?!

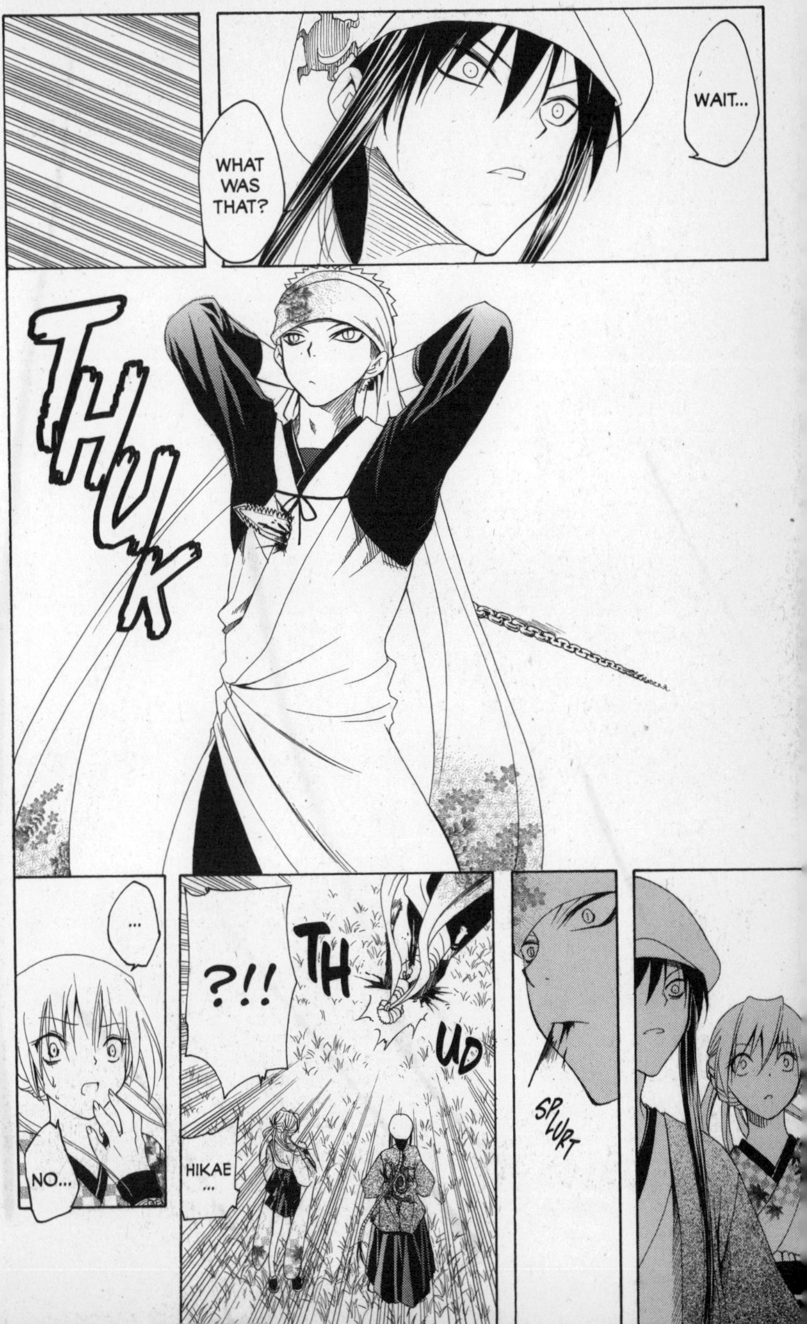
WAIT...
WHAT WAS THAT?
THUK
SPLURT
TH
?!!
UD
HIKAE ...
...
NO...

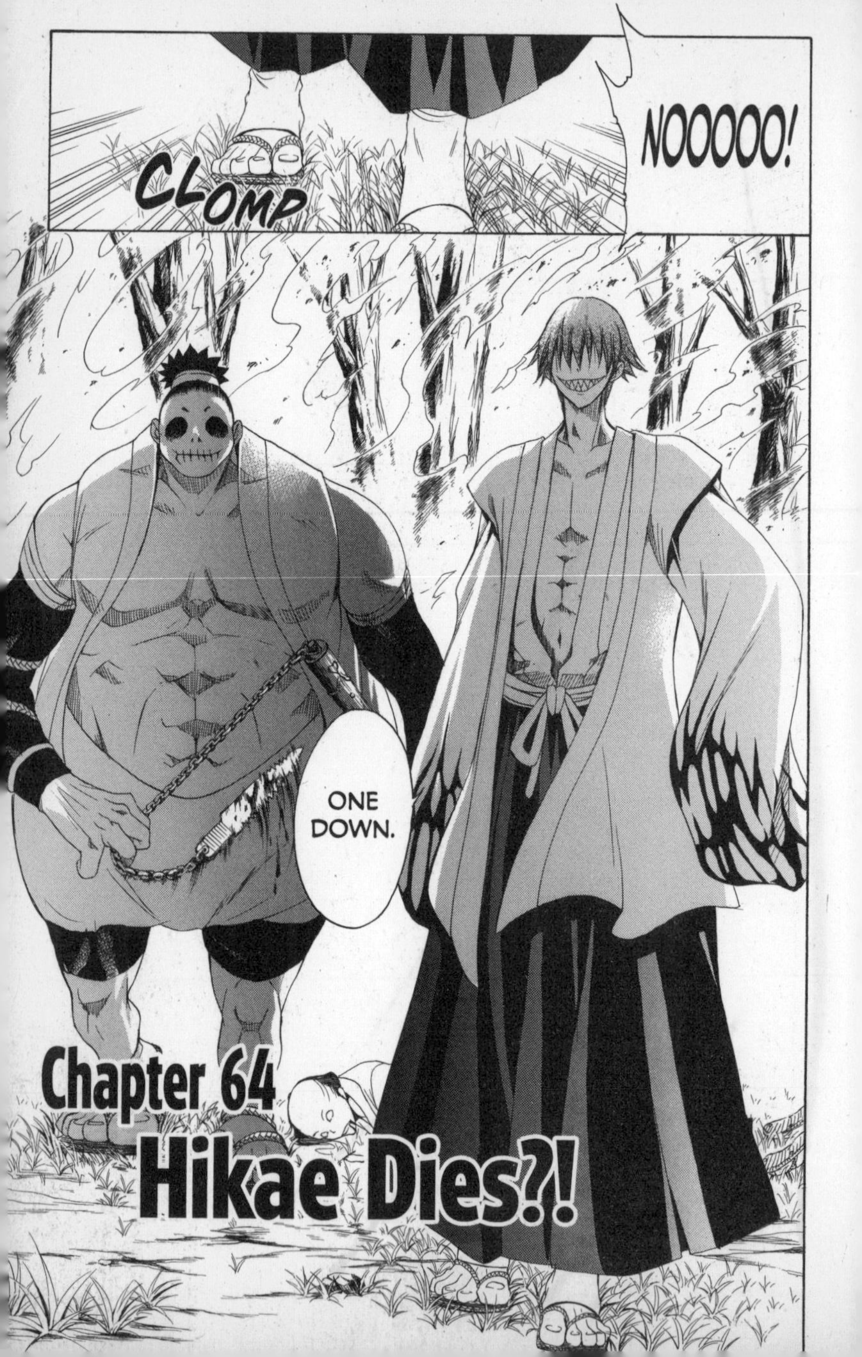
NOOOOO!
CLOMP
ONE DOWN.
Chapter 64
Hikae Dies?!

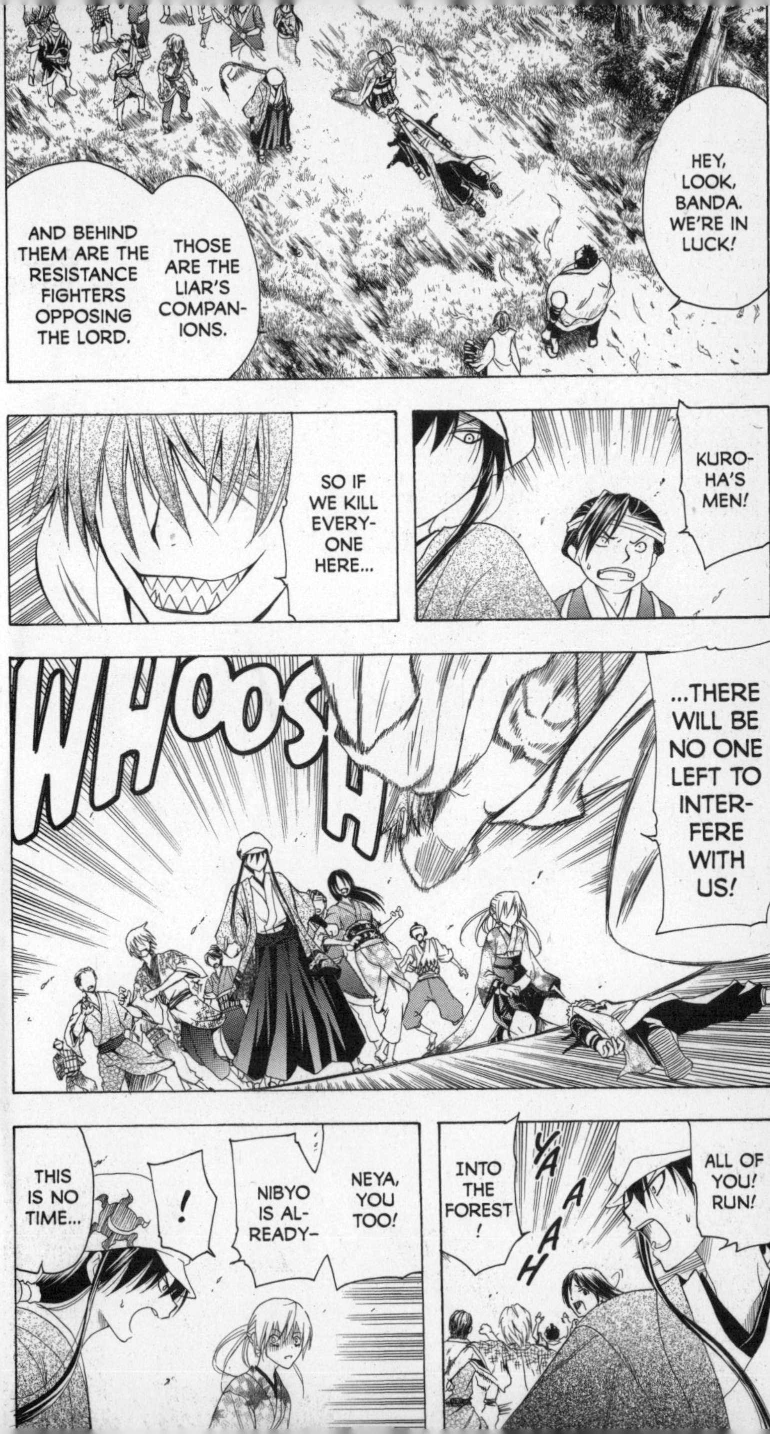

HEY, LOOK, BANDA. WE'RE IN LUCK!
THOSE ARE THE LIAR'S COMPANIONS.
AND BEHIND THEM ARE THE RESISTANCE FIGHTERS OPPOSING THE LORD.
KUROHA'S MEN!
SO IF WE KILL EVERYONE HERE...
...THERE WILL BE NO ONE LEFT TO INTERFERE WITH US!
WHOOSH
ALL OF YOU! RUN!
YAAAAH
INTO THE FOREST!
NEYA, YOU TOO!
NIBYO IS ALREADY-
!
THIS IS NO TIME...

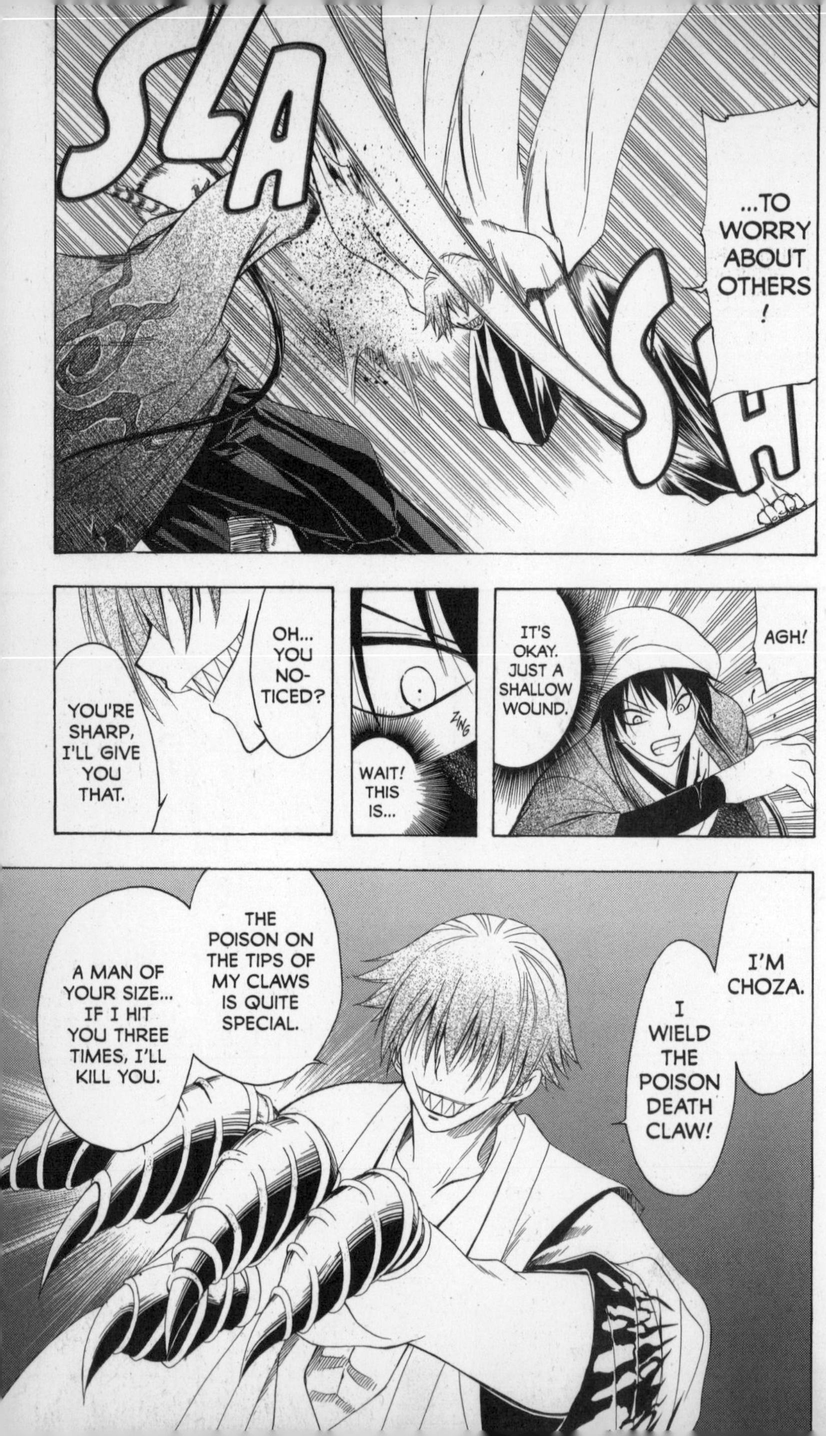
...TO WORRY ABOUT OTHERS!
SLA
SH
AGH!
IT'S OKAY. JUST A SHALLOW WOUND.
ZING
WAIT! THIS IS...
OH... YOU NO-TICED?
YOU'RE SHARP, I'LL GIVE YOU THAT.
I'M CHOZA.
I WIELD THE POISON DEATH CLAW!
THE POISON ON THE TIPS OF MY CLAWS IS QUITE SPECIAL.
A MAN OF YOUR SIZE... IF I HIT YOU THREE TIMES, I'LL KILL YOU.

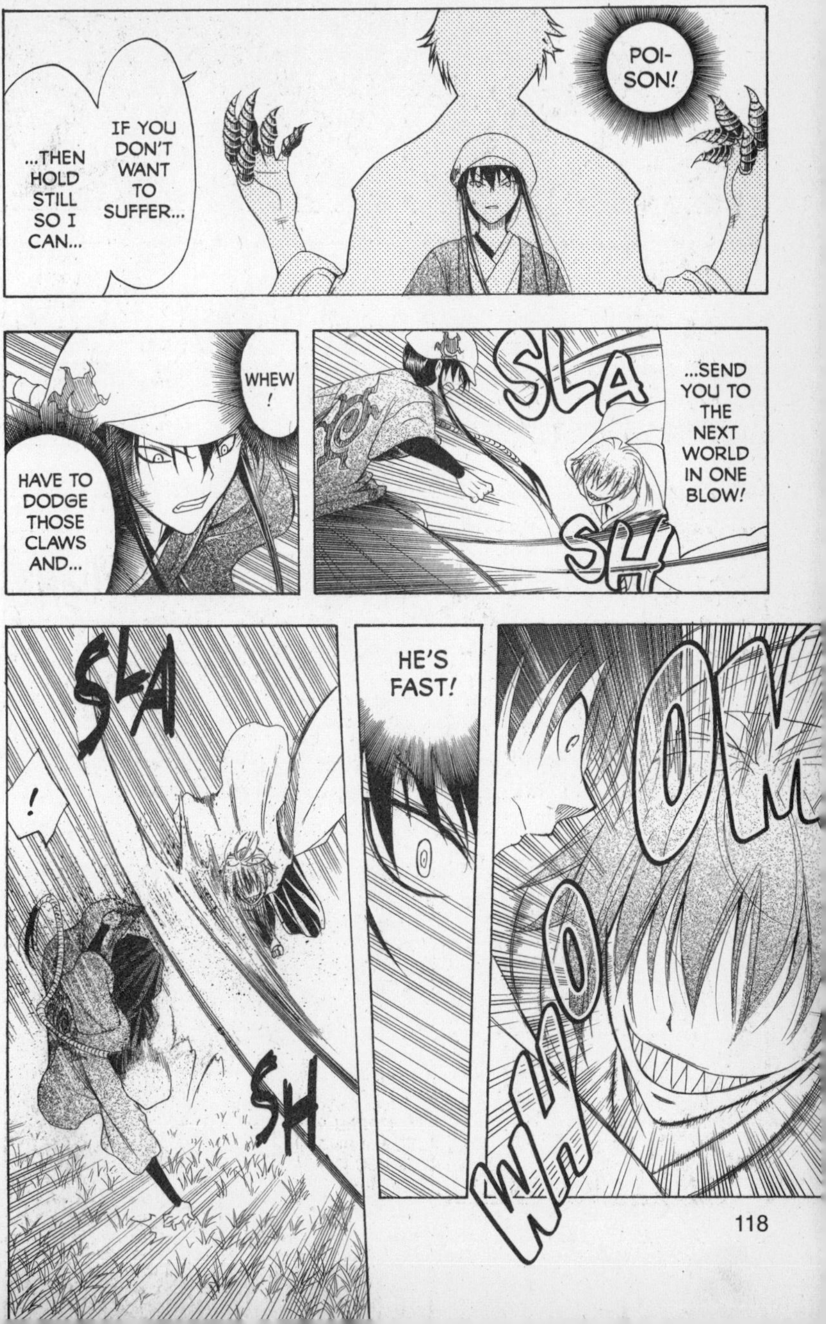

POI-SON!
IF YOU DON'T WANT TO SUFFER...
...THEN HOLD STILL SO I CAN...
SLA
...SEND YOU TO THE NEXT WORLD IN ONE BLOW!
SH
WHEW!
HAVE TO DODGE THOSE CLAWS AND...
WHOOOM
HE'S FAST!
SLA
!
SH

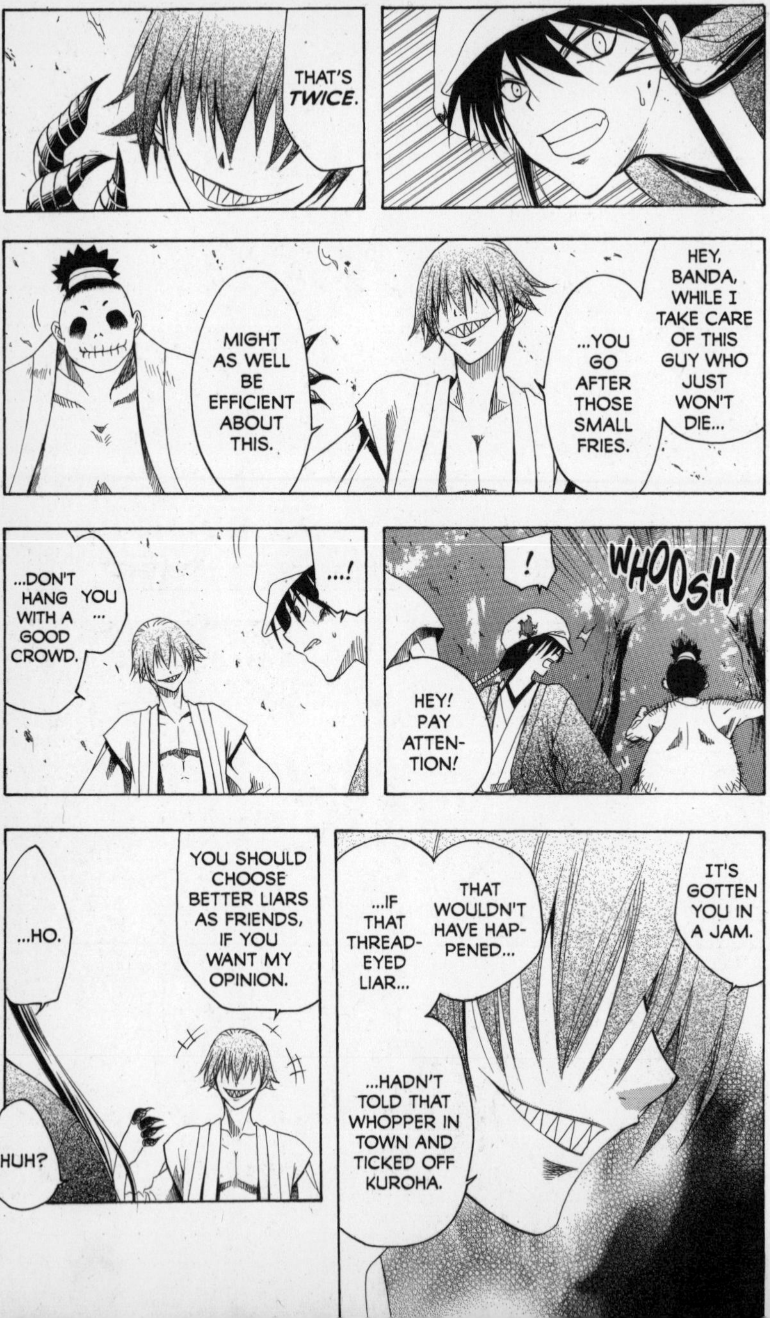
THAT'S *TWICE*.
HEY, BANDA, WHILE I TAKE CARE OF THIS GUY WHO JUST WON'T DIE...
...YOU GO AFTER THOSE SMALL FRIES.
MIGHT AS WELL BE EFFICIENT ABOUT THIS.
WHOOSH
!
HEY! PAY ATTENTION!
...!
YOU ...
...DON'T HANG WITH A GOOD CROWD.
IT'S GOTTEN YOU IN A JAM.
THAT WOULDN'T HAVE HAPPENED...
...IF THAT THREAD-EYED LIAR...
...HADN'T TOLD THAT WHOPPER IN TOWN AND TICKED OFF KUROHA.
YOU SHOULD CHOOSE BETTER LIARS AS FRIENDS, IF YOU WANT MY OPINION.
...HO.
HUH?

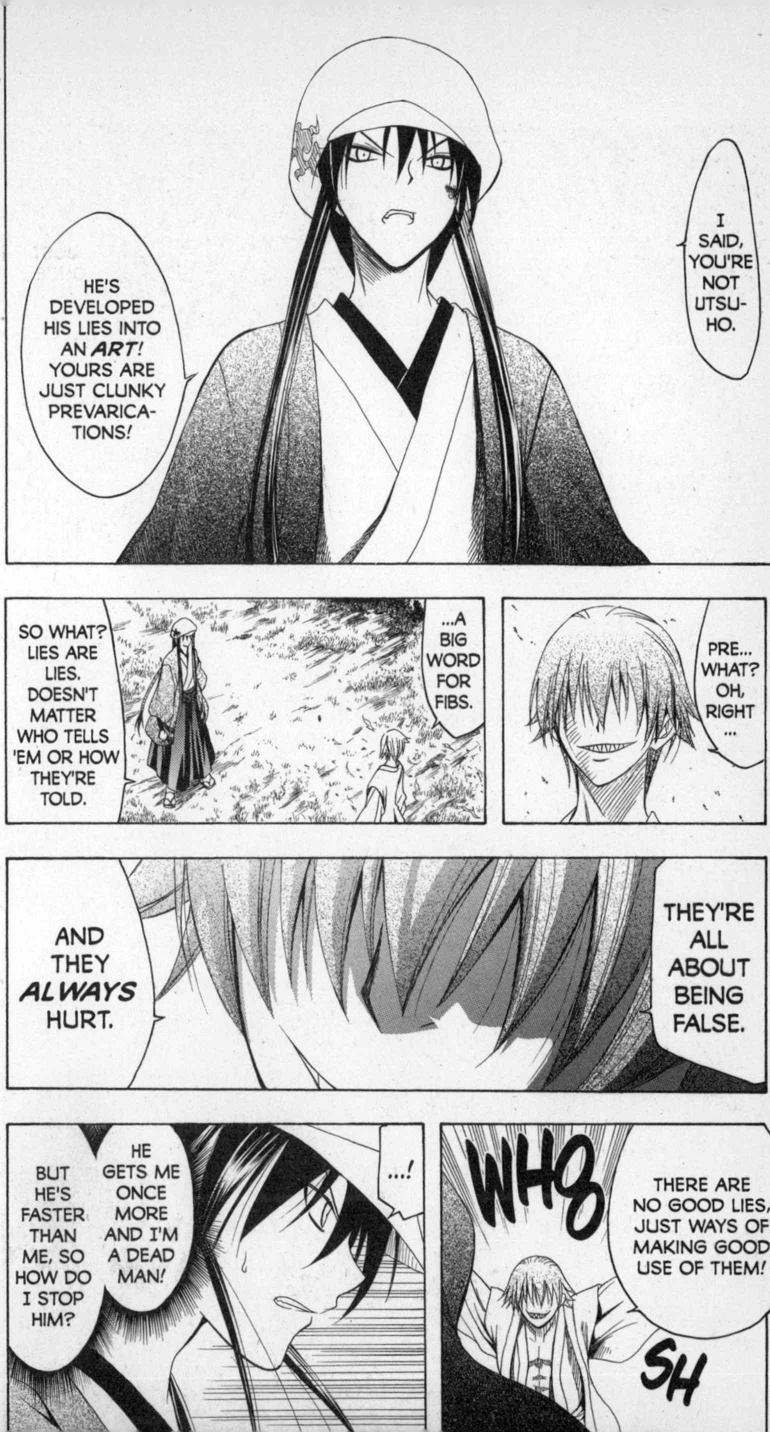
I SAID, YOU'RE NOT UTSU-HO.
HE'S DEVELOPED HIS LIES INTO AN *ART*! YOURS ARE JUST CLUNKY PREVARICATIONS!
PRE... WHAT? OH, RIGHT ...
...A BIG WORD FOR FIBS.
SO WHAT? LIES ARE LIES. DOESN'T MATTER WHO TELLS 'EM OR HOW THEY'RE TOLD.
THEY'RE ALL ABOUT BEING FALSE.
AND THEY *ALWAYS* HURT.
WHO
THERE ARE NO GOOD LIES, JUST WAYS OF MAKING GOOD USE OF THEM!
SH
...!
HE GETS ME ONCE MORE AND I'M A DEAD MAN!
BUT HE'S FASTER THAN ME, SO HOW DO I STOP HIM?

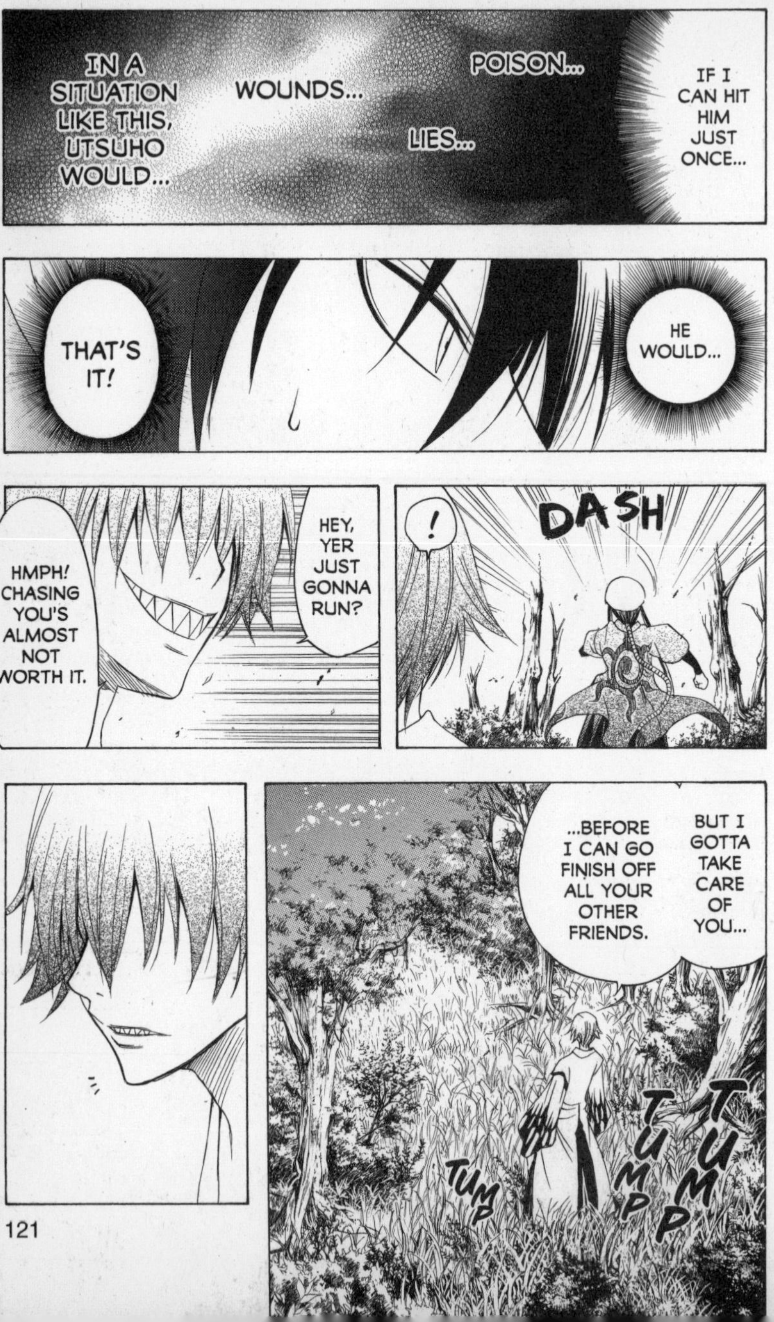
IF I CAN HIT HIM JUST ONCE...
POISON...
WOUNDS...
LIES...
IN A SITUATION LIKE THIS, UTSUHO WOULD...
HE WOULD...
THAT'S IT!
DASH
!
HEY, YER JUST GONNA RUN?
HMPH! CHASING YOU'S ALMOST NOT WORTH IT.
BUT I GOTTA TAKE CARE OF YOU...
...BEFORE I CAN GO FINISH OFF ALL YOUR OTHER FRIENDS.
TUMP
TUMP
TUMP

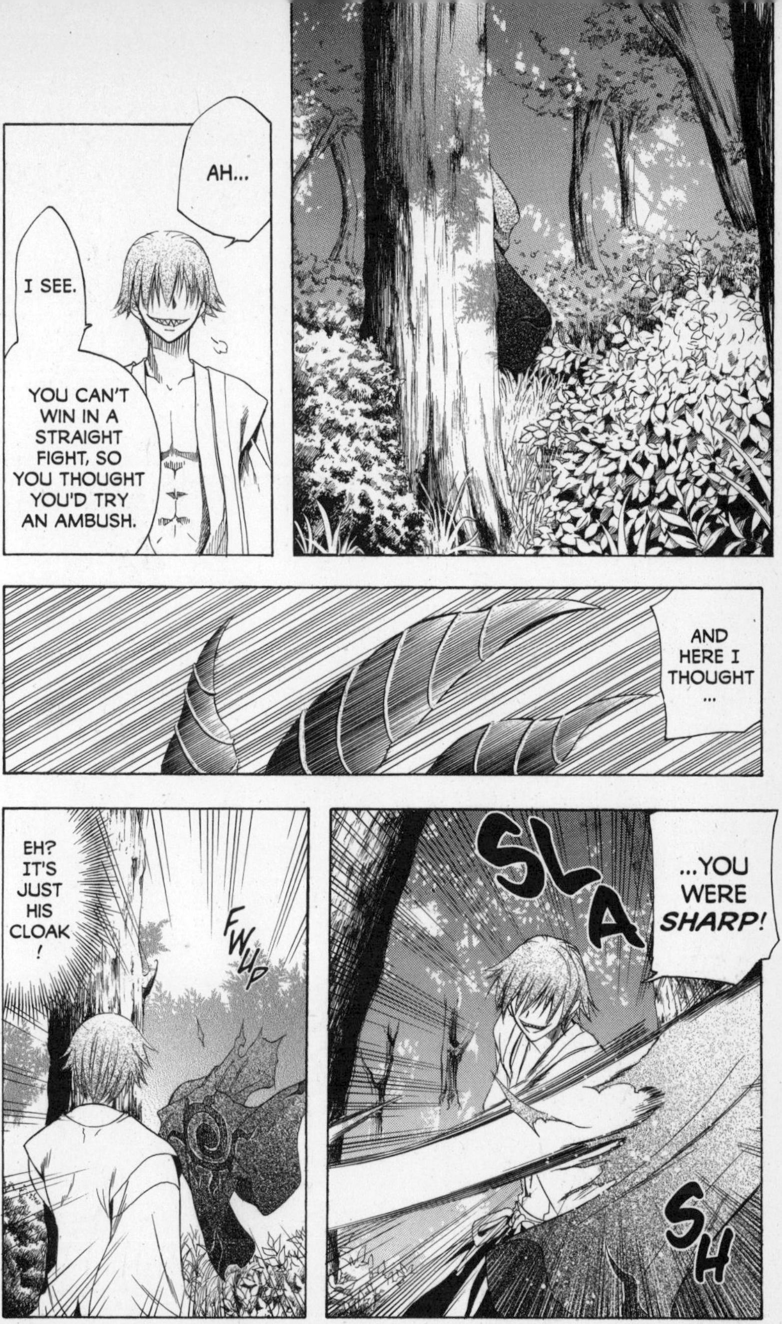
AH...
I SEE.
YOU CAN'T WIN IN A STRAIGHT FIGHT, SO YOU THOUGHT YOU'D TRY AN AMBUSH.
AND HERE I THOUGHT ...
SLA
...YOU WERE *SHARP!*
SH
EH? IT'S JUST HIS CLOAK!
FWUP

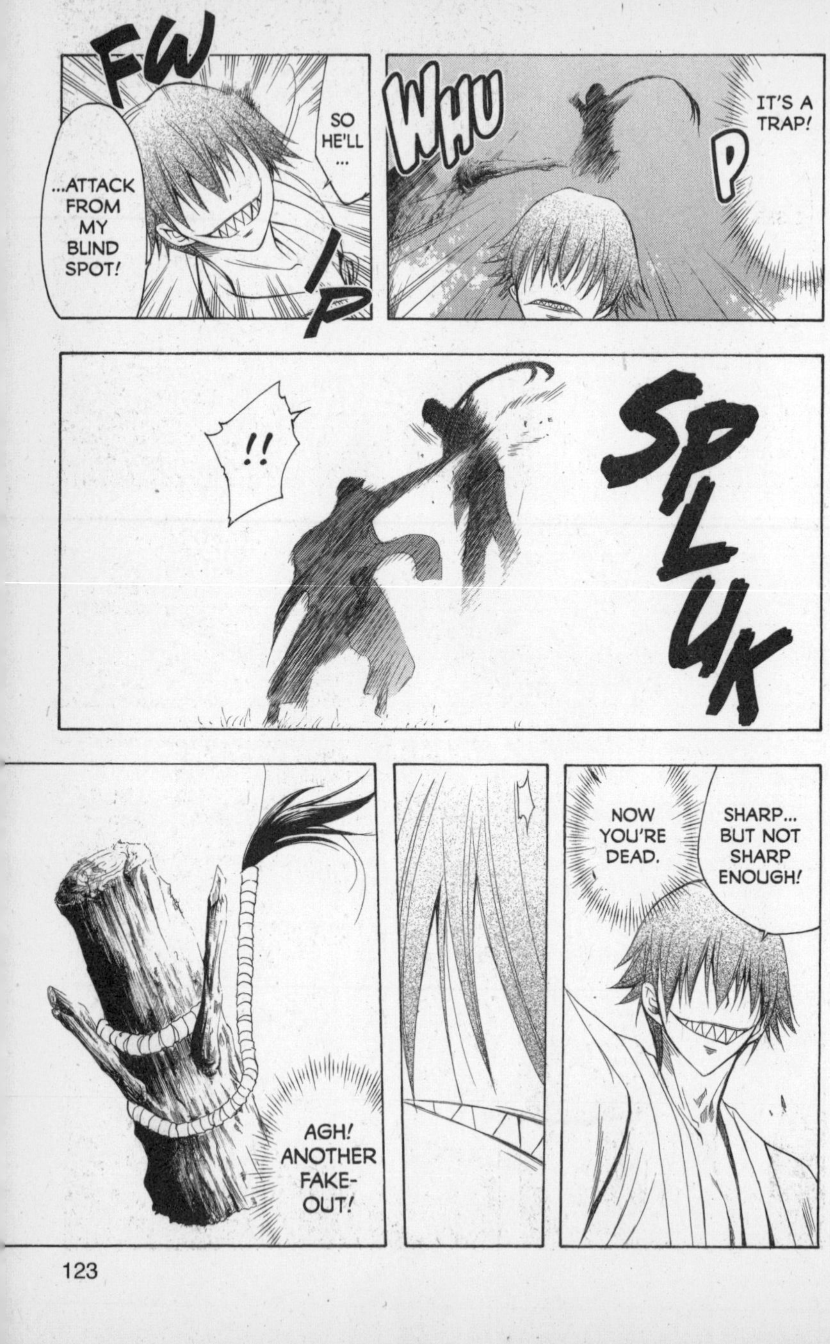
IT'S A TRAP!
WHUP
SO HE'LL...
...ATTACK FROM MY BLIND SPOT!
FWIP
SPLUK
!!
SHARP... BUT NOT SHARP ENOUGH!
NOW YOU'RE DEAD.
AGH! ANOTHER FAKE-OUT!

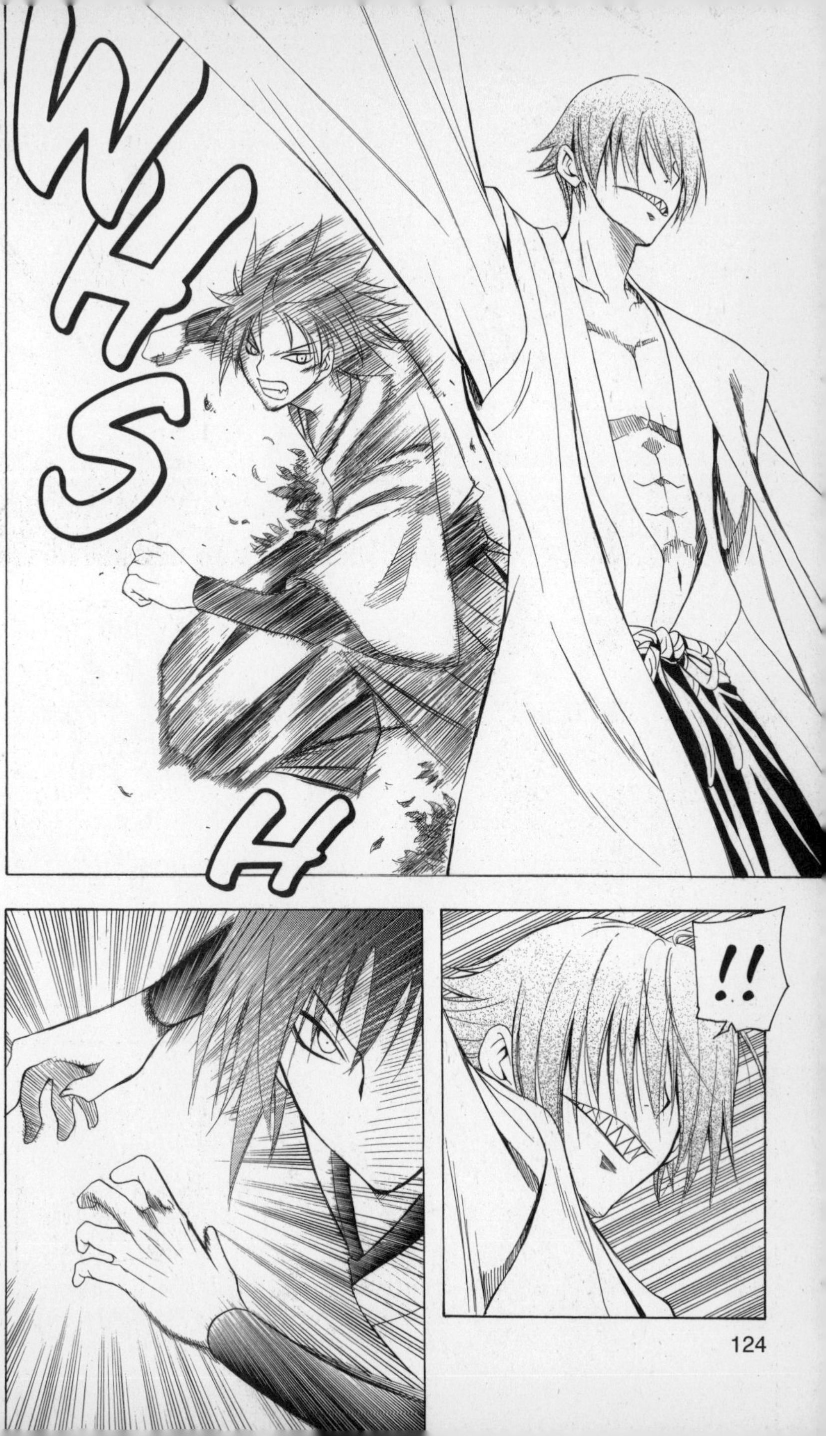
WHISH
!!

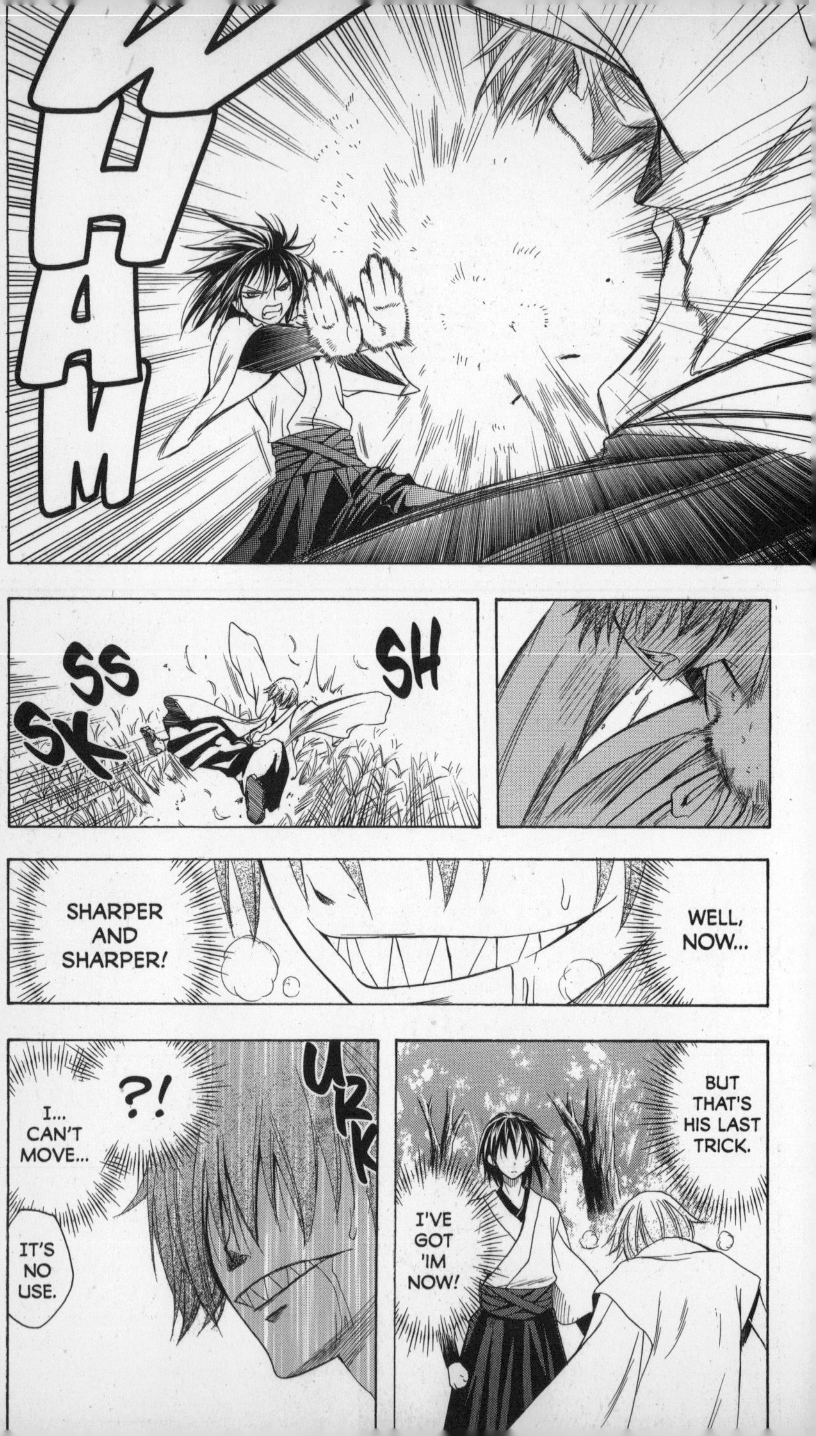
WHAM
SH
SSSK
WELL, NOW...
SHARPER AND SHARPER!
BUT THAT'S HIS LAST TRICK.
I'VE GOT 'IM NOW!
URK
?!
I... CAN'T MOVE...
IT'S NO USE.

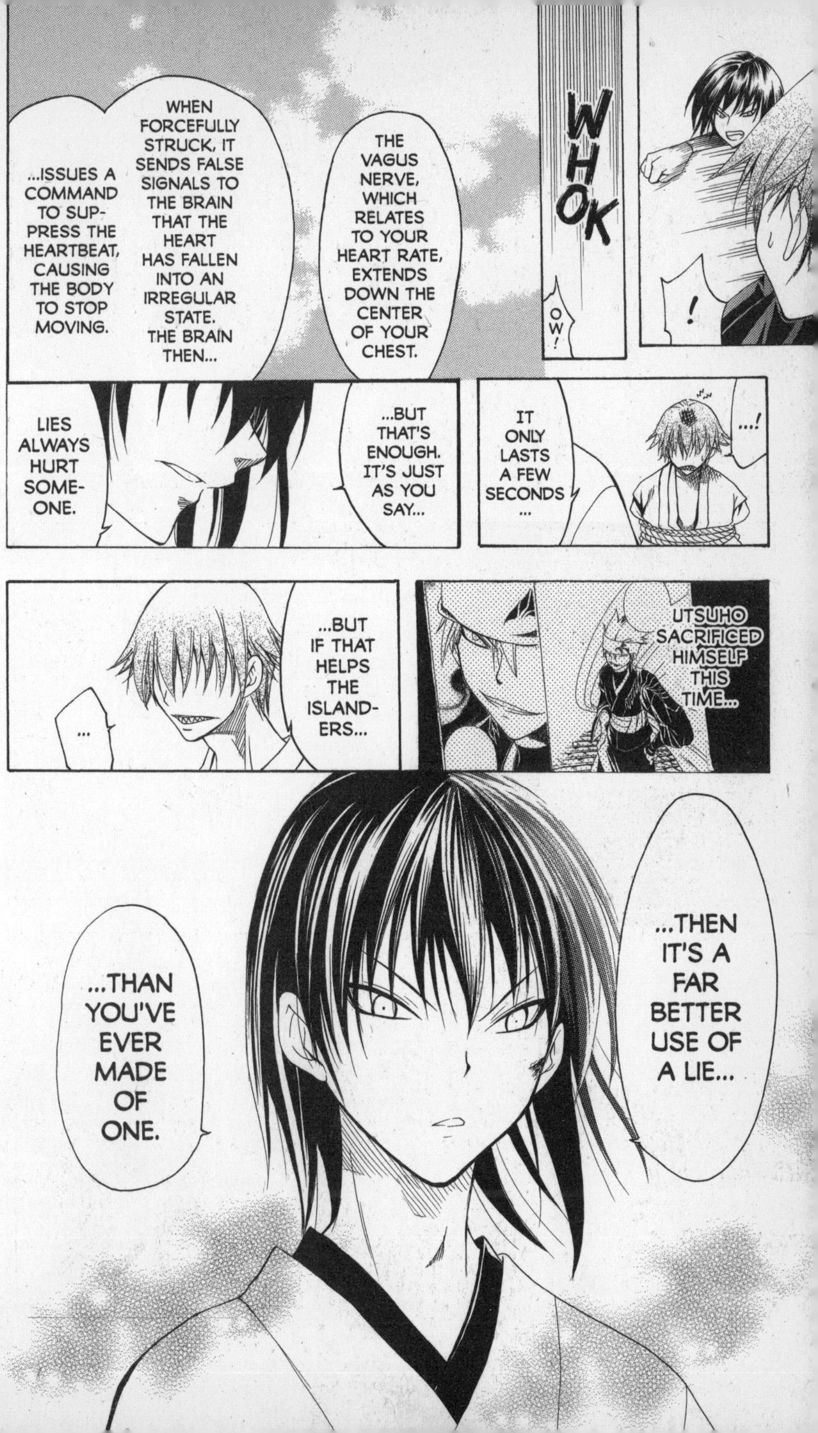
!
WHOK
OW!
THE VAGUS NERVE, WHICH RELATES TO YOUR HEART RATE, EXTENDS DOWN THE CENTER OF YOUR CHEST.
WHEN FORCEFULLY STRUCK, IT SENDS FALSE SIGNALS TO THE BRAIN THAT THE HEART HAS FALLEN INTO AN IRREGULAR STATE. THE BRAIN THEN...
...ISSUES A COMMAND TO SUP-PRESS THE HEARTBEAT, CAUSING THE BODY TO STOP MOVING.
...!
IT ONLY LASTS A FEW SECONDS...
...BUT THAT'S ENOUGH. IT'S JUST AS YOU SAY...
LIES ALWAYS HURT SOME-ONE.
UTSUHO SACRIFICED HIMSELF THIS TIME...
...BUT IF THAT HELPS THE ISLAND-ERS...
...
...THEN IT'S A FAR BETTER USE OF A LIE...
...THAN YOU'VE EVER MADE OF ONE.

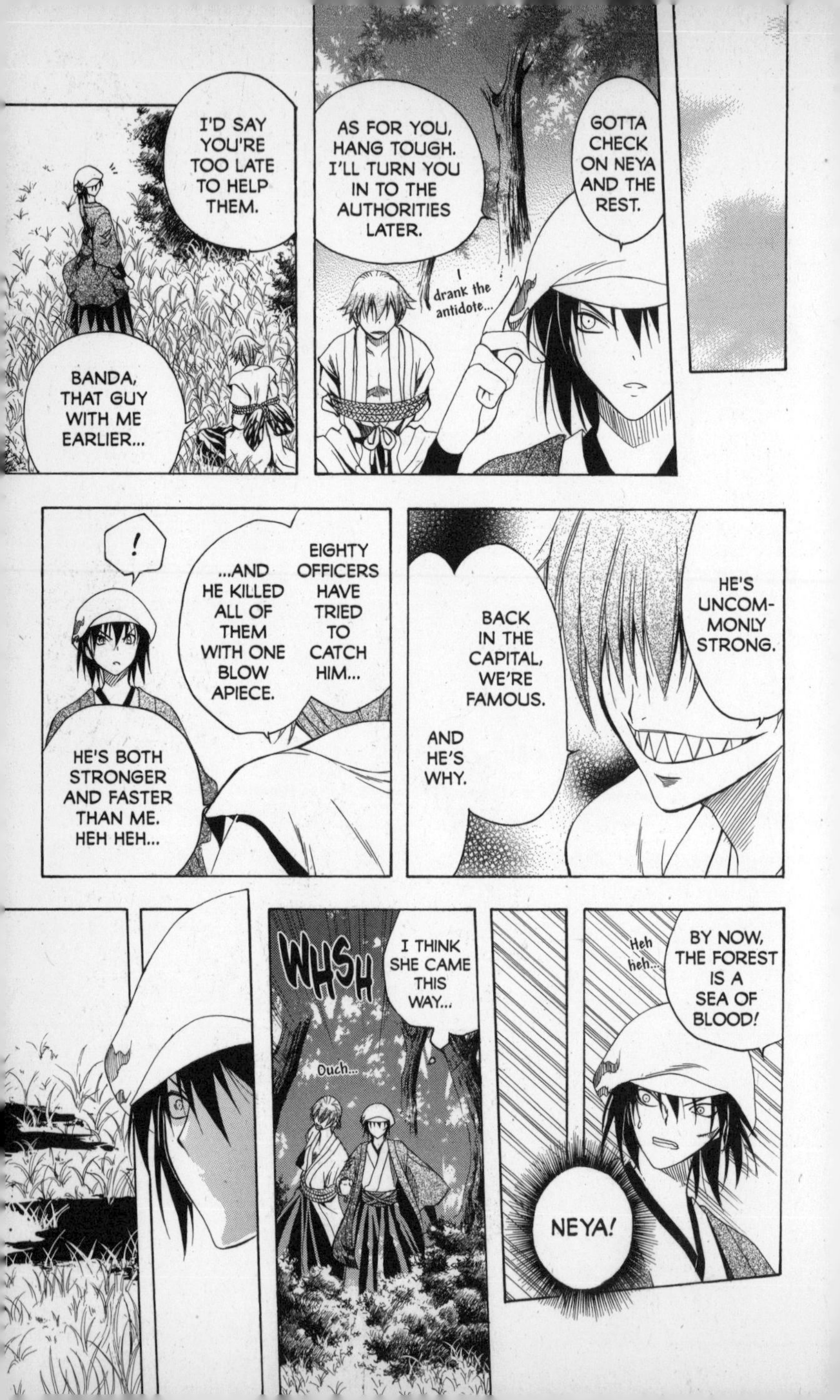
GOTTA CHECK ON NEYA AND THE REST.
AS FOR YOU, HANG TOUGH. I'LL TURN YOU IN TO THE AUTHORITIES LATER.
I drank the antidote...
I'D SAY YOU'RE TOO LATE TO HELP THEM.
BANDA, THAT GUY WITH ME EARLIER...
HE'S UNCOMMONLY STRONG.
BACK IN THE CAPITAL, WE'RE FAMOUS.
AND HE'S WHY.
EIGHTY OFFICERS HAVE TRIED TO CATCH HIM...
...AND HE KILLED ALL OF THEM WITH ONE BLOW APIECE.
!
HE'S BOTH STRONGER AND FASTER THAN ME. HEH HEH...
BY NOW, THE FOREST IS A SEA OF BLOOD!
Heh heh...
NEYA!
WHSH
I THINK SHE CAME THIS WAY...
Ouch...

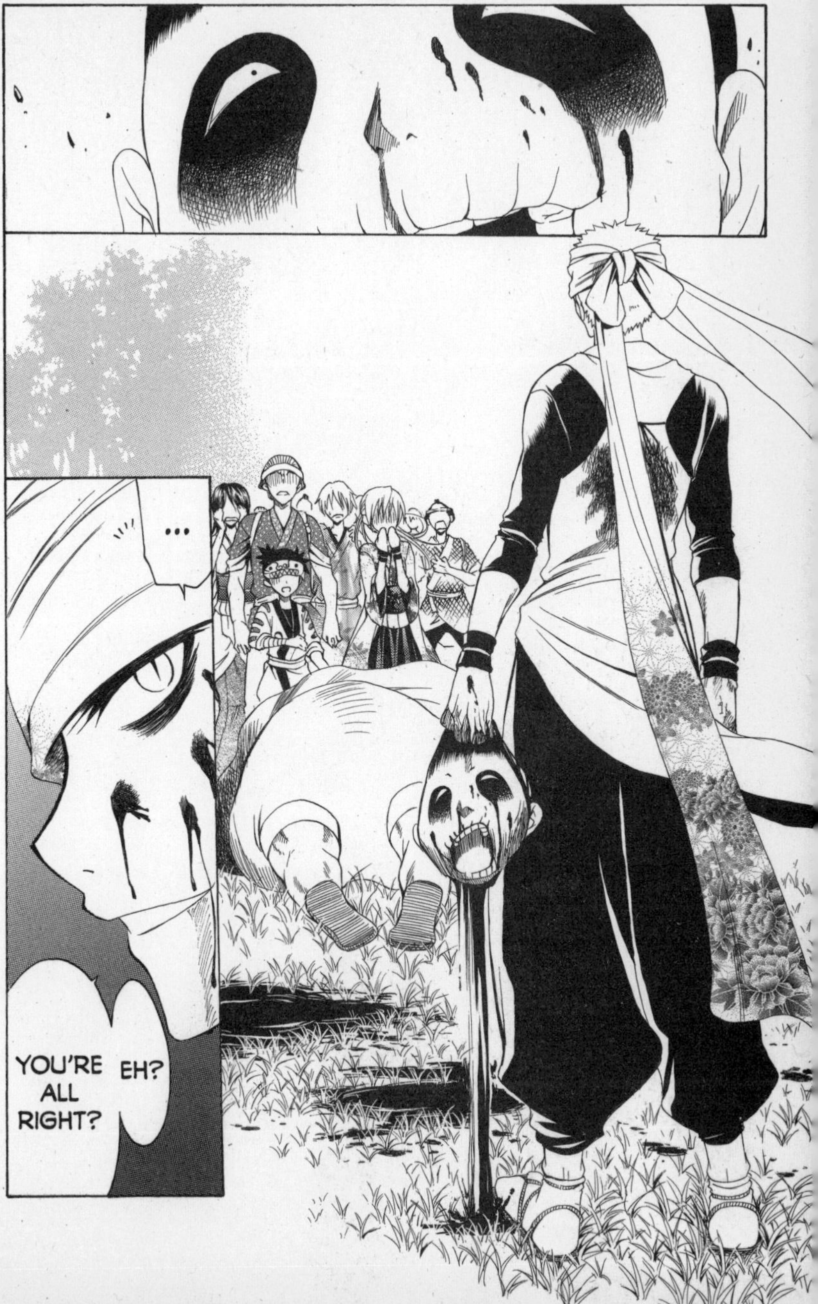
...
EH?
YOU'RE ALL RIGHT?

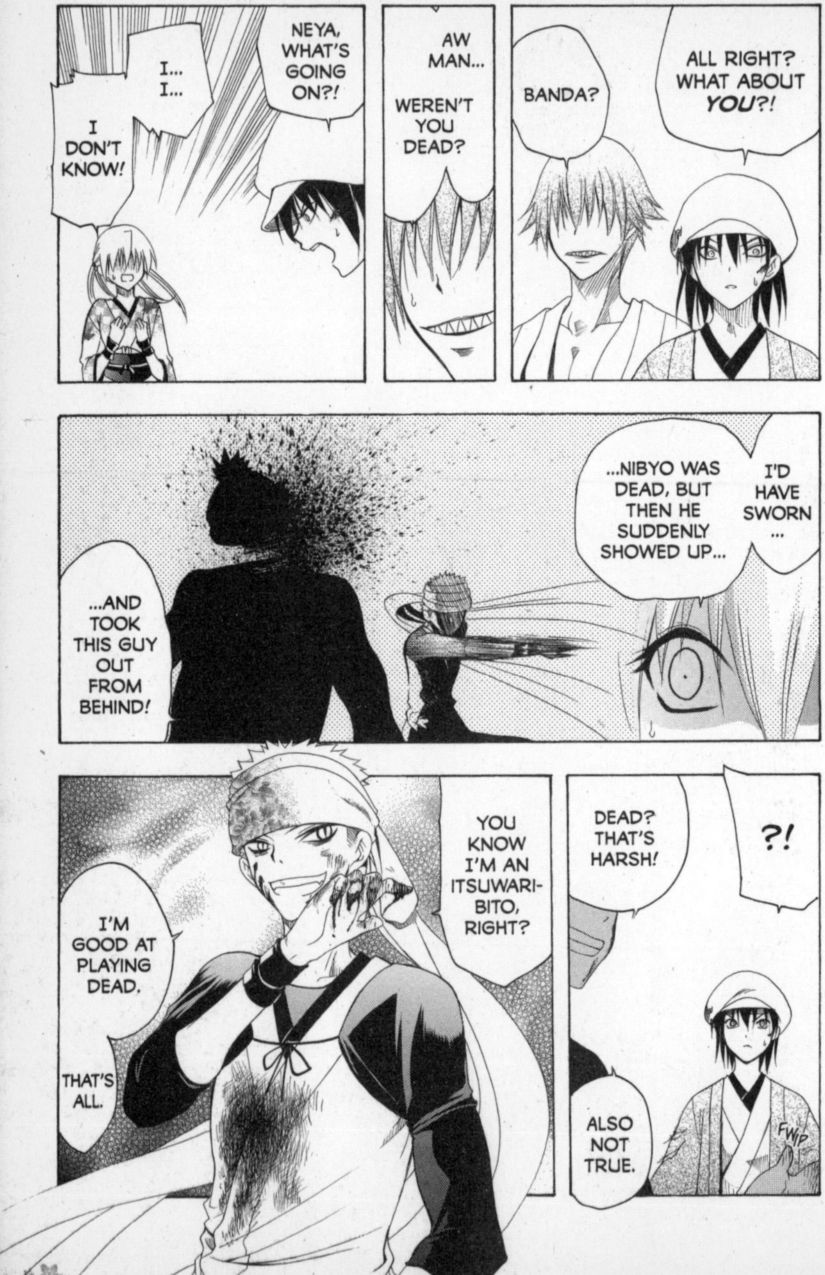
ALL RIGHT? WHAT ABOUT *YOU*?!
BANDA?
AW MAN...
WEREN'T YOU DEAD?
NEYA, WHAT'S GOING ON?!
I... I...
I DON'T KNOW!
I'D HAVE SWORN ...
...NIBYO WAS DEAD, BUT THEN HE SUDDENLY SHOWED UP...
...AND TOOK THIS GUY OUT FROM BEHIND!
?!
DEAD? THAT'S HARSH!
ALSO NOT TRUE.
FWIP
YOU KNOW I'M AN ITSUWARI-BITO, RIGHT?
I'M GOOD AT PLAYING DEAD.
THAT'S ALL.

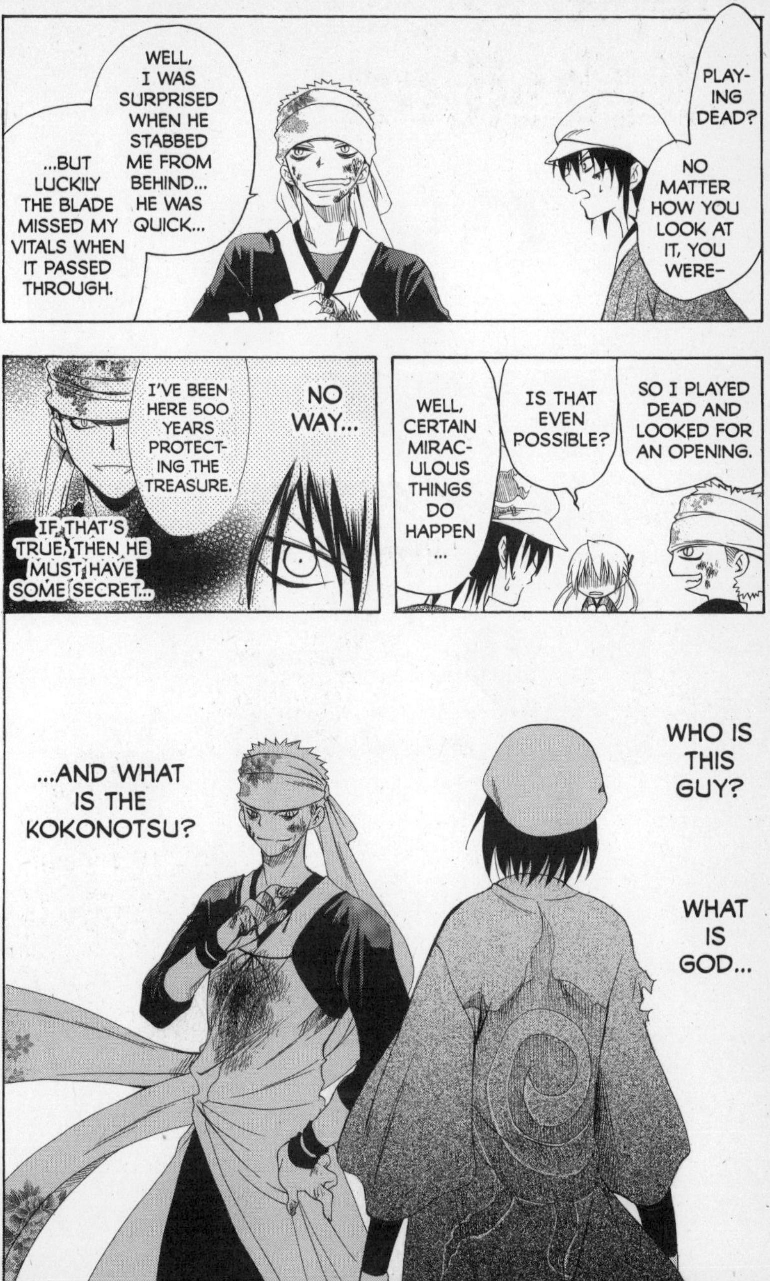
PLAYING DEAD?
NO MATTER HOW YOU LOOK AT IT, YOU WERE–
WELL, I WAS SURPRISED WHEN HE STABBED ME FROM BEHIND... HE WAS QUICK...
...BUT LUCKILY THE BLADE MISSED MY VITALS WHEN IT PASSED THROUGH.
SO I PLAYED DEAD AND LOOKED FOR AN OPENING.
IS THAT EVEN POSSIBLE?
WELL, CERTAIN MIRACULOUS THINGS DO HAPPEN ...
NO WAY...
I'VE BEEN HERE 500 YEARS PROTECTING THE TREASURE.
IF THAT'S TRUE, THEN HE MUST HAVE SOME SECRET...
WHO IS THIS GUY?
WHAT IS GOD...
...AND WHAT IS THE KOKONOTSU?

Chapter 65
Rebellion

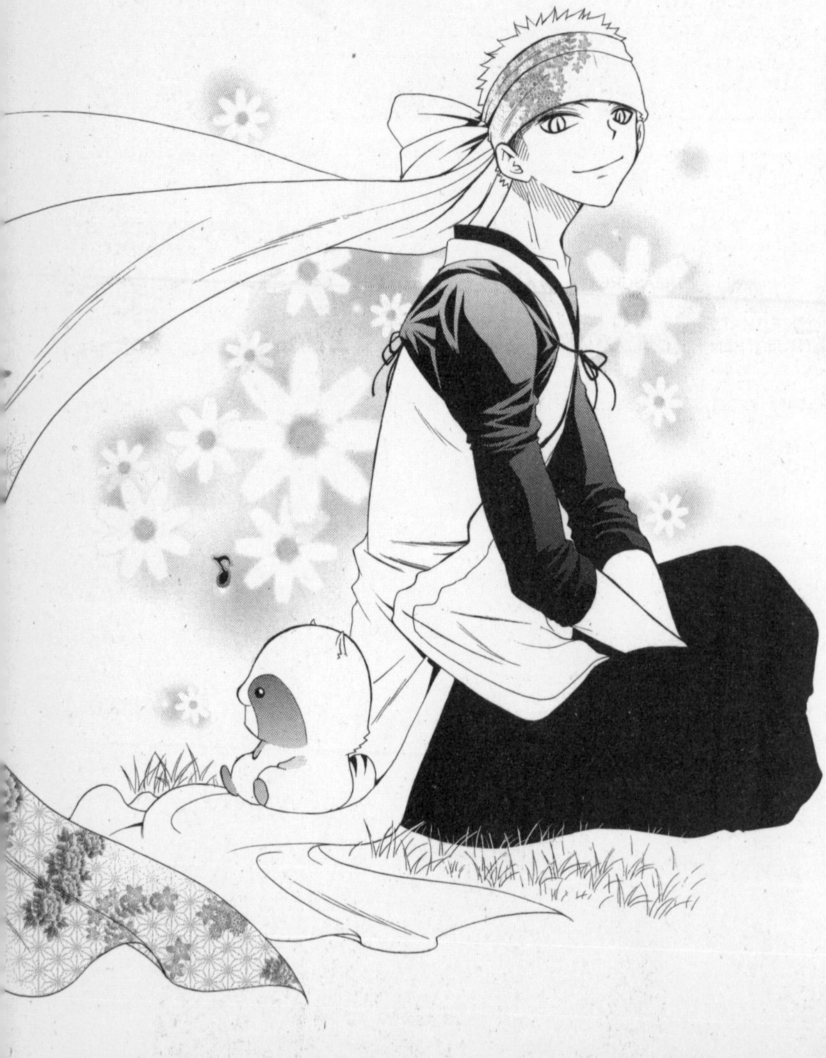

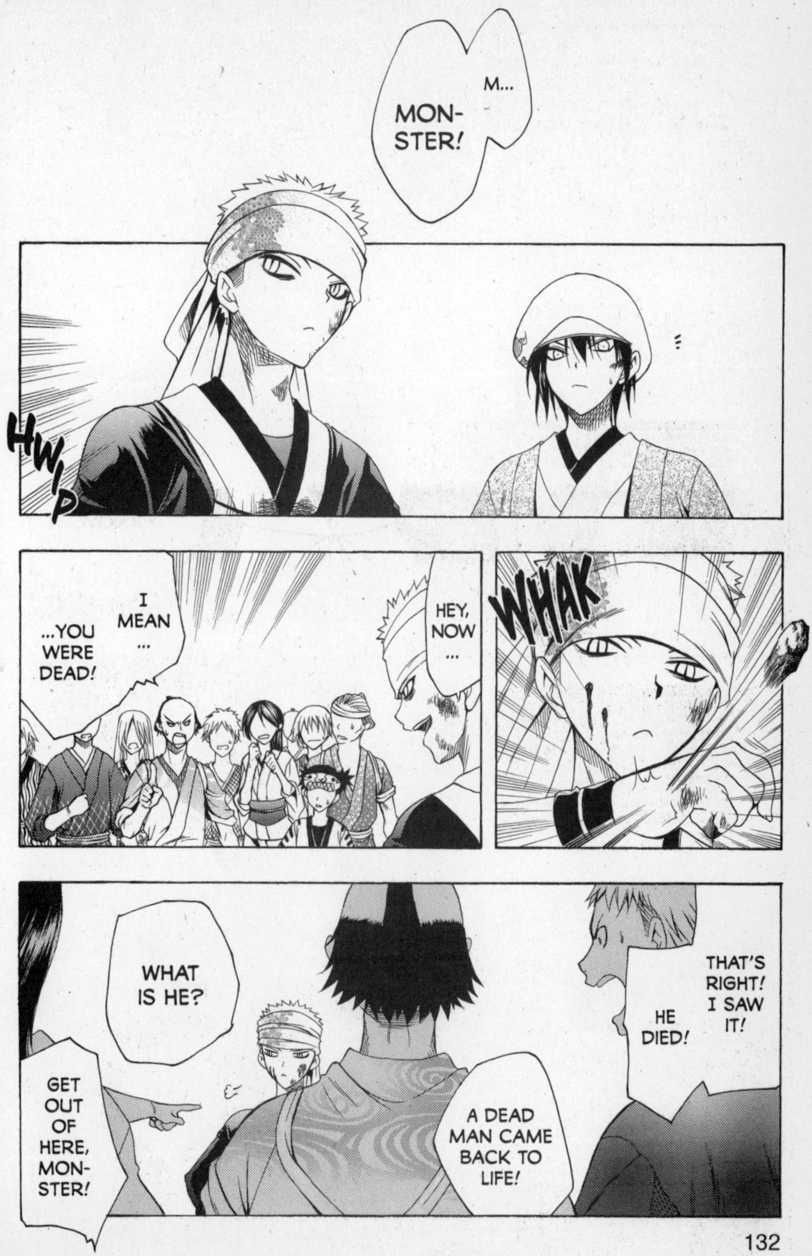

M... MON-STER!
HWIP
WHAK
HEY, NOW...
I MEAN...
...YOU WERE DEAD!
THAT'S RIGHT! I SAW IT!
HE DIED!
A DEAD MAN CAME BACK TO LIFE!
WHAT IS HE?
GET OUT OF HERE, MON-STER!

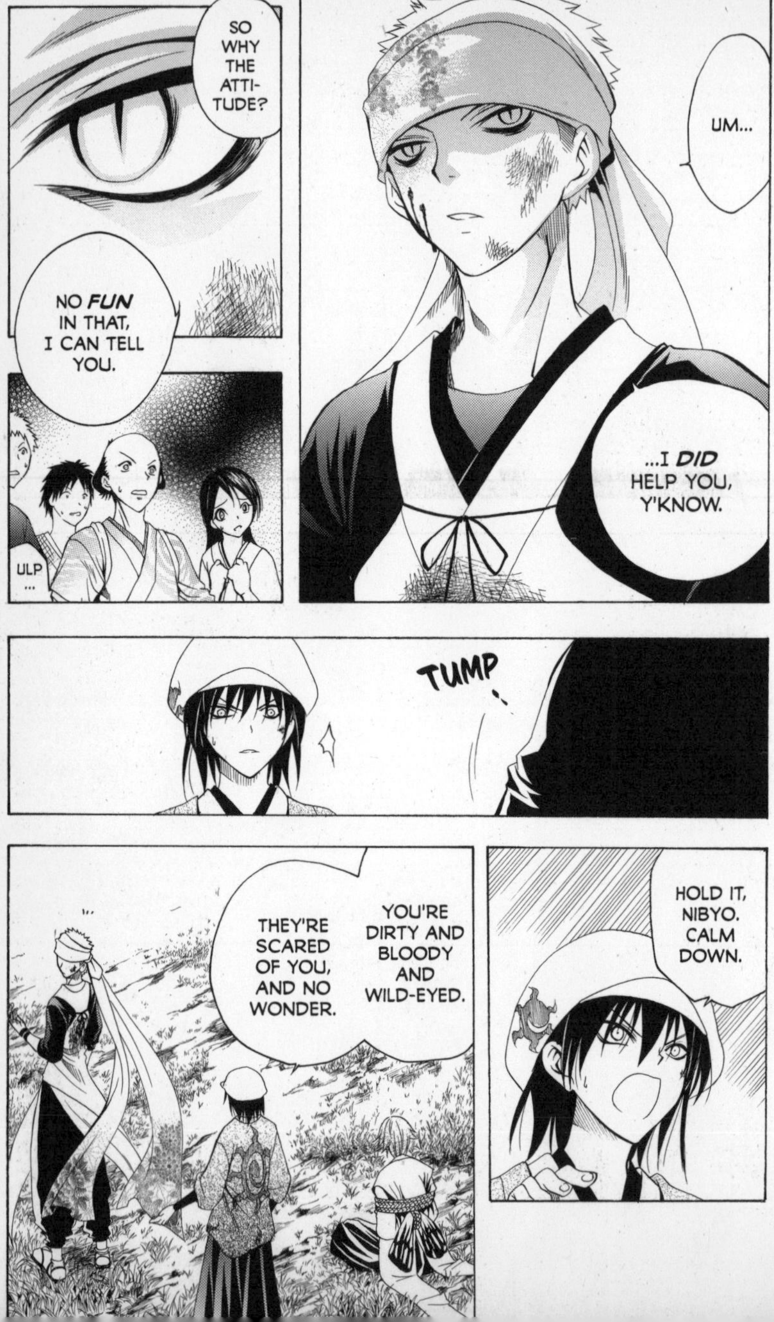
UM...
...I DID HELP YOU, Y'KNOW.
SO WHY THE ATTI-TUDE?
NO FUN IN THAT, I CAN TELL YOU.
ULP...
TUMP
HOLD IT, NIBYO. CALM DOWN.
YOU'RE DIRTY AND BLOODY AND WILD-EYED.
THEY'RE SCARED OF YOU, AND NO WONDER.
...

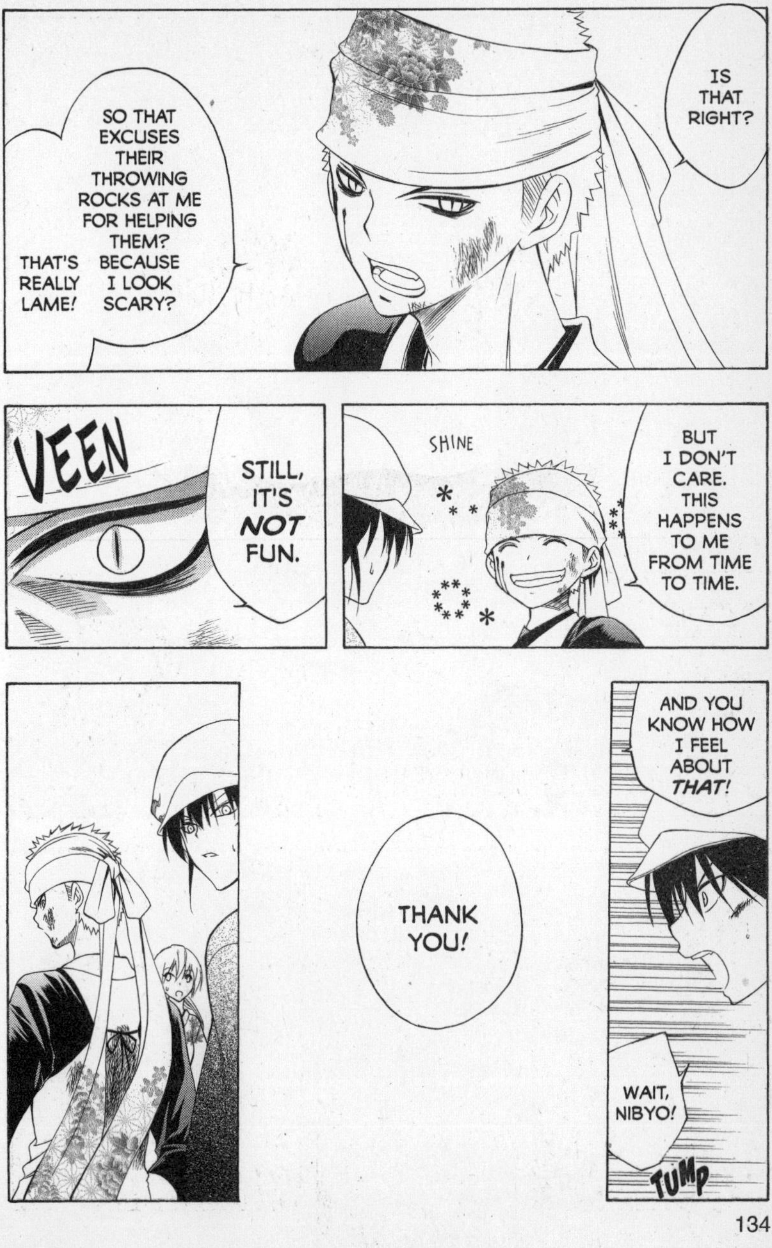
IS THAT RIGHT?
SO THAT EXCUSES THEIR THROWING ROCKS AT ME FOR HELPING THEM? BECAUSE I LOOK SCARY?
THAT'S REALLY LAME!
BUT I DON'T CARE. THIS HAPPENS TO ME FROM TIME TO TIME.
SHINE
STILL, IT'S *NOT* FUN.
VEEN
AND YOU KNOW HOW I FEEL ABOUT *THAT*!
WAIT, NIBYO!
TUMP
THANK YOU!

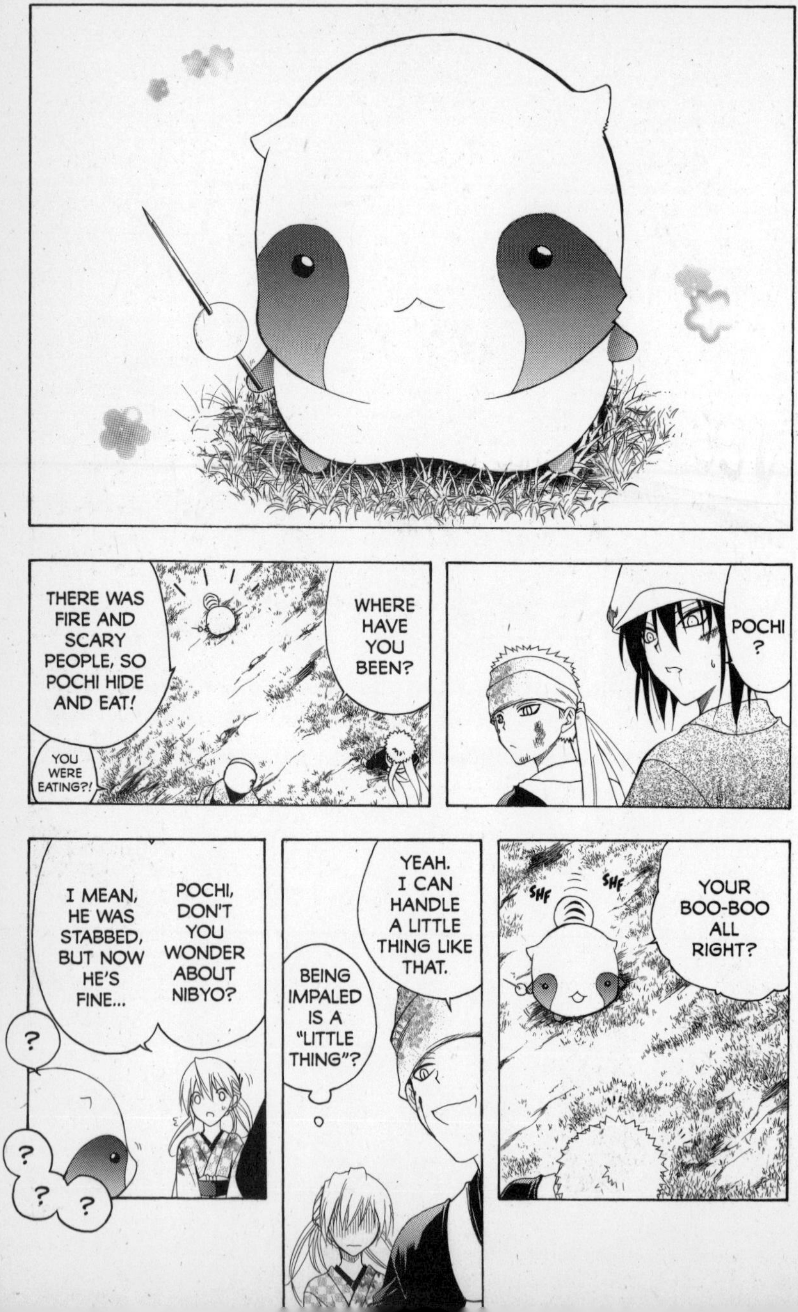
POCHI?
WHERE HAVE YOU BEEN?
THERE WAS FIRE AND SCARY PEOPLE, SO POCHI HIDE AND EAT!
YOU WERE EATING?!
SHF
SHF
YOUR BOO-BOO ALL RIGHT?
YEAH. I CAN HANDLE A LITTLE THING LIKE THAT.
BEING IMPALED IS A "LITTLE THING"?
POCHI, DON'T YOU WONDER ABOUT NIBYO?
I MEAN, HE WAS STABBED, BUT NOW HE'S FINE...
?
?
?
?

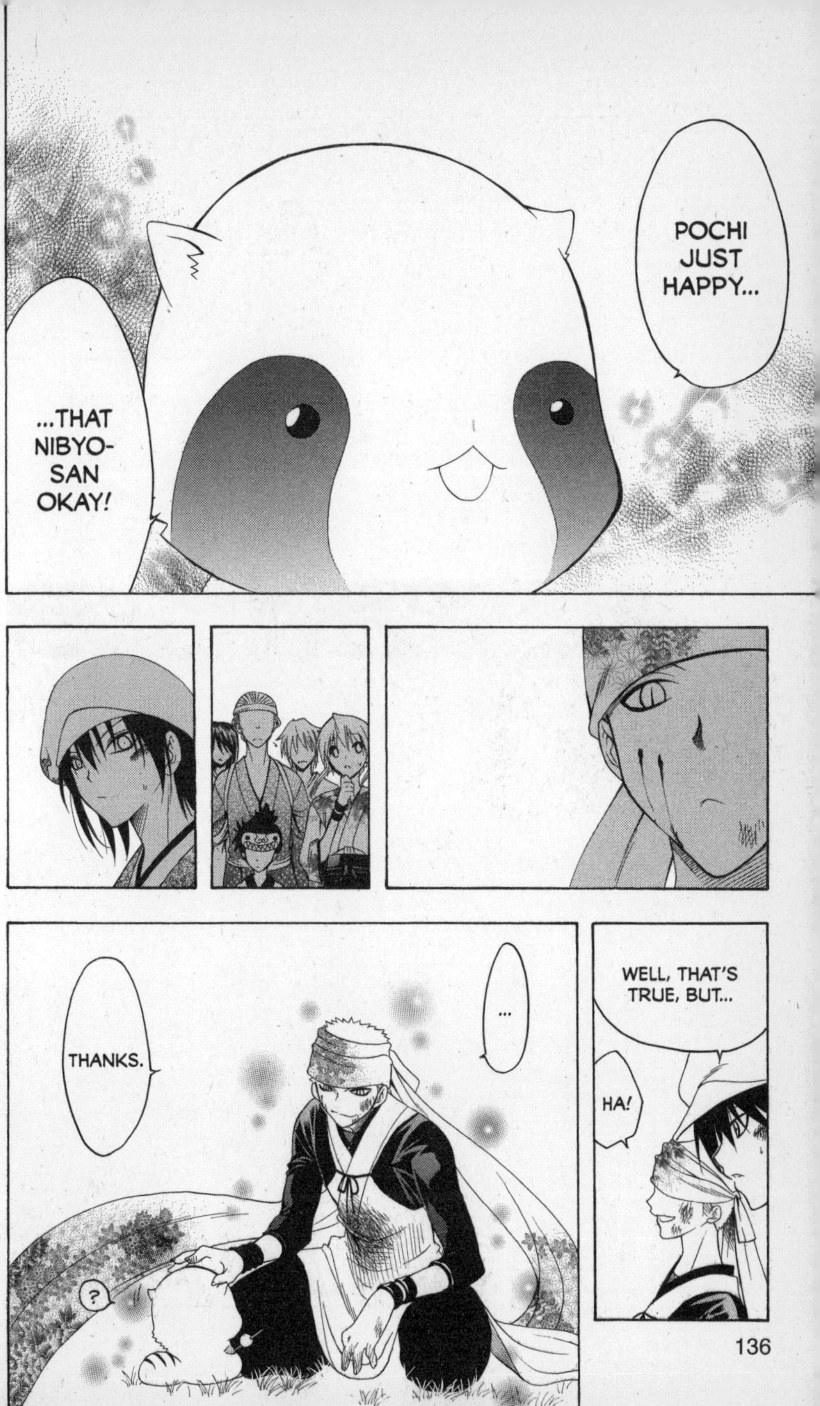

POCHI JUST HAPPY...
...THAT NIBYO-SAN OKAY!
WELL, THAT'S TRUE, BUT...
HA!
...
THANKS.
?

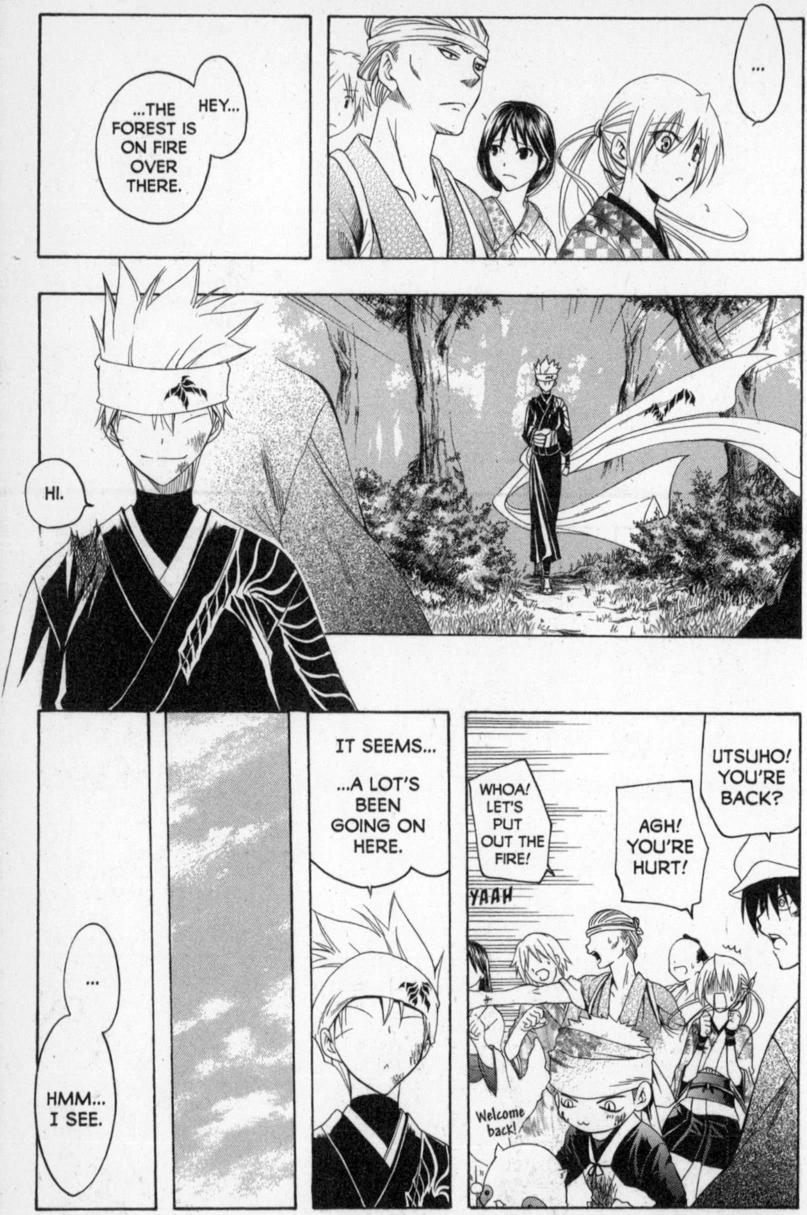
...
HEY...
...THE FOREST IS ON FIRE OVER THERE.
HI.
UTSUHO! YOU'RE BACK?
AGH! YOU'RE HURT!
WHOA! LET'S PUT OUT THE FIRE!
YAAH
Welcome back!
IT SEEMS...
...A LOT'S BEEN GOING ON HERE.
...
HMM... I SEE.

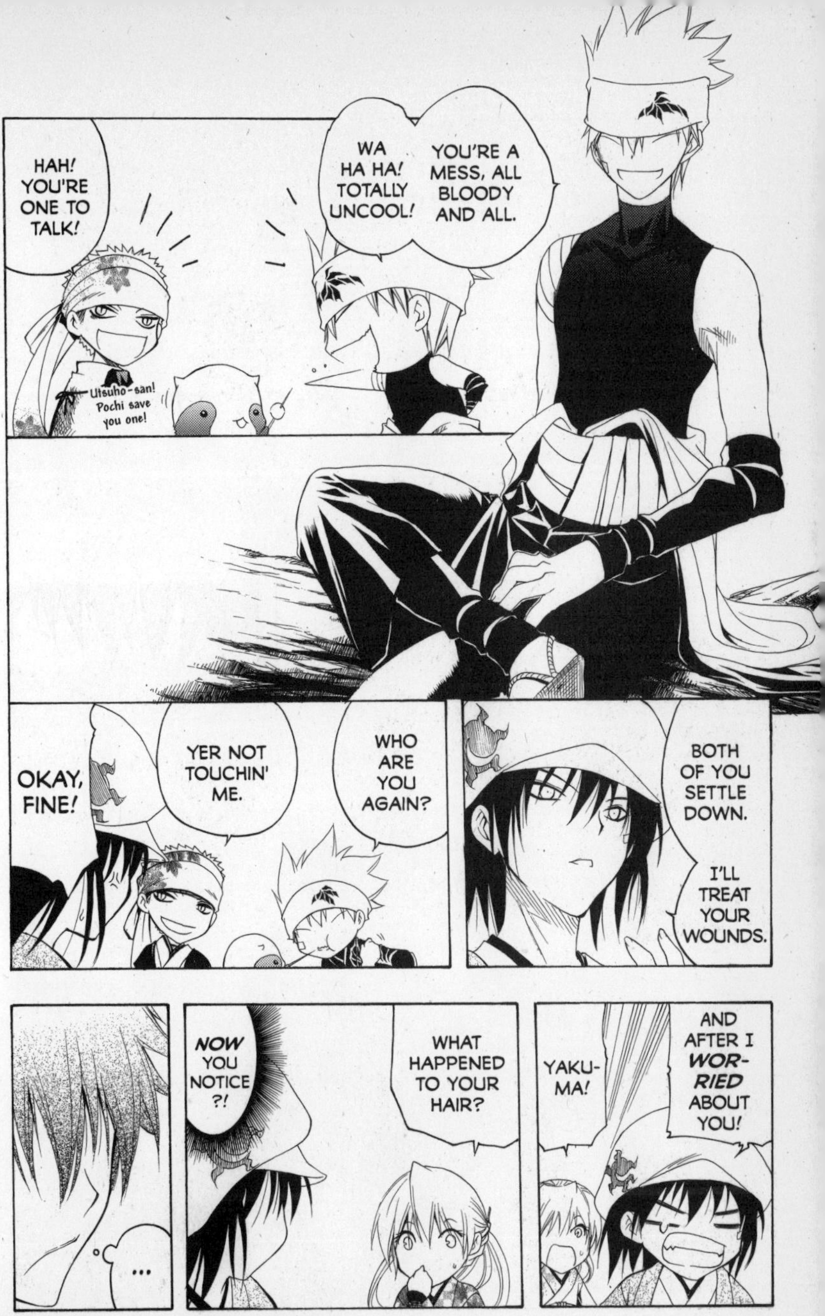

YOU'RE A MESS, ALL BLOODY AND ALL.
WA HA HA! TOTALLY UNCOOL!
HAH! YOU'RE ONE TO TALK!
Utsuho-san! Pochi save you one!
BOTH OF YOU SETTLE DOWN.
I'LL TREAT YOUR WOUNDS.
WHO ARE YOU AGAIN?
YER NOT TOUCHIN' ME.
OKAY, FINE!
AND AFTER I *WOR-RIED* ABOUT YOU!
YAKU-MA!
WHAT HAPPENED TO YOUR HAIR?
NOW YOU NOTICE?!
...

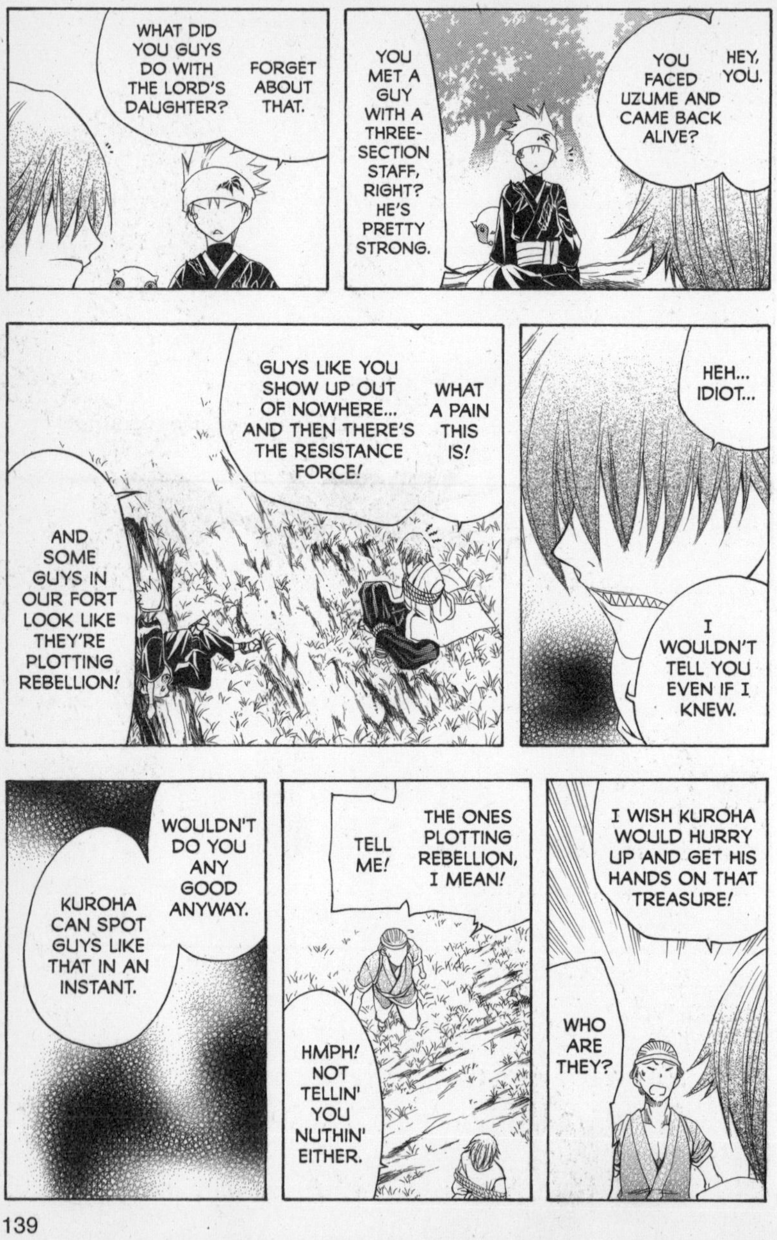
HEY, YOU.
YOU FACED UZUME AND CAME BACK ALIVE?
YOU MET A GUY WITH A THREE-SECTION STAFF, RIGHT? HE'S PRETTY STRONG.
FORGET ABOUT THAT.
WHAT DID YOU GUYS DO WITH THE LORD'S DAUGHTER?
HEH... IDIOT...
I WOULDN'T TELL YOU EVEN IF I KNEW.
WHAT A PAIN THIS IS!
GUYS LIKE YOU SHOW UP OUT OF NOWHERE... AND THEN THERE'S THE RESISTANCE FORCE!
AND SOME GUYS IN OUR FORT LOOK LIKE THEY'RE PLOTTING REBELLION!
I WISH KUROHA WOULD HURRY UP AND GET HIS HANDS ON THAT TREASURE!
WHO ARE THEY?
TELL ME! THE ONES PLOTTING REBELLION, I MEAN!
HMPH! NOT TELLIN' YOU NUTHIN' EITHER.
WOULDN'T DO YOU ANY GOOD ANYWAY.
KUROHA CAN SPOT GUYS LIKE THAT IN AN INSTANT.

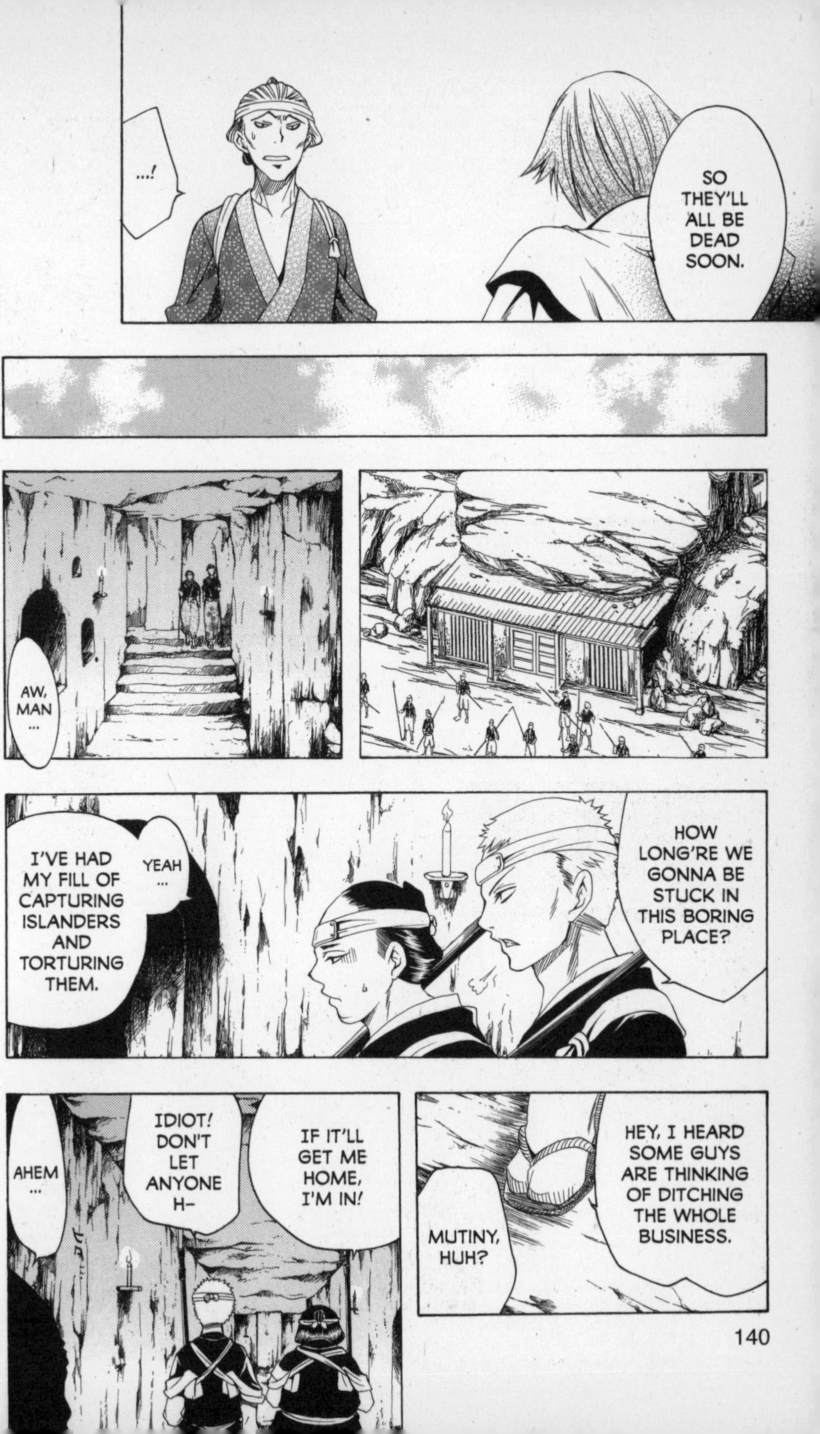

SO THEY'LL ALL BE DEAD SOON.
...!
AW, MAN ...
HOW LONG'RE WE GONNA BE STUCK IN THIS BORING PLACE?
YEAH ...
I'VE HAD MY FILL OF CAPTURING ISLANDERS AND TORTURING THEM.
HEY, I HEARD SOME GUYS ARE THINKING OF DITCHING THE WHOLE BUSINESS.
MUTINY, HUH?
IF IT'LL GET ME HOME, I'M IN!
IDIOT! DON'T LET ANYONE H-
AHEM ...

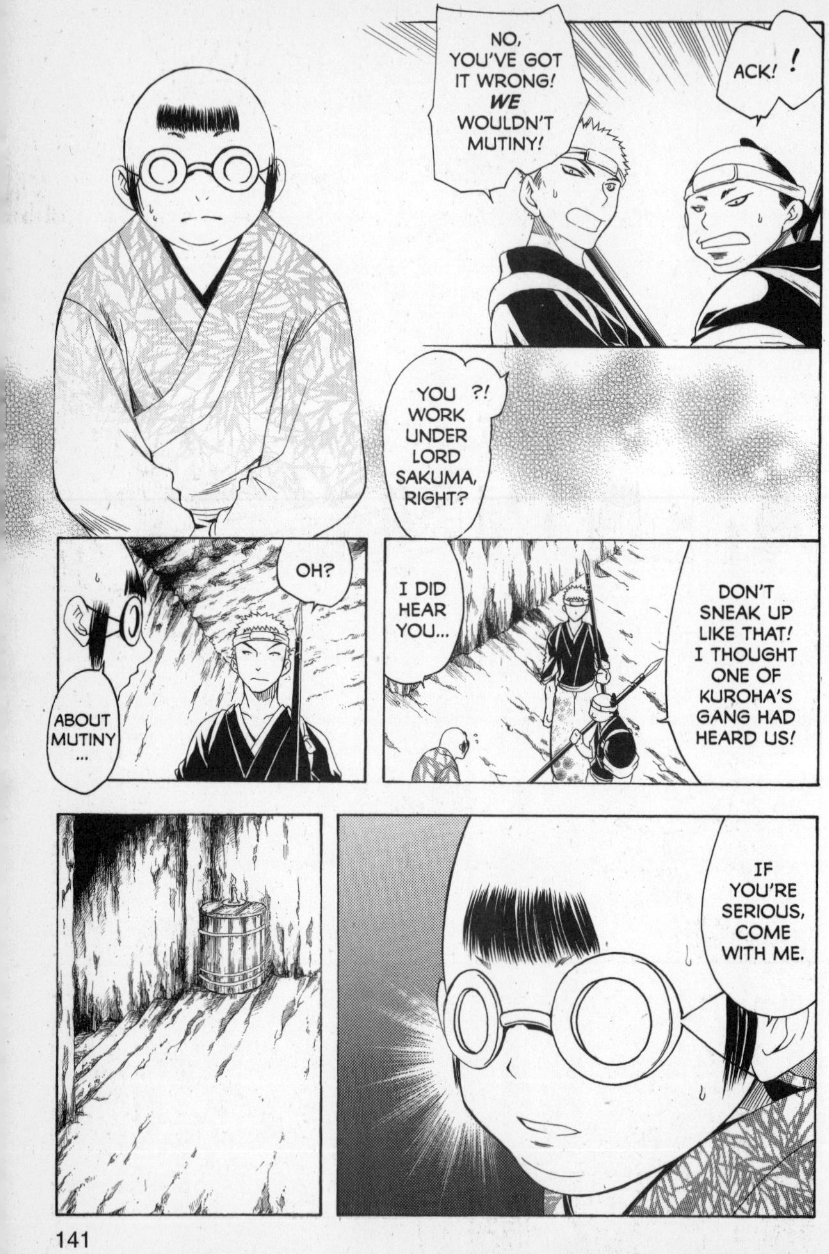
ACK! !
NO, YOU'VE GOT IT WRONG! ***WE*** WOULDN'T MUTINY!
YOU ?! WORK UNDER LORD SAKUMA, RIGHT?
DON'T SNEAK UP LIKE THAT! I THOUGHT ONE OF KUROHA'S GANG HAD HEARD US!
I DID HEAR YOU...
OH?
ABOUT MUTINY ...
IF YOU'RE SERIOUS, COME WITH ME.

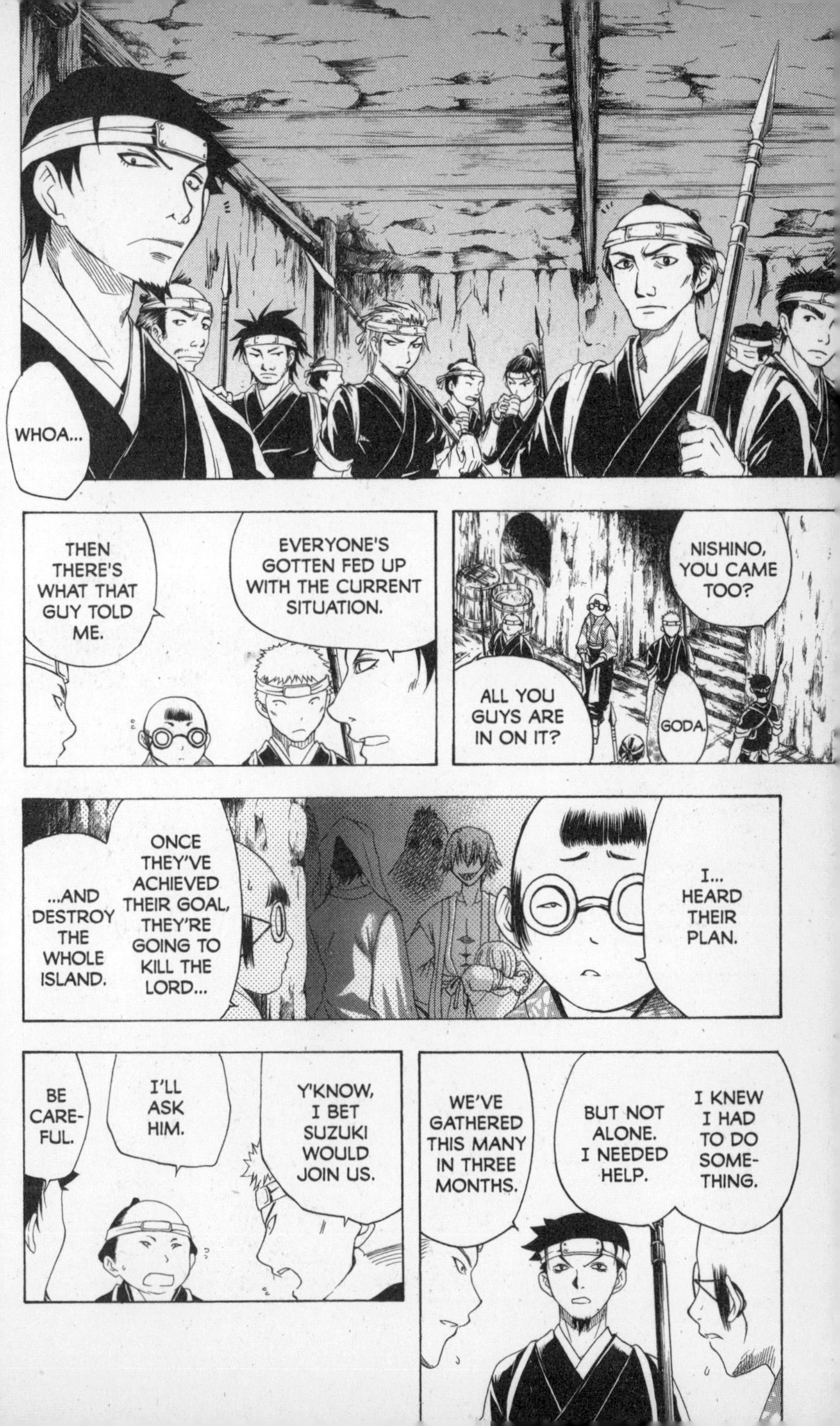
WHOA...
NISHINO, YOU CAME TOO?
GODA.
ALL YOU GUYS ARE IN ON IT?
EVERYONE'S GOTTEN FED UP WITH THE CURRENT SITUATION.
THEN THERE'S WHAT THAT GUY TOLD ME.
I... HEARD THEIR PLAN.
ONCE THEY'VE ACHIEVED THEIR GOAL, THEY'RE GOING TO KILL THE LORD...
...AND DESTROY THE WHOLE ISLAND.
I KNEW I HAD TO DO SOME-THING.
BUT NOT ALONE. I NEEDED HELP.
WE'VE GATHERED THIS MANY IN THREE MONTHS.
Y'KNOW, I BET SUZUKI WOULD JOIN US.
I'LL ASK HIM.
BE CARE-FUL.

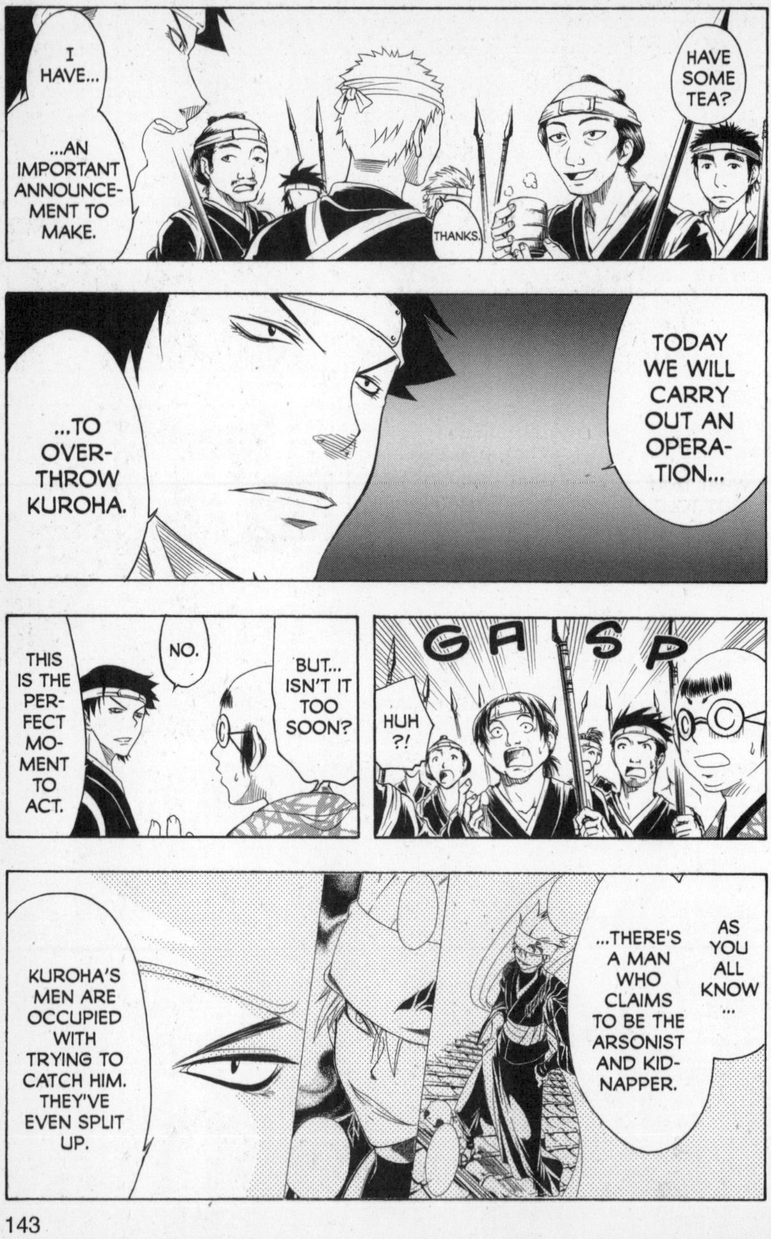
HAVE SOME TEA?
THANKS.
I HAVE...
...AN IMPORTANT ANNOUNCEMENT TO MAKE.
TODAY WE WILL CARRY OUT AN OPERATION...
...TO OVERTHROW KUROHA.
GASP
HUH?!
BUT... ISN'T IT TOO SOON?
NO.
THIS IS THE PERFECT MOMENT TO ACT.
AS YOU ALL KNOW...
...THERE'S A MAN WHO CLAIMS TO BE THE ARSONIST AND KIDNAPPER.
KUROHA'S MEN ARE OCCUPIED WITH TRYING TO CATCH HIM. THEY'VE EVEN SPLIT UP.

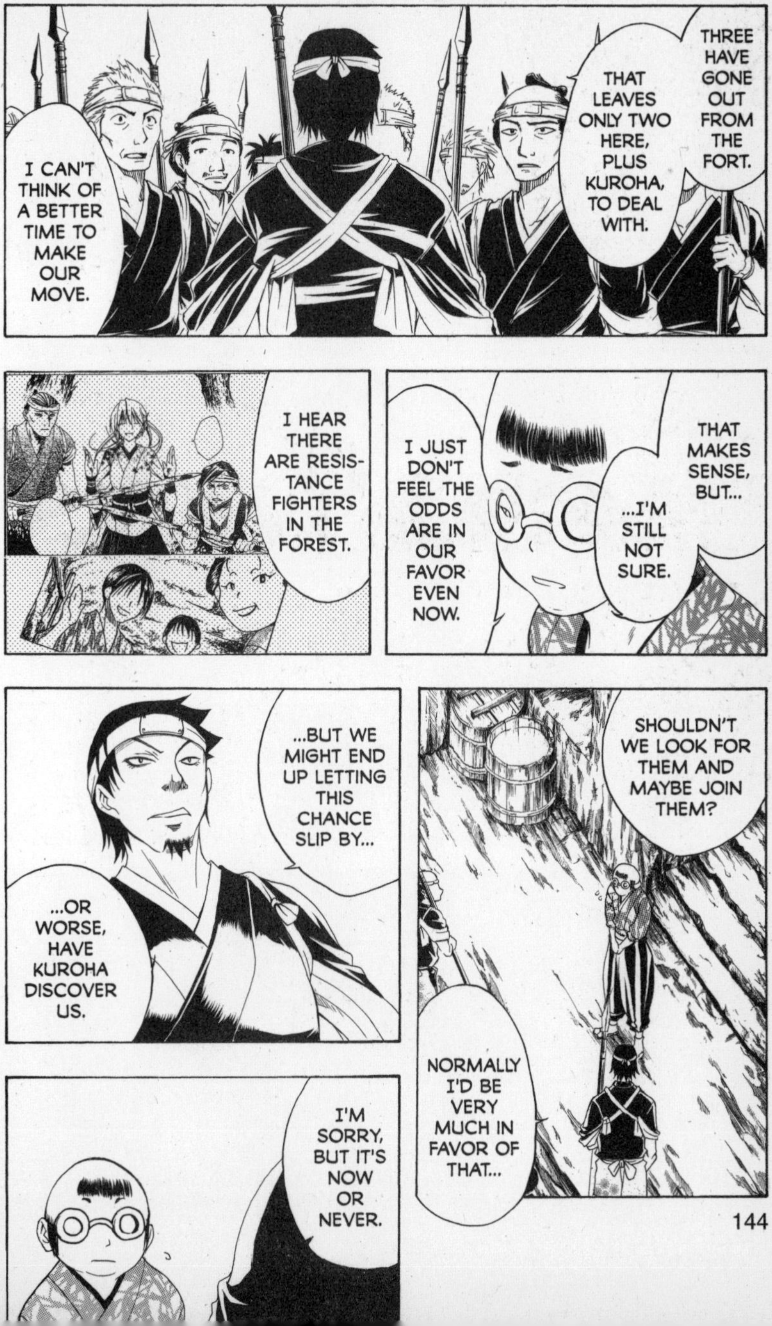
THREE HAVE GONE OUT FROM THE FORT.
THAT LEAVES ONLY TWO HERE, PLUS KUROHA, TO DEAL WITH.
I CAN'T THINK OF A BETTER TIME TO MAKE OUR MOVE.
THAT MAKES SENSE, BUT...
...I'M STILL NOT SURE.
I JUST DON'T FEEL THE ODDS ARE IN OUR FAVOR EVEN NOW.
I HEAR THERE ARE RESIS-TANCE FIGHTERS IN THE FOREST.
SHOULDN'T WE LOOK FOR THEM AND MAYBE JOIN THEM?
NORMALLY I'D BE VERY MUCH IN FAVOR OF THAT...
...BUT WE MIGHT END UP LETTING THIS CHANCE SLIP BY...
...OR WORSE, HAVE KUROHA DISCOVER US.
I'M SORRY, BUT IT'S NOW OR NEVER.

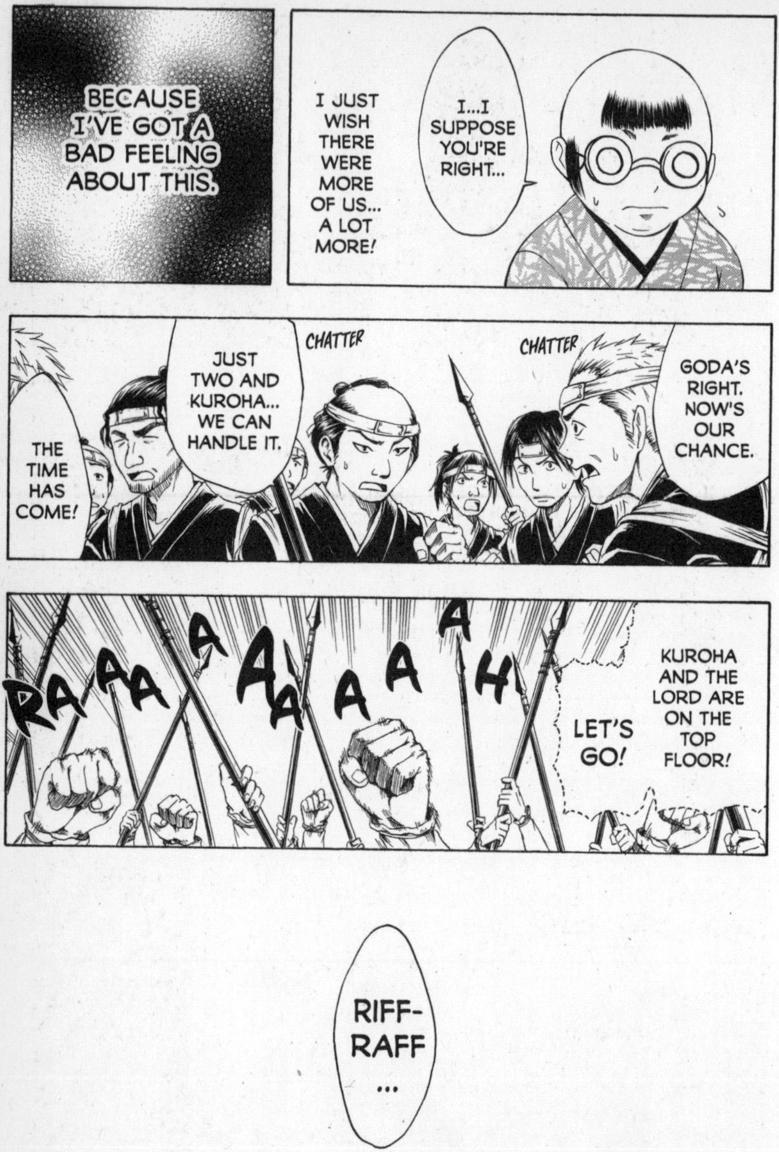
I...I SUPPOSE YOU'RE RIGHT...
I JUST WISH THERE WERE MORE OF US... A LOT MORE!
BECAUSE I'VE GOT A BAD FEELING ABOUT THIS.
GODA'S RIGHT. NOW'S OUR CHANCE.
CHATTER
CHATTER
JUST TWO AND KUROHA... WE CAN HANDLE IT.
THE TIME HAS COME!
KUROHA AND THE LORD ARE ON THE TOP FLOOR!
LET'S GO!
RAAAAAAAAAH
RIFF-RAFF ...

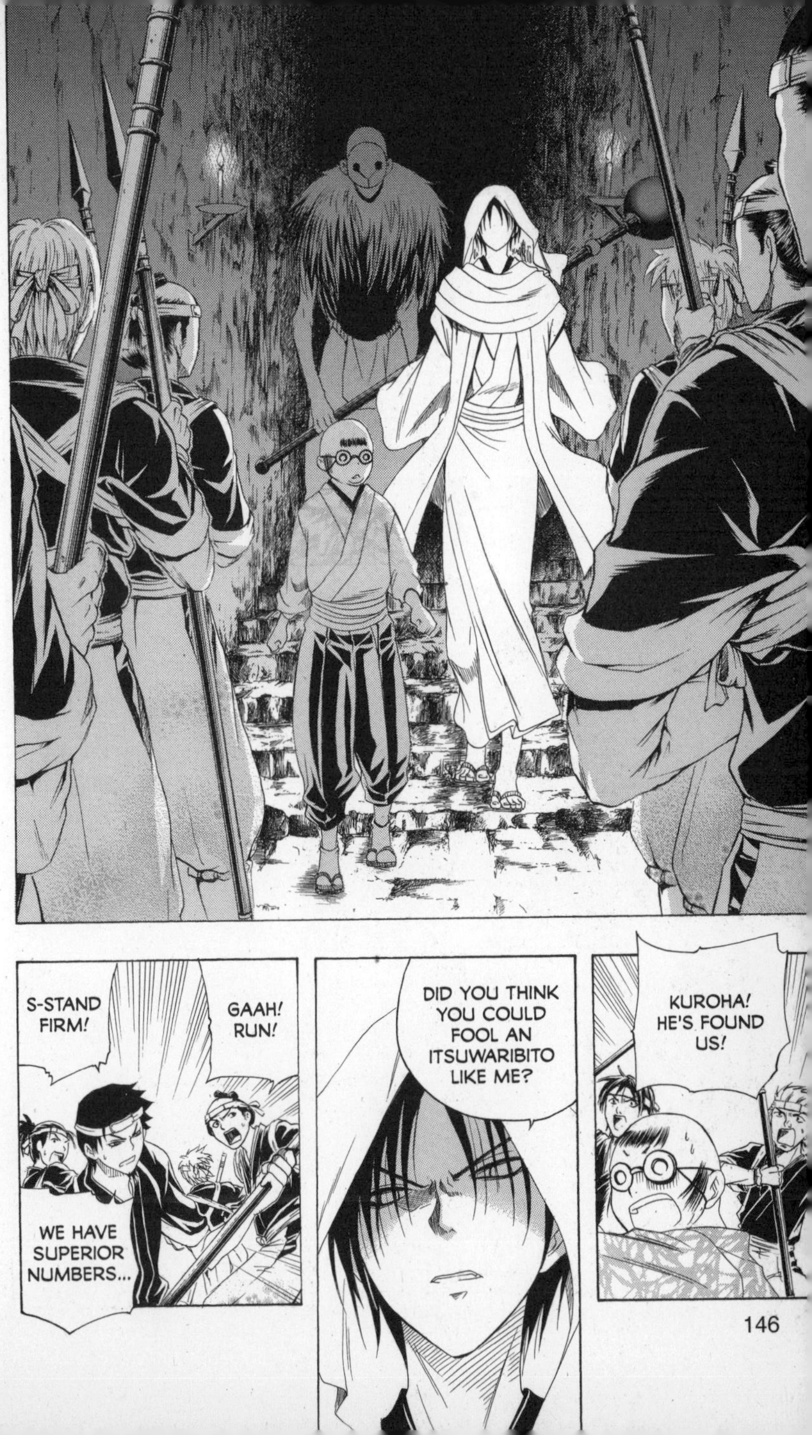
KUROHA! HE'S FOUND US!
DID YOU THINK YOU COULD FOOL AN ITSUWARIBITO LIKE ME?
GAAH! RUN!
S-STAND FIRM!
WE HAVE SUPERIOR NUMBERS...

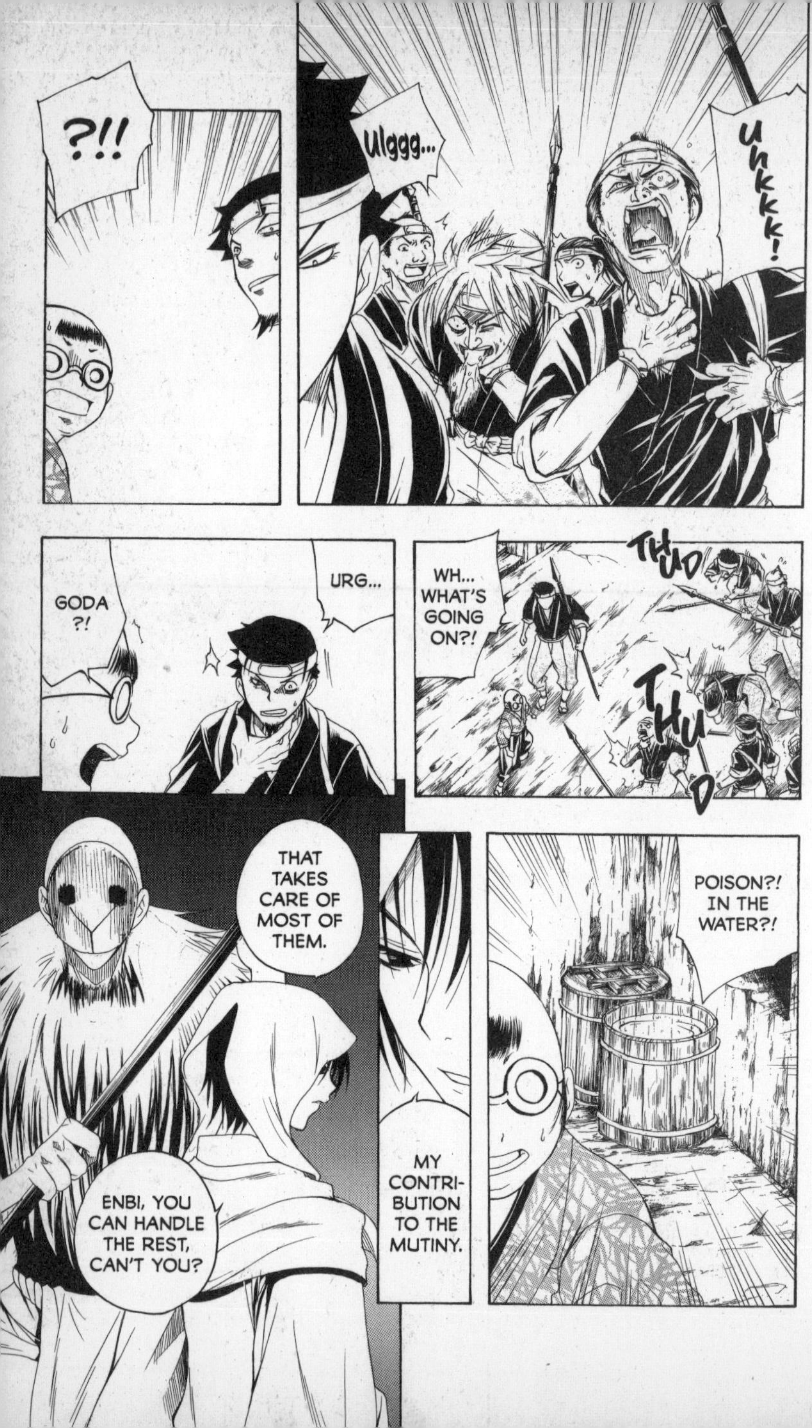
UNKKKK!
Ulggg...
?!!
WH... WHAT'S GOING ON?!
THUD
THUD
URG...
GODA ?!
POISON?! IN THE WATER?!
MY CONTRIBUTION TO THE MUTINY.
THAT TAKES CARE OF MOST OF THEM.
ENBI, YOU CAN HANDLE THE REST, CAN'T YOU?

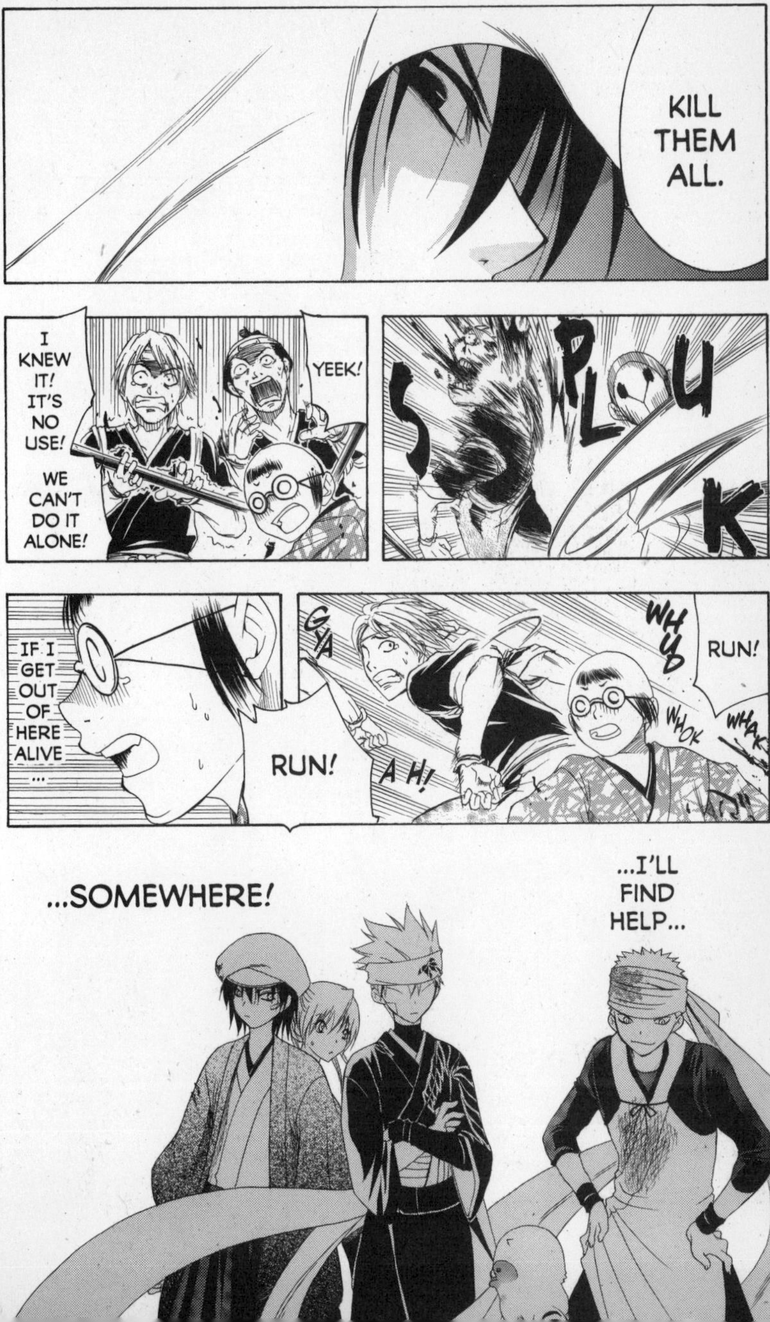
KILL THEM ALL.
PLUK
YEEK!
I KNEW IT! IT'S NO USE!
WE CAN'T DO IT ALONE!
RUN!
WHUD
WHAK
WHOK
GYA
AH!
RUN!
IF I GET OUT OF HERE ALIVE ...
...I'LL FIND HELP...
...SOMEWHERE!

Chapter 66 Raid

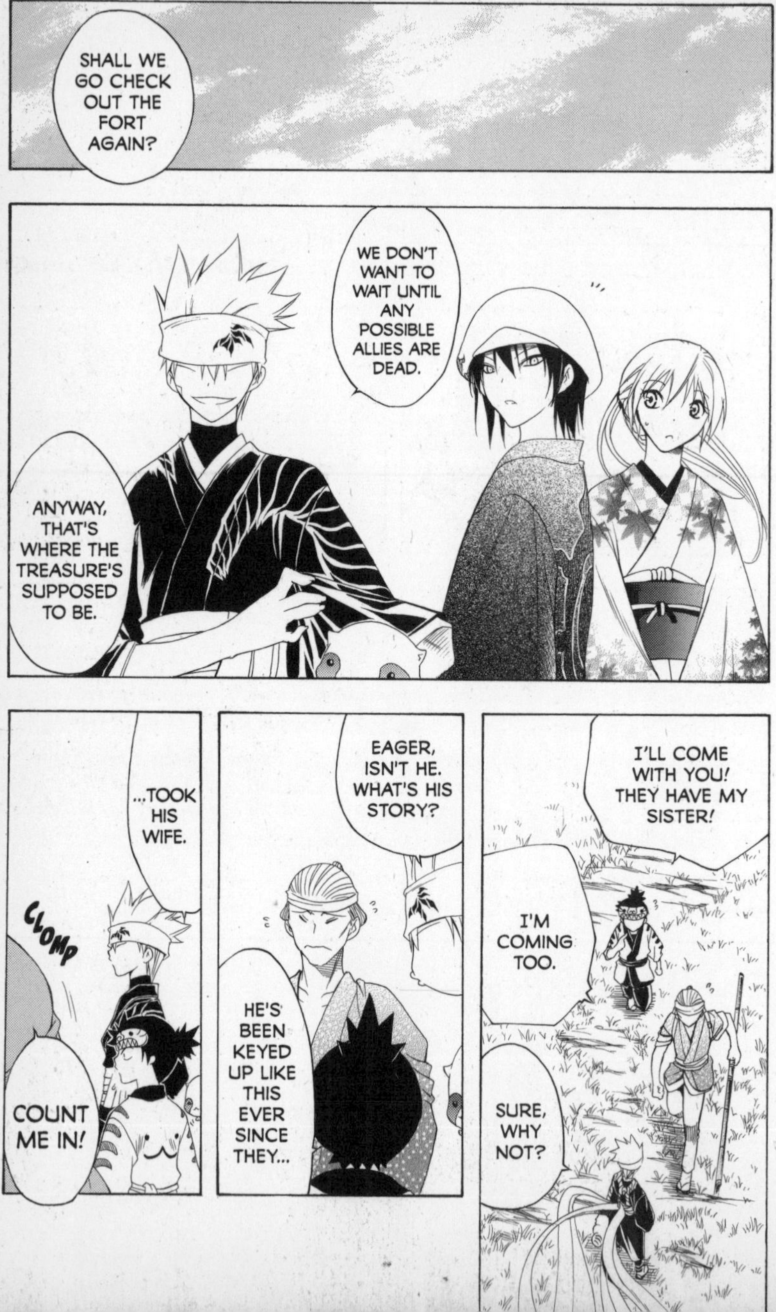

SHALL WE GO CHECK OUT THE FORT AGAIN?
WE DON'T WANT TO WAIT UNTIL ANY POSSIBLE ALLIES ARE DEAD.
ANYWAY, THAT'S WHERE THE TREASURE'S SUPPOSED TO BE.
I'LL COME WITH YOU! THEY HAVE MY SISTER!
I'M COMING TOO.
SURE, WHY NOT?
EAGER, ISN'T HE. WHAT'S HIS STORY?
HE'S BEEN KEYED UP LIKE THIS EVER SINCE THEY...
...TOOK HIS WIFE.
CLOMP
COUNT ME IN!

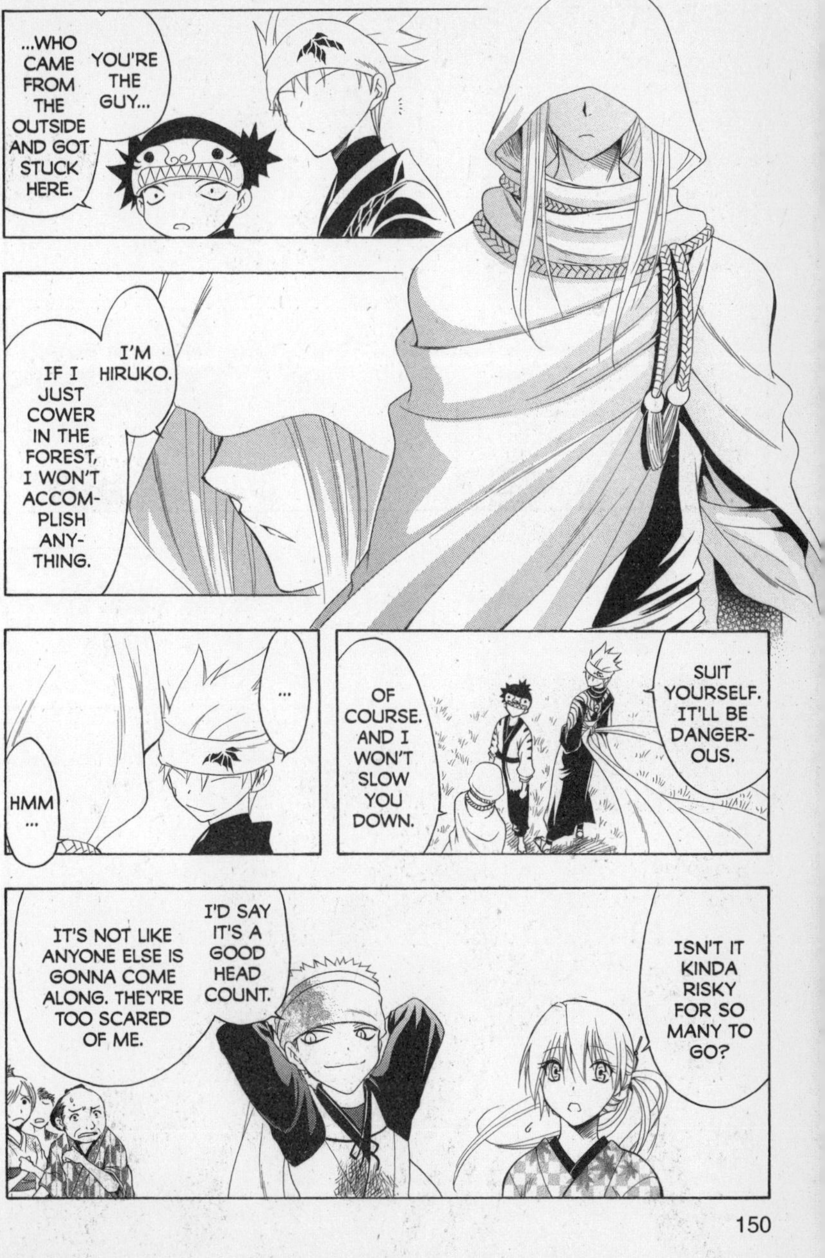
YOU'RE THE GUY...
...WHO CAME FROM THE OUTSIDE AND GOT STUCK HERE.
I'M HIRUKO.
IF I JUST COWER IN THE FOREST, I WON'T ACCOMPLISH ANYTHING.
SUIT YOURSELF. IT'LL BE DANGEROUS.
OF COURSE. AND I WON'T SLOW YOU DOWN.
...
HMM ...
ISN'T IT KINDA RISKY FOR SO MANY TO GO?
I'D SAY IT'S A GOOD HEAD COUNT.
IT'S NOT LIKE ANYONE ELSE IS GONNA COME ALONG. THEY'RE TOO SCARED OF ME.

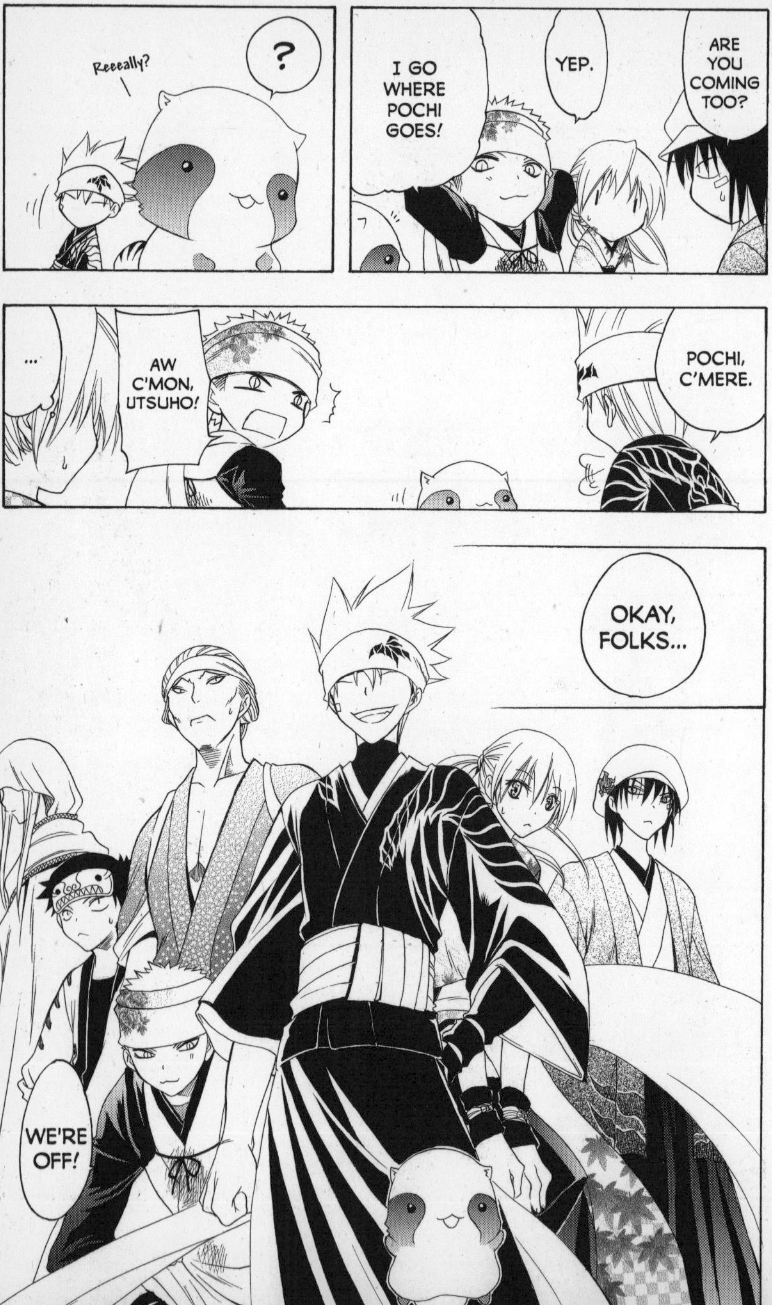
ARE YOU COMING TOO?
YEP.
I GO WHERE POCHI GOES!
?
Reeeally?
POCHI, C'MERE.
AW C'MON, UTSUHO!
...
OKAY, FOLKS...
WE'RE OFF!

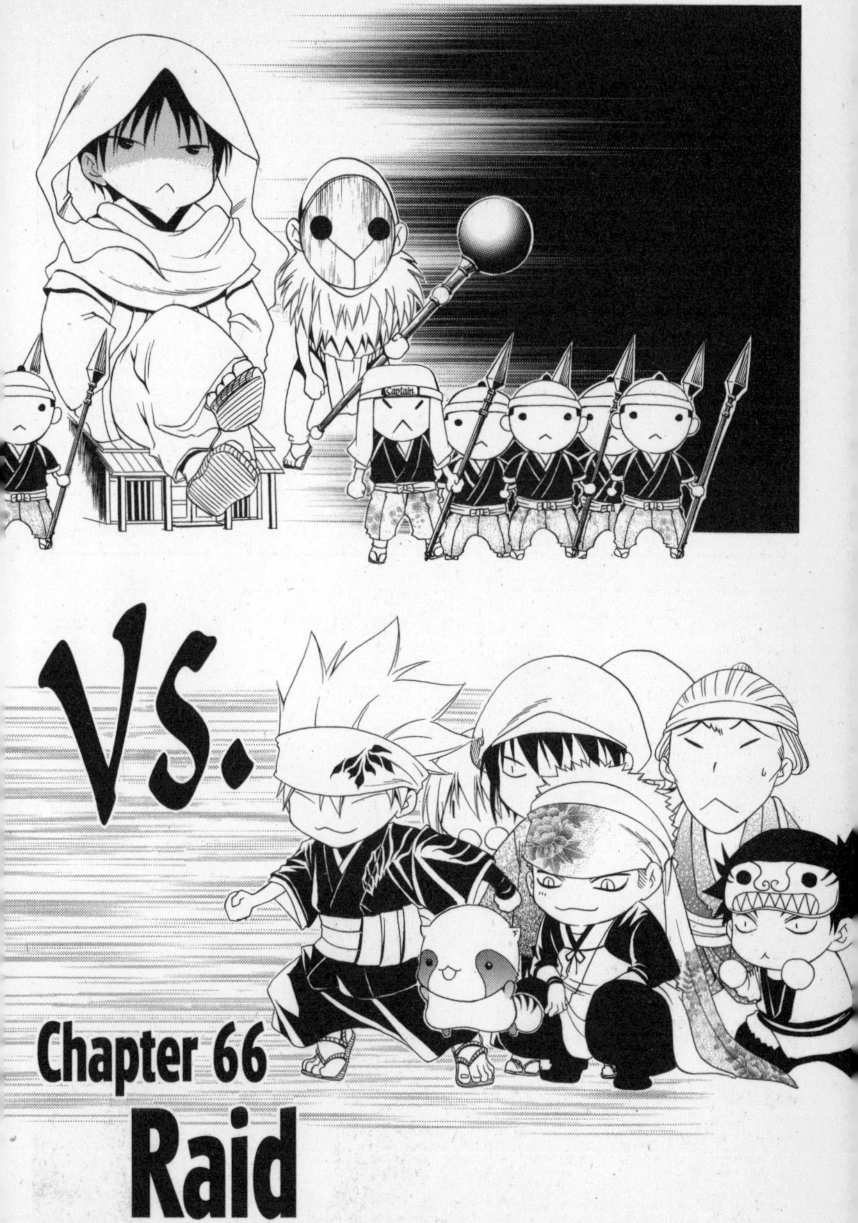
Captain
VS.

Chapter 66
Raid

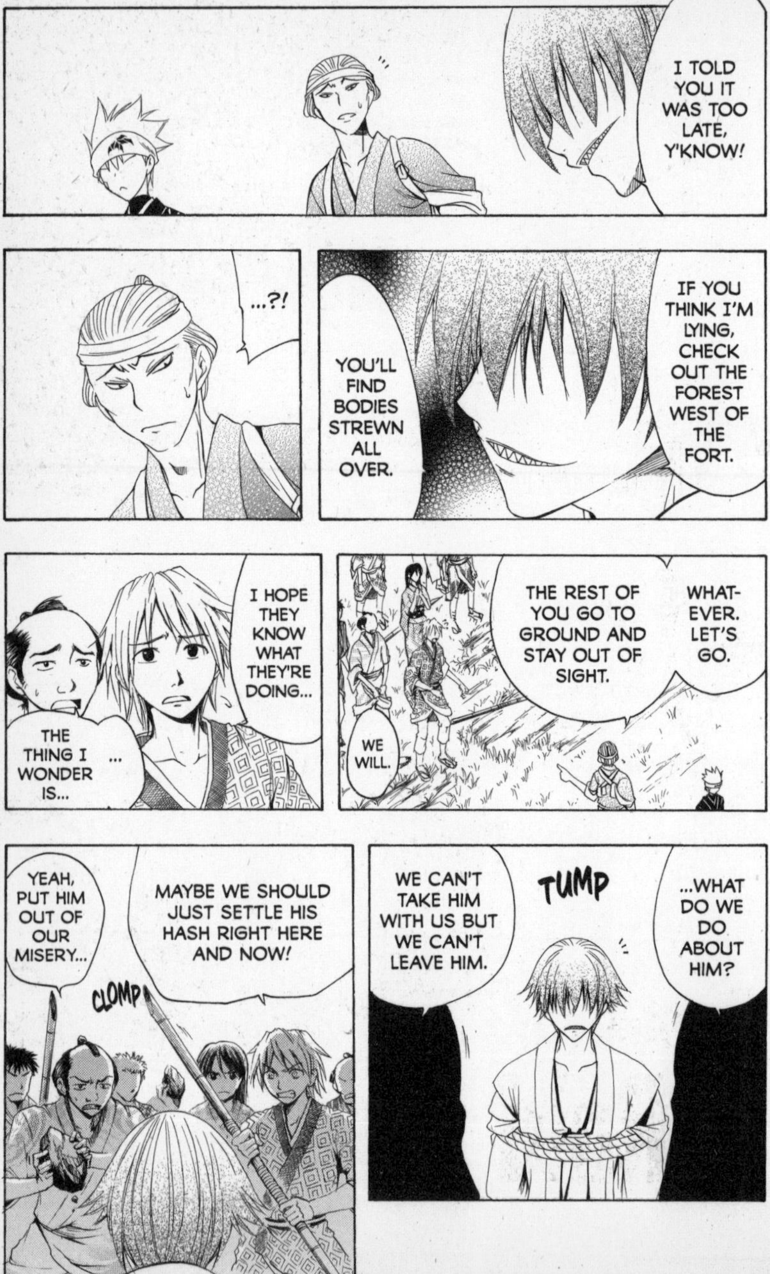
I TOLD YOU IT WAS TOO LATE, Y'KNOW!
IF YOU THINK I'M LYING, CHECK OUT THE FOREST WEST OF THE FORT.
YOU'LL FIND BODIES STREWN ALL OVER.
...?!
WHAT-EVER. LET'S GO.
THE REST OF YOU GO TO GROUND AND STAY OUT OF SIGHT.
WE WILL.
I HOPE THEY KNOW WHAT THEY'RE DOING...
...
THE THING I WONDER IS...
...WHAT DO WE DO ABOUT HIM?
TUMP
WE CAN'T TAKE HIM WITH US BUT WE CAN'T LEAVE HIM.
MAYBE WE SHOULD JUST SETTLE HIS HASH RIGHT HERE AND NOW!
CLOMP
YEAH, PUT HIM OUT OF OUR MISERY...

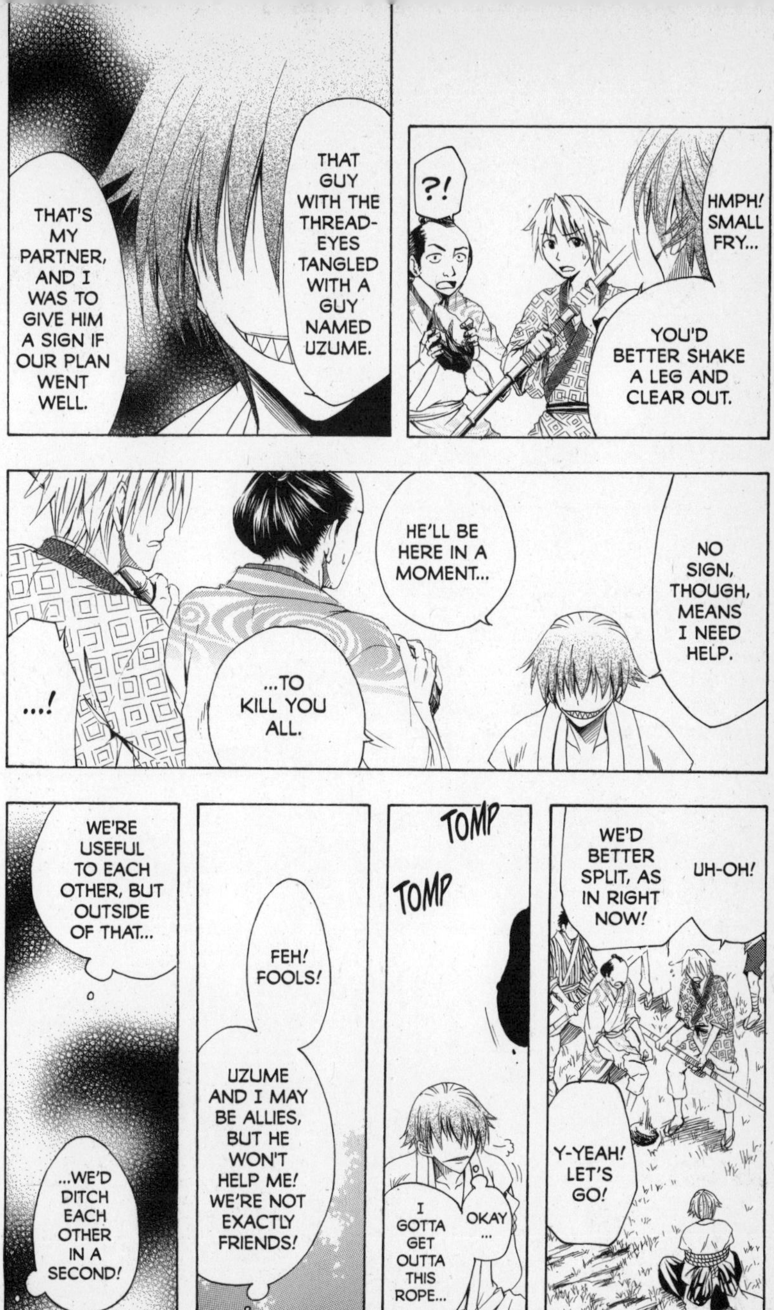
HMPH! SMALL FRY...
?!
YOU'D BETTER SHAKE A LEG AND CLEAR OUT.
THAT GUY WITH THE THREAD-EYES TANGLED WITH A GUY NAMED UZUME.
THAT'S MY PARTNER, AND I WAS TO GIVE HIM A SIGN IF OUR PLAN WENT WELL.
NO SIGN, THOUGH, MEANS I NEED HELP.
HE'LL BE HERE IN A MOMENT...
...TO KILL YOU ALL.
...!
UH-OH!
WE'D BETTER SPLIT, AS IN RIGHT NOW!
Y-YEAH! LET'S GO!
TOMP
TOMP
OKAY...
I GOTTA GET OUTTA THIS ROPE...
FEH! FOOLS!
UZUME AND I MAY BE ALLIES, BUT HE WON'T HELP ME! WE'RE NOT EXACTLY FRIENDS!
WE'RE USEFUL TO EACH OTHER, BUT OUTSIDE OF THAT...
...WE'D DITCH EACH OTHER IN A SECOND!

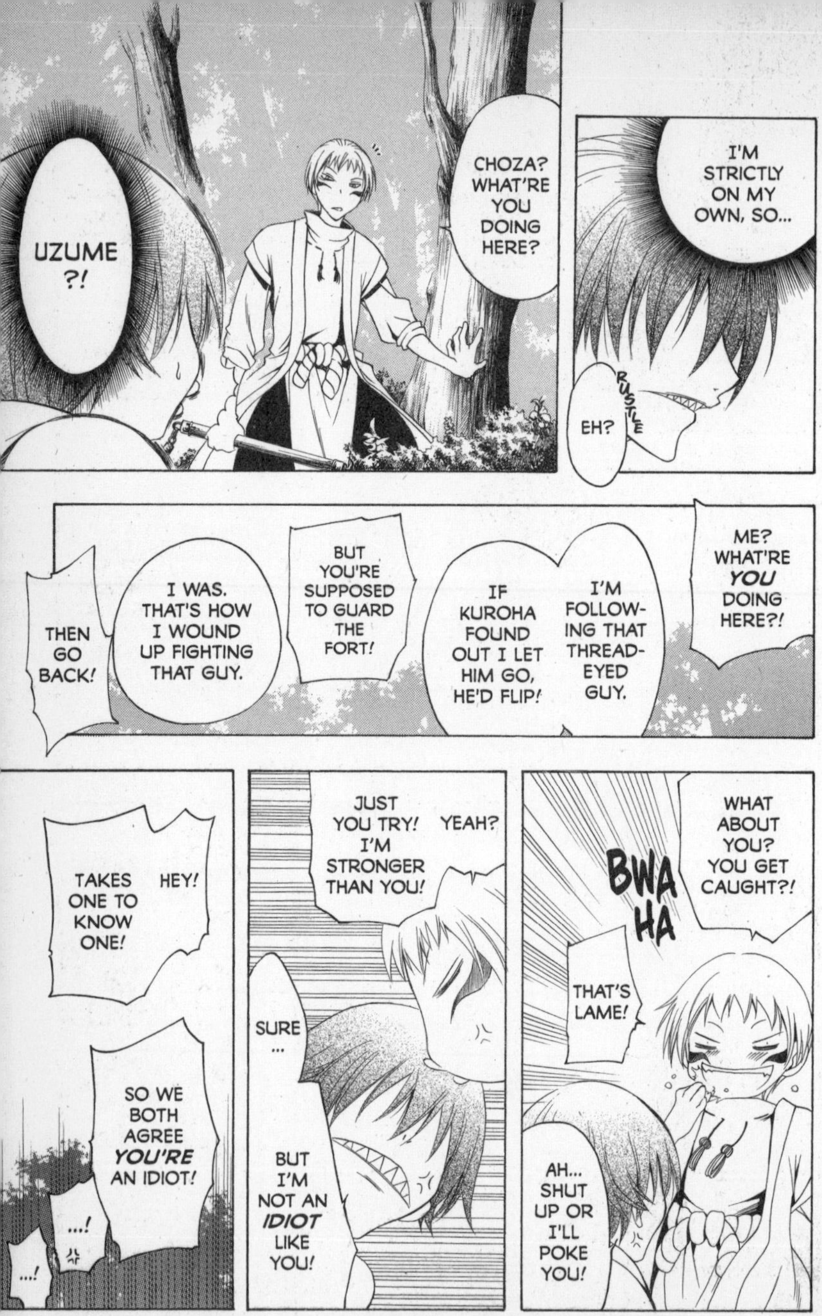

I'M STRICTLY ON MY OWN, SO...
RUSTLE
EH?
CHOZA? WHAT'RE YOU DOING HERE?
UZUME ?!
ME? WHAT'RE *YOU* DOING HERE?!
I'M FOLLOW-ING THAT THREAD-EYED GUY.
IF KUROHA FOUND OUT I LET HIM GO, HE'D FLIP!
BUT YOU'RE SUPPOSED TO GUARD THE FORT!
I WAS. THAT'S HOW I WOUND UP FIGHTING THAT GUY.
THEN GO BACK!
WHAT ABOUT YOU? YOU GET CAUGHT?!
BWA HA
THAT'S LAME!
AH... SHUT UP OR I'LL POKE YOU!
YEAH?
JUST YOU TRY! I'M STRONGER THAN YOU!
SURE ...
BUT I'M NOT AN *IDIOT* LIKE YOU!
HEY!
TAKES ONE TO KNOW ONE!
SO WE BOTH AGREE *YOU'RE* AN IDIOT!
...!
...!

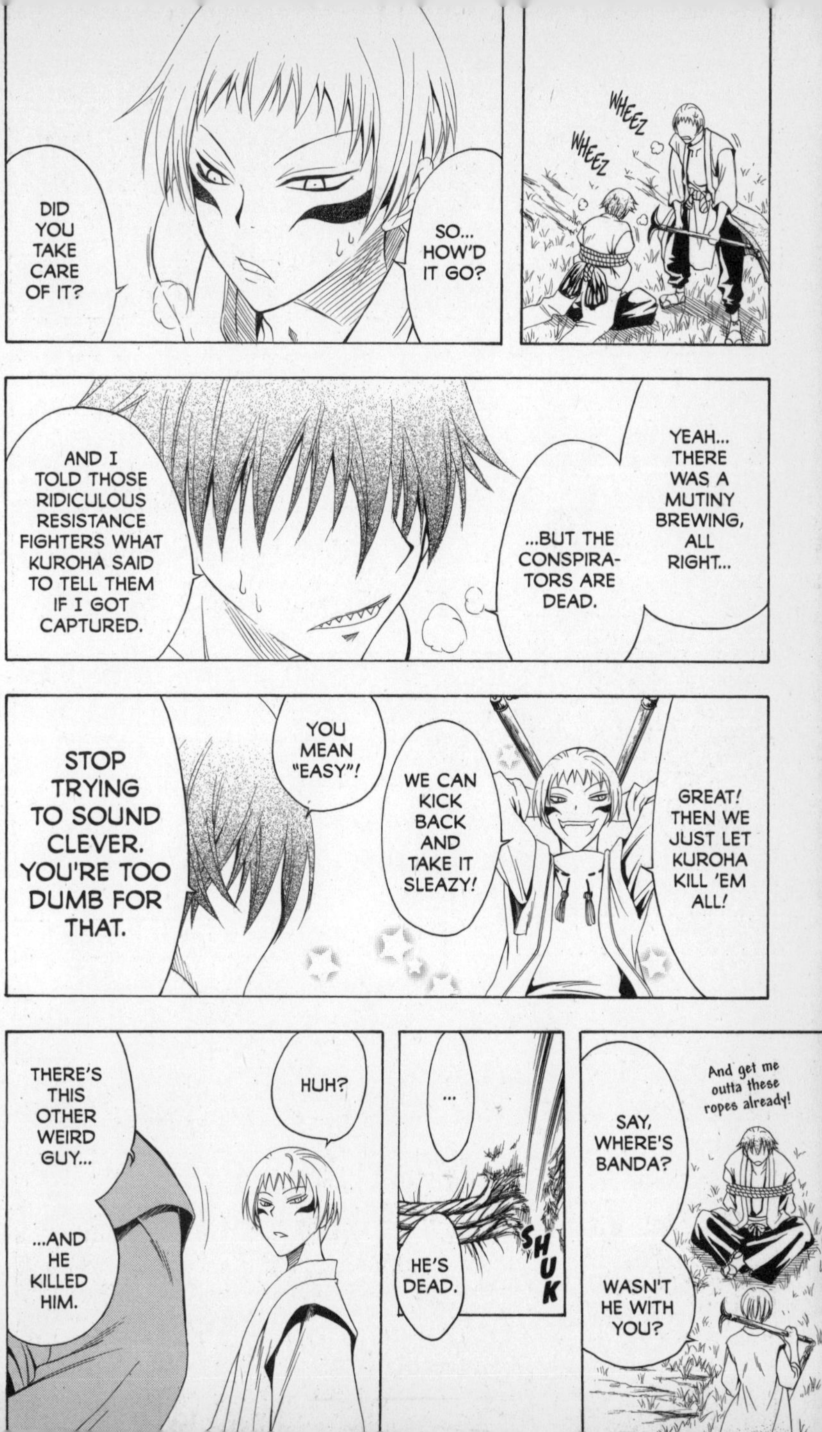

WHEEZ
WHEEZ
SO... HOW'D IT GO?
DID YOU TAKE CARE OF IT?
YEAH... THERE WAS A MUTINY BREWING, ALL RIGHT...
...BUT THE CONSPIRATORS ARE DEAD.
AND I TOLD THOSE RIDICULOUS RESISTANCE FIGHTERS WHAT KUROHA SAID TO TELL THEM IF I GOT CAPTURED.
GREAT! THEN WE JUST LET KUROHA KILL 'EM ALL!
WE CAN KICK BACK AND TAKE IT SLEAZY!
YOU MEAN "EASY"!
STOP TRYING TO SOUND CLEVER. YOU'RE TOO DUMB FOR THAT.
And get me outta these ropes already!
SAY, WHERE'S BANDA?
WASN'T HE WITH YOU?
...
SHUK
HE'S DEAD.
HUH?
THERE'S THIS OTHER WEIRD GUY...
...AND HE KILLED HIM.

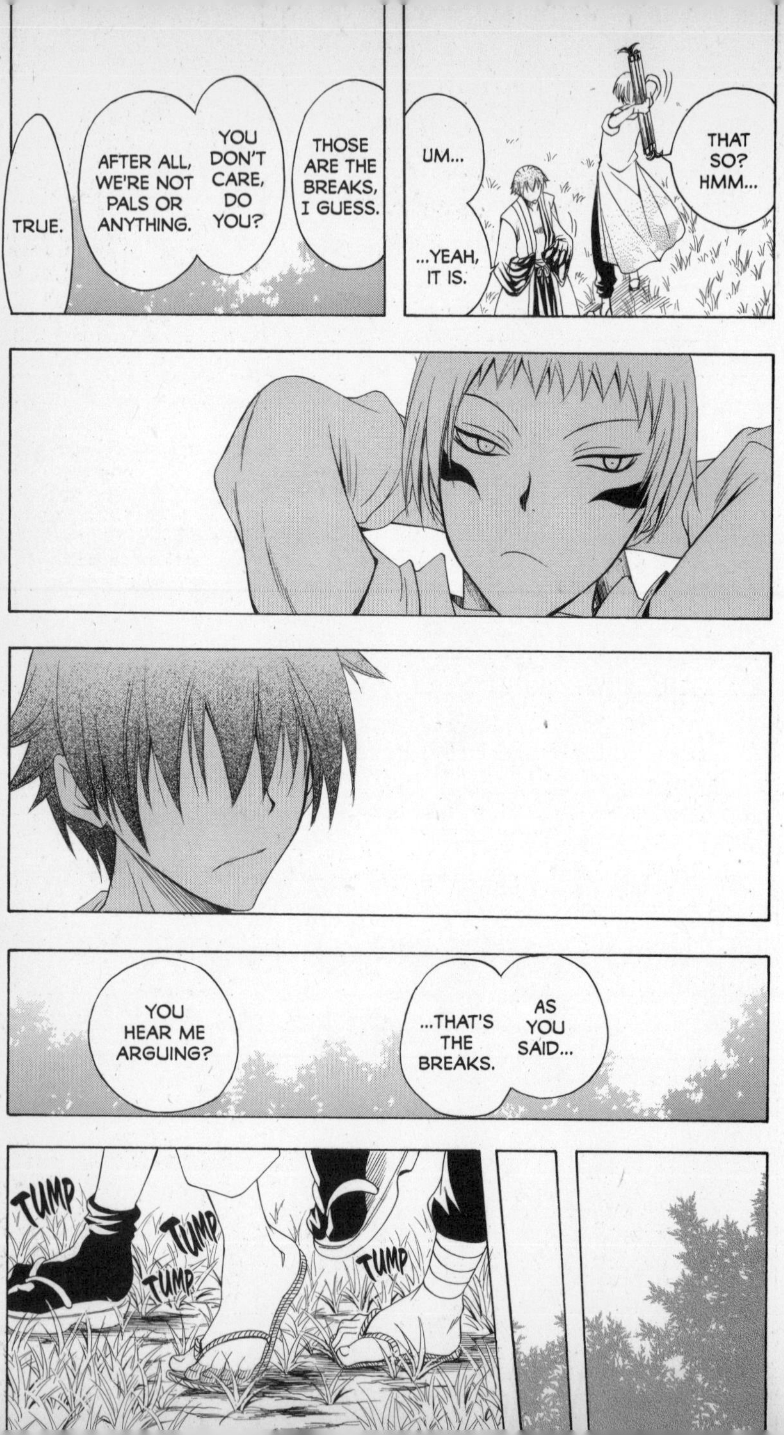
THAT SO? HMM...
UM...
...YEAH, IT IS.
THOSE ARE THE BREAKS, I GUESS.
YOU DON'T CARE, DO YOU?
AFTER ALL, WE'RE NOT PALS OR ANYTHING.
TRUE.
AS YOU SAID...
...THAT'S THE BREAKS.
YOU HEAR ME ARGUING?
TUMP
TUMP
TUMP
TUMP

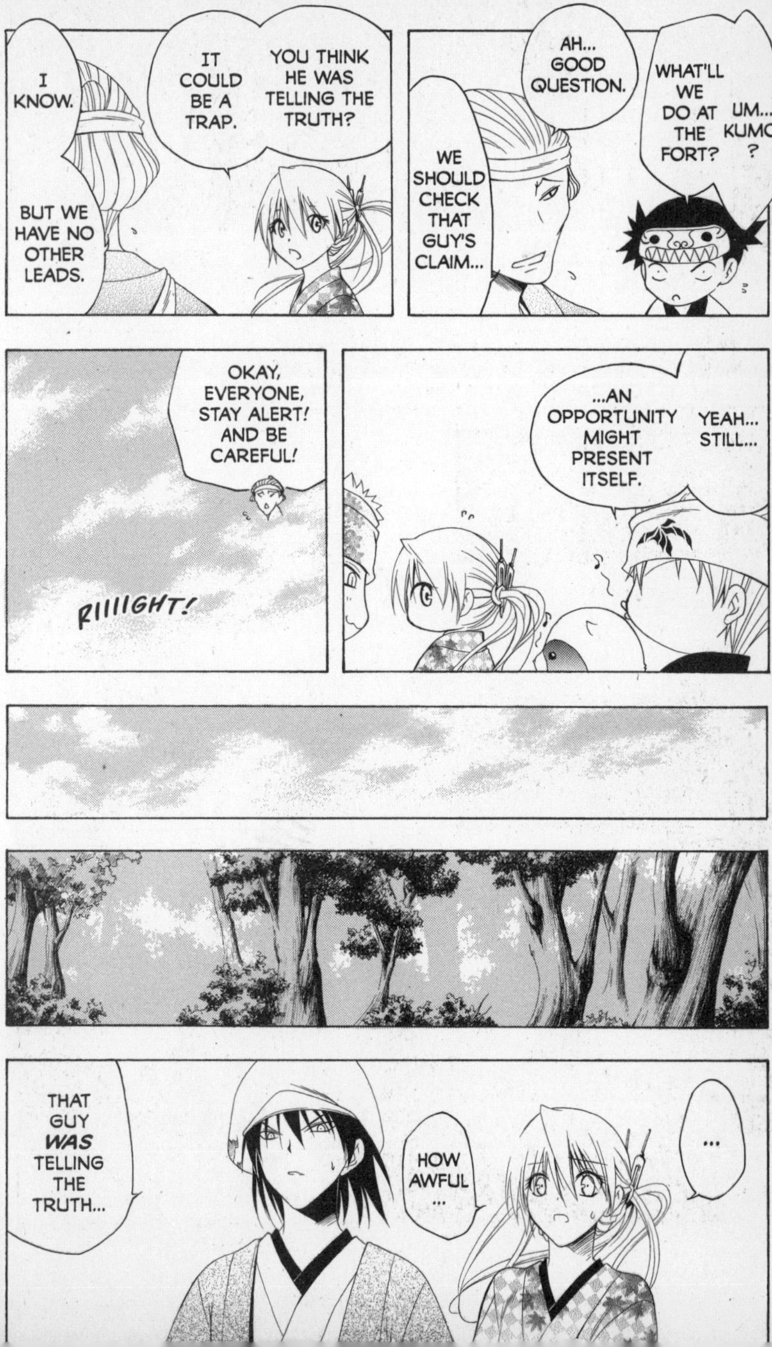
UM... KUMOI?
WHAT'LL WE DO AT THE FORT?
AH... GOOD QUESTION.
WE SHOULD CHECK THAT GUY'S CLAIM...
YOU THINK HE WAS TELLING THE TRUTH?
IT COULD BE A TRAP.
I KNOW.
BUT WE HAVE NO OTHER LEADS.
YEAH... STILL...
...AN OPPORTUNITY MIGHT PRESENT ITSELF.
OKAY, EVERYONE, STAY ALERT! AND BE CAREFUL!
RIIIIGHT!
...
HOW AWFUL...
THAT GUY *WAS* TELLING THE TRUTH...

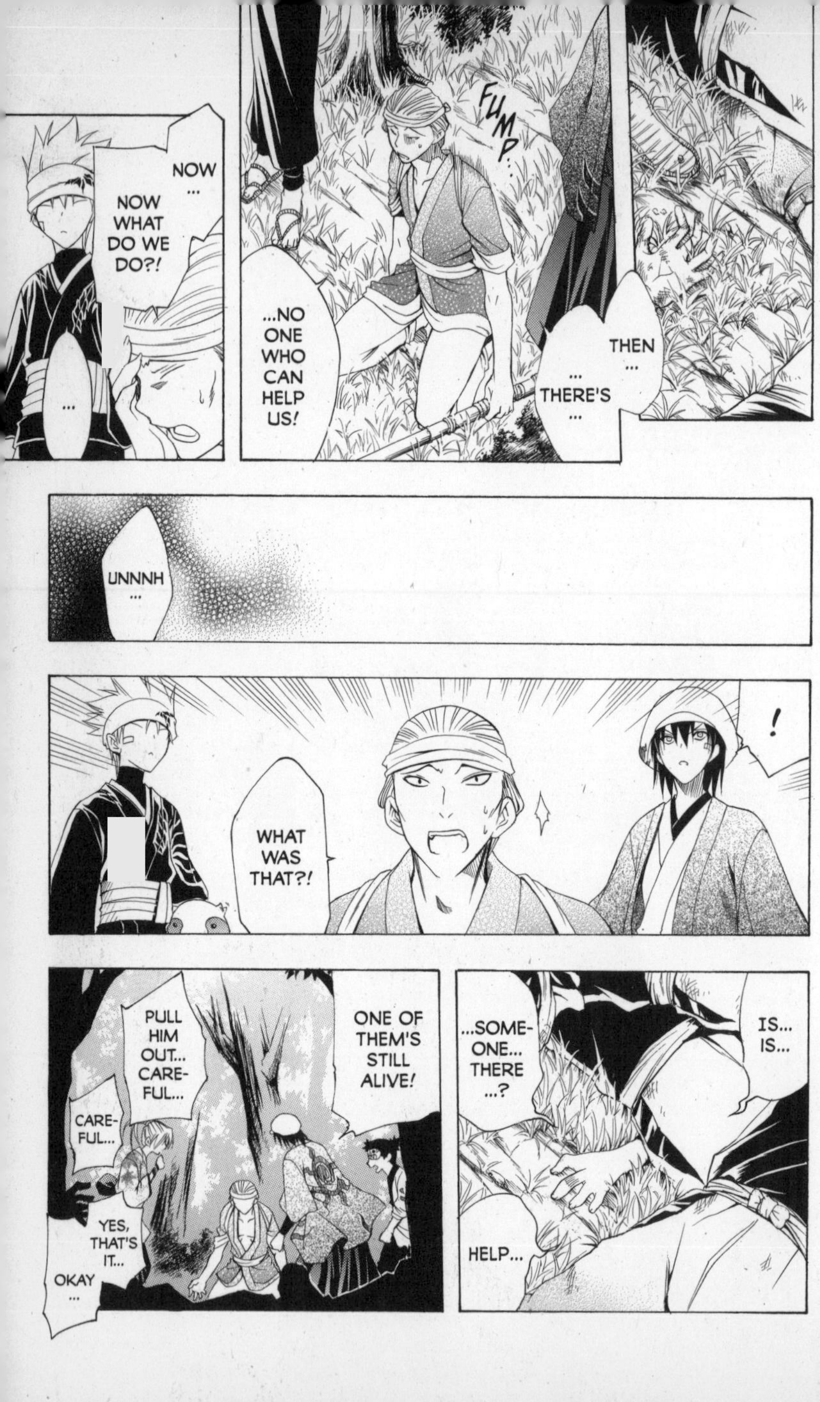
THEN...
...THERE'S...
FUMP...
...NO ONE WHO CAN HELP US!
NOW...
NOW WHAT DO WE DO?!
...
UNNNH...
!
WHAT WAS THAT?!
IS... IS...
...SOME-ONE... THERE...?
HELP...
ONE OF THEM'S STILL ALIVE!
PULL HIM OUT... CARE-FUL...
CARE-FUL...
YES, THAT'S IT...
OKAY...

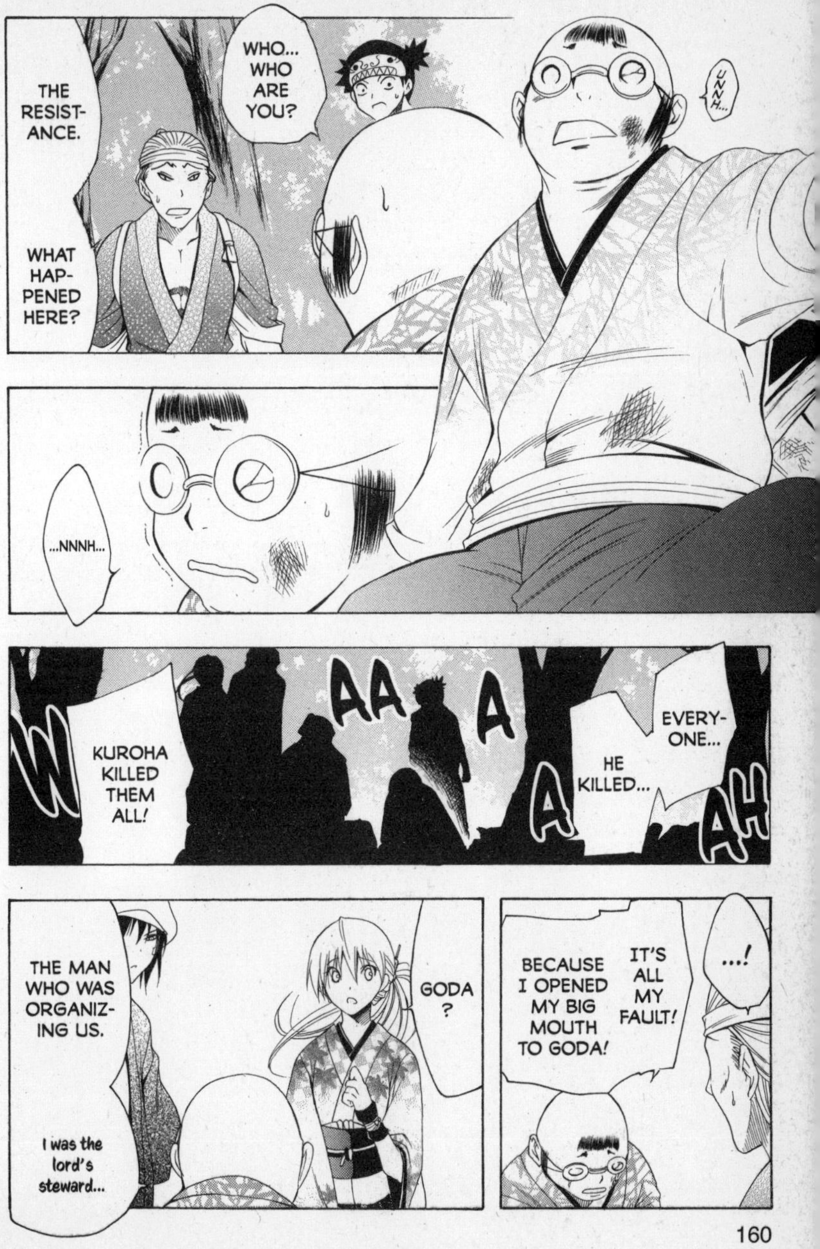
UNNH...
WHO... WHO ARE YOU?
THE RESISTANCE.
WHAT HAPPENED HERE?
...NNNH...
EVERYONE...
HE KILLED...
KUROHA KILLED THEM ALL!
W AA A A AH
...!
IT'S ALL MY FAULT!
BECAUSE I OPENED MY BIG MOUTH TO GODA!
GODA?
THE MAN WHO WAS ORGANIZING US.
I was the lord's steward...

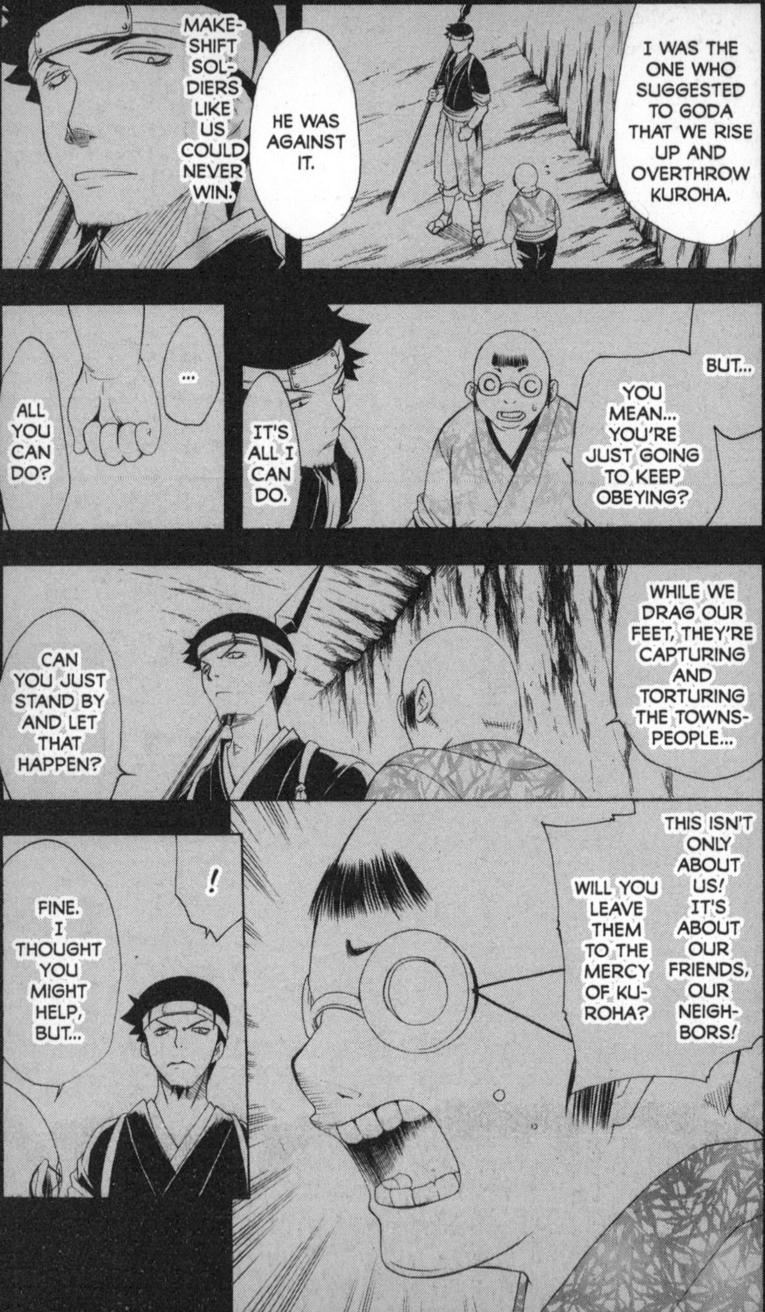
I WAS THE ONE WHO SUGGESTED TO GODA THAT WE RISE UP AND OVERTHROW KUROHA.
HE WAS AGAINST IT.
MAKESHIFT SOLDIERS LIKE US COULD NEVER WIN.
BUT...
YOU MEAN... YOU'RE JUST GOING TO KEEP OBEYING?
IT'S ALL I CAN DO.
...
ALL YOU CAN DO?
WHILE WE DRAG OUR FEET, THEY'RE CAPTURING AND TORTURING THE TOWNSPEOPLE...
CAN YOU JUST STAND BY AND LET THAT HAPPEN?
THIS ISN'T ONLY ABOUT US! IT'S ABOUT OUR FRIENDS, OUR NEIGHBORS!
WILL YOU LEAVE THEM TO THE MERCY OF KUROHA?
!
FINE. I THOUGHT YOU MIGHT HELP, BUT...

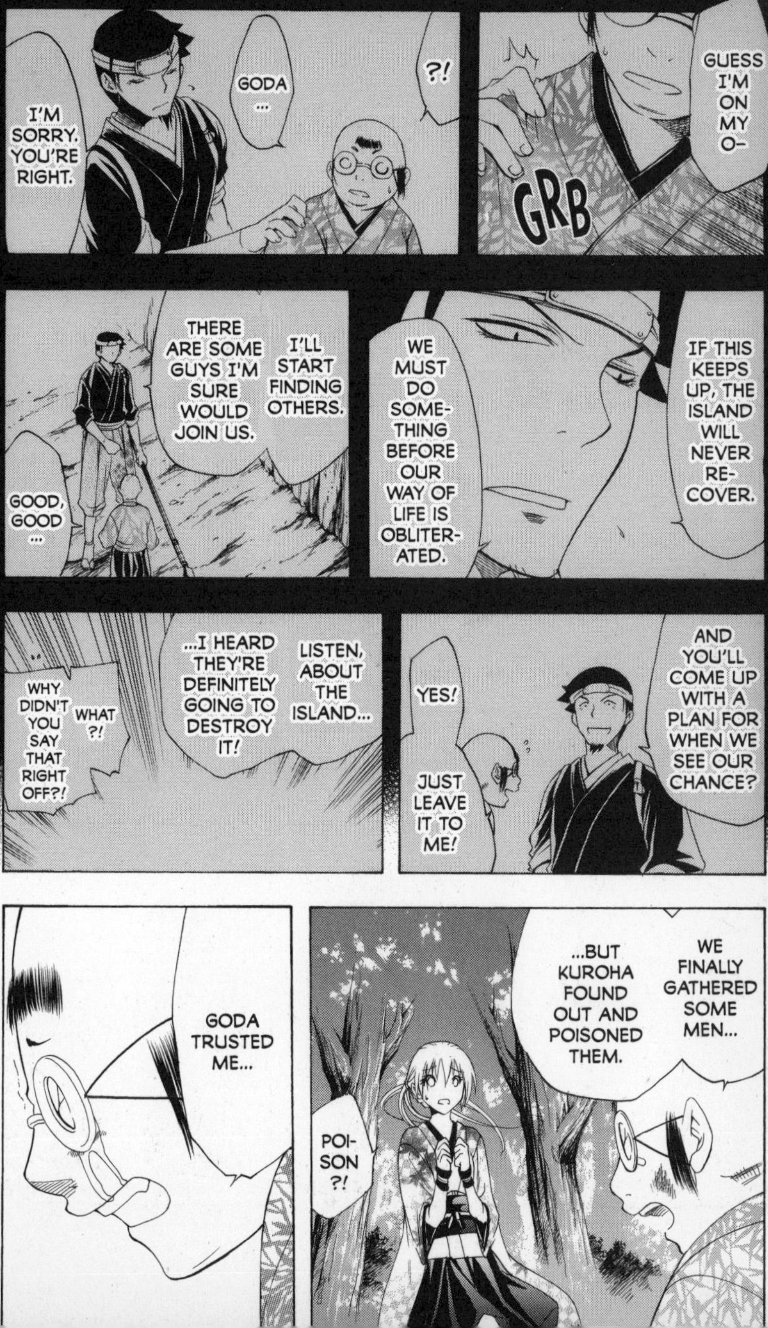
GUESS I'M ON MY O-
GRB
?!
GODA ...
I'M SORRY. YOU'RE RIGHT.
IF THIS KEEPS UP, THE ISLAND WILL NEVER RE-COVER.
WE MUST DO SOME-THING BEFORE OUR WAY OF LIFE IS OBLITER-ATED.
I'LL START FINDING OTHERS.
THERE ARE SOME GUYS I'M SURE WOULD JOIN US.
GOOD, GOOD ...
AND YOU'LL COME UP WITH A PLAN FOR WHEN WE SEE OUR CHANCE?
YES!
JUST LEAVE IT TO ME!
LISTEN, ABOUT THE ISLAND...
...I HEARD THEY'RE DEFINITELY GOING TO DESTROY IT!
...
WHAT ?!
WHY DIDN'T YOU SAY THAT RIGHT OFF?!
WE FINALLY GATHERED SOME MEN...
...BUT KUROHA FOUND OUT AND POISONED THEM.
POI-SON ?!
GODA TRUSTED ME...

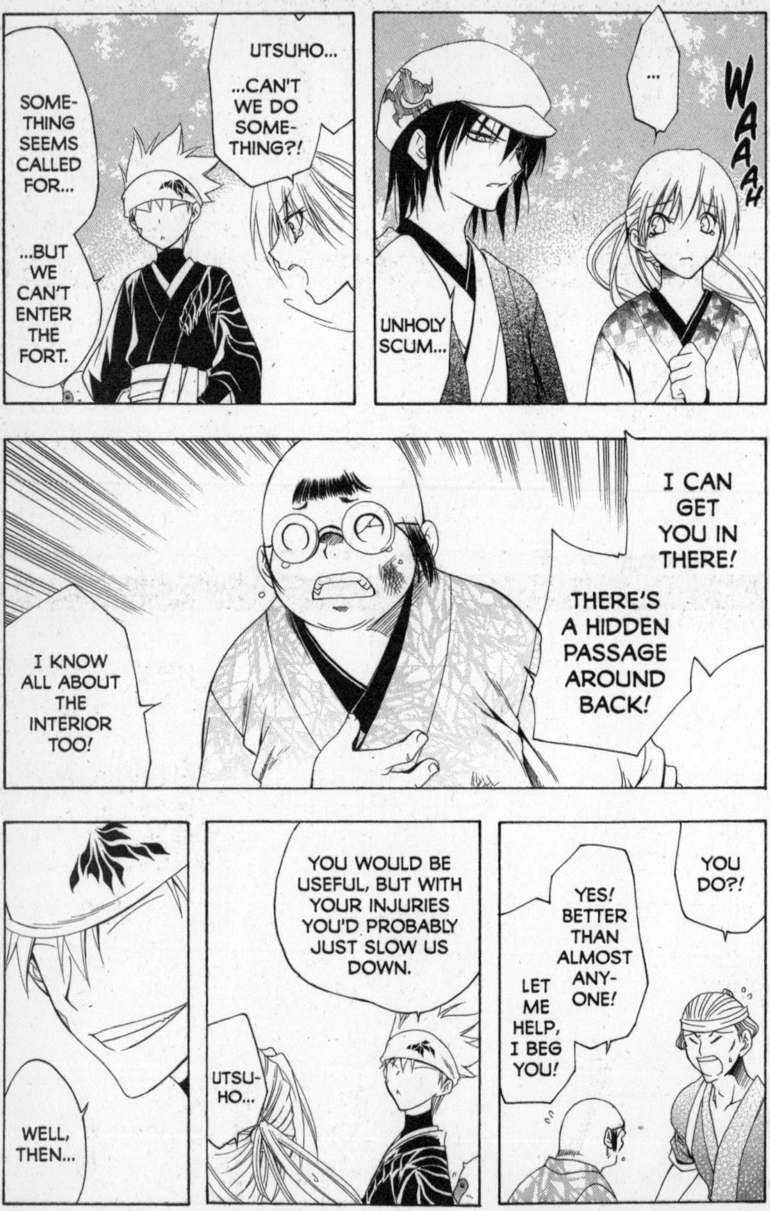
...
WAAAH
UNHOLY SCUM...
UTSUHO... ...CAN'T WE DO SOMETHING?!
SOMETHING SEEMS CALLED FOR... ...BUT WE CAN'T ENTER THE FORT.
I CAN GET YOU IN THERE!
THERE'S A HIDDEN PASSAGE AROUND BACK!
I KNOW ALL ABOUT THE INTERIOR TOO!
YOU DO?!
YES! BETTER THAN ALMOST ANYONE!
LET ME HELP, I BEG YOU!
YOU WOULD BE USEFUL, BUT WITH YOUR INJURIES YOU'D PROBABLY JUST SLOW US DOWN.
UTSUHO...
WELL, THEN...

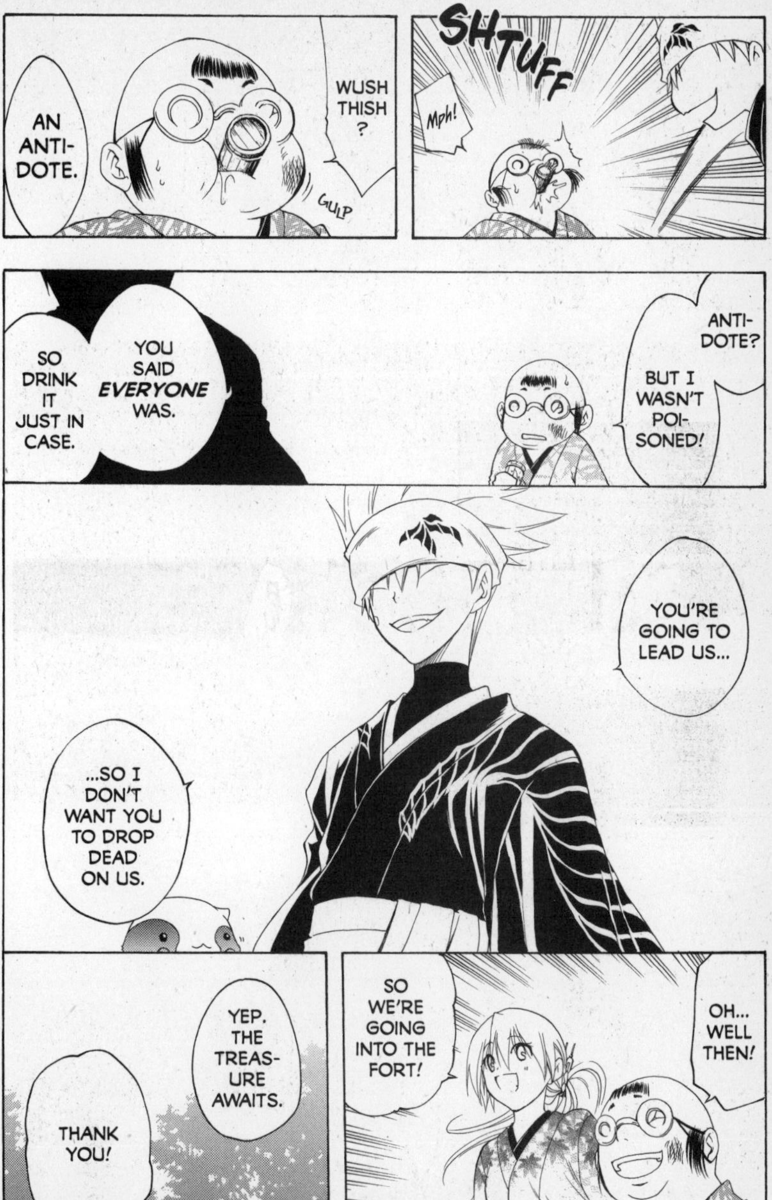
SHTUFF
Mph!
WUSH THISH?
AN ANTIDOTE.
GULP
ANTIDOTE?
BUT I WASN'T POISONED!
YOU SAID *EVERYONE* WAS.
SO DRINK IT JUST IN CASE.
YOU'RE GOING TO LEAD US...
...SO I DON'T WANT YOU TO DROP DEAD ON US.
OH... WELL THEN!
SO WE'RE GOING INTO THE FORT!
YEP. THE TREASURE AWAITS.
THANK YOU!

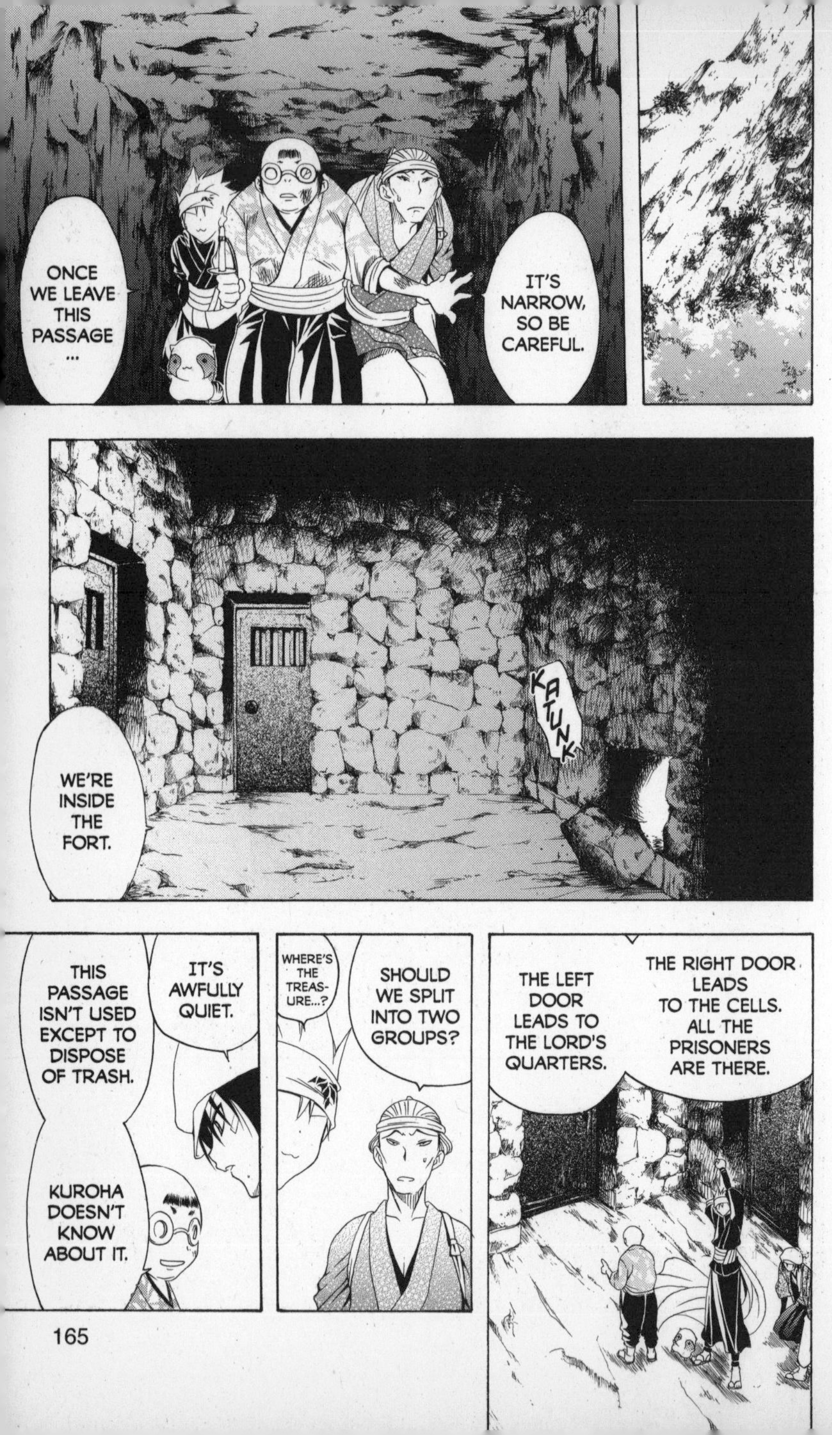
IT'S NARROW, SO BE CAREFUL.
ONCE WE LEAVE THIS PASSAGE...
KATUNK
WE'RE INSIDE THE FORT.
THE RIGHT DOOR LEADS TO THE CELLS. ALL THE PRISONERS ARE THERE.
THE LEFT DOOR LEADS TO THE LORD'S QUARTERS.
SHOULD WE SPLIT INTO TWO GROUPS?
WHERE'S THE TREASURE...?
IT'S AWFULLY QUIET.
THIS PASSAGE ISN'T USED EXCEPT TO DISPOSE OF TRASH.
KUROHA DOESN'T KNOW ABOUT IT.

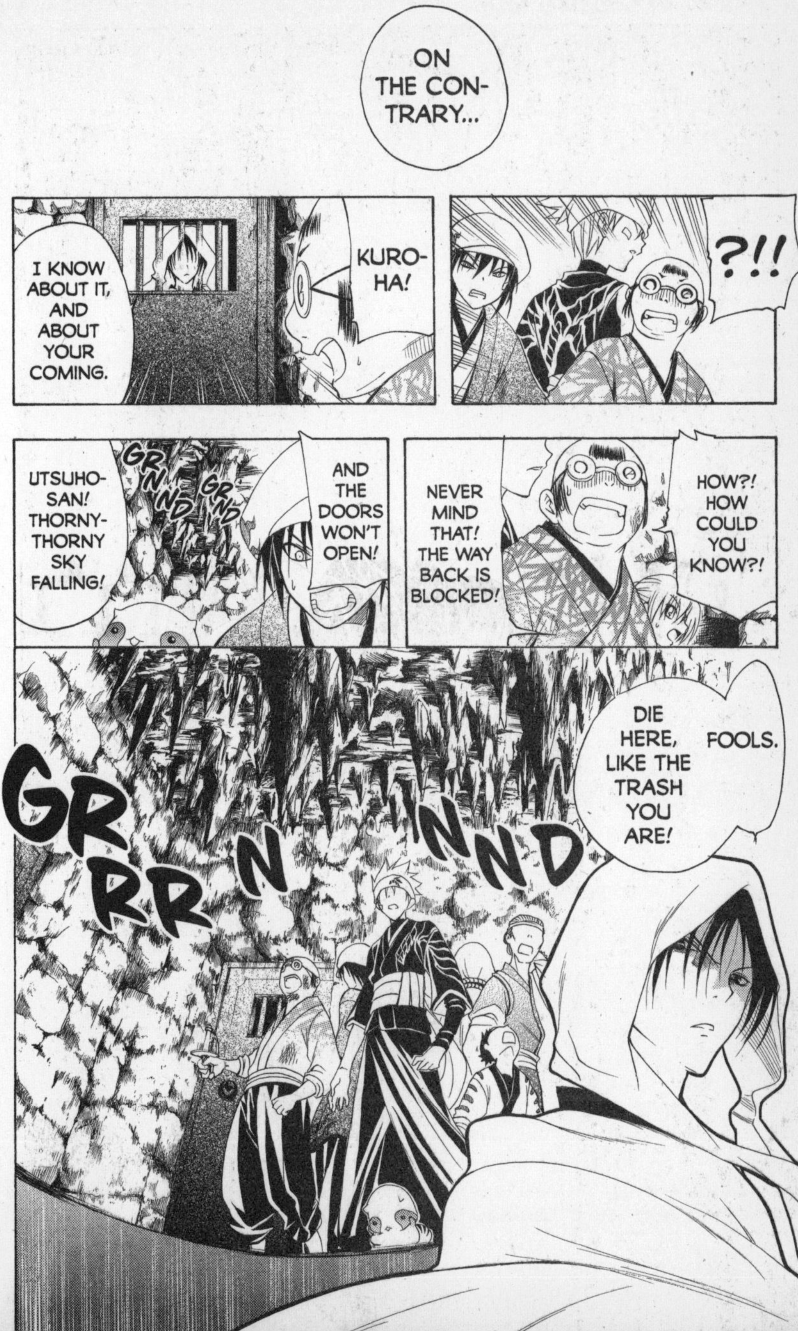
ON THE CON-TRARY...
?!!
KURO-HA!
I KNOW ABOUT IT, AND ABOUT YOUR COMING.
HOW?! HOW COULD YOU KNOW?!
NEVER MIND THAT! THE WAY BACK IS BLOCKED!
AND THE DOORS WON'T OPEN!
GRNND GRND
UTSUHO-SAN! THORNY-THORNY SKY FALLING!
FOOLS.
DIE HERE, LIKE THE TRASH YOU ARE!
GRRRNNNND

Chapter 67 Split Up

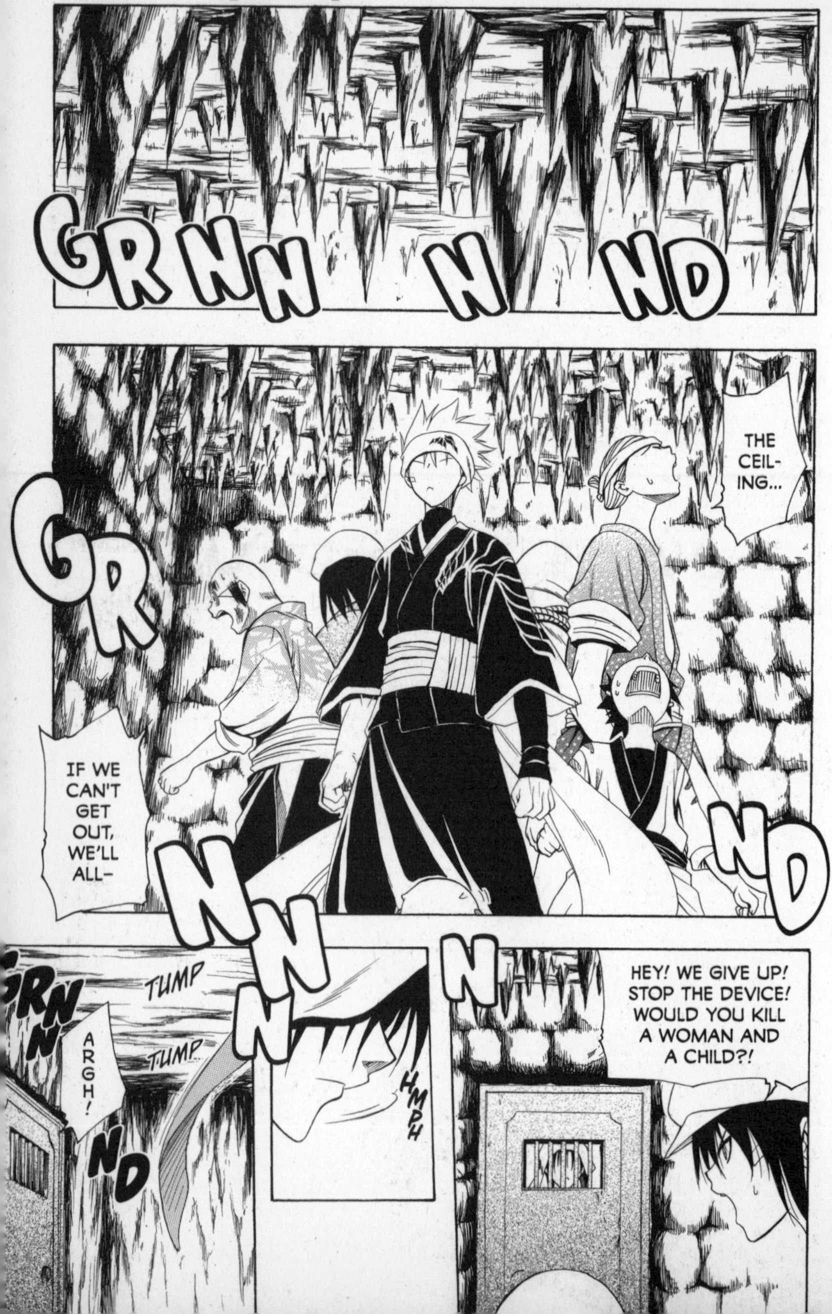
GRNN N ND
THE CEIL-ING...
GR
IF WE CAN'T GET OUT, WE'LL ALL–
NNNN ND
HEY! WE GIVE UP! STOP THE DEVICE! WOULD YOU KILL A WOMAN AND A CHILD?!
HMPH
TUMP
TUMP
ARGH!
GRNN ND

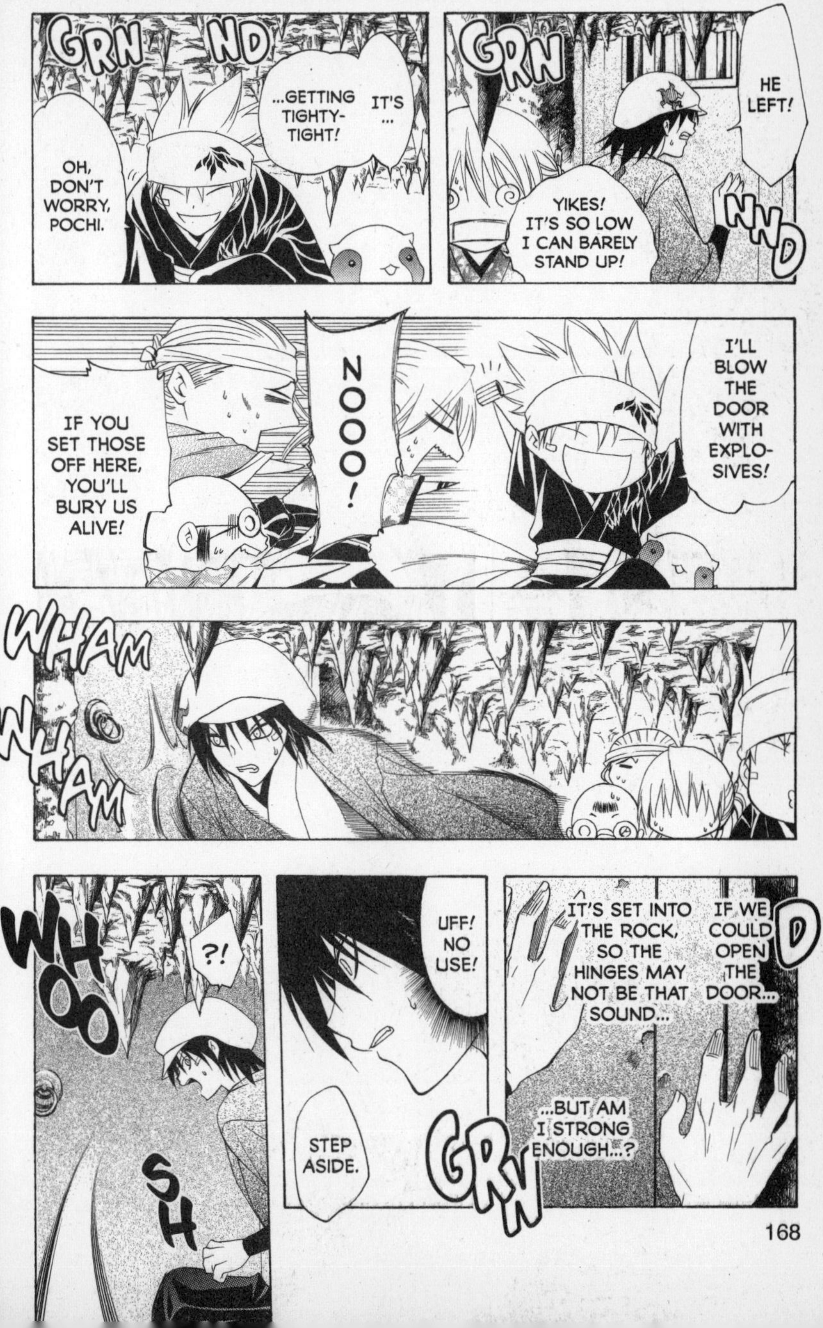
GRN
HE LEFT!
NND
YIKES! IT'S SO LOW I CAN BARELY STAND UP!
GRN ND
IT'S ...
...GETTING TIGHTY-TIGHT!
OH, DON'T WORRY, POCHI.
I'LL BLOW THE DOOR WITH EXPLOSIVES!
NOOO!
IF YOU SET THOSE OFF HERE, YOU'LL BURY US ALIVE!
WHAM
WHAM
D
IF WE COULD OPEN THE DOOR...
IT'S SET INTO THE ROCK, SO THE HINGES MAY NOT BE THAT SOUND...
...BUT AM I STRONG ENOUGH...?
GRN
UFF! NO USE!
STEP ASIDE.
?!
WHOO
SH

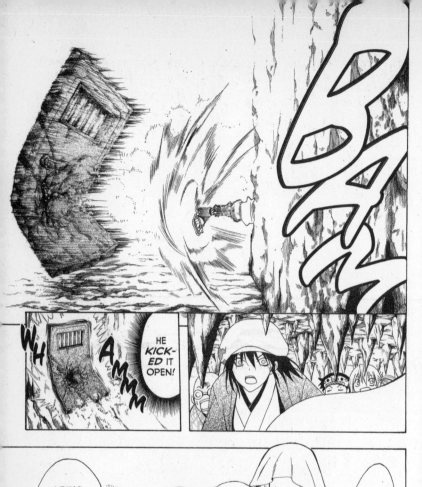

BAMM

WH AMMM

HE *KICK-ED* IT OPEN!

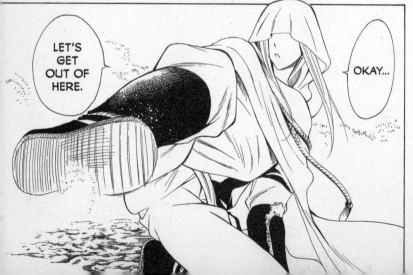

LET'S GET OUT OF HERE.

OKAY...

Chapter 67
Split Up

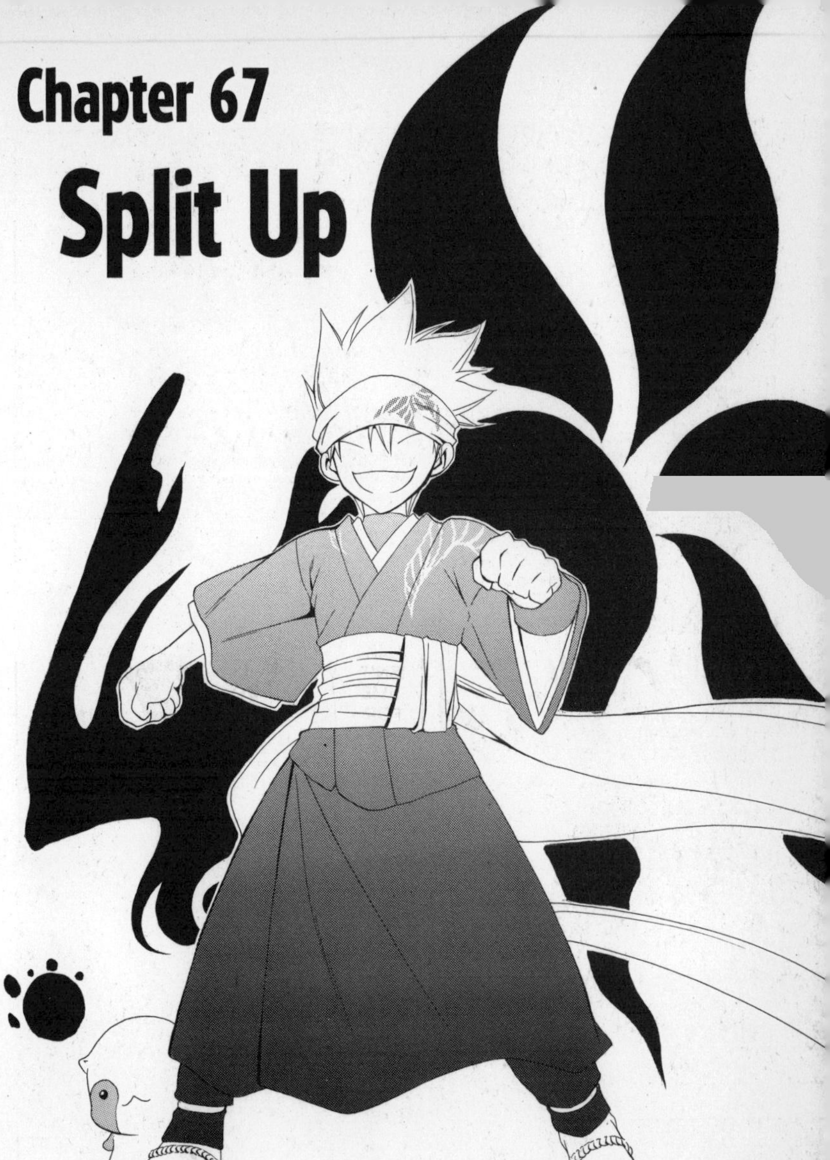

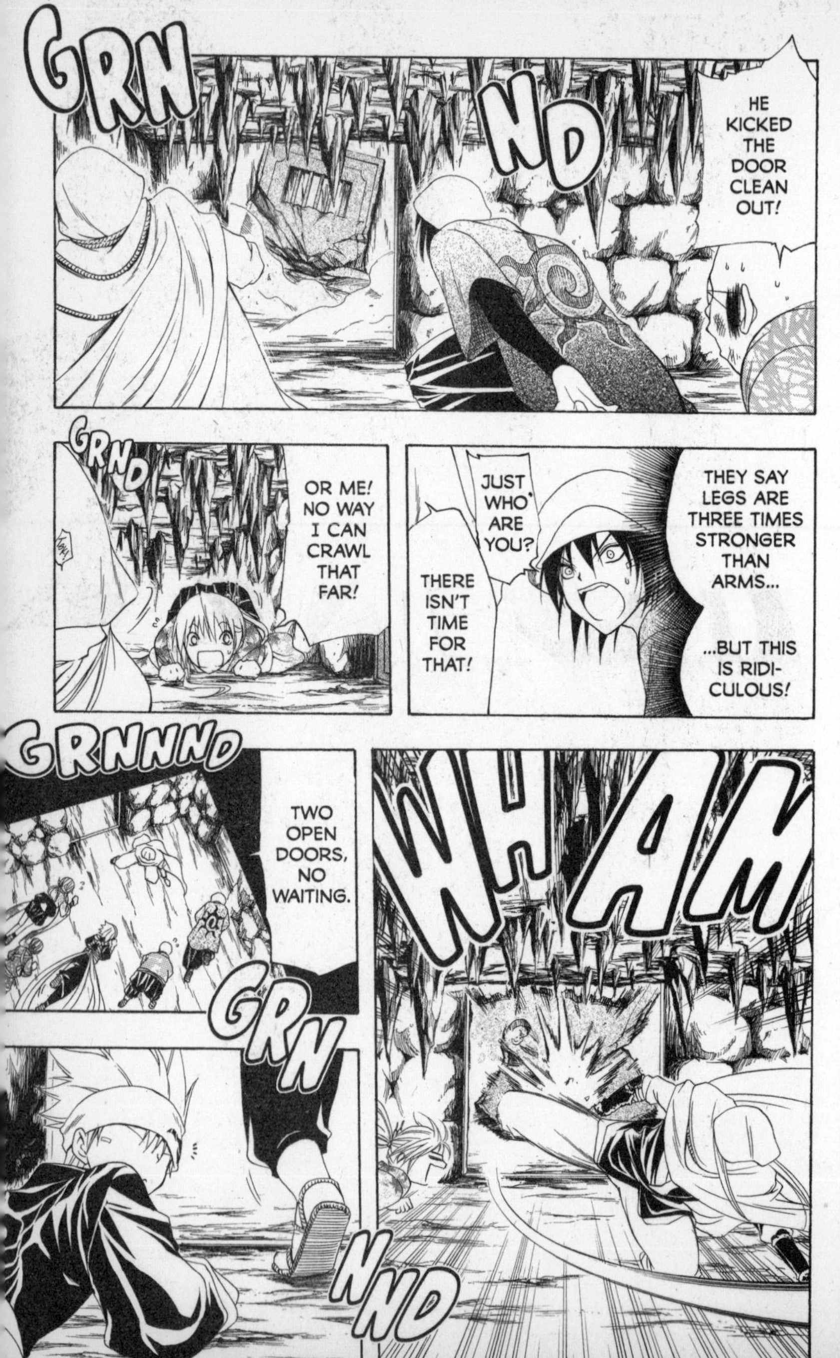
GRN
ND
HE KICKED THE DOOR CLEAN OUT!
THEY SAY LEGS ARE THREE TIMES STRONGER THAN ARMS...
...BUT THIS IS RIDI-CULOUS!
JUST WHO ARE YOU?
THERE ISN'T TIME FOR THAT!
GRND
OR ME! NO WAY I CAN CRAWL THAT FAR!
WHAM
GRNNND
TWO OPEN DOORS, NO WAITING.
GRN
NND

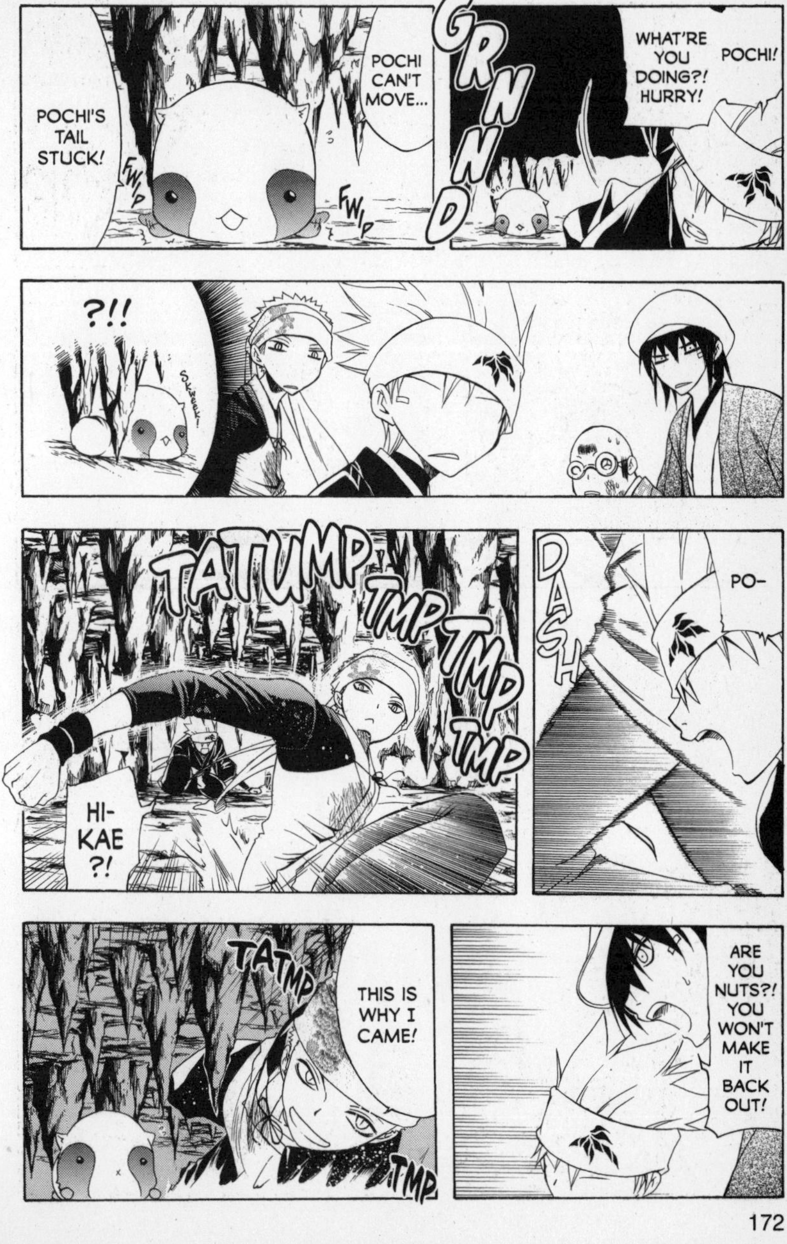
POCHI!
WHAT'RE YOU DOING?! HURRY!
GRNND
POCHI CAN'T MOVE...
POCHI'S TAIL STUCK!
FWIP
FWIP
?!!
SKWEEK!
PO-
DASH
TATUMP
TMP TMP TMP
HI-KAE?!
ARE YOU NUTS?! YOU WON'T MAKE IT BACK OUT!
TATMP
THIS IS WHY I CAME!
TMP

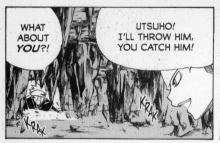

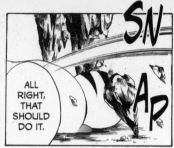

SNAP
ALL RIGHT, THAT SHOULD DO IT.
UTSUHO! I'LL THROW HIM, YOU CATCH HIM!
WHAT ABOUT *YOU*?!
KRAK
KRAK
DON'T WORRY ABOUT ME!
FWISH
IT'LL JUST HURT A LITTLE.
POCHI, WHAT'RE YOU DOING?
WHAT ABOUT NIBYO-SAN?
I'LL BE FINE.
YOU KNOW I CAN'T DIE, DON'T YOU?
GRNNNND
YES, BUT...

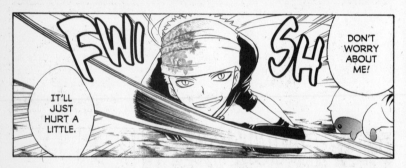

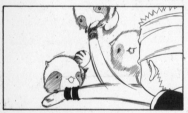

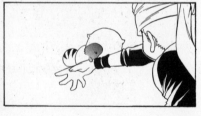

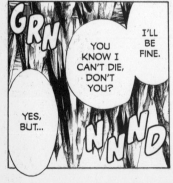

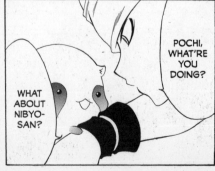

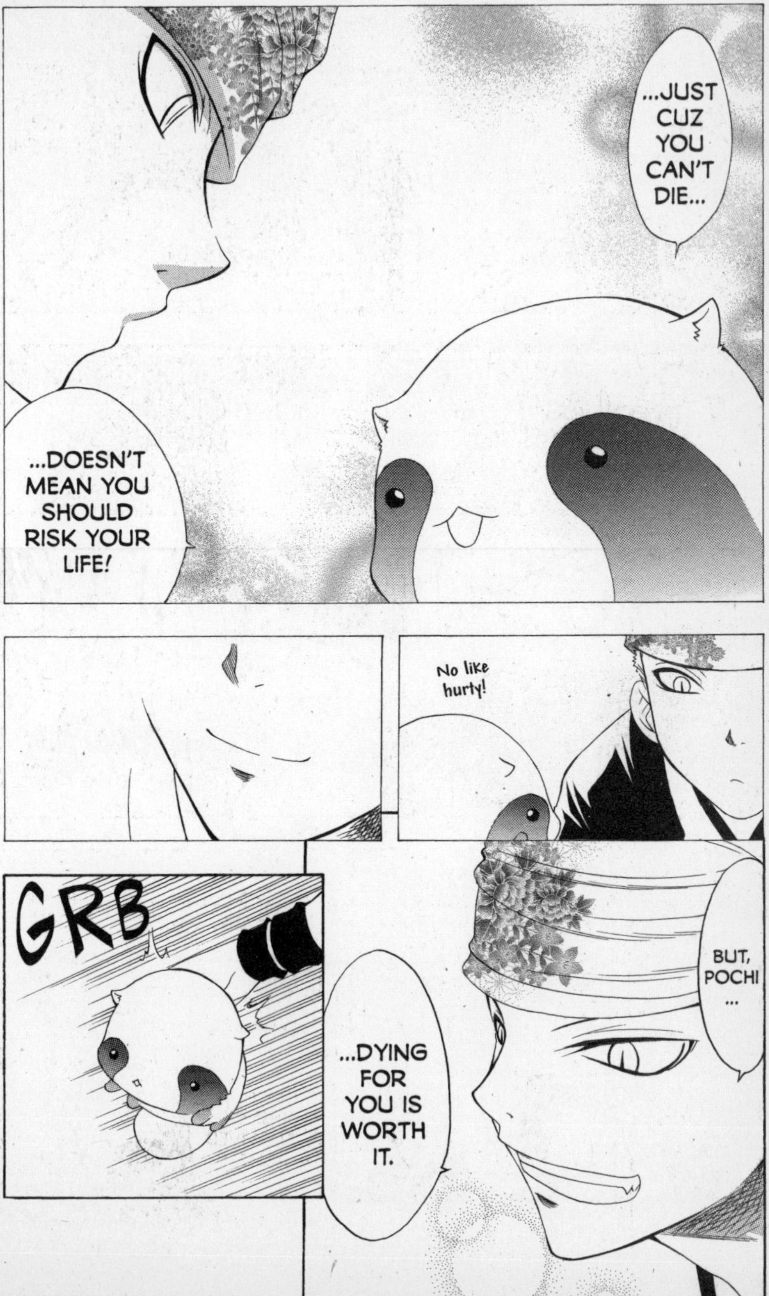
...JUST CUZ YOU CAN'T DIE...
...DOESN'T MEAN YOU SHOULD RISK YOUR LIFE!
No like hurty!
BUT, POCHI...
...DYING FOR YOU IS WORTH IT.
GRB

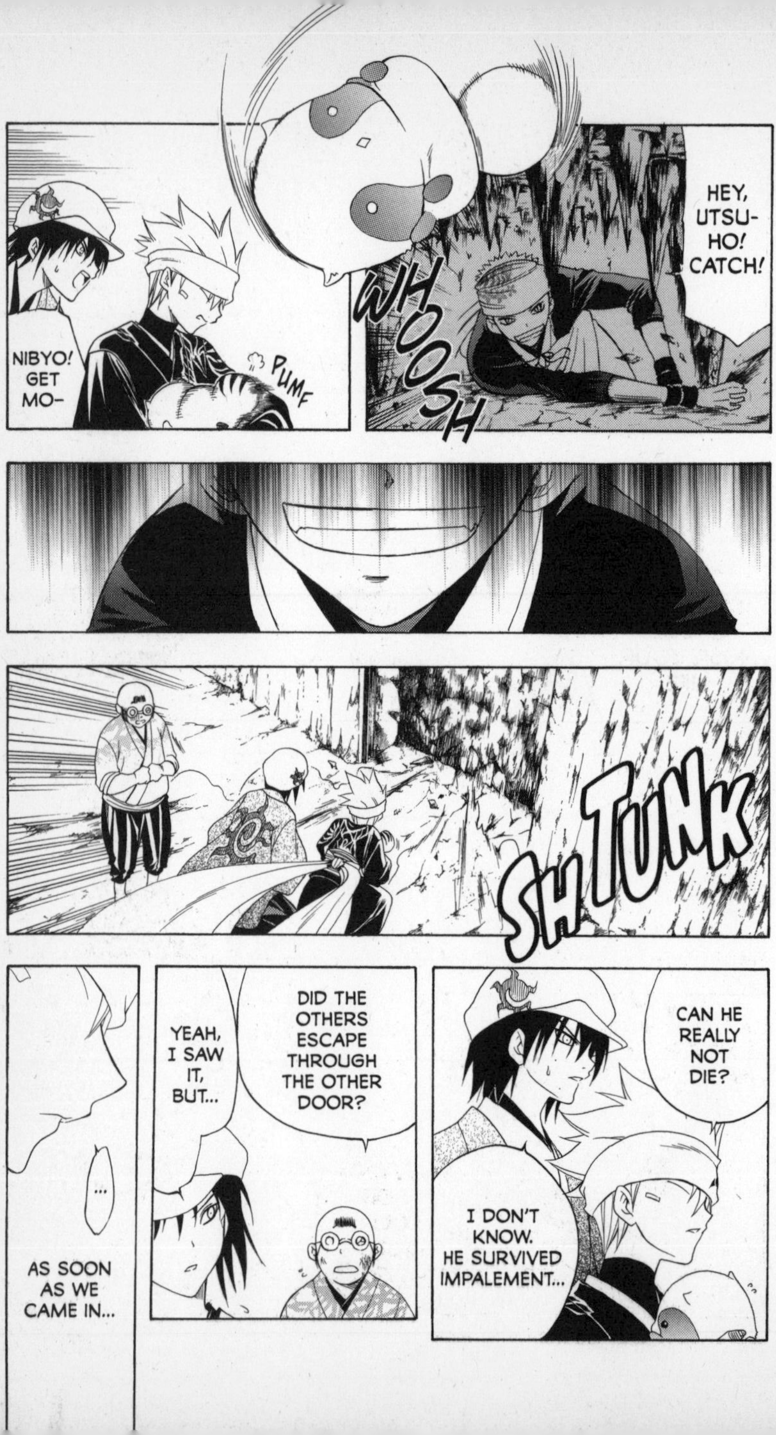
HEY, UTSU-HO! CATCH!
WHOOSH
NIBYO! GET MO-
PUMF
SHTUNK
CAN HE REALLY NOT DIE?
I DON'T KNOW. HE SURVIVED IMPALEMENT...
DID THE OTHERS ESCAPE THROUGH THE OTHER DOOR?
YEAH, I SAW IT, BUT...
...
AS SOON AS WE CAME IN...

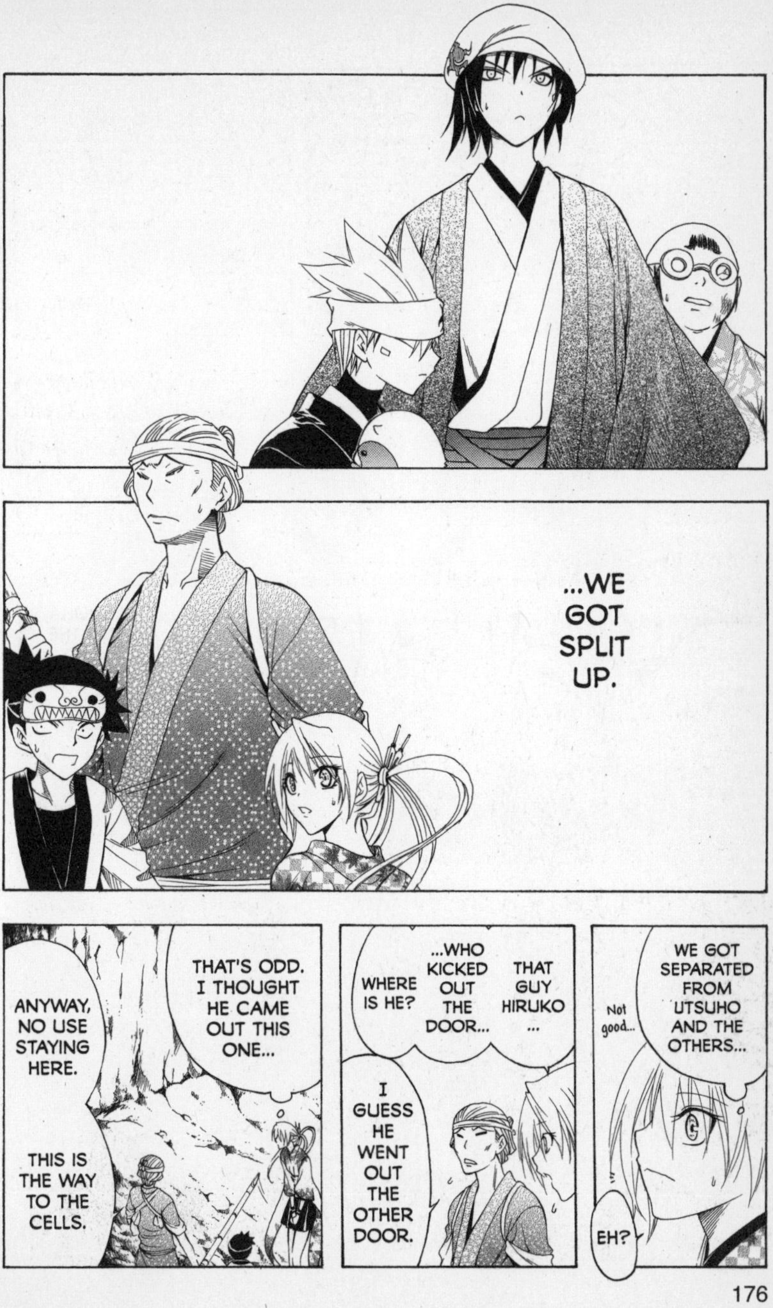
...WE GOT SPLIT UP.
WE GOT SEPARATED FROM UTSUHO AND THE OTHERS...
Not good...
EH?
THAT GUY HIRUKO ...
...WHO KICKED OUT THE DOOR...
WHERE IS HE?
I GUESS HE WENT OUT THE OTHER DOOR.
THAT'S ODD. I THOUGHT HE CAME OUT THIS ONE...
ANYWAY, NO USE STAYING HERE.
THIS IS THE WAY TO THE CELLS.

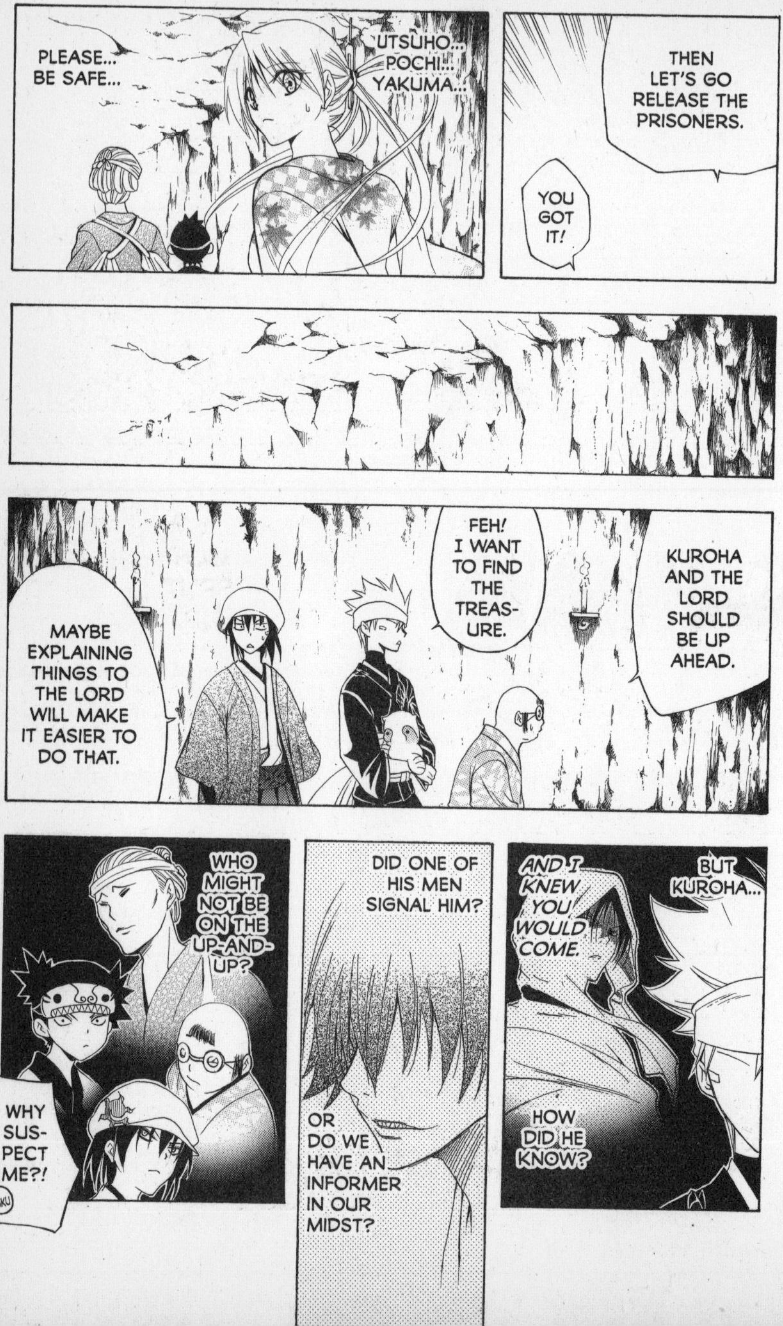
THEN LET'S GO RELEASE THE PRISONERS.
YOU GOT IT!
UTSUHO... POCHI... YAKUMA...
PLEASE... BE SAFE...
KUROHA AND THE LORD SHOULD BE UP AHEAD.
FEH! I WANT TO FIND THE TREAS-URE.
MAYBE EXPLAINING THINGS TO THE LORD WILL MAKE IT EASIER TO DO THAT.
BUT KUROHA...
AND I KNEW YOU WOULD COME.
HOW DID HE KNOW?
DID ONE OF HIS MEN SIGNAL HIM?
OR DO WE HAVE AN INFORMER IN OUR MIDST?
WHO MIGHT NOT BE ON THE UP-AND-UP?
WHY SUS-PECT ME?!
YAKU

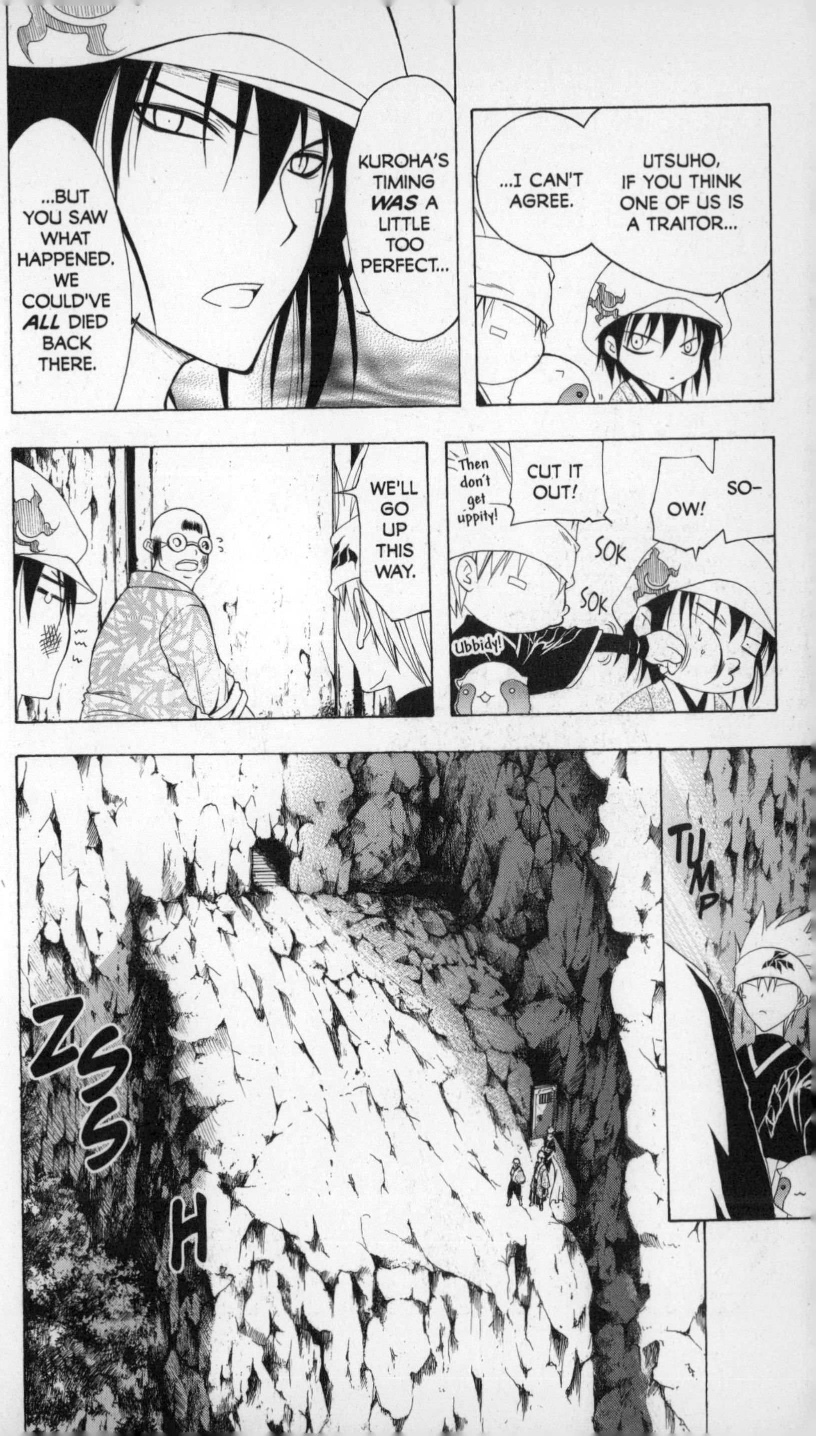
UTSUHO, IF YOU THINK ONE OF US IS A TRAITOR...
...I CAN'T AGREE.
KUROHA'S TIMING *WAS* A LITTLE TOO PERFECT...
...BUT YOU SAW WHAT HAPPENED. WE COULD'VE *ALL* DIED BACK THERE.
SO-
OW!
CUT IT OUT!
Then don't get uppity!
SOK
SOK
Ubbidy!
WE'LL GO UP THIS WAY.
TUMP
ZSSH

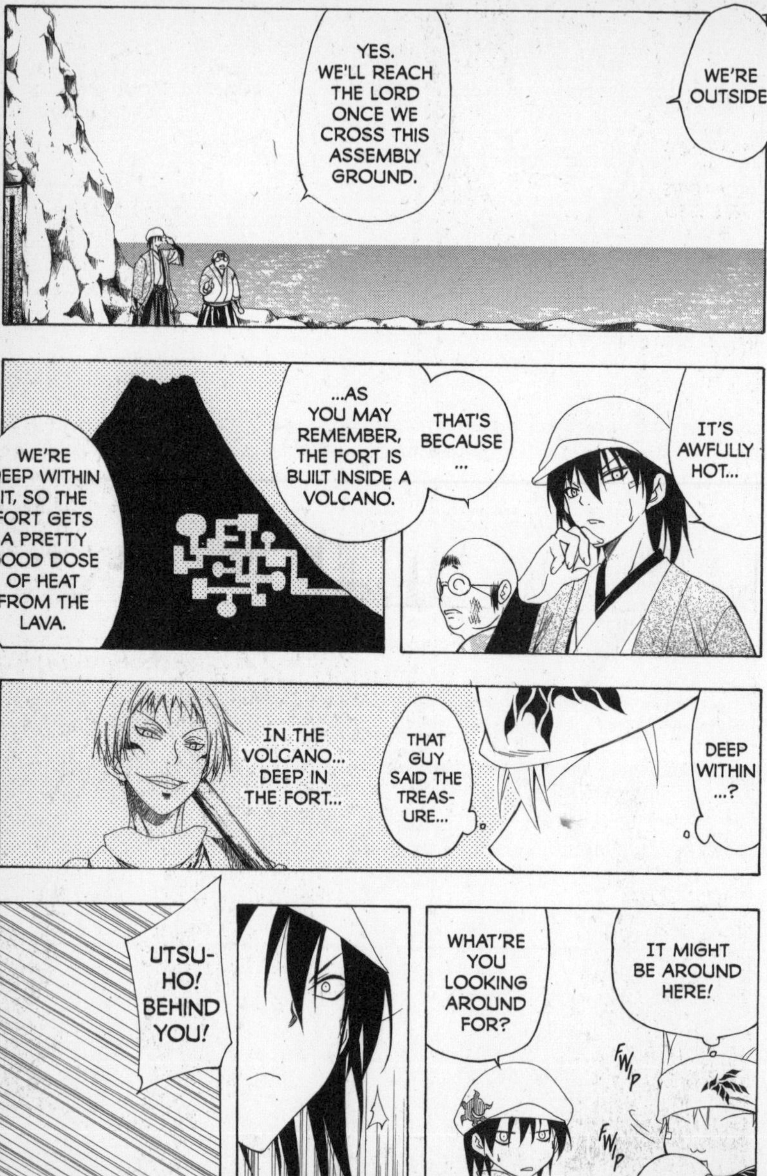

WE'RE OUTSIDE.
YES. WE'LL REACH THE LORD ONCE WE CROSS THIS ASSEMBLY GROUND.
IT'S AWFULLY HOT...
THAT'S BECAUSE ...
...AS YOU MAY REMEMBER, THE FORT IS BUILT INSIDE A VOLCANO.
WE'RE DEEP WITHIN IT, SO THE FORT GETS A PRETTY GOOD DOSE OF HEAT FROM THE LAVA.
DEEP WITHIN ...?
THAT GUY SAID THE TREAS- URE...
IN THE VOLCANO... DEEP IN THE FORT...
IT MIGHT BE AROUND HERE!
FWIP
FWIP
WHAT'RE YOU LOOKING AROUND FOR?
UTSU- HO! BEHIND YOU!

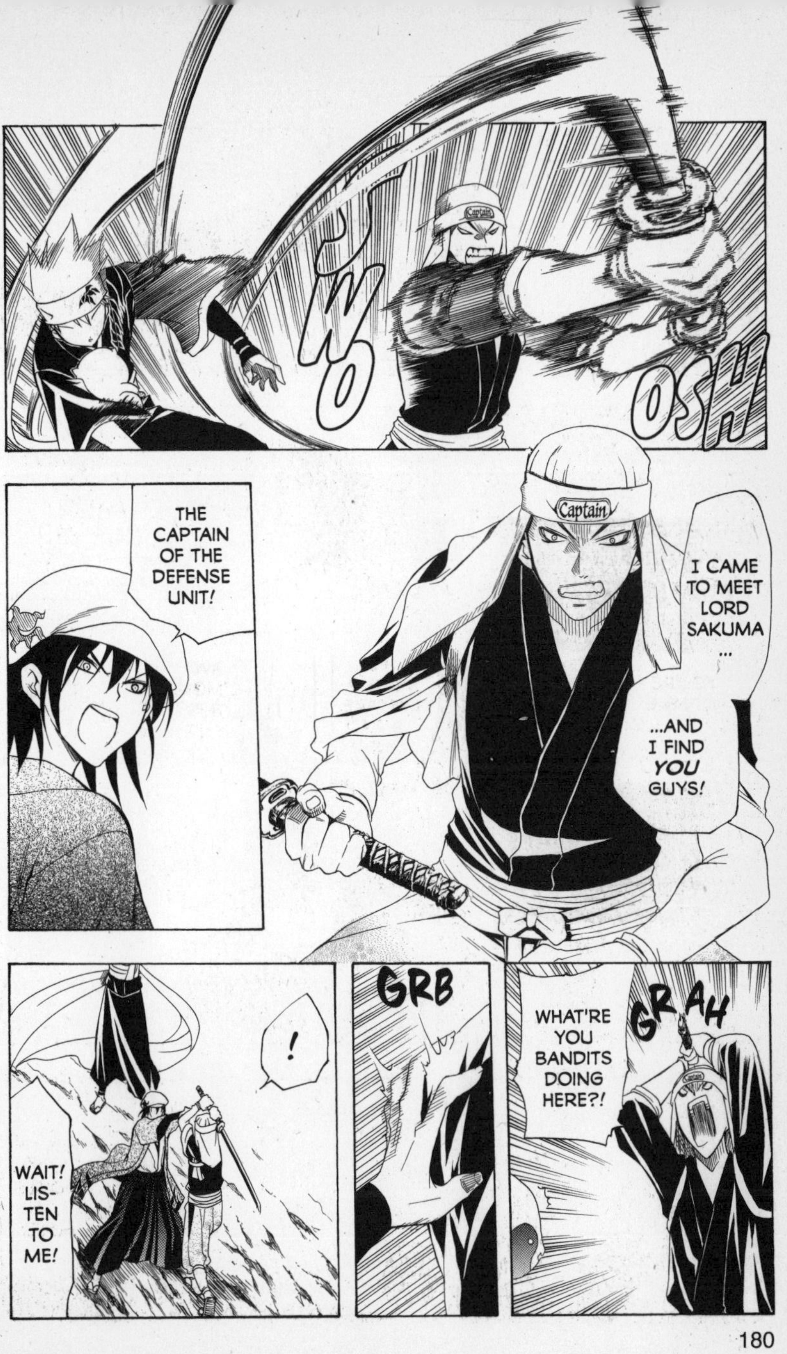
WHO
OSH
I CAME TO MEET LORD SAKUMA ...
...AND I FIND *YOU* GUYS!
THE CAPTAIN OF THE DEFENSE UNIT!
GRAH
WHAT'RE YOU BANDITS DOING HERE?!
GRB
!
WAIT! LIS-TEN TO ME!

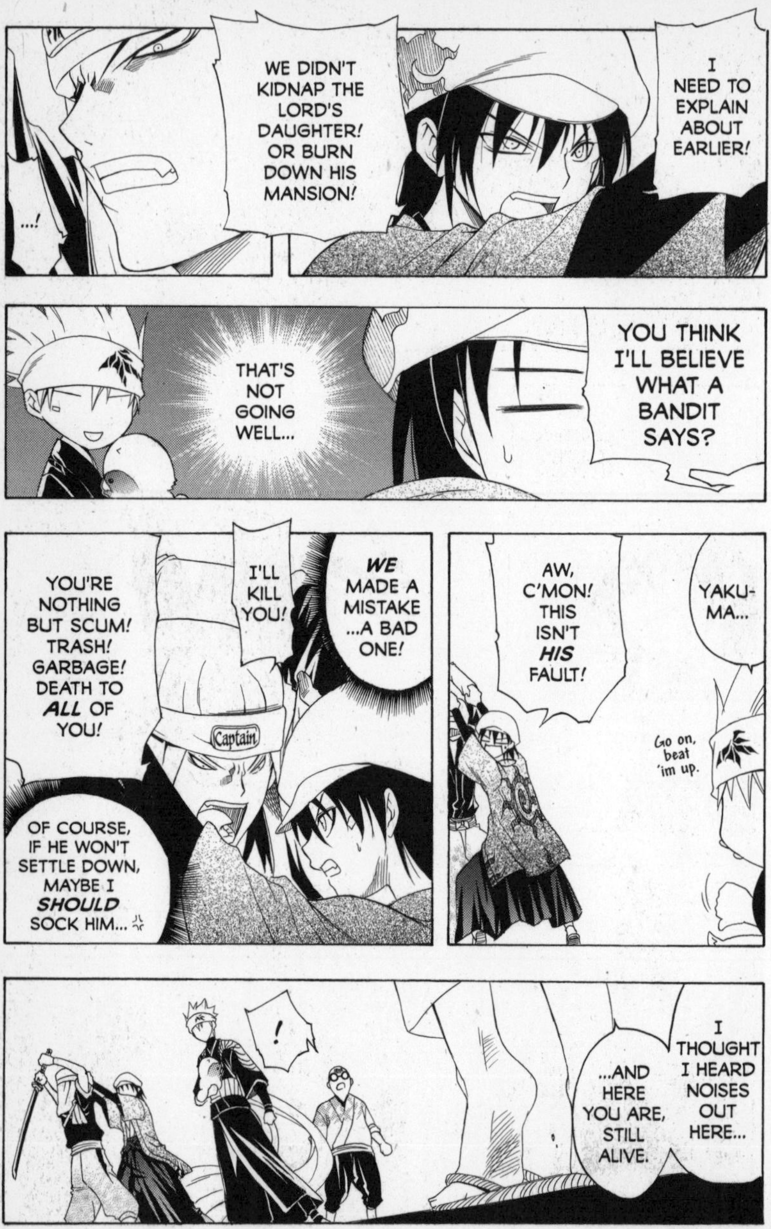
I NEED TO EXPLAIN ABOUT EARLIER!
WE DIDN'T KIDNAP THE LORD'S DAUGHTER! OR BURN DOWN HIS MANSION!
...!
YOU THINK I'LL BELIEVE WHAT A BANDIT SAYS?
THAT'S NOT GOING WELL...
YAKU-MA...
AW, C'MON! THIS ISN'T *HIS* FAULT!
Go on, beat 'im up.
WE MADE A MISTAKE ...A BAD ONE!
I'LL KILL YOU!
YOU'RE NOTHING BUT SCUM! TRASH! GARBAGE! DEATH TO *ALL* OF YOU!
Captain
OF COURSE, IF HE WON'T SETTLE DOWN, MAYBE I *SHOULD* SOCK HIM...
I THOUGHT I HEARD NOISES OUT HERE...
...AND HERE YOU ARE, STILL ALIVE.
!

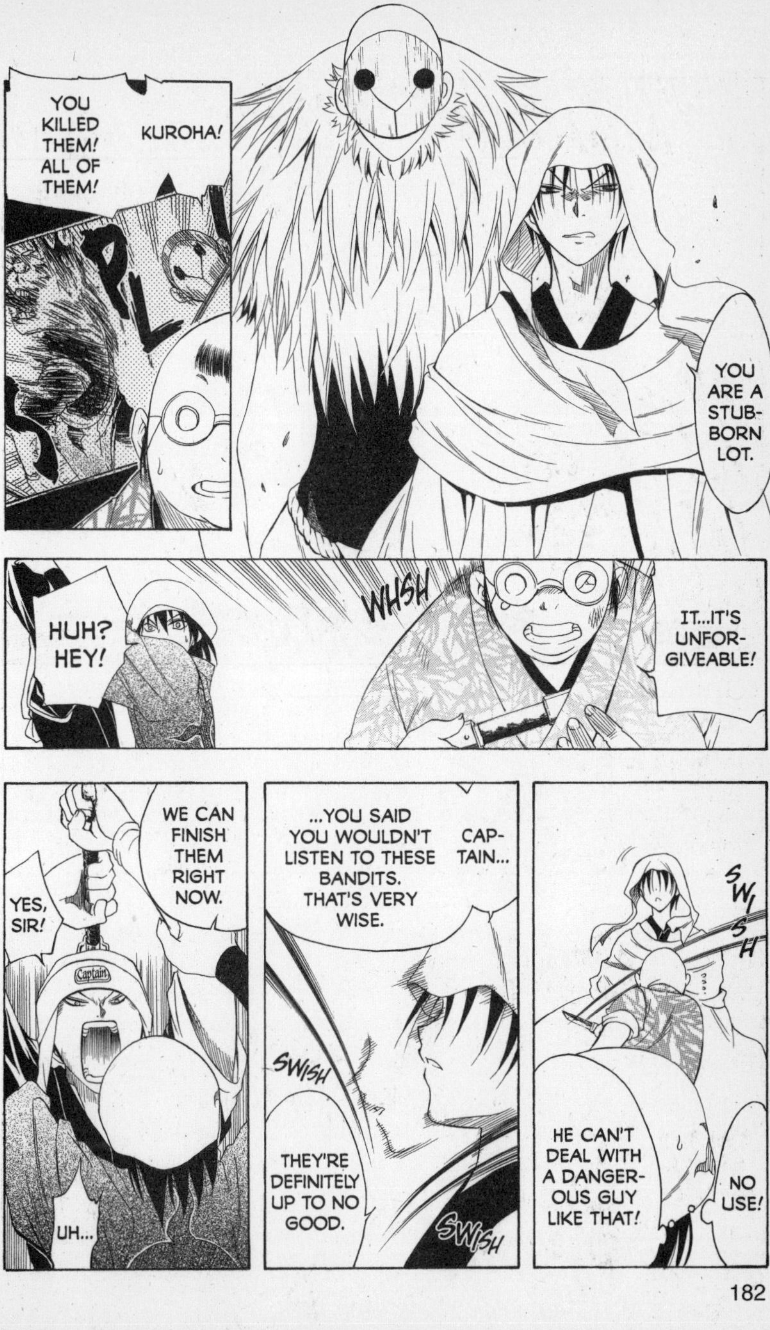
KUROHA!
YOU KILLED THEM! ALL OF THEM!
YOU ARE A STUBBORN LOT.
IT...IT'S UNFORGIVEABLE!
WHSH
HUH? HEY!
SWISH
HE CAN'T DEAL WITH A DANGEROUS GUY LIKE THAT!
NO USE!
CAPTAIN...
...YOU SAID YOU WOULDN'T LISTEN TO THESE BANDITS. THAT'S VERY WISE.
SWISH
THEY'RE DEFINITELY UP TO NO GOOD.
SWISH
WE CAN FINISH THEM RIGHT NOW.
YES, SIR!
Captain
UH...

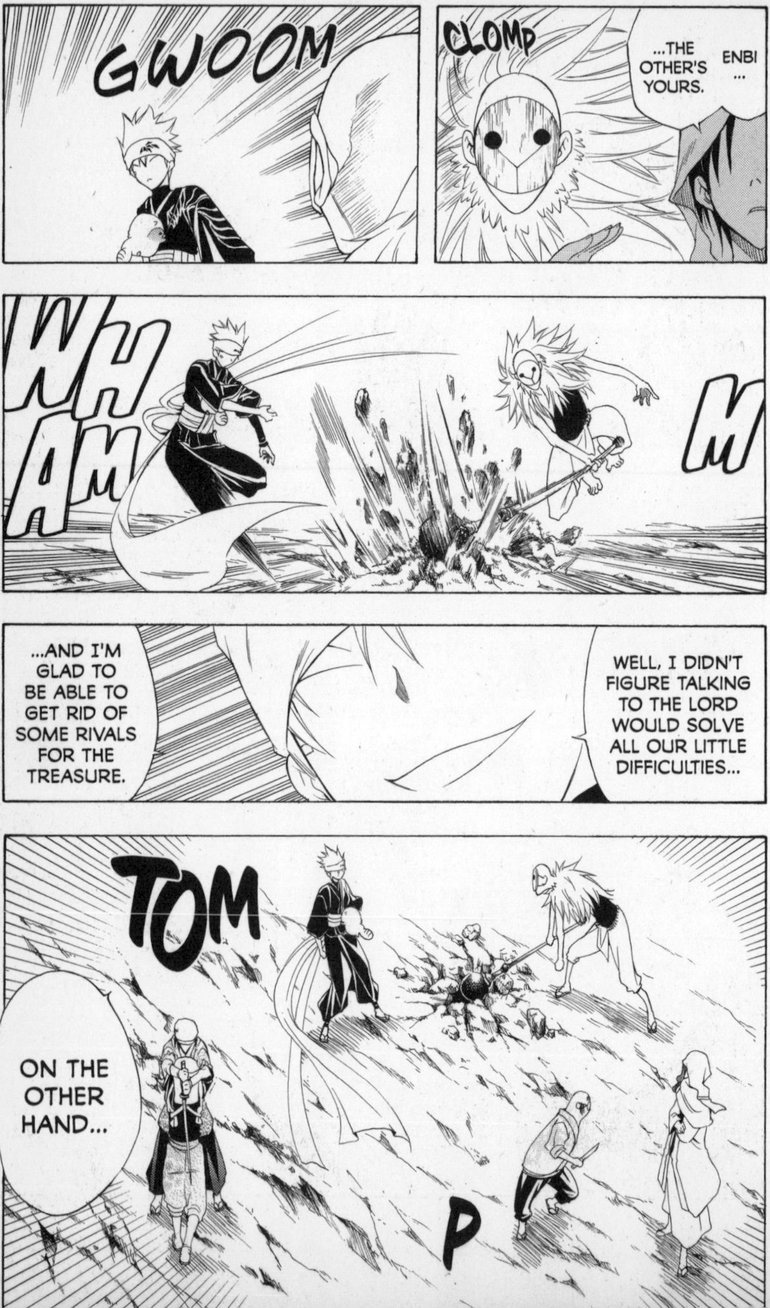
ENBI ...
...THE OTHER'S YOURS.
CLOMP
GWOOM
M
WHAM
WELL, I DIDN'T FIGURE TALKING TO THE LORD WOULD SOLVE ALL OUR LITTLE DIFFICULTIES...
...AND I'M GLAD TO BE ABLE TO GET RID OF SOME RIVALS FOR THE TREASURE.
TOM
ON THE OTHER HAND...
P

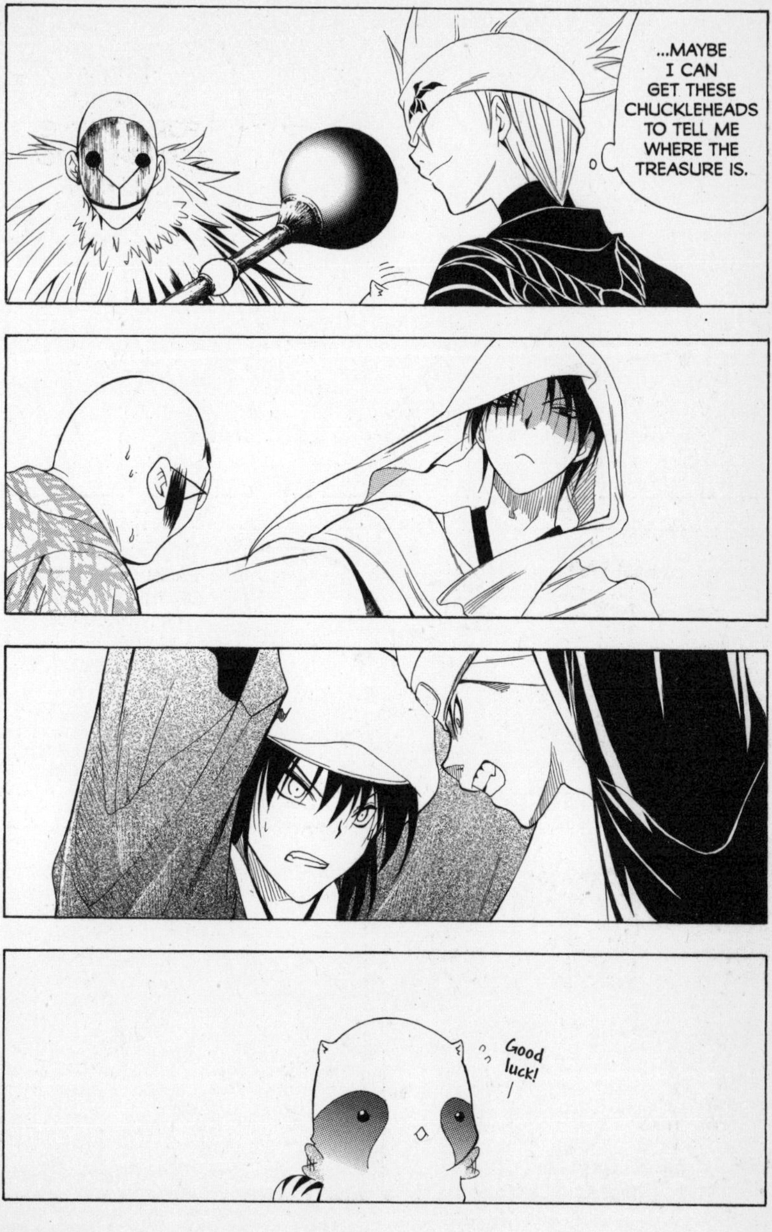
...MAYBE I CAN GET THESE CHUCKLEHEADS TO TELL ME WHERE THE TREASURE IS.
Good luck!

◆ Bonus Manga ◆

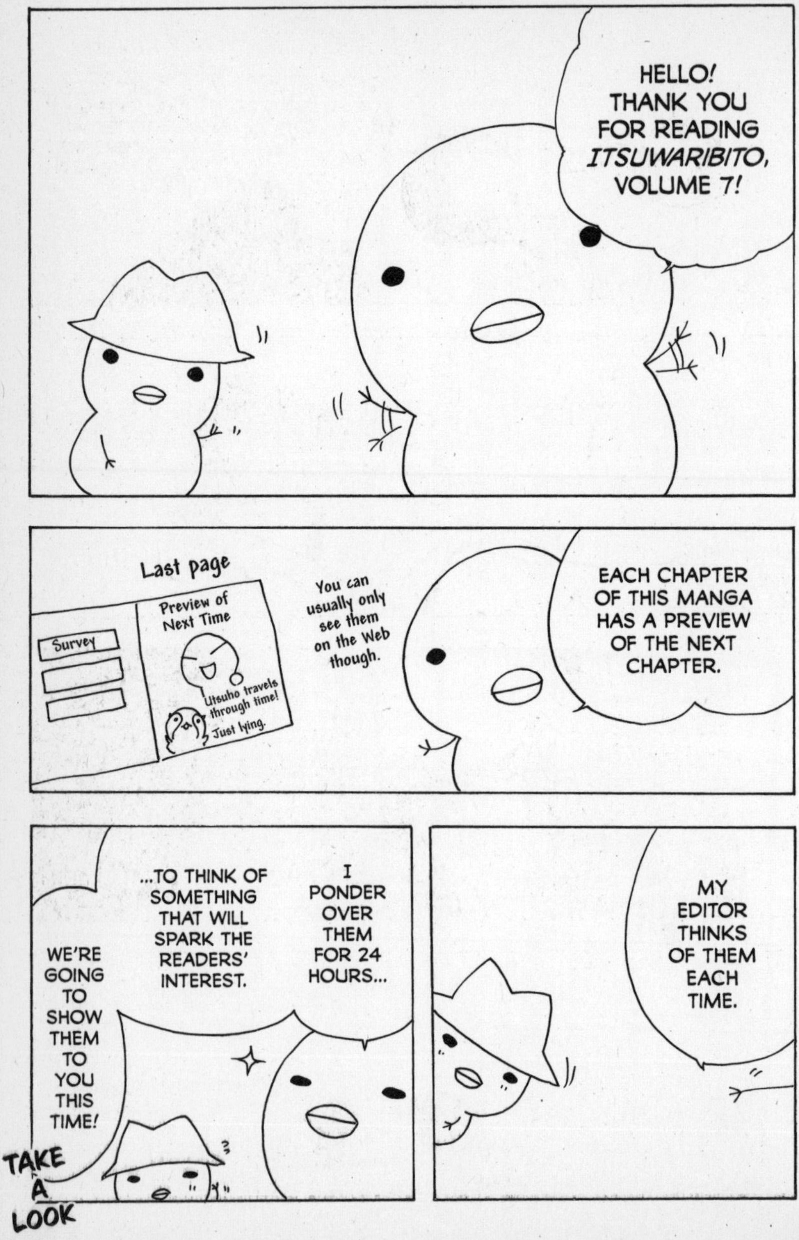
HELLO! THANK YOU FOR READING *ITSUWARIBITO*, VOLUME 7!
EACH CHAPTER OF THIS MANGA HAS A PREVIEW OF THE NEXT CHAPTER.
You can usually only see them on the Web though.
Last page
Preview of Next Time
Survey
Utsuho travels through time!
Just lying.
MY EDITOR THINKS OF THEM EACH TIME.
I PONDER OVER THEM FOR 24 HOURS...
...TO THINK OF SOMETHING THAT WILL SPARK THE READERS' INTEREST.
WE'RE GOING TO SHOW THEM TO YOU THIS TIME!
TAKE A LOOK

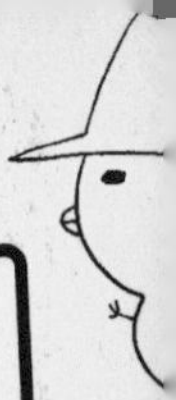

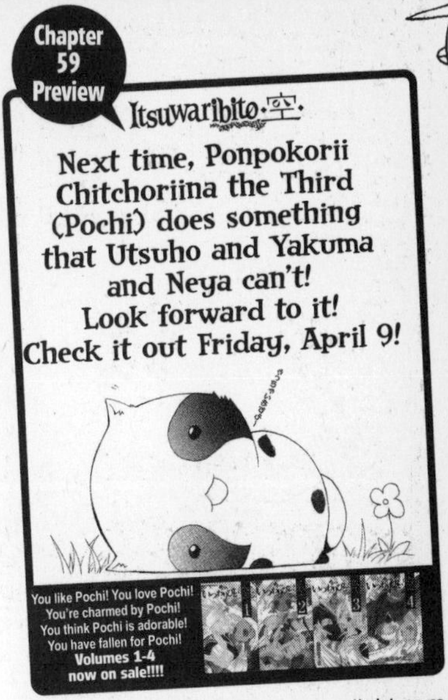
Chapter 59 Preview
Itsuwaribito 空
Next time, Ponpokorii Chitchoriina the Third (Pochi) does something that Utsuho and Yakuma and Neya can't!
Look forward to it!
Check it out Friday, April 9!
You like Pochi! You love Pochi! You're charmed by Pochi! You think Pochi is adorable! You have fallen for Pochi!
Volumes 1-4 now on sale!!!!

I, the editor, will offer some light commentary as you take a look. –*Editor*

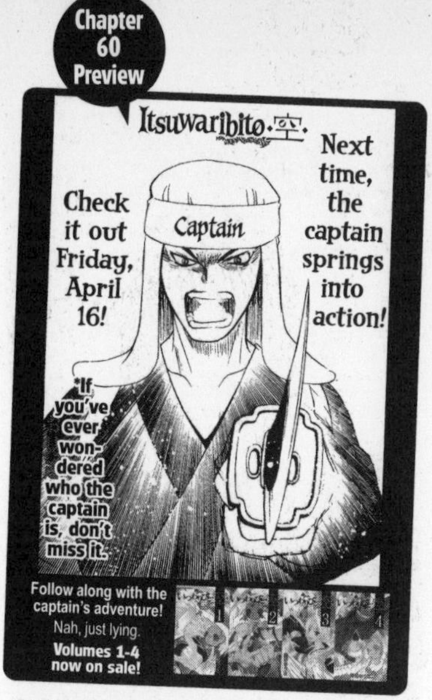
Chapter 60 Preview
Itsuwaribito 空
Next time, the captain springs into action!
Captain
Check it out Friday, April 16!
*If you've ever wondered who the captain is, don't miss it.
Follow along with the captain's adventure!
Nah, just lying.
Volumes 1-4 now on sale!

The advertisement for the graphic novels at the bottom is from when the preview appeared, so don't be confused! –*Editor*

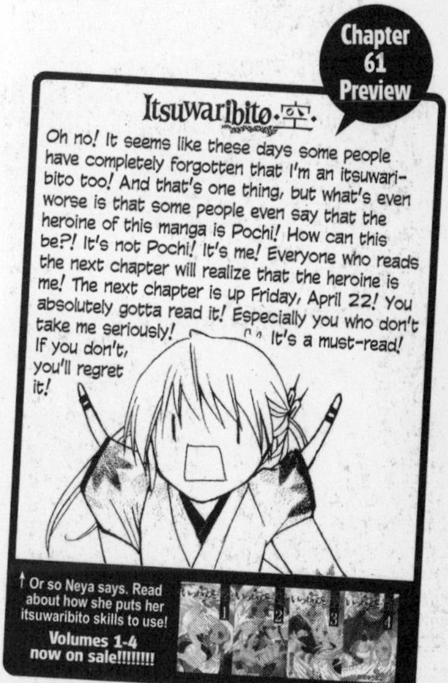
Chapter 61 Preview
Itsuwaribito 空
Oh no! It seems like these days some people have completely forgotten that I'm an itsuwaribito too! And that's one thing, but what's even worse is that some people even say that the heroine of this manga is Pochi! How can this be?! It's not Pochi! It's me! Everyone who reads the next chapter will realize that the heroine is me! The next chapter is up Friday, April 22! You absolutely gotta read it! Especially you who don't take me seriously! It's a must-read!
If you don't, you'll regret it!
↑ Or so Neya says. Read about how she puts her itsuwaribito skills to use!
Volumes 1-4 now on sale!!!!!!!!

The date is wrong. It's a secret that the new chapter went up on April 23, not 22. –*Editor*

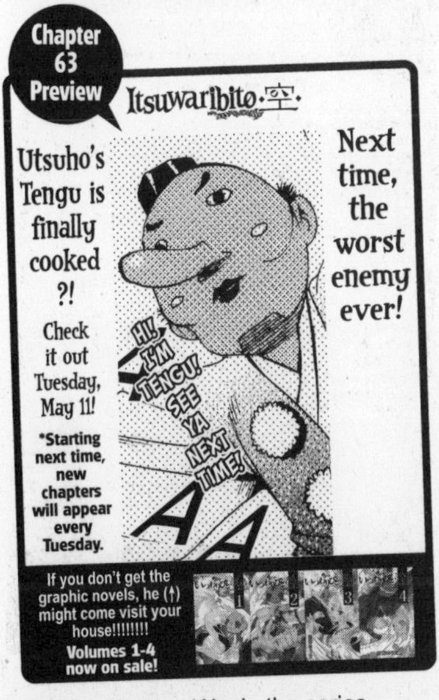
Chapter 63 Preview
Itsuwaribito 空
Next time, the worst enemy ever!
Utsuho's Tengu is finally cooked?!
Check it out Tuesday, May 11!
*Starting next time, new chapters will appear every Tuesday.
HI! I'M TENGU! SEE YA NEXT TIME!
If you don't get the graphic novels, he (↑) might come visit your house!!!!!!!!
Volumes 1-4 now on sale!

After Golden Week, the series started appearing on Tuesday each week. –*Editor*

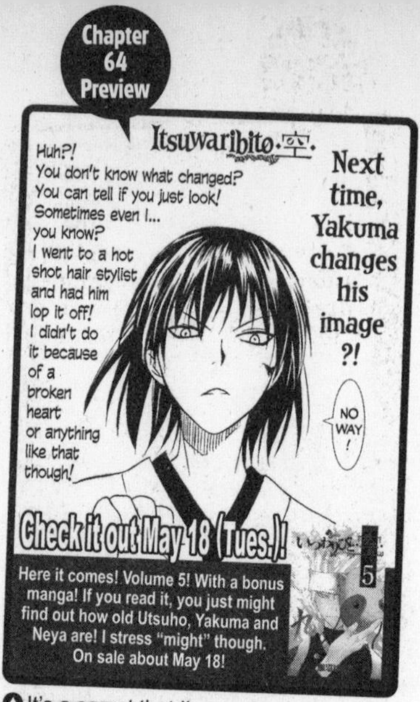
Chapter 64 Preview
Itsuwaribito 空
Huh?! You don't know what changed? You can tell if you just look! Sometimes even I... you know? I went to a hot shot hair stylist and had him lop it off! I didn't do it because of a broken heart or anything like that though!
Next time, Yakuma changes his image?!
NO WAY!
Check it out May 18 (Tues.)!
Here it comes! Volume 5! With a bonus manga! If you read it, you just might find out how old Utsuho, Yakuma and Neya are! I stress "might" though. On sale about May 18!

It's a secret that Iinuma Sensei got mad at me for revealing too much. *–Editor*

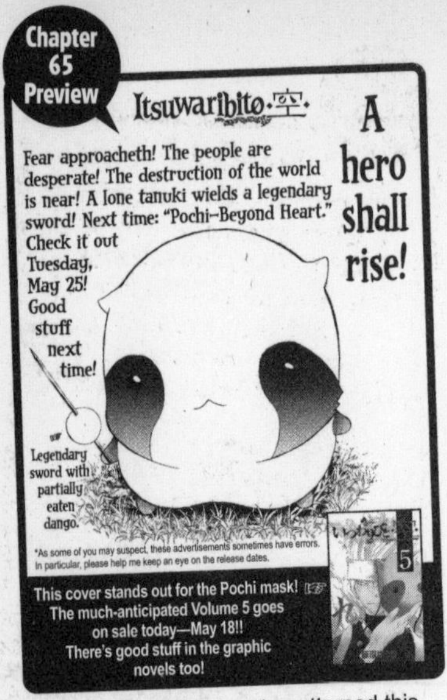
Chapter 65 Preview
Itsuwaribito 空
Fear approacheth! The people are desperate! The destruction of the world is near! A lone tanuki wields a legendary sword! Next time: "Pochi–Beyond Heart." Check it out Tuesday, May 25! Good stuff next time!
A hero shall rise!
Legendary sword with partially eaten dango.
*As some of you may suspect, these advertisements sometimes have errors. In particular, please help me keep an eye on the release dates.
This cover stands out for the Pochi mask! The much-anticipated Volume 5 goes on sale today—May 18!! There's good stuff in the graphic novels too!

It's a secret that I sorta patterned this after Evan◯lion. *–Editor*

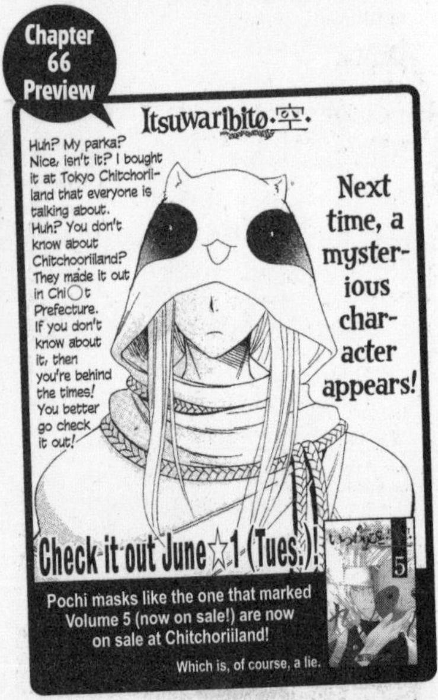
Chapter 66 Preview
Itsuwaribito 空
Huh? My parka? Nice, isn't it? I bought it at Tokyo Chitchoriiland that everyone is talking about. Huh? You don't know about Chitchooriiland? They made it out in Chi◯t Prefecture. If you don't know about it, then you're behind the times! You better go check it out!
Next time, a mysterious character appears!
Check it out June☆1 (Tues.)!
Pochi masks like the one that marked Volume 5 (now on sale!) are now on sale at Chitchoriiland!
Which is, of course, a lie.

"Chitchoriiland" is correct. It's a secret that it's misspelled "Chitchooriiland" at one spot. *–Editor*

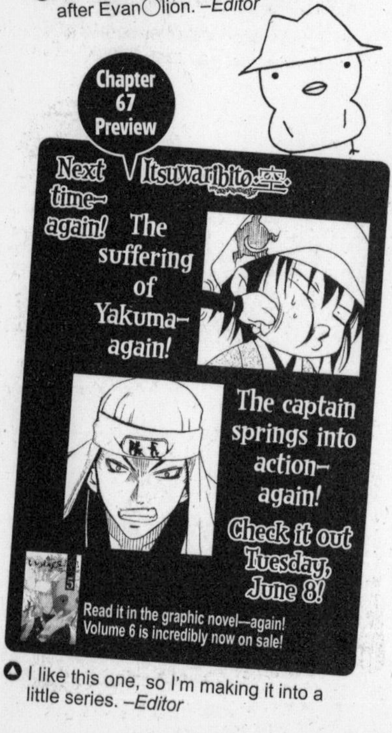
Chapter 67 Preview
Next time—again!
Itsuwaribito 空
The suffering of Yakuma—again!
The captain springs into action—again!
Check it out Tuesday, June 8!
Read it in the graphic novel—again! Volume 6 is incredibly now on sale!

I like this one, so I'm making it into a little series. *–Editor*

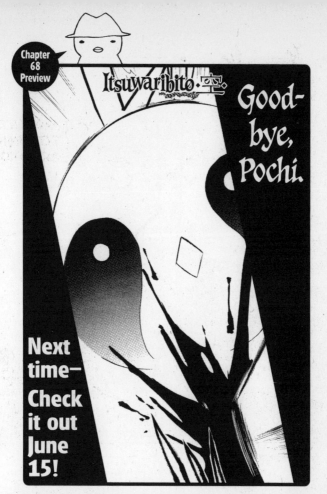

Chapter 68 Preview

Itsuwaribito

Good-bye, Pochi.

Next time—Check it out June 15!

⛰ Volume 7 contains up through Chapter 67, so this preview also serves as a preview of the next volume. What happens to Pochi?! Look forward to the next volume!! Usually, I take the picture for a preview from the next chapter. I can do that because Iinuma Sensei finishes the scripts so fast! Applaud the sensei while you wait for the next volume! –*Editor*

THAT'S ALL.

ANYWAY, THAT'S WHAT THEY'RE LIKE.

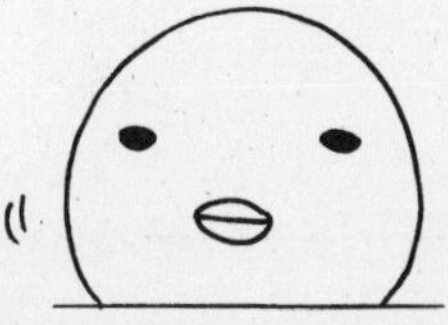

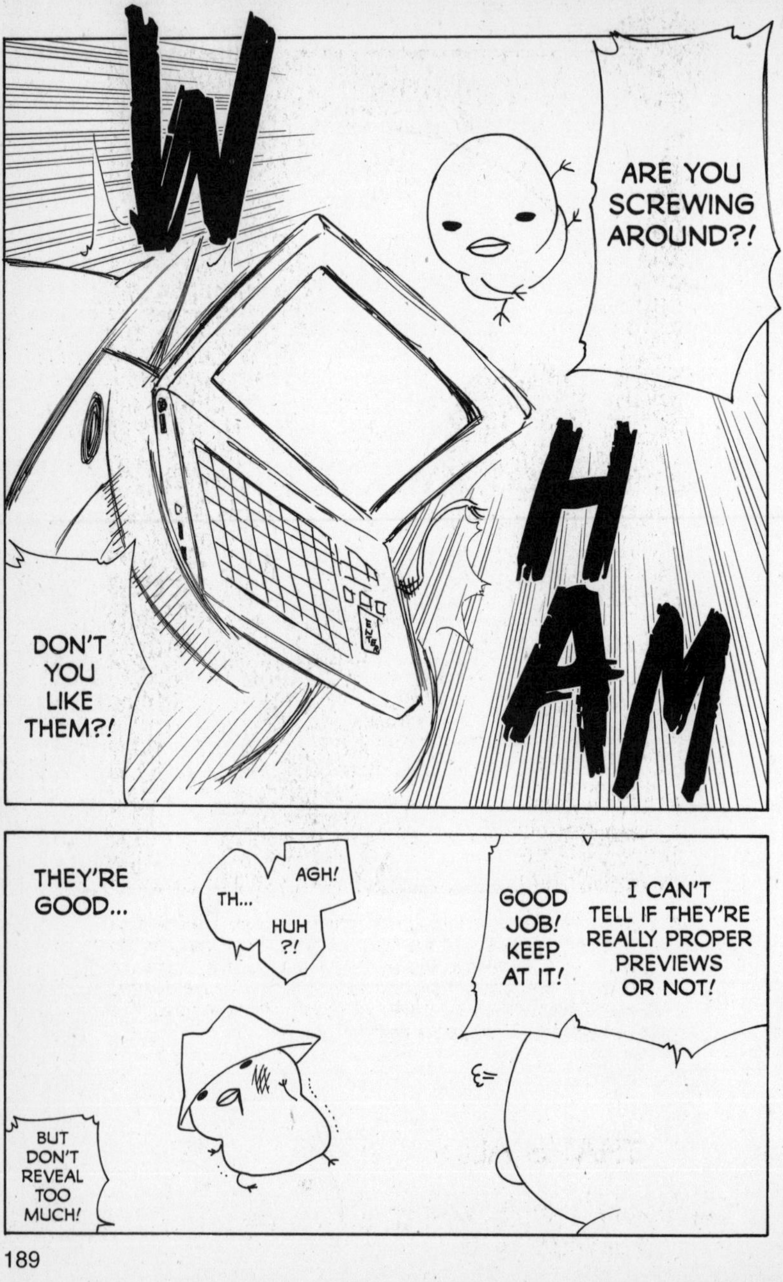
ARE YOU SCREWING AROUND?!
WHAM
DON'T YOU LIKE THEM?!
I CAN'T TELL IF THEY'RE REALLY PROPER PREVIEWS OR NOT!
GOOD JOB! KEEP AT IT!
THEY'RE GOOD...
AGH! TH... HUH?!
BUT DON'T REVEAL TOO MUCH!

ITSUWARIBITO

Volume 7
Shonen Sunday Edition

Story and Art by
YUUKI IINUMA

© 2009 Yuuki IINUMA/Shogakukan
All rights reserved.
Original Japanese edition "ITSUWARIBITO UTSUHO"
published by SHOGAKUKAN Inc.

Translation/John Werry
Touch-up Art & Lettering/Susan Daigle-Leach
Design/Matt Hinrichs
Editor/Gary Leach

Printed in Canada

Published by VIZ Media, LLC
P.O. Box 77010
San Francisco, CA 94107

10 9 8 7 6 5 4 3 2 1
First printing, December 2012

www.viz.com
WWW.SHONENSUNDAY.COM

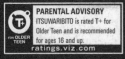

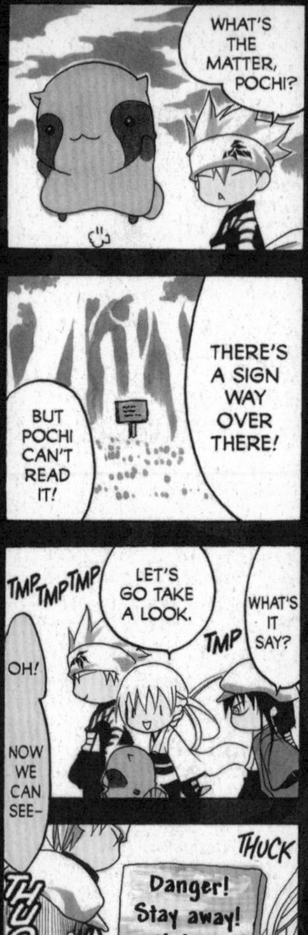
WHAT'S THE MATTER, POCHI?
THERE'S A SIGN WAY OVER THERE!
BUT POCHI CAN'T READ IT!
WHAT'S IT SAY?
TMP
LET'S GO TAKE A LOOK.
TMP TMP TMP
OH!
NOW WE CAN SEE–
THUCK
Danger! Stay away! Holes!
THUCK

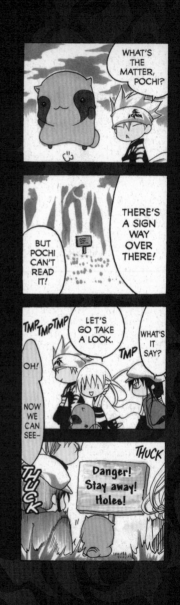

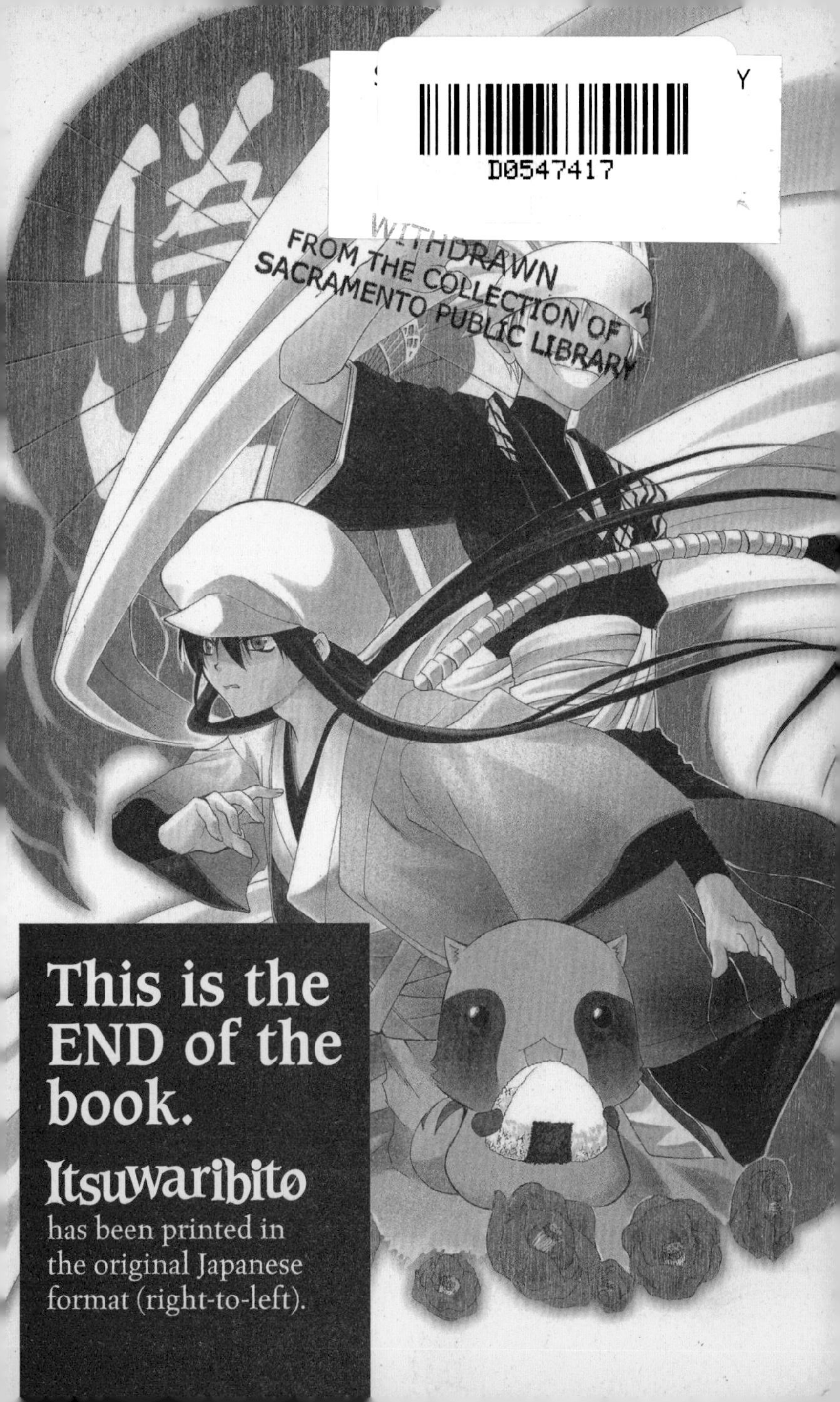

This is the END of the book.

Itsuwaribito
has been printed in the original Japanese format (right-to-left).